Saints, Sinners, and the God of the World

Numen Book Series

Studies in the History of Religions

Texts and Sources in the History of Religions

VOLUME 133

Saints, Sinners, and the God of the World

The Hartford Sermon Notebook Transcribed, 1679–1680

By

Andrew Phillips Mallory

BRILL

LEIDEN • BOSTON
2011

On the cover: Page 2 of Isaac Foster's November 14, 1680 Sacrament Day sermon. Image is courtesy of the Indian and Colonial Research Center, Old Mystic Connecticut.

This book is printed on acid-free paper.

Library of Congress Cataloging-in-Publication Data

Saints, sinners, and the God of the world : the Hartford sermon notebook transcribed, 1679–1680 / by Andrew Phillips Mallory.
p. cm. — (Numen book series ; v. 133. Studies in the history of religions)
Includes bibliographical references (p.) and index.
ISBN 978-90-04-19242-3 (hardback : alk. paper) 1. Puritans—Connecticut—Hartford—History—17th century. 2. Hartford (Conn.)—Church history—17th century. 3. Sermons, American—17th century. 4. Puritans—Sermons. I. Mallory, Andrew Phillips, 1966- II. Title. III. Series.

BX9355.H37S25 2011
252'.0959—dc22

2010048235

ISSN 0169-8834
ISBN 978 90 04 19242 3

FSC
Mixed Sources
Product group from well-managed forests and other controlled sources
www.fsc.org Cert no. SGS-COC-006767
©1996 Forest Stewardship Council

PRINTED BY A-D DRUK BV - ZEIST, THE NETHERLANDS

For
Isaac

CONTENTS

ACKNOWLEDGMENTS

This project has been a fascinating journey into the mind and soul of Puritan history and theology, and a significant intellectual experience for my own mind and soul. Many people have been involved in this project both directly and indirectly. First, I would express my greatest appreciation to the Indian and Colonial Research Center in Old Mystic, Connecticut. The ICRC holds the original sermon notebook, along with hundreds of other manuscript sources that await the attention of historians. The ICRC is an excellent archive, and without the specific assistance of Joan Cohn and Michael Spellmon, this book would not have happened. Thank you so much, Joan and Michael. In the spring of 2010, southeastern Connecticut experienced serious flooding on a scale seldom seen in this region. The Indian and Colonial Research Center was flooded out. Fortunately, the contents were spared serious damage, but the building is in need of major renovations, making the future of this wonderful archive doubtful at best.

To Maarten Frieswijk at Brill, the Netherlands. I have enjoyed our correspondence over the past three years, and I am pleased to call you a friend. Throughout this process you were supportive and encouraging. Thank you Maarten. Now I will always cheer for the Dutch in the World Cup, unless they play the USA!

Professional historians share a love of the subject, but are driven to understand its mysteries. Writing history requires patience, stubbornness, intellect, and most importantly, collaboration. It requires a special reliance on the research and ideas of colleagues, especially where primary sources no longer exist. I have always been reading and debating history, but to the extent that I have successfully written history in the form of this book, I am indebted to the many excellent historians who have shared their many tools and insights.

Most recently, to the history professors at Central Connecticut State University, whose excellence and combined efforts have improved my scholarship in the subject I love. History is a craft, and as such requires considerable training and preparation for those who would practice it. My specific gratitude extends to Louise Williams, and Norton Mezvinsky. To Glenn Sunshine, whose seminars and lectures will not soon be forgotten. And lastly, Katherine Hermés, who has guided much of my research throughout this project, and perhaps most importantly, introduced me to the Indian and Colonial Research Center. Thank you Kathy for your patient guidance. You were right, this should be a book.

Lastly, I would thank my family. Phyllis and Charles Nason. You have both always embraced me as a son, and it has been great to be part of your wonderful family. My siblings and virtual siblings, Becky, Daren, and Jennifer, Gene, Ann, and Kevin, for always supporting my endeavors. My aunt Harriet and uncle Albert. Thanks for all the books "Auntie." Grandpa Ray. I'm glad I got to know you and I miss your stories. To the greatest historian ever, my grandmother Georgia. How I wish you could have seen this, and your grandchildren. We love and miss you Gram. To Dad. Your love of history and of writing shaped much of what is here. We miss you very much.

My mother Virginia. You have always supported me in all endeavors and encouraged me to pursue my interests. You are a great mom. Your love of history shaped these pages and their author in countless ways, but you already know that. I love you Mom.

My children, Andrew and Evelyn, "the greatest kids in the world," you never complained, even when Dad was dragging you along to a cemetery, or spending hour after hour reading and writing. It has been a pleasure to watch you both grow as this book has grown.

And to my dearest friend and loving wife Rhonda Nason Mallory, whose unfailing interest and constant support always inspire me. We have been through so much together and I could not have completed this book without your support and encouragement. More importantly, you have taught me about myself, in ways that you and I alone understand, and which matter far more than any singular success I may ever experience. I will always love you.

To God alone belongs the glory…

LIST OF ILLUSTRATIONS

INTRODUCTION

The *Hartford Sermon Notebook* is a compact, bound series of notes taken during sermons delivered by a variety of different ministers in Hartford, Connecticut during the years 1679 and 1680. Figure 7 is an illustration of the notebook's actual size. The notebook's authorship is unknown, but whoever took the notes did a meticulous job, and the sermons contained in the notebook are nearly all complete. Initially, my interest in transcribing the notebook was motivated by its antiquity, since the colony of Connecticut was only fifty years old when the notebook was created. However, as I worked with the notebook, its value as an untapped primary source for Connecticut's earliest history quickly revealed itself, and I knew it had to be transcribed.

The movements of history are varied and complex, and are seldom adequately explained by any single motive force. It is true that ideas, economic crises, wars, political strains, and religious pressures have often "made history", but by themselves these forces are just pieces of history, and as causes of historical change should be taken as a sum rather than a difference. This project does not limit itself by relying on any one particular historical discipline, nor is it a haphazard venture; I simply believe that relying on a wide range of scholarship is an effective way to unpack and sort out the contents of the Hartford Sermon Notebook.

The idea of multi-causality can be applied to the historical implications of a seventeenth century sermon notebook because, while theology alone might explain the notebook's significance, theology alone would also end the usefulness of a multi-causal approach, and would severely limit the variety of sources from which this book could draw. Simply put, the structure of this book relies on many expert opinions within the varied fields of intellectual, theological, and social history to guide its explanations of what the sermons actually meant to the people who heard them, and I am indebted to the many scholars whose insightful interpretations fuel so much of what follows.

A century and a half before America declared its independence from England, small groups of English religious dissenters began arriving on the shores of New England in search of a new beginning for their lives and their faith. Their story is complex, as most history tends to be, and therefore challenging to write. Perhaps the greatest scholar of Puritan history, Perry Miller says, "It is not easy to restrain one's own prejudices and to exercise the sort of historical imagination that is required for the understanding of a portion of the past according to its own intentions before we allow ourselves to judge it by our own standards."[1] There was no better instruction for my effort to understand the mysterious notebook I had uncovered.

The sermon notebook required a complete transcription of sixty-two previously unknown sermons. Until I began this process, I did not know whether these were "Puritan" sermons, or even where they came from. I was able to discern that they originated from seventeenth-century Hartford, Connecticut, by comparing the notebook's sermons to others in the area and reading histories of both the Puritans and the Connecticut River Valley. I had to avoid the urge to label these sermons too quickly and let the document reveal itself to me as I deciphered the handwriting, decoded symbols, and struggled to understand what passages meant literally, not figuratively. Interpretation had to be held at bay until the evidence suggested avenues of investigation; investigation then yielded help in my attempts to transcribe the text. I understood what Perry Miller meant by "historical imagination," which is not a license to create fiction, but an obligation to think creatively about one's sources.

The first goal of this book was to complete an accurate transcription of over two hundred pages of colonial handwriting from a sermon notebook of unknown authorship, while its second objective was to provide a thorough analysis of the content of the sermons, to show how they might fit into existing theories of New England Puritan society and theology. The analysis necessarily deals with only a small number of themes in the historiography of the New England Puritans, with emphasis on the final decades of the seventeenth century.

New England's ministers of the late seventeenth century were nearly all graduates of Harvard College, and all but one of the ministers whose sermons appear in the *Hartford Sermon Notebook* were Harvard graduates. At Harvard, the course of study included not only

[1] Perry Miller and Thomas H. Johnson eds., *The Puritans: A Sourcebook of their Writings* (Mineola New York: Dover Publications, Inc., 2001), 5.

the requisite theological topics necessary to preach the word of God, but also included the scholastic subjects of the day, including rhetoric, science, and logic. The sermons that the ministers delivered contained a variety of subjects ranging from covenant doctrines, the natural man and the saint, the processes of regeneration, conversion, sanctification, justification, the power of sin and the glory of grace among others. The sermons transcribed in this book deal not only with the broader subjects of reformed theology, but also contain exhortations on intemperance and its effect on Indians, and the pervasiveness of the Devil in the lives of the congregation.

The multiple themes that appear throughout the notebook provide an excellent opportunity to test the conclusions of other scholars in the field of New England Puritan studies, and to investigate a limited number of questions. The principal question is whether certain specific conclusions of New England Puritan scholars are supported by the *Hartford Sermon Notebook*. The notebook contains a remarkably complete two-year record of preaching in Hartford, Connecticut, during the years 1679 and 1680. This book does not tackle every theme found in the notebook, but it does deal with several important subjects from the historiography of New England Puritanism.

The sermon notebook supports the claims of Puritan scholars regarding covenant theology. Specifically, the concept of the covenant appears often in the sermons, and the language of Hartford's ministers regarding covenants supports our current understanding of New England Puritan covenant theology in the seventeenth century. The themes of conversion/regeneration, justification, redemption, and election or visible sainthood as examined by other scholars also appear to be supported by the sermons of Hartford's ministers. Finally, the sermons preached in Hartford were diverse, including several "occasional" sermons, Thanksgiving Day sermons, ordination sermons, and sacrament day sermons. Along with the more frequent "regular" sermons found in the notebook, these occasional sermons are an important addition to the extant New England Puritan sermon texts currently available for study.[2]

[2] Occasional sermons were those preached during the week, regular sermons were preached on Sunday. For complete descriptions of "occasional" and "regular" sermons see Harry Stout's the *New England Soul: Preaching and Religious Culture in Colonial New England* (New York: Oxford University Press, 1986).

Rather than select a narrow research question of limited breadth, I have chosen a wider approach for my analysis. After years of transcribing and editing over 60 sermons, I believe it is reasonable to be the first to comment on them, and I have not limited myself by dealing with only one or two themes. The scholarship that I seek to demonstrate builds on the work of a number of excellent historians, and this book sustains their conclusions more often than it refutes them.

Much of the best material concerning New England Puritan sermons is contained in broader studies in which sermons play a secondary role, but there are some exceptions, especially in the work of Harry Stout.[3] The following books are well known secondary sources in New England Puritan historiography and have guided much of my analysis, while the final bibliography contains many other sources that have shaped my understanding of New England's Puritan ministers and the sermons they preached.

[3] The following is not an exhaustive list, but offers a variety of sources that deal with various Puritan sermon themes, including the structure of the Puritan sermon. I have benefited from all of these sources both in terms of my understanding of the subject, and also for specific citations used in my analysis of the *Hartford Sermon Notebook*: Daniel A. Cohen, "In Defense of the Gallows: Justifications of Capital Punishment in New England Execution Sermons, 1674–1825." *American Quarterly* 40, no. 2 (June 1988): 147–164; Emory Elliot, "The Development of the Puritan Funeral Sermon and Elegy: 1660–1750." *Early American Literature* 40, (1980): 151–164; Emory Elliot, *Power and the Pulpit in Puritan New England* (Princeton: Princeton University Press, 1975) Alfred Habegger, "Preparing the Soul for Christ: The Contrasting Sermon Forms of John Cotton and Thomas Hooker." *American Literature* 41, no. 3 (November 1969): 342–354; Charles E. Hambrick-Stowe, *The Practice of Piety: Puritan Devotional Disciplines in Seventeenth-Century New England* (Chapel Hill: The University of North Carolina Press, 1982) Marvin Xavier Lesser, "'All for Profit': The Plain Style and the Massachusetts Election Sermons in the Seventeenth Century," (Ph.D. diss., Columbia University, 1967); Etta Madden, "Resurrecting Life Through Rhetorical Ritual: A Buried Value of the Puritan Funeral Sermon." *Early American Literature* 26, (1991): 232–250; Charles W. Mignon, "Christ the Glory of All Types: The Initial Sermon from Edward Taylor's 'Upon the Types of the Old Testament'." *The William and Mary Quarterly* 37, no. 2 (April 1980): 286–301; Perry Miller, *The New England Mind, Vol. 1: The Seventeenth Century* (Cambridge Massachusetts: The Belknap Press of the Harvard University Press, 1982); Perry Miller, "Preparation for Salvation in Seventeenth-Century New England." *Journal of the History of Ideas* 4, no. 3 (June 1943): 253–286; Edmund S. Morgan, "Light on the Puritans From John Hull's Notebooks." *The New England Quarterly* 15, no. 1 (March 1942): 95–101; Mary Morrisey, "Interdisciplinarity and the Study of Early Modern Sermons." *The Historical Journal* 42, no. 4 (December 1999): 1111–1123 and Mary Morrisey, "Scripture, Style and Persuasion in Seventeenth-Century English Theories of Preaching." *The Journal of Ecclesiastical History* 53, no. 4 (October 2002): 1–19. Leland Ryken, *Worldly Saints: The Puritans as They Really Were* (Grand Rapids, MI: Academie Books, 1986).

As a primer, the compilation of William S. Johnson and John H. Leith, *Reformed Reader: A Sourcebook in Christian Theology* is a great place to begin. It is a perfect combination of expert analysis and carefully chosen primary source materials from the most important reformers of the sixteenth and seventeenth centuries. Particularly impressive is its coverage of John Calvin, arguably the most important of the reformers. Many of the books listed in this bibliography contain introductory chapters covering the history of the Puritans and their movement, or are surveys on the subject, and I have benefited greatly by the works of Francis Bremer, Stephen Foster, and Sargent Bush. Their works are not only first-rate scholarship, but are a pleasure to read.

Once I had determined that the Hartford Sermon Notebook was a Puritan source, I quickly realized the need to immerse myself in their history and theology, beginning with the works of Perry Miller. On the reverse of the 1982 reprinting of Miller's *The New England Mind: The Seventeenth Century*, a reviewer wrote, "For many years to come every serious student of American Puritanism will still have to begin by reading *The New England Mind*."[4] First published in 1939, *The New England Mind* continues to play an important role as the classic intellectual history of New England Puritan thought, although many of Miller's theories have been challenged, including the Puritan relationship to Calvinism, the overriding importance of the Puritan intellect, typology, and even critiques of the number of sources used by Miller in his works.[5]

---

[4] Perry Miller, *The New England Mind, Vol. 1: The Seventeenth Century* (Cambridge Massachusetts: The Belknap Press of the Harvard University Press, 1982)

[5] Were we to gauge the influence of Perry Miller by his impact on the minds of other historians, we might declare that the historical field of American Puritan studies was his creation. More specifically, Perry Miller's intellectual history helped to firmly establish the force of ideas as a shaper of history. In the half-century since his death, historians have continually sought to critique Miller's work, while adapting new theories to his Puritans. The essays that follow represent varying criticisms of Miller's work, because I believe that reading "about" Miller's ideas is at least as important as the ideas themselves. For apologists see: David Harlan, "A People Blinded from Birth: American History According to Sacvan Bercovitch." *The Journal of American History* 78, no. 3 (December 1991), 949–971. Harlan's assessment of Miller is that he "transformed seventeenth-century Puritanism from a dull and barren period into one of the most vital and important episodes in the history of American thought." Also, see David Hollinger, "Perry Miller and Philosophical History." *History and Theory* 7, no. 2 (1968), 189–202. Miller's adversarial critics are numerous and have forwarded important alternatives. See: Francis T. Butts, "The Myth of Perry Miller." The American

Miller's *Errand into the Wilderness*, published in 1956 and *The New England Mind*, offer valuable insights into Puritan sermon terminology, along with Miller's interesting interpretations and definitions of what many Puritan religious concepts were. He writes about grace, sin, covenants, regeneration, and many other themes found in the *Hartford Sermon Notebook.*

David Hall's *The Faithful Shepherd: A History of the New England Ministry in the Seventeenth Century* is another intellectual interpretation of Puritan history that argues more for similarities with the European experience, rather than the popular isolated Puritan in the wilderness ideal associated with Perry Miller. Hall argues that Puritanism's roots are those of Calvin, and that the New England ministry was forced to deal with the idea that after escaping from their persecutors in Europe, their newfound problems in New England may have been worse. Principally, the ministers had to establish a system of control based on Calvin as much as reformed English Protestantism. As with *The New England Mind, the Faithful Shepherd* is useful in analyzing the intellectual concepts contained in the sermon notebook, since many of the Puritan religious concepts that both authors discuss flourish in the Hartford sermons.

David Hall's *Worlds of Wonder, Days of Judgment* presents a wide range of New England Puritan religious and intellectual concepts, because it opens up our understanding of how ordinary people thought about religion. While Perry Miller's exposition of federal theology was the reconstruction of elite, theological ideas, the person copying sermons into a notebook on Sunday doubtless understood many of the theological concepts his minister lay before him, and as Hall reminds us, there was another world of less intellectual rigor and religiosity among the Puritans.

Historical Review 87, no. 3 (June 1982), 665–694; Arne Delfs, "Anxieties of Influence: Perry Miller and Sacvan Bercovitch." The New England Quarterly 70, no. 4 (December 1997), 601–615; Everett Emerson, "Perry Miller and the Puritans: A Literary Scholar's Assessment." *The History Teacher* 14, no. 4 (August 1981), 459–467; David D. Hall, "A Reader's Guide to The New England Mind, Vol. 1: The Seventeenth Century." American Quarterly 34, no. 1 (Spring 1982), 31–36. George Selement, "Perry Miller: A Note on His Sources in The New England Mind, Vol. 1: The Seventeenth Century." The William and Mary Quarterly 31, no. 3 (July 1974), 453–464, and more recently, David A. Weir's "Early New England: A Covenanted Society." (Grand Rapids, MI: William B. Eerdmans Publishing Company, 2005).

Harry Stout's *The New England Soul* turned away from Miller's analysis of published sermons to examine the kind of sermon given on regular Sundays in churches all over New England. These are exactly the same kinds of sermons that appear in the notebook. Stout's analysis regarding the elements of the sermon, the various themes that sermons addressed, and important speculations about the meaning of the sermons in the lives of the people who heard them is essential for establishing the context of the notebook. His book is a five part generational study of the New England sermon from 1620 to 1776, with a section covering the period from 1666–1700. This period of New England history is important because it represents the first generation of New Englanders to be born in New England. The indigenous culture and religious nature of these earliest "Americans" began to have uniqueness, and represents the start of the process of defining what would eventually become a sovereign nation.

Paul Lucas's *The Valley of Discord: Church and Society Along the Connecticut River, 1636–1725* is an important source for the history of Connecticut during the years of the notebook. It is similar to Stout's work as a chronological, societal based interpretation, though Stout and Lucas both provide significant intellectual interpretations. Lucas addresses a variety of themes that characterize the ecclesiastical dissension and conflict of the Connecticut River Valley in the seventeenth century. I have used *The Valley of Discord* to look for connections between events in Hartford, and more broadly, events in New England during the years of the Hartford sermons, 1679 and 1680, that may correlate with the subject matter of the sermons. Intellectually, Lucas is concerned with presenting a view of Puritan New England that suggests a marked lack of unification in religious, governmental, and social structures. This book partly explores whether or not the Hartford sermons support this view.

Edmund Morgan's *Visible Saints* deals with the origins and history of what became a peculiar style of Puritanism in New England, a style that focused on accepting only truly tested saints for membership. His book discusses the origins of the Half-Way Covenant, and more importantly it describes the nature of what a saint in New England actually was, a concept that can initially be difficult to grasp. The Hartford sermons periodically refer to saints and the Elect. Morgan's book has helped me make reasonable claims about these terms and what they mean in the context of the notebook's sermons. It has also been an essential source for the Puritan history found in Chapter 1.

Charles Hambrick Stowe's *The Practice of Piety: Puritan Devotional Disciplines in Seventeenth-Century New England* was written by a scholar who is both historian and pastor. His insights have been invaluable to my understanding of Puritan theology, and I site his work often. Stowe is an intellectual counter-weight to Perry Miller in that he offers many contrary arguments. Ultimately, the scholarship of both Miller and Stowe allows us to understand the New England Puritan in both "heart" and "mind."

The following secondary sources have also shaped my understanding of New England's Puritans, especially regarding their theology. Each of these books became miniature classrooms, as I sought to understand the sermons I had transcribed. The body of work involving the Puritans is staggering, and the sources so far listed, combined with this book's entire bibliography, represent only the sources I have read and benefited from so far.

Stephen Foster's *The Long Argument: English Puritanism and the Shaping of New England Culture, 1570–1700*. Lisa M. Gordis, *Opening Scripture: Bible Reading and Interpretive Authority in Puritan New England*. E. Brooks Holifield, *Theology in America: Christian Thought from the Age of the Puritans to the Civil War*. Norman Pettit, The *Heart Prepared: Grace and Conversion in Puritan Spiritual Life* and The *Heart Renewed: Assurance of Salvation in New England Spiritual Life*. David A. Weir's *Early New England: A Covenanted Society* completes the list. While by no means an exhaustive listing, scholars of the Puritans will certainly be familiar with all of these works.

The seventeenth century Puritan sermons of Massachusetts, especially those in print, are well known and well examined; however, the absence of works by Connecticut's ministers during this period makes the study of Connecticut's Puritans a bit more challenging. I am not suggesting that the *Hartford Sermon Notebook* is the only manuscript of its kind, but after reading numerous secondary sources on Puritanism in New England, and especially after reading the books of many acclaimed historians of Puritanism and consulting their bibliographies, the unpublished sermons of Connecticut's Puritans appear far less often in the literature than those of Massachusetts. In most cases, the bibliographies contained in the secondary sources do not list any repositories or locations for the unpublished sermons of Connecticut's ministers during the seventeenth century.

It has been argued that New England Puritan ministers were similar intellectually. Virtually all of the ministers from the second generation,

(1666 to 1700) were Harvard educated, so that the word as preached in Massachusetts was akin to that of Connecticut. Based on that statement, there is little chance that the sermons of Hartford's preachers were radically different from those of Massachusetts relative to Puritan theology. David Hall's homogenous characterization of the Puritan ministers of New England supports this view: "Dispersed throughout a hundred towns, the clergy helped maintain a common system. They had all been trained alike; they all thought alike," and after reading all of Hall's major published works, the ministers were definitely like-minded theologically.[6]

Fully transcribed, the *Hartford Sermon Notebook* is valuable because it contains the sermons of at least five different ministers. Five different Puritan minds and souls are contained in one seventeenth-century document, including Isaac Foster, Ben Woodbridge, Caleb Watson, John Whiting and Thomas Cheever from Malden, Massachusetts.[7]

Ultimately, the most important aspect of this book may be the transcription itself, a process that has consumed much of the last three years, and transcribing the notebook has been one of the most rewarding intellectual pursuits of my life. I have chosen to maintain the pagination of the notebook in the transcription. Unquestionably, a thematic arrangement of the sermons might prove interesting, but there are many examples in the notebook where the sermons flow from one to the next chronologically and thematically, especially regarding the "sermon series" arrangements of Isaac Foster.

---

[6] David D. Hall, *Worlds of Wonder, Days of Judgment: Popular Religious Belief in Early New England* (Cambridge Massachusetts: Harvard University Press, 1990), 6.

[7] It has been suggested that Perry Miller's work leans too heavily toward Puritan thought rather than Puritan heart. For a thorough introduction to the New England Puritans, I suggest the work of David Hall, Harry Stout, Edmund Morgan, and Charles Hambrick Stowe. Together, their books cover a wide spectrum of Puritan religious, intellectual, and cultural beliefs. For a discussion of the pastor/teacher dynamic in colonial New England churches see David D. Hall, *The Faithful Shepherd: A History of the New England Ministry in the Seventeenth Century* (Cambridge Massachusetts: Harvard University Press for Harvard Theological Studies, 2006), 95. For an interesting but somewhat dated discussion of the subject, see Vergil V. Phelps, "The Pastor and Teacher in New England." *Harvard Theological Review* 4 (July 1911): 388–399. Generally, the teacher defined the various elements of scripture, while the preacher exhorted the congregation to live by them. The important distinction here is that Caleb Watson was Hartford's schoolmaster not its teacher. The teacher/pastor dynamic was a Calvinist structure that came with the Puritans to the new world, but which had virtually disappeared from New England's churches by the end of the seventeenth century.

The structure of the book is in three parts. Part one includes a concise history of the Puritans, along with some of the elements that help define Puritanism. Part one also includes biographies of the ministers whose sermons appear in the notebook. Here I provide only a brief introduction to Puritan religious history, with a focus on some of the specific characteristics of Puritan ministers. The intention is to contextualize the sermons with a background history of the Puritans in both the Old World and New. Again, this book is principally concerned with the transcription and analysis of the sermons themselves, but the sermons are far more interesting when we know something about the lives and ideas of the ministers who preached them.

Part two deals with the paleography and transcription of the notebook. Many of the shorthand characteristics found in the notebook made the paleography extremely challenging, and are worth describing in some detail. Photocopied examples from the original notebook are included to show some of the more interesting transcription challenges encountered.

Part three contains the transcription of the notebook's 62 sermons. To preserve the transcription as a unique document, my analysis of the sermons appears in the introduction of each sermon or sermon series, and in footnotes. By separating my analysis of the sermons from the transcription itself, my purpose is for other scholars to be more easily able to analyze the transcribed sermons as original primary sources.

In the analysis, certain sermons receive more attention than others do, which is simply a function of the subjective nature of the book, and not indicative of the importance of any particular sermon. While constrained as an exhaustive study of the doctrines and ideas contained in the sermon notebook, the analysis mainly serves to complement the transcription.

PART ONE

HISTORY AND BIOGRAPHY

CHAPTER ONE

A SHORT HISTORY OF THE PURITANS

The Hartford Sermon Notebook is a product of the Reformation, and with the rise of humanism and the popularity of the cults of antiquity, Europeans since before the time of Luther and Calvin had been reaching back many centuries for answers to questions about their world. Donatism, with its pursuit of a perfect church on Earth, and St. Augustine's distinction between the visible and invisible churches, are only fragmentary examples of the impact of early Christianity on what would become Protestantism, and ultimately for this book, Puritanism.[1] In other words, Puritanism did not spontaneously erupt somewhere in England during the sixteenth century. The ideas that shaped it took centuries to grow, and in terms of the Reformation as a movement, the story of the Puritans is but one of its chapters.

In *The New England Mind: the Seventeenth Century*, Perry Miller tells us, "The soul of Puritan theology is the hidden God, who is not fully revealed even in His own revelation. The Bible is His declared will; behind it always lies His secret will."[2] Miller notes that the Puritan religious ethos as determined by scripture was not restrained to Sunday devotions. Puritans used the Bible as a kind of blueprint for behavior, and not simply personal behavior, but in matters of theology, politics, economics and military exploits, the Bible was the instructive source.[3]

---

[1] Edmund S. Morgan, *Visible Saints: the History of a Puritan Idea* (Ithaca: Cornell University Press, 1963), 2–3. In addition, in an interesting article "Were There Any Puritans in New England?" *The New England Quarterly* 74, no. 1 (March 2001), 118–138, the historian Michael Winship argues that the very meaning of the term "Puritan" is problematic and in need of reassessment. This book uses the term "Puritan" throughout its pages. I believe "Puritan" is a recognizable historical term that, while objectionable to some, is an accepted point of reference for most historians and theologians.

[2] Perry Miller, *The New England Mind, Vol. 1: The Seventeenth Century* (Cambridge Massachusetts: The Belknap Press of the Harvard University Press, 1982), 21.

[3] Perry Miller and Thomas H. Johnson eds., *The Puritans: A Sourcebook of their Writings*, 43.

Similarly, the historian David Hall credits the uniqueness of the Bible over all other books by virtue of its status as the "Word." "All other texts were copies of this one original; all other forms of truth were incomplete or partial next to Scripture. It was the living speech of God, the "voice" of Christ, a text that people heard."[4] The important distinction made by Hall is that people "heard" the sermon, which enhances the uniqueness of the *Hartford Sermon Notebook*, since the sermons it contains were not edited or prepared for the printing press. Indeed, as Paul Lucas writes in *The Valley of Discord,* seventeenth century Connecticut had no printing press of its own, which clearly limited the publishing possibilities for its ministers.[5]

Puritans were English Protestants, and England's Reformation spanned the years 1527–1660. According to the historian and minister Charles Hambrick-Stowe, "Puritanism in England, whatever else it accomplished in the economic, ecclesiastical, political, and social turmoil of the period, was a devotional movement dedicated to the spiritual regeneration of individuals and society."[6] As mainland Europe struggled over the ideas of men like Luther and Calvin, England wrestled with its own Protestant Reformation.

England's Protestant movement was rooted in the fourteenth century dissenter tradition of John Wycliffe, the Oxford theologian. Wycliffe, like Luther, insisted that lay people improve themselves spiritually by reading the Bible.[7] In 1519, Luther discovered that his work was influencing England, and that an Augustinian friar named Robert Barnes, in Cambridge, at a place called the White Horse Inn, was leading discussions there. Known as "Little Germany," the island, like the mainland, was moving toward its divorce from Rome.[8]

In *Puritans in the New World*, David Hall briefly explores the origin of the name "Puritan," as an interesting historical aside. Hall's reference is from Bradford's *Of Plymouth Plantation*, where the term

---

[4] David D. Hall, *Worlds of Wonder, Days of Judgment*, 24.

[5] Paul R. Lucas, *Valley of Discord: Church and Society along the Connecticut River, 1636–1725* (Hanover New Hampshire: The University Press of New England, 1976), 212.

[6] Charles E. Hambrick-Stowe, *The Practice of Piety: Puritan Devotional Disciplines in Seventeenth-Century New England* (Chapel Hill: The University of North Carolina Press, 1982), 23.

[7] James D. Tracy, *Europe's Reformations, 1450–1650* (Lanham Maryland: Rowman & Littlefield, 1999), 185.

[8] Ibid.

"Puritan" is traced to the fourth century C.E., and was apparently a kind of mockery that grew from a controversy within the Christian church. The name grew legs in the sixteenth century and became a caricature in popular theater: "the Puritan as a zealous busybody."[9] As Hall explains it, the Puritans of the seventeenth century embraced the term, and it became more generally associated with piety and commitment to God.[10]

During the Reformation, the English monarchy tended to bounce back and forth between Catholicism and Protestantism, depending on who held the reins of power. Henry VIII's split with Rome is well known (1534–1547),[11] but his children were no less controversial in English religious history. Henry was followed by the Protestant period of Edward VI (1547–1553), which was reversed by Mary Tudor who briefly reestablished Catholicism (1553–1558). Elizabeth I revived English Protestantism (1558–1603),[12] and was succeeded by Scotland's James I (1603–1625). Ultimately, James produced an heir in Charles I, who leaned toward the Episcopal Church and who was later beheaded by Oliver Cromwell's forces, ushering in a period of parliamentary control better known as the "Commonwealth" (1646–1658).[13]

Monarchs were not the only victims of the executioner's axe or the flames of the stake. Often beheaded or burned alive, England's religious martyrs fared no better during the Reformation.[14] To say the least, a cursory study of this period of English history reveals a tendency toward violent resolution to religious conflict and dissent, but

---

9 David D. Hall, *Puritans in the New World: A Critical Anthology* (Princeton: Princeton University Press, 2004), x.

10 Ibid.

11 As discussed by Edmund Morgan in *Visible Saints,* Henry VIII did something else that would have a tremendous impact on England's reformation when he allowed the translation of the Bible into English, thus spreading the "Word" to a wider audience on the island. Morgan, *Visible Saints*, 5.

12 Even though Elizabeth was a Protestant, she was also a shrewd politician, who constantly played Catholic and Protestant sympathies against one another to suit her needs. According to Edmund Morgan "In spite of Elizabeth's political skill, the Puritans increased their numbers steadily and continued to demand further reforms. But by the close of Elizabeth's reign they had made little headway." Morgan, *Visible Saints*, 5–6.

13 Tracy, *Europe's Reformations*, 186.

14 In his essay, "Contesting Control of Orthodoxy Among the Godly: William Pynchon Reexamined." *The William and Mary Quarterly* 54, no. 4 (October 1997), 796, Michael Winship reveals that the last English Burning of a Heretic, the Arian Edward Wightman, took place in 1612.

the specific nature of the Puritan struggle in England is what gave rise to "New England" and is where we must turn to contextualize the sermons contained in the *Hartford Sermon Notebook.*

In general, if we think of the Puritans as Protestants, we can cautiously summarize their beliefs. Certain Protestant concepts were generally accepted by Puritans; that Rome and the Pope were the enemies of Christ, that the Catholic list of sacraments was too long, and that what was needed most was an end to the centuries of obedience to Catholic priests, who by the close of the sixteenth century were often less versed in scripture than the people they were preaching to. Puritans expressed their ire with certain ministers calling them "Dumme Dogs, Unskilful sacrificing priestes, Destroyeing Drones, or rather Catepillars of the Word."[15] In his works, Perry Miller often uniquely describes "who" the Puritans were, and he describes them with a comfortable ease of familiarity unlike few other Puritan scholars. Writing in the 1930's, in response to other scholar's attempts at classification of the Puritans, Miller says:

> It is important to note that the Puritans were fully aware of the figure they cut. They did not, like some of their modern apologists, argue that a man can have a 'good time' even though a Puritan. Living was serious business, and those who took it gaily here would come to a reckoning hereafter. What made it supportable to them was not the incidental amusements along the way but the one engrossing joy of saints' communion with the God who had made them and had redeemed them (Miller, *The New England Mind*, 60).

By the end of the sixteenth century, Puritans had established much of their belief system, which, as James Tracy describes it, consisted of "a more general demand for purging the liturgy of a long list of "popish" elements, like saints' days, candles, the exchange of rings at marriage, prayers at the graveside, and the religious celebration of Christmas."[16] Personal behavior, one's external qualities, mattered very much to the Puritan, as revealed by Edmund Morgan's example that Puritans "did not differ from their contemporaries in their views

---

[15] *Seconde Parte of a Register*, II, 211. As cited in Morgan, *Visible Saints*, 7. Included in Morgan's book are examples from the Registers of various "undesirable" men who had become preachers, including one "Mr Levit, parson of Leden Roding, a notorious swearer, a dicer, a carder, a hawker and hunter, a verie careless person, he had a childe by a maid since he was instituted and inducted..." *Visible Saints*, 8.

[16] Tracy, *Europe's Reformations*, 195.

about the importance of salvation as much as they did in their views about behavior... they wrote hundreds of books explaining the exact conduct demanded by God in every human situation."[17]

As the end of Elizabeth's monarchy approached, certain key elements of the Protestant ethos remained contentious, and one of the most important concepts prevailing was John Calvin's predestination.[18] When simplified, predestination is just about as it sounds, certain Christians were predestined for an afterlife in heaven, or conversely, damnation in hell. Calvin declared that predestination was "God's eternal decree, by which he compacted with himself what he willed to become of each man... eternal life is foreordained for some, eternal damnation for others. Therefore, as any man has been created to one or the other of these ends, we speak of him as predestined to life or death."[19]

The many implications of predestination are interesting. One might have asked the question, how do I know if I am predestined, and what might I be predestined for? These questions were born of Calvin's conception of predestination, and New England's Puritans searched for answers to them as they sought to create a community of the Elect. Predestination was also important to Reformed Theology because it went side by side with the doctrine of justification by grace alone.[20] In other words, grace and predestination are God's divine choice, and you could not have one without the other.

Perry Miller's definition of Puritans as Calvinists is helpful: "It is true, the Puritans were Calvinists, if we mean that they more or less agreed with the great theologian of Geneva."[21] Calvinism had an important influence on Puritan theology. The extreme exclusivity of the Puritan system, the church of the elect, was staggering, and even more so in the hands of New England's Puritans, who placed 3000 miles of ocean

---

[17] Edmund S. Morgan, *The Puritan Family: Religion and Domestic Relations in Seventeenth-Century New England* (New York: Harper and Row Publishers, 1966), 2. The *Hartford Sermon Notebook* contains dozens of references to the internal and external man, and I believe these words are meant in the behavioral sense. It is this appearance of piety, which ties directly into Puritan concerns about the unknown hypocrites among them.

[18] Tracy, *Europe's Reformations*, 195.

[19] William Stacy Johnson ed., *Reformed Reader: A Sourcebook in Christian Theology* (Louisville, Kentucky: Westminster/John Knox Press, 1993), 93.

[20] Ibid., 86.

[21] Miller and Johnson, *The Puritan Source Book*, 56.

between themselves and any major competing forms. The Hartford Sermon Notebook contains many examples of this exclusivity, and its preachers make a clear distinction between the regenerated elect, and the unregenerate damned.[22]

The historian David Hall points to a particular Calvinist doctrine known as Calvin's "middle way," and as it pertained to the ministry, it went roughly as follows: "Calvin warned that some Protestants erred in assigning no special privileges to the ministry, while others exaggerated its power beyond measure."[23] Calvin sought a structure for the ministry that was somewhere in between the poles, a "middle way." According to Hall, Calvin formulated this concept of the ministry from the apostle Paul, who believed his actions were a response to the Holy Spirit, independent of his own force of will. Calvin understood the ministry to be fuelled by God's Holy Spirit, without which ministers would simply be lecturers, rather than men of God.[24] In other words, Calvin did not believe that the ministry possessed any special sacramental power, and that without the Holy Spirit, the word of God had no power to save.[25]

Calvin's theology includes much more than the nature of the ministry, but it is an important distinction here because of the nature of Hartford's ministry, circa 1679–1680. Calvin's concept of the ministry plays out in the *Hartford Sermon Notebook*, in Isaac Foster's ordination sermon, and in other sermons where Foster seemed to have been a mediator for God. Hartford's ministers, especially Foster, implored the congregation of Hartford to seek Christ for the assurance of eternal salvation that can only come from the son of God, but there are also

[22] Article VII from the Synod of Dort defines the elect in Calvin's terms, making it clear that election comes before salvation, and only by the grace of God: "Election is the unchangeable purpose of God, whereby, before the foundation of the world, he hath, out of mere grace, according to the sovereign good pleasure of his own will, chosen, from the whole human race, which had fallen through their own fault, from their primitive state of rectitude, into sin and destruction, a certain number of persons to redemption in Christ, whom he from eternity appointed the Mediator and head of the elect, and the foundation of salvation." William Stacy Johnson ed., *Reformed Reader: A Sourcebook in Christian Theology* (Louisville, Kentucky: Westminster/John Knox Press, 1993), 98.

[23] David D. Hall, *The Faithful Shepherd: A History of the New England Ministry in the Seventeenth Century* (Cambridge Massachusetts: Harvard University Press for Harvard Theological Studies, 2006), 9.

[24] Ibid.

[25] Hall, *The Faithful Shepherd*, 10.

many warnings in the sermons, whose general message is the exhortation that life without Christ is the surest way to damnation.

John Calvin influenced the Puritans as much as he did any other reformed church of the sixteenth and seventeenth centuries, but there were important differences between Calvin and the Puritans, especially concerning the covenant. The basic definition of the covenant as it relates to the Puritans in New England was a gathered church of voluntary believers, seeking perfection as visible saints under the watchful eye of God.

According to Edmund Morgan, after Mary's death, the church of England "Swept in Papist and Protestant alike in the wholesale conversion of the realm...Elizabeth had swept the whole people of England into her so-called church just as Calvin had allegedly done with the people of Geneva. Every Englishman had been automatically transformed by government decree into a member of the new Anglican Church. There had been no voluntary gathering of believers."[26] The essential difference, and what was especially significant to the Puritans who settled and formed churches in New England, is the subtly important point of voluntary membership. Puritans were not interested in making everyone a member of the church, nor did they need to. Instead, Puritans in New England who were members of their church were able to make church attendance and ministerial upkeep mandatory for everyone, while keeping membership and sacramental benefits to themselves, the Elect, the "visible saints." In other words, the Puritans had created a much more exclusive system that did not seek a "middle way." The Puritan system was more orthodox, and in general, New England's Puritans did not believe in making concessions to those unfortunate souls among them not counted as members, though many of the sermons in the Hartford Sermon Notebook are exhortations to non-members.

The often-prolonged process New England Puritans employed to "call" a minister seems very Calvinist given that the congregation decided the fate of their minister before, during, and after his ordination, instead of some distant bishopric. The account of Isaac Foster's call and ordination as it related to the ministers "call" is especially interesting. Harry Stout describes the power of New England's ministers as "awesome", yet he also explains that it was not arbitrary power,

[26] Morgan, *Visible Saints*, 24–25.

but rather, that New England's ministers simply possessed the formal education required, and via ordination, a kind of license to practice as preachers. The ministers were not necessarily any more inspired than most laymen were, they simply earned the right to be the preacher. Stout also points out that when these ministers abused their right to preach, they could be, and at times were, dismissed by the congregation.[27] The Thomas Cheever biography in chapter two, Cheever was harshly reprimanded and dismissed by his congregation, demonstrates the authority of New England's congregations. The point is simply that Puritan ministers were not untouchable, and the sermon notebook contains several examples where its ministers implore the congregation to support them.

The ministers of colonial New England were part of a large but mostly decentralized system of belief, whose ultimate goal was to guide God's elect to a final reunion with Christ. The ministers of the *Hartford Sermon Notebook* are commonly referred to as those of the second generation, and they functioned within a system that was very different from that of the Old World.[28]

David Hall's comparison of the relationship of church and state in the Old and New Worlds reveals some important differences among ministers on both sides of the Atlantic. The European model entailed a very close relationship between church and state. The church was everyone's church, with the king at the top. The church was closely associated with political and social functions, and many times, the church imposed its will through the civil courts. This dynamic tended to arouse a spirit of anti-clericalism, and general disdain for the clergy.[29]

The colonial experience in New England was quite different. Church courts were non-existent, and church membership was voluntary. There were no Inquisitions, and the civil magistrate imposed the penalties. The power of the clergy in New England was spiritual, and not part of the state apparatus. Hall asserts that these important differences created an environment that was less anti-clerical than that of Europe.[30]

---

[27] Stout, *The New England Soul*, 19.

[28] See Harry Stout's *The New England Soul* for a thorough description of the generational breakdown of New England's ministers.

[29] David Hall, *World of Wonders, Days of Judgment*, 6.

[30] Ibid.

New England's ministers may have been less likely to arouse anti-clericalism than their counterparts in England, but the ordination day sermons of Isaac Foster contain an imploring element where he and Woodbridge seem to plead with the congregation to support Foster's ministry, as if support would not be forthcoming unless they did so. As a young preacher, Foster was very much in need of mutual acceptance on the part of his congregation; he knew they could send him packing, but given the chance, he could prove himself worthy.

Puritanism was a set of beliefs, it was a separate formulation of Protestantism with its own unique structure, but it was not yet a separate church.[31] Tracy tells us "Puritans had a distinctive tendency to personalize the doctrine of predestination, searching within their own experience for a moment of conversion at which God's grace had entered their lives."[32] Within this Puritan way there grew two very distinct systems that would later present many challenges to Puritans in New England, namely, Presbyterianism and Congregationalism. While Calvin influenced both systems, differences existed between them. The Presbyterian design consisted of a system of representative ecclesiastical bodies that functioned together as a larger church. This was in marked contrast to Congregationalism, which refused "to recognize any larger church body," and was known as the Independent wing. Independents "believed decisions on all important matters must be made by each congregation."[33]

The social historian T.H. Breen provides a diversion from the specifically religious nature of the Reformation and its impact on the colonization of New England. Breen's book *Puritans and Adventurers: Change and Persistence in Early America* analyzes the forces in England that contributed to the New World exodus of the seventeenth century.[34] The book contains a series of essays that cover a geographic spectrum of immigration from New England to Virginia, and his description of the decay of the provincial localized villages of England is very

[31] Tracy, *Europe's Reformations*, 195.
[32] Ibid.
[33] Ibid., 196.
[34] An excellent launching pad for Puritan social history begins with Edmund Morgan, and I would also suggest the works of David Hall. These historians do not easily classify into one methodological camp, and for my purposes, they do not need to. I would suggest that they both qualify as historians of many methods, and that their intellectual insights are second to none regarding New England in the seventeenth century.

interesting. Breen argues that forces other than religious zeal contributed greatly to patterns of immigration.[35] However, while Breen does not completely dismiss the impetus of religious independence, he argues that its role was secondary to that of the dynamic changes imposed on local loyalties by the English monarchy, and that the particularism that dominated so much of the English countryside in the seventeenth century was under attack.[36]

While Breen offers a compelling argument for forces of immigration other than religion, there were several motivations at work, not the least of which was religious freedom. The historian David Weir suggests that we should be aware of many possible contributors to the immigrants of seventeenth century New England. "The complexity of the human psyche cannot simply be reduced to any one motivating force for migration: any individual could have numerous reasons for migrating to the new world...Economic, political, and religious factors were certainly often public and primary..."[37] Clearly, a variety of influences including religious preference, contributed to the complex migration of English people to New England.

Perhaps the most well known Puritans were the Separatists. This group includes the Pilgrims, who because of their views regarding baptism, they believed it was sacrilegious to baptize infants, were harassed by the Church of England. The Pilgrims separated from the Church of England and fled to Holland in 1607. Despite the relative freedom of worship the Pilgrims experienced in the Dutch Republic, the fear of Dutch acculturation provided much of the impetus for an Atlantic crossing and the famed voyage of the Mayflower.[38]

In 1620, the Pilgrims completed their Atlantic crossing and settled in Plymouth, but it is important to recognize that the Pilgrims were refugees from England, unlike the waves of English who followed them; non-separating Puritans like John Winthrop and John Cotton, who established the Massachusetts Bay colony at Boston, and Thomas Hooker's Hartford, Connecticut. The Bay Company was not running away from the problems of religious intolerance in England, rather,

---

[35] T.H. Breen, *Puritans and Adventurers: Change and Persistence in Early America* (New York: Oxford University Press, 1980), 10.
[36] Ibid., 7.
[37] David A. Weir, *Early New England: A Covenanted Society*, 28–29.
[38] Tracy, *Europe's Reformations*, 196.

it was a "task force of Christians" whose goal was the completion of Europe's reformation in the Puritan image.[39]

Massachusetts Bay was a chartered colony of England that generally recognized the Church of England as a real church and enjoyed agreeable commerce with the mother country, but more importantly to its first settlers, the Bay Colony enjoyed a religious independence in the New World that simply was not possible had they remained in England. Under the leadership of Thomas Hooker, Hartford's earliest settlers found agreeable acreage and greater autonomy on the banks of the Connecticut River, but neither Massachusetts Bay nor Connecticut sought outward separation from the Church of England, they simply put an ocean between England's church and their own desired form of worship.

[39] Perry Miller, *Errand Into the Wilderness* (Cambridge Massachusetts: The Belknap Press of the Harvard University Press, 1956), 11.

CHAPTER TWO

HARTFORD'S MINISTERS (1679–1680)

Five different ministers preached the sermons contained in the *Hartford Sermon Notebook*. Most of the New England ministers of the late seventeenth century were graduates of Harvard College, and with the exception of Benjamin Woodbridge, all of the ministers in the *Hartford Sermon Notebook* graduated from Harvard. At Harvard, the course of study included not only the requisite theological topics necessary to preach the word of God, but also the scholarly subjects of the day, including rhetoric, art, science, and logic.[1] That the ministers were highly educated was a function of the religious system they themselves had designed, which would never have sustained itself in New England without Harvard College.[2]

The need for Harvard in early New England, as described by Edmund Morgan, shows the importance of preaching and erudition among Puritans: "Puritans set much store by preaching, which they considered the principal means ordained by God for instructing people in the great truths revealed by Scriptures."[3] To stay in the pulpit, preachers had to know their scripture "inside and out," or the literate, instructed congregations of New England would have replaced them.[4] The literate, learned nature of the "common man" in New England is well documented. These merchants and farmers were highly instructed,

---

1 Miller and Johnson, *The Puritan Source Book*, 20.

2 For additional sources on early Harvard curriculum see: T.G. Hahn, "Urian Oakes's Elegie on Thomas Shepard and Puritan Poetics." *American Literature* 45, no. 2 (May 1973), 163–181; Joe W. Kraus, "The Development of a Curriculum in the Early American Colleges." *History of Education Quarterly* 1, no. 2 (June 1961), 64–76; Samuel Eliot Morison, The *Founding of Harvard College* (Cambridge: Harvard University Press, 1935) and, Samuel Eliot Morison, "The Harvard School of Astronomy in the Seventeenth Century." *The New England Quarterly* 7, no. 1 (March 1934), 3–24. See also Lisa M. Gordis, *Opening Scripture: Bible Reading and Interpretive Authority in Puritan New England.* (Chicago: The University of Chicago Press, 2003).

3 Morgan, *Visible Saints*, 7.

4 David Hall's *Worlds of Wonder Days of Judgment* and Charles Hambrick Stow's *The Practice of Piety* both contain in-depth analysis of the extent to which New England's Puritans could read, write, and converse with one another on many levels regarding scripture and Christianity. As these books point out, the Puritans were an intellectually savvy group, and were well versed in the tenets of their faith.

and well versed in theology, and they often discussed important topics such as predestination and infant damnation.[5]

Not surprisingly, the scholarly nature of Puritan preachers and their congregations held true in Hartford. The sermons that Hartford's ministers preached contained a variety of subjects ranging from covenant doctrines, the processes of regeneration, conversion, salvation, the power of sin and the glory of grace. The sermons transcribed in this study include these subjects and others, including intemperance and its effects on Indians, and the pervasiveness of the Devil in the lives of the congregation.

This book is primarily concerned with the transcription and analysis of the notebook's sermons, but as with the previous chapter on Puritan history, the sermons are more interesting when the ministers who preached them are given some life, making biographical backgrounds useful. John Langdon Sibley's *Biographical Sketches of the Graduates of Harvard University* guides the biographies. Sibley's work is important because, as Paul Lucas discusses in *Valley of Discord*, many eighteenth and nineteenth century histories relied on primary sources that no longer exist.[6] Were it not for the work of these historians, who very often quoted heavily from the primary source documents, much of colonial New England's history would be lost. This is especially true for Connecticut, where extant documents from the seventeenth century are quite rare.

The notebook contains only one first or "Christian" name, that of Ben Woodbridge, and with two exceptions in which no names appear, all of the sermons begin with the salutation Mr., followed by the minister's last name and the date. There are slight variations in the order of name and date for a small number of the sermons, but in general, the order adheres to the preachers name followed by the date. Based on colonial period class rosters from Harvard College, an examination of the ecclesiastical and church records at the Connecticut State Library, manuscripts from the Massachusetts Historical Society, and brief appearances by these ministers in other primary and secondary sources cited here, I am confident that my identifications of the notebook's ministers are accurate.

---

[5] Miller and Johnson, *The Puritan Source Book*, 14.

[6] Lucas, *Valley of Discord*, 209–210. In his bibliographic essay, Lucas discusses the importance of eighteenth and nineteenth century histories as pseudo primary sources for documents that no longer exist.

As previously stated, the *Hartford Sermon Notebook* is valuable partly because it contains the sermons of at least five different ministers, including Isaac Foster, Ben Woodbridge, Caleb Watson (school-master), John Whiting and Thomas Cheever from Malden Massachusetts. Cheever may have been visiting his sister who lived in Farmington. John Whiting was pastor of the First Church in Hartford until 1670, when he became pastor of the newly founded Second Church, a result of a schism in Hartford over the contentiousness of the Half-Way Covenant.[7] Caleb Watson's tenure as a schoolmaster in Hartford is well documented, and the grave of Isaac Foster is located in Hartford's Ancient Burial Ground, on Main Street, at the property of the First Congregational Church. Foster is buried near Timothy Woodbridge who succeeded him as minister in 1682 or 1683 upon Foster's death, the result of an epidemic that was sweeping through the colony.[8]

It is very likely that the six sermons of "Mr. Woodbridge" are all the work of Ben Woodbridge, who had been pastor of the Windsor church, and somewhat less likely that they are the work of John Woodbridge who was the pastor in Wethersfield, or Timothy Woodbridge, Foster's successor. Based on information contained in *The Colonial Clergy and the Colonial Churches of New England*, Timothy Woodbridge was settled in Kittery, Maine from 1680–1682. Foster and Timothy Woodbridge very likely had some kind of friendship, since Foster was a tutor at Harvard when Timothy Woodbridge was a student. I have included brief biographies for both John and Timothy Woodbridge mainly to be thorough. The Woodbridge sermons could be the work of John or Timothy, but the likelihood that they are all the work of Ben Woodbridge seems more plausible based on the themes of these sermons. I will present evidence for the details of this conclusion in the Ben Woodbridge biography and in analysis of the Woodbridge sermons.

Timothy Woodbridge received his B.A. from Harvard in 1675 and his M.A. in 1678.[9] In 1683, he settled in Hartford and was ordained

[7] The John Whiting biography that follows discusses the breakup of Hartford's church.

[8] Written sources indicate Foster died in August 1682, while his marker at the cemetery indicates 1683.

[9] John Langdon Sibley, *Biographical Sketches of Graduates of Harvard University, Volume II 1659–1677* (Cambridge, Massachusetts: Charles William Sever, 1881), 465.

minister of the First Church on November 18, 1685.[10] Timothy Woodbridge was one of the original founders of Yale University. He fought unsuccessfully to locate the school in Wethersfield, and New Haven won the honor of becoming the location for Connecticut's premier university. He served as pastor of the First Church in Hartford until his death in 1732.[11]

Obituaries of the day said of Timothy Woodbridge that he "was a learned, well accomplished and grave Divine. His natural and acquired Endowments, in conjunction with his steady piety, Prudence, and Zeal, and Faithfulness in his Lord's Work, render'd him truly great, a star of the first magnitude..."[12]

John Woodbridge, an older brother of Timothy, received his B.A. from Harvard in 1664. He was first a preacher in Killingworth (Clinton), Connecticut where he was ordained in 1669–1670. John Haynes of Hartford, the predecessor to Isaac Foster, imposed hands.[13] Sibley does not indicate why, but in 1678–9, John Woodbridge resigned as minister in Killingworth and settled in Wethersfield, becoming their minister in 1679. He preached in Wethersfield until his death in 1691.

Sibley's biography also includes some interesting facts concerning fortifications constructed for John Woodbridge when he was pastor at Killingworth (Clinton), Connecticut in 1675. The fortifications were a reaction to the beginnings of King Philip's War. Note also, that in colonial New England, while the town meetinghouse was the center of civic and spiritual gatherings, it was also the town's innermost fortification for any final stand against invaders. From the summer of 1675 to the summer of 1676, Metacom, King Philip was his English name, a Wampanoag chief, led an uprising of his tribe that quickly spread over much of New England involving most of New England's Algonquian tribes. It was an extremely bloody conflict, and as the sermons of Isaac

---

[10] Ibid.

[11] Sibley, *Harvard Graduates*, 465.

[12] Ibid., 467.

[13] Ibid., 156. Imposing hands was part of the ordination rite. It was a tradition that has been traced to Christ's forgiveness of those disciples who had doubted him. See Paul Bernier's *Ministry in the Church: A Pastoral Approach* (Mystic CT: Twenty-Third Publications, 1992), 71.

Foster attest, the impact of the war left a considerable mark on the consciousness of the colonists.[14]

Sibley also notes that John Woodbridge was infirm for some years before he died, and that in 1682 the town of Wethersfield voted to give him an additional twenty pounds to defray the costs of his "extraordinary charges."[15] I do not know exactly what this means, but it is clear that John Woodbridge was not a completely healthy man around the time of the *Hartford Sermon Notebook's* creation. Therefore, it is possible to infer that the Woodbridge sermons may not be his, due to some physical infirmity that may have prevented him from traveling or preaching. I acknowledge that this is sheer speculation, but as previously stated, conclusive proof of the Woodbridge identities has little impact on the value of the sermons, and is more of an interesting aside.

Benjamin Woodbridge is not included in *Sibley's Harvard Graduates* because he did not graduate, but he did attend Harvard. He was also a central figure in Windsor, Connecticut's lengthy doctrinal struggle over church government, to be or not to be Presbyterian, and the Half-Way Covenant. This covenant held that a child of a church member, upon reaching adulthood, but not themselves able to relate an experience of conversion sufficient enough to earn membership in the church, would still be able to have their children baptized. This sounds more confusing than it actually is. The bottom line is simply that a generation of New Englanders was reaching maturity, and many of them had not become fully-fledged members of the church, but although they were not yet part of that exclusive group known as the Elect, they nevertheless were able to obtain the baptismal sacrament for their children.[16]

For orthodox Puritans, this was simply unacceptable, and the resultant conflict saw many New England churches split in two. Hartford endured its schism in 1670, when John Whiting and his followers created Hartford's Second Church. Whiting and his supporters were of

---

[14] Two excellent recent sources on King Philip's War include: *The Name of War: King Philip's War and the Origins of American Identity* by Jill Lepore, and *King Philip's War: The History and Legacy of America's Forgotten Conflict* by Eric Schultz and Michael Tougias.

[15] Sibley, *Harvard Graduates*, 157.

[16] See: Robert G Pope. *The Half-Way Covenant: Church Membership in Puritan New England* (Princeton: Princeton University Press, 1969).

the "we don't like it ilk." While Hartford's churches diverged on the issues of church membership and baptism, sermons from both sides appear in the notebook. I would cautiously suggest that this indicates a somewhat greater tolerance among Puritans for divergent ideas, with the understanding that the "word" mattered most on Sunday, rather than the Half-Way leanings of one's neighbors.[17] It is also important to remember that Puritans, as with many Protestants, did not believe in the large number of sacraments practiced by the Catholic Church. Essentially, baptism and the Eucharist completed their list of acceptable, biblically inspired sacraments, which helps to explain why baptism became such a contentious issue to the Puritans of New England.

As for Ben Woodbridge, it seems that being able to preach the word may have mattered more than a preacher's educational credentials since, even though he did not graduate from Harvard, he was Windsor's preacher from 1670 to 1681. During this time, Windsor was embroiled in its own Presbyterian/Congregational struggle for power, and according to the research of Paul Lucas, there were several casualties. The town had decided to let Woodbridge and his Presbyterian followers have their own church in much the same way as Hartford had done. Apparently, this arrangement was initially successful, but not sustainable. According to Lucas, it was an uneasy truce, but the final factor in the demise of the Presbyterians was money. "The town grew tired of its new creation and refused to support Second Church as liberally as it supported First."[18]

The membership rolls at Second Church in Windsor began to shrink, and sometime around 1677 the members of Second Church decided to disband and rejoin First Church. The bitterness of their initial fight is revealed by the refusal of First Church to allow their wayward neighbors to return unless they offered themselves up for a new public examination concerning their fitness for membership, keeping in mind that the same people they had formerly covenanted within First Church would be the people testing their fitness. Of course, the members of Second Church refused to subject themselves to what must have seemed nothing short of public humiliation. Eventually, an

---

[17] There are many excellent books and articles pertaining to the Half-Way covenant and New England church politics in the seventeenth century. Pope's *Half-Way Covenant* is the standard source, and many other sources that discuss New England's Puritan history devote some analysis to it.

[18] Lucas, *Valley of Discord*, 69.

accord was temporarily reached when both First and Second Church fired their ministers Ben Woodbridge and Nathaniel Chauncey, since the two men had become the unfortunate symbols of the conflict.[19]

Ben Woodbridge may have sought refuge in Hartford's First Church, which leaned toward Presbyterianism, and perhaps his sermon appears because he may have stayed in Hartford while waiting for his next call. After close readings of the Woodbridge sermons, and based on the contentious history of Windsor's church regarding the Half-Way covenant and church membership, I am inclined to believe that all of the Woodbridge sermons are the work of Ben Woodbridge. Lastly, the idea that all of the Woodbridge sermons are those of Ben Woodbridge seems even more likely considering the infirmity of John Woodbridge in Wethersfield, and Timothy's excursion to Kittery from 1680 to 1682.

Isaac Foster's sermons furnish the bulk of the *Hartford Sermon Notebook*, and after his ordination on July 14, 1680, the notebook essentially becomes his legacy. I have been able to locate very little documentation regarding Isaac Foster. With the exception of the recent work of Paul Lucas and some older nineteenth century historians, Foster is a virtual unknown in the historiography of New England's Puritans. Because Foster died so young at the age of 30, he never had an opportunity for fame, though after studying his sermons it is doubtful that he was interested in glory. In fact, his sermons are the exertions of a much wiser man, and the message he delivered to his congregation, while not uncommon as Puritan preaching goes, contains a solemn maturity that must have moved his listeners. His Sacrament Day sermon in particular, contains a stirring description of the trials and crucifixion of Christ.

Foster was a Fellow and Tutor at Harvard, and graduated first in a class of twelve in 1671. He was born around 1652, and was the son of William Foster, a merchant from Charlestown. In October 1671, only a few months after earning his first degree at Harvard, Turks captured Isaac on a voyage with his father to Balboa.[20] It is an event recorded in the nineteenth century source *Lossing's American Historical Record*.[21]

---

[19] Ibid., 70.

[20] Sibley, *Harvard Graduates*, 336.

[21] Benson J. Lossing ed., *The American Historical Record and Repertory of Notes and Queries* (Philadelphia: Chase and Town Publishers, 1872), 372. This source, along with

I have included copies of the two pages from *Lossing's American Historical Record* that tell the story of Foster's captivity, Figure 6, and a poem by Michael Wigglesworth that celebrates his return, Figure 7.

According to Sibley, in 1677 following the death of Thomas Shepard, the ministers Increase Mather, Urian Oakes, and Samuel Willard recommended Foster for the position of Pastor of the church in Charlestown, but the final decision granted settlement to Shepard's son Thomas Shepard, Jr.[22] In the Spring of 1678, Foster was recommended by Governor Hinckley for settlement in Barnstable, Massachusetts. In a series of letters, Hinckley urged Foster to "Come over to Barnstable and help them, setting forth not only the earnest desires both of the church and town; but the opportunity to promote Christ's work amongst the poor Indians there..."[23] In the meantime, Windsor had fired all of its preachers, and was looking for a new candidate to lead their reunified church. Sibley does not indicate why Foster passed on the opportunity at Barnstable, but he quickly became a candidate for the vacancy in Windsor.

The process Windsor endured to find a new minister involved the highest levels of New England church leadership. Paul Lucas discusses the various intrigues in *Valley of Discord*. As previously stated, Windsor had fired both of its ministers and was pursuing new leadership for its church. "Two men emerged as likely candidates, Samuel Mather, cousin of Increase Mather, of Milford and Isaac Foster of Charlestown, Massachusetts. Mather especially wanted to leave Milford, because he detested the congregation. In a 1678 letter to his relative, Increase of Boston, he wrote of his low salary, lack of authority, and his objections to the obstinacy of the brethren..."[24] Both men went through what amounted to interrogations to determine how they would respect the autonomy of Windsor's fraternity of brethren. Ultimately, both men received rather cool receptions by the discerning Elect of Windsor, though some preference was shown for Foster due to his qualities as "the better preacher."[25]

---

many others from the nineteenth century, can be accessed in its entirety in the public domain via Google books.

22 Sibley, 336.

23 Ibid., 338.

24 Lucas, *Valley of Discord*, 118.

25 Ibid., 119.

In *The Faithful Shepherd*, David Hall suggests that after the breakup of Windsor's First Church, the factions sought an "Ambidexter" who could please them both.[26] However, the dynamic described by Lucas does not resemble a cooperative stance between the groups, at least not until the very end of the conflict, when the two sides finally decided to settle their differences. Ultimately, resolution to the Windsor dispute depended more on the urgency of finding a preacher than the actual settlement of theological differences.

In early 1679, Windsor held an election to determine their new minister. In what may have resembled something of a seventeenth century landslide, Foster defeated Mather 83 to 44.[27] Samuel Mather had been defeated in the "popular vote," notwithstanding the final authority of his relative in Boston, whose influence truly covered the length and breadth of New England. Increase Mather had interviewed Isaac Foster while Foster was still in Boston to determine his suitability for the call in Windsor. The following exchange of letters from the Collections of the Massachusetts Historical Society between Increase Mather and John Whiting of Hartford's Second Church, reveal the kind of scrutiny that ministerial candidates experienced in seventeenth century New England. Receiving the Mather stamp of approval must have been the most important hurdle for many preachers seeking a home to ply the word.

The details provided by Paul Lucas suggest that the committee in Windsor took Mather's letter to heart. It is unclear what John Whiting's official role may have been. A number of his sermons appear in the *Hartford Sermon Notebook*. He may have been acting as an advisor to the committee in Windsor as they struggled to find a new minister. Apparently, Increase was more interested in advancing the career of his relative Samuel. In his letter to Whiting, Increase expresses his concerns about Foster's position on church government, and that Foster will be too badly missed at Harvard, where he was a fellow and tutor, which might preclude him from accepting the call in Windsor. Lucas indicates that due to this exchange of letters, and there were probably other letters as well, the committee in Windsor requested another grilling of Foster on his church government position, was he Presbyterian or Congregational? Not surprisingly, Foster refused to be

[26] Hall, *The Faithful Shepherd*, 187.
[27] Lucas, *Valley of Discord*, 119.

JOHN WHITING TO INCREASE MATHER.

These for the Reverend Mr Increase Mather, Teacher of a Church in Boston.

REV^D AND DEAR SIR, — The particular errand of these lines is to informe that the two Congregations in Windsor having mutually ingaged themselves to submitt to the advice of a Councill in the difficulties depending among them, they are accordingly advised to a re-union and walk in the Congregationall way according to Synods 48 and 62; and for their further settlement to seeke out for another minister, Mr Woodbridge being left to his liberty and Mr. Chancy looked att by some, not so throughly furnished to lead so great a people, tho: his doctrine is sound, and his conversation eminently pious: The Councill (under whose guidance the matter yet remaines) have proposed your kinsman Mr Samuell Mather, (in whose piety, parts and perswasion (?) some that know him are greatly satisfied) and in case of non-concurrence in him, to M^r ffoster † of Charlstown. Mr Mather they fall not in with (though the Church, as I heare, is generally for him). The Councill g^d desires that you would be pleased (with the Revd Mr Oakes, to whom I have also written to that end) to intimate in a few words whither M^r ffoster be free from ingagement, and then, how qualified in respect of godlines and learning, (we are strangers to him on all accounts) and particularly what his judgement is in respect of church order; whether indeed declaredly Congregationall, that being of considerable weight to the settlement and welfare of that people, as well as the comfort of their neighbours. I beseech you S^r, according to wonted candor and

* Rev. John Whiting [H. C. 1658] was a tutor of the College, but called to preach at Salem, in 1657. He remained there two years without being settled. In 1660 he went to Hartford, and was ordained as colleague with Rev. Samuel Stone.

† Rev. Isaac Foster. See p. 98 in this volume.

Figure 1. Copy of John Whiting's letter to Increase Mather discussing the suitability of Isaac Foster as a candidate for minister in Windsor Connecticut.

464 THE MATHER PAPERS. [1678-9.

faithfulnes, give us an account of him therein. There are some thoughts that Mr Mather's being indeed Congregationall (though Synodically) is that which diverts their thoughts from him, who was first coměnded to their enquiry. You have the summ of the matter, wherein I earnestly intreate a plaine and speedy answer. We desire to mourne with them that mourne, and sympathise with them (especially saints) that are in sorrow. The Lord pitty and heale poore New Eng'd.* Alas, what have we done? Our God humble and helpe: News would be very welcome, especially if you have any certainty in that great busines about the King: Harty respects from, with desire of prayer for

Yours sincerely in our deare Saviour,

JNO WHITING.

HARTFORD, ffeb: 27. 78: [9]

REVEREND SR, — Being desired by the Councill to joyne with Mr Whitting in desiring of yourselfe & Mr Oakes to grant us information concerning Mr Foster; the opportunity being so suddain & not known by me till just now, I can onely request your favour herein, which will greatly oblidg

Your humble servant, JOHN ALLYN.†

Figure 2. Second page of John Whiting's letter to Increase Mather.

INCREASE MATHER TO JOHN WHITING.*

BOSTON 1 mo. 10 day, 167$\frac{8}{9}$

REVEREND & DEAR SIR, —I reeeived your lr̃e (with Capt Allyn's† name also subscribed) wherein you desire information concerning Mr Isaac Foster.‡ I beleeve hee is truly godly. I know that hee is of good parts, both nat[l] & acquired; & indeed more ꝑsed in preaching than most that I have known of his standing. As for his judg[t] respecting church order I have not heard him fully declare himselfe. When he joyned to the church in Charlestown he . . . that he was not satisfyed in that practice of imposing . . . respecting the work of grace, upon such as they admitted into full com̃union; when some here regarded him to be a Presbyterian. This day, hee was with me in my study. I desired him to tell me playnly what his notions were as to matters referring to church govt. His answer was, that he believed he knew the reason of my proposal, for . . . had acquainted him with what yourse[lf had] written to Mr. Oakes & me, & upon that account hee was not so free to express himselfe; onely s[d] that he had never upon any occasion declared against the way Congregational. To be sure he is as large respecting the subject of Baptisme as the Synod in 62. You cannot expect that Mr O. & myselfe (being members of the Corporation) shld be forward in removing any of the Fellows from the Colledge, that are desirable; of which nũbr Mr. Foster is one. And I question whether his friends will be willing that hee shd goe so far as Windsor is from these ꝑts. Yet if you see cause to promote an invitation that way, I shall not discourage you. The Grace of the L[d] Jesus be with your Spirit.

I am yours vnfeignedly I. M.

* Rev. John Whiting [H. C. 1653]. See note to his letters in this volume.

† John Allyn, of Windsor, and also of Hartford. See note on p. 87.

‡ Rev. Isaac Foster [H. C. 1671] was son of William Foster, merchant, of Charlestown. He was Fellow of Harvard College, minister of Hartford in 1680, and died August 20, 1682. See the letter referred to in this volume.

Figure 3. Increase Mather's reply to John Whiting regarding the suitability of Isaac Foster as a candidate for the minister of Windsor Connecticut.

subjected to any more scrutiny by the Bay ministers and he informed Windsor that he was not coming.[28] Eventually, the wounds in Windsor healed and its church was reunited, but peace would come without the spiritual guidance of Isaac Foster.

Foster's eventual call to Hartford First Church came only after what seems like a rapid series of lost opportunities to settle in any other New England township.[29] The fact that he was actively pursued by these towns says more about his ability as a preacher than any ministerial vacancy. After all, New England towns often went years without a settled minister. Choosing a minister involved elders and brethren, and was often a complex political process wrought with many obstacles, especially regarding the difficulties associated with the Half-Way Covenant and the Presbyterian/Congregational conflicts prevailing in the last decades of the seventeenth century.[30] Clearly, the history of the churches in Hartford and especially Windsor, demonstrate the controversial nature of New England church politics as completely as any other towns of the period.

The exact date of Foster's death is somewhat unclear. His epitaph reads January 1683, which corresponds to archival records at the Connecticut State Library, but sources contemporary to Foster state that he died in the summer of 1682, the victim of an epidemic.[31]

Caleb Watson was a schoolmaster not a minister. He received his M.A. from Harvard in 1664. In 1665, he began an eight-year tenure as the

[28] Lucas, *Valley of Discord*, 119.

[29] In chapter II of his social history *The Puritan Family*, Edmund Morgan describes the nature of a person's "call" or their "calling." This term was not reserved for ministers, but was established at an early age in the life of a New England Puritan. The most important element of one's call was that it adheres strictly to the will of God, whatever that call or occupation may be.

[30] Two sources that thoroughly address the complications of the Half-Way covenant and the Presbyterian/Congregational antagonisms of the seventeenth century are Robert G. Pope's *The Half-Way Covenant: Church Membership in Puritan New England* and *Valley of Discord* by Paul Lucas.

[31] Foster's grave is located on the property of Hartford's First Church in what is popularly known as the Ancient Burial Ground. John Whiting's letter to Increase Mather dated October 25, 1682 mentions Foster's death but does not provide an exact date. Similarly, a letter from John Bishop of Stamford Connecticut dated September 16, 1682 also mentions his death and that "many Indians also died thereabouts." *Collections of the Massachusetts Historical Society*, Vol. VIII. pp. 311 and 465. Church records from the archives of the Connecticut State Library indicate that Foster died in 1683. Connecticut Church Records, Reel #500, LDS #1009610, Hartford First Church of Christ, V1-1684-1910.

Figure 4. Isaac Foster's gravestone inscription at Hartford's Ancient Burial Ground.

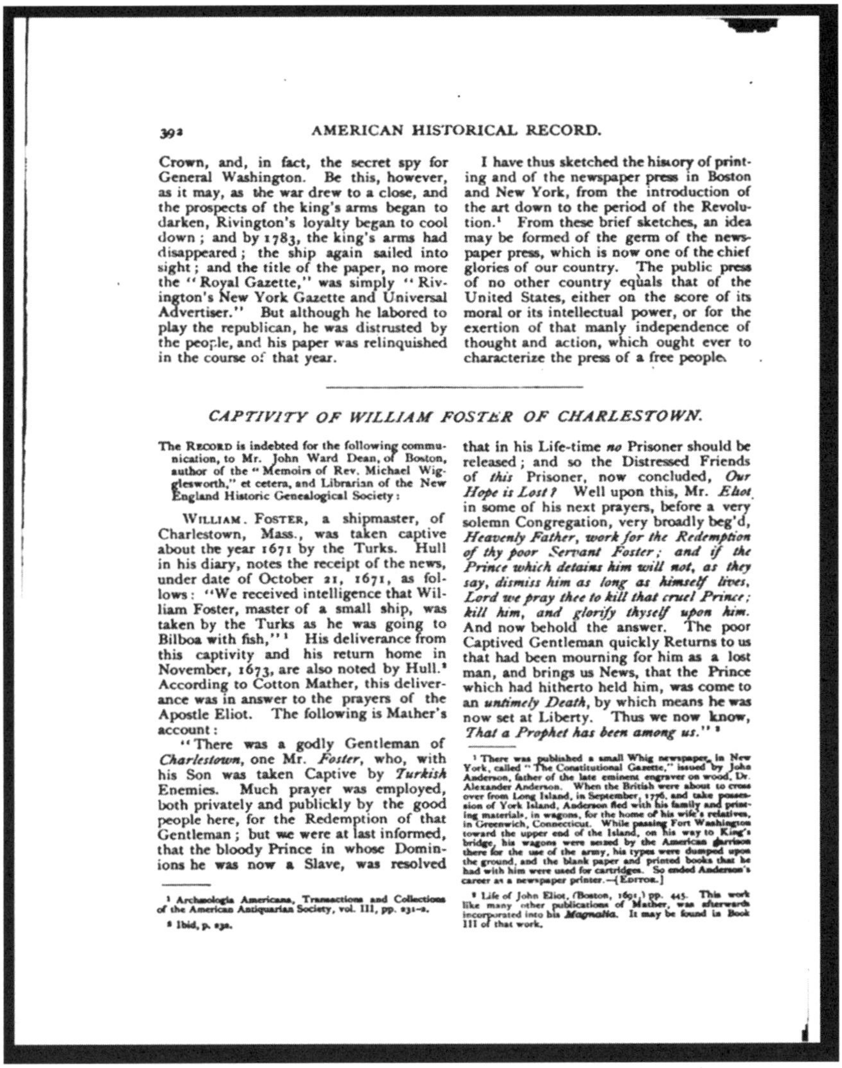

392 AMERICAN HISTORICAL RECORD.

Crown, and, in fact, the secret spy for General Washington. Be this, however, as it may, as the war drew to a close, and the prospects of the king's arms began to darken, Rivington's loyalty began to cool down; and by 1783, the king's arms had disappeared; the ship again sailed into sight; and the title of the paper, no more the "Royal Gazette," was simply "Rivington's New York Gazette and Universal Advertiser." But although he labored to play the republican, he was distrusted by the people, and his paper was relinquished in the course of that year.

I have thus sketched the history of printing and of the newspaper press in Boston and New York, from the introduction of the art down to the period of the Revolution.[1] From these brief sketches, an idea may be formed of the germ of the newspaper press, which is now one of the chief glories of our country. The public press of no other country equals that of the United States, either on the score of its moral or its intellectual power, or for the exertion of that manly independence of thought and action, which ought ever to characterize the press of a free people.

CAPTIVITY OF WILLIAM FOSTER OF CHARLESTOWN.

The RECORD is indebted for the following communication, to Mr. John Ward Dean, of Boston, author of the "Memoirs of Rev. Michael Wigglesworth," et cetera, and Librarian of the New England Historic Genealogical Society:

WILLIAM FOSTER, a shipmaster, of Charlestown, Mass., was taken captive about the year 1671 by the Turks. Hull in his diary, notes the receipt of the news, under date of October 21, 1671, as follows: "We received intelligence that William Foster, master of a small ship, was taken by the Turks as he was going to Bilboa with fish,"[1] His deliverance from this captivity and his return home in November, 1673, are also noted by Hull.[2] According to Cotton Mather, this deliverance was in answer to the prayers of the Apostle Eliot. The following is Mather's account:

"There was a godly Gentleman of *Charlestown*, one Mr. *Foster*, who, with his Son was taken Captive by *Turkish* Enemies. Much prayer was employed, both privately and publickly by the good people here, for the Redemption of that Gentleman; but we were at last informed, that the bloody Prince in whose Dominions he was now a Slave, was resolved that in his Life-time *no* Prisoner should be released; and so the Distressed Friends of *this* Prisoner, now concluded, *Our Hope is Lost!* Well upon this, Mr. *Eliot* in some of his next prayers, before a very solemn Congregation, very broadly beg'd, *Heavenly Father, work for the Redemption of thy poor Servant Foster; and if the Prince which detains him will not, as they say, dismiss him as long as himself lives, Lord we pray thee to kill that cruel Prince; kill him, and glorify thyself upon him.* And now behold the answer. The poor Captived Gentleman quickly Returns to us that had been mourning for him as a lost man, and brings us News, that the Prince which had hitherto held him, was come to an *untimely Death*, by which means he was now set at Liberty. Thus we now know, *That a Prophet has been among us.*"[3]

[1] Archæologia Americana, Transactions and Collections of the American Antiquarian Society, vol. III, pp. 231–2.

[2] Ibid, p. 232.

[1] There was published a small Whig newspaper, in New York, called "The Constitutional Gazette," issued by John Anderson, father of the late eminent engraver on wood, Dr. Alexander Anderson. When the British were about to cross over from Long Island, in September, 1776, and take possession of York Island, Anderson fled with his family and printing materials, in wagons, for the home of his wife's relatives, in Greenwich, Connecticut. While passing Fort Washington toward the upper end of the Island, on his way to King's bridge, his wagons were seized by the American garrison there for the use of the army, his types were dumped upon the ground, and the blank paper and printed books that he had with him were used for cartridges. So ended Anderson's career as a newspaper printer.—[EDITOR.]

[3] Life of John Eliot, (Boston, 1691,) pp. 445. This work like many other publications of Mather, was afterwards incorporated into his *Magnalia*. It may be found in Book III of that work.

Figure 5. Page from the *American Historical Record* describing the captivity and return of William and Isaac Foster.

Rev. Michael Wigglesworth, of Malden, Mass. author of *The Day of Doom*, wrote a poem of eight stanzas upon this event, which has never been printed. I transcribe it for the Record, from the author's autograph copy, which was lately generously presented to me by Rev. George E. Ellis, D. D. of Boston:

Upon ye return of my dear friend Mr Foster wth his son out of captivity undr ye Moors.

A Song of Praise to keep in remembrance the loving kindness of ye Lord.

1

Come hither, hearken unto me,
  All ye that God do fear,
And what he hath done for my soul
  I will to you declare.
I to ye Lord fro my distress
  Did cry & he gave ear,
Out of Hell's belly I did cry,
  And he my prayer did hear.

2

I shall not die, but live, and shall
  The works of Jah declare:
The Lord did sorely chasten mee
  Yet mee from death did spare.
O set wide open unto mee
  The gates of righteousness.
I will go into them, & will
  The praise of Jah confess.

3

Bless thou the Lord, my soul, & all
  In me, his holy name
Bless thou ye Lord, my soul, & all
  His boundless minde the same.
With me together o do yee
  Jehovah magnify!
And let us all herein agree
  To lift his name on high.

4

The God hee of Salvation is
  That is our God most strong
And to ye Lord Jehovah doth
  Issues of Death belong.
The Right-hand of Jehovah is
  Exalted upon high:
The Right-hand of Jehovah is
  A working valiantly.

5

On Pıinces poure contempt doth Hee
  Lays Tyrants in ye dust
Who proudly crush the innocent
  To satisfy their lust.
He breaks ye teeth of cruel Beasts
  That raven for ye prey
Out of ye Lion's bloody jawes
  Hee plucks ye sheep away.

6

Thou broken hast ye iron Barrs
  And loos'd ye fetters strong,
Thou rescu'd hast ye poor-opprest
  From all that did them wrong.
Out of ye Dungeon dark & deep
  Thou hast my soul set free
So long as I a being have
  My praise shall be of thee.

7

How beautiful Jehovah is
  Oh taste, & see likewise
Oh great is that man's blessedness
  Whose trust on him relies!
Upon ye Lord for evermore
  See that yor selves you stay
For there is with Jehovah store
  Of strength yt lasts for ay.

8

O love ye Lord all yee his saints
  The :aithful he doth guard
But he unto proud doers grants
  A plentyfull reward.
Because ye Lord ye poor doth hear
  Nor 's prisoners doth despise
Let Heav'n, earth, sea, him praise, and all
  That moves therein likewise.

An account of Mr. Foster and his descendants, by Dr. E. J. Forster and W. S. Appleton, Esq. appeared in the *Historical and Genealogical Register*, vol. XXV, pp 67—71. Mr. Foster died May 8, 1698. Messrs. Forster and Appleton, in the article above referred to, express the opinion that the son who was taken captive with him, was the eldest son, Rev. Isaac Foster, who was born about 1652, graduated at Harvard College in 1671, settled as pastor of the church at Hartford, Ct. 1671, and died August 20, 1682.

Figure 6. Michael Wigglesworth's poem celebrating Foster's return. The *American Historical Record.*

first schoolmaster of Hadley, Massachusetts. For a number of years in New England, congregational churches employed a dual system of minister and teacher. Many times, both men would address the congregation on Sunday. Generally, the teacher taught the details of scripture while the minister exhorted the congregation to live by those details in the way of Jesus Christ.[32] Again, the distinction must be made that Caleb Watson was not Hartford's teacher he was its schoolmaster. The Calvinist pastor/teacher structure ended in Hartford in the 1650's, with the death of Samuel Stone. Nevertheless, based on his sermons, Watson was clearly very educated. Therefore, while Hartford may not have officially endorsed the pastor/teacher arrangement, its schoolmaster still played an important role regarding biblical instruction via the pulpit.

Sibley does not say why, but in 1674, Watson took up residence as the schoolmaster in Hartford. His position in the community was of some importance and his school "came to be regarded, not as county school, or a high school, but as the main reliance of the town for the education of all its children, old and young..."[33] In 1681, Connecticut's General Court granted him 200 acres of land, and in 1683 he was granted freemanship. In 1700, the committee for the management of the prudentials authorized the displacement of the position of schoolmaster in Hartford in what resembled a kind of forced retirement, and Watson was left unemployed.[34] According to Sibley, Watson received a pension of sorts in that he no longer had to pay any taxes. Sibley also says that Watson filled in from time to time as preacher in Farmington, and that "he died in 1725–6, probably at Windsor, an 'old man,' much respected."[35]

Thomas Cheever was the son of the famous New England schoolmaster Ezekiel Cheever. Thomas Cheever graduated from Harvard in 1677 and began preaching in Malden, Massachusetts in 1679, where he was ordained in 1681.[36] The sermon notebook contains only one sermon from Thomas Cheever, and it was a challenge transcribing his

---

[32] For a discussion of the teacher-pastor relationship that existed in seventeenth century New England. Again, see: Vergil V. Phelps, "The Pastor and Teacher in New England."

[33] Sibley, *Harvard Graduates*, 96.

[34] Ibid., 97.

[35] Ibid.

[36] Ibid., 502.

name. Were it not for the fact that the notebook's author included the name Maulden, a common seventeenth-century spelling of Malden, Massachusetts, after Mr. Cheever, it might not have been possible to make the connection, but after some patient paleography and genealogical investigation, I am confident that we are dealing with Thomas Cheever.[37]

Sibley writes about a great scandal in the life of Thomas Cheever in which, in 1686, while serving as the minister in Malden, he was accused of blaspheming the name of God. Cheever denied the validity of the charges, but the ecclesiastical council thought otherwise, and he was relieved of his duties. Cheever moved to Rumney Marsh (Chelsea, Massachusetts), where he became that town's minister. He remained the minister of Rumney Marsh until his replacement in 1747 due to infirmities associated with age. He died in 1749.[38]

John Whiting graduated from Harvard in 1653. He was the son of William Whiting, a wealthy merchant and one time treasurer of the Colony of Connecticut. Sibley writes that Whiting was born in England, and later immigrated to New England. He served as a ministerial assistant to Edmund Norris in Salem, Massachusetts, and in 1660 moved his family to Hartford. At the time of his ordination in Hartford First Church, Joseph Haynes was also serving in the capacity of minister, and the conflict over the Half-Way Covenant drove a wedge between the two men. As a result, the church split, but unlike their neighboring church in Windsor, the schism stuck. From 1670 on, Hartford had two churches, and if Lucas is correct in *Valley of Discord*, Connecticut's seventeenth-century Presbyterian/Congregational conflict had claimed another victim.[39]

---

[37] Based on the genealogical record *Descendants of Richard of Sychdin Llewys*, http://www.lewisstreet.com/historical_society/family_group_sheets/Report01.html, Mary Cheever, sister of Thomas Cheever, was married to William Lewis of Farmington Connecticut. This note is included to support the transcription of Cheever's name. It is not unreasonable to suggest that Thomas Cheever might have visited his sister in Farmington, and while there spent some time in Hartford where he delivered a sermon as a sort of "guest preacher." Additionally, Cheever and Foster were classmates at Harvard, which may also account for his presence in Hartford.

[38] Sibley, *Harvard Graduates*, 503.

[39] Ibid., 345, 346.

Whiting served as minister to the army of the Colony of Connecticut during King Phillip's War.[40] He remained pastor of the Second Church in Hartford until his death in 1689.[41] John Whiting is the only preacher in the *Hartford Sermon Notebook* to be published during his lifetime. Samuel Green of Boston published Whiting's Election Day sermon *The Way of Israel's* Welfare in 1686.[42]

---

[40] Ibid., 346.

[41] Ibid.

[42] For a detailed account of publications by Puritan Ministers see George Selement, "Publication and the Puritan Minister" *The William and Mary Quarterly*, 37, no. 2 (April 1980), 219–241. Also see Robert M. Benton's *An Annotated Check List of Puritan Sermons Published in America Before 1700*, "Bulletin of the New York Public Library" (New York: Peter Smith, 1941). Benton's source is valuable because each sermon's opening text and doctrine is included, which makes this source somewhat more useful than a simple list of sermons with titles and authors.

PART TWO

TRANSCRIPTION AND PALEOGRAPHY

CHAPTER THREE

TRANSCRIPTION METHODOLOGY

The sermons contained in the *Hartford Sermon Notebook* are typical of "The Plain Style," a sermon style characterized by a logically ordered sequence of points in which the introductory text is followed by various examples of Doctrines, Reasons, and Uses. [1] Generally, each point of Doctrine, Reason or Use precedes a logically ordered sequence of sub-points. While this may appear stilted and unimaginative, "The Plain Style" is an invaluable aid to paleography. It is not particularly difficult to follow the minister's thought process, simply look for the next ordered number in the sermon. Point follows point from beginning to end. This style of preaching must have been useful for someone trying to write down everything being said, especially if that person was educated enough to anticipate what was coming next, as many of New England's Puritans were.[2]

The transcription methodology used for the notebook was not complicated since the notebook's author recorded the sermons by attempting to write down every word the minister said, as he said them.[3] Accordingly, each section of the sermon is prefaced by the word

[1] Perry Miller's *The Puritan Mind* provides one of the most in depth discussions available regarding the "Plain Style," but many of the works cited in this book provide some discussion of it, especially the works that deal specifically with Puritan sermon themes and structure. Marvin Xavier Lesser's Ph.D. dissertation "'All for Profit': The Plain Style and the Massachusetts Election Sermons in the Seventeenth Century," Columbia University, 1967, has been very useful, especially regarding the "Plain Style" as it existed in the latter part of the century.

[2] Many Puritan scholars reflect on the learned nature of New England's Puritans, but an excellent source for this subject is David Hall's *Worlds of Wonder, Days of Judgment*. Among its many insights, this fascinating book shows the importance of literacy and the importance of print culture in Colonial New England.

[3] In his paper "Light on the Puritans from John Hull's Notebooks," *The New England Quarterly*, 15, no. 1 (March 1942), 95, Edmund Morgan refers to "the industrious Puritan who followed the practice of 'writing after the preacher.'" Clearly, the *Hartford Sermon Notebook* is of that same tradition, and one wonders how many other sermon notebooks remain in hidden places throughout New England. Lisa Gordis tells us that New Englanders "were taught to be active readers not only of the Bible itself, but of the biblical text as presented in their ministers' sermons, on which they were expected to take notes..." *Opening Scripture, 97*. The image that evolves becomes one of active participation, rather than simply a passive listening experience.

Doctrine, Reason, or Use. Each time one of these words appeared in the notebook, I started a new paragraph in the transcription. Many published Puritan sermons follow this general format, so it seems an appropriate way to format the completed, typed transcription.[4]

I have retained all of the notebook's original spelling. The only exceptions are words whose spelling was not discernable, but recognizable contextually, in which case I used the modern English spelling. I chose this method because of the Puritan tendency to forgo any standardized spelling regimen.[5] In fact, there are examples in the notebook where a word is spelled in two or three different ways in the same sermon. To a modern reader raised on the importance of proper spelling, the seventeenth-century version of written English will definitely raise an eyebrow. In addition, abbreviations in the original have been expanded.

I chose to capitalize all references to God, which in the notebook is represented by a shorthand symbol that resembles a backwards upper case L. I also used the upper case for the first word of each sentence, a practice the author of the notebook largely ignores. To improve readability, I have inserted punctuation, except in cases where I could not determine logical breaks, in which case no punctuation appears. Generally, the notebook contains only terminal punctuation or none at all, but where punctuation does exist in the notebook, I have not altered it. Primarily used as a period at the end of sentences, the colon appears often in the notebook. The colons that appear after the words

---

For many Puritans, the Sunday and weekday sermons they heard were as much about edification as they were regeneration.

[4] John Whiting's *The Way of Israel's Welfare* is a good comparative source, along with the work of Edward Taylor, who was a contemporary of the preachers in the *Hartford Sermon Notebook*. Taylor's sermon form is reproduced in Charles W. Mignon, "Christ the Glory of All Types: The Initial Sermon from Edward Taylor's 'Upon the Types of the Old Testament'" *The William and Mary Quarterly*, 37, no. 2 (April 1980), 286–301. There are many other sources available including Perry Miller's *Puritan Sourcebook*, and I would also refer scholars to an interesting internet website entitled *Fire and Ice*, which contains dozens of Puritan sermons, most of which can be downloaded from the site. Finally, if one has access to *Evans Early American Imprints*, this database contains hundreds of primary sources from the 17th century. I used this site to familiarize myself with New England sermon forms published contemporary to the Hartford Sermon Notebook. This database can be accessed at http://infoweb.newsbank.com/, and through many university library/ media centers.

[5] Alice Morse Earle's *The Sabbath in Puritan New England*. New York: Charles Scribner's Sons, 1891, discusses the wayward nature of Puritan spelling, but it is interesting to note that Puritans paid much more attention to standardized spelling in their printed works.

Doctrine, Reason, and Use are generally mine, as are all question marks contained in the transcription.

Each biblical reference has been fully enclosed in parentheses. Many times in the notebook the sub points, which are nearly always preceded by a sequential number, are written directly after a biblical reference. It has been a challenge to separate the two, a task made easier by referring to the *1560 Geneva Bible, and the King James Bible of 1611*. It is important to note that the sermon notebook in its original form is an unfinished product. The person who created it needed to use every square inch of paper available, no doubt for reasons of economy, considering the relative scarcity of notebook paper in seventeenth-century Hartford. Had he or she been able to rewrite the notebook or publish its contents, the grammar would likely have been cleaned up. The published New England sermons from the late seventeenth century incorporate a much more thorough grammatical structure.[6] Words that could not be transcribed have been enclosed in brackets, and I have included discernable letters where possible. In cases where I lacked absolute confidence in the transcription of a word, it has been bracketed.

Figures 8 through 11 that follow include some of the more interesting paleographic challenges encountered in the transcription. The highlighted words are only a small sample of the entire notebook's personality. I found it interesting that much of the transcription challenge came from the smaller parts of speech rather than complex words, and that once I unlocked these smaller parts of speech, my ability to transcribe with greater speed and accuracy improved greatly.

In a number of the notebook's sermons, sentences are incomplete. I believe this is a function of the author simply not writing fast enough, or perhaps not hearing what the minister said. Based on the writing style, I am sure the notebook is the product of one person. Readability in the notebook varies, sometimes drastically. It is impossible to know exactly why, but fatigue, and no doubt the preaching styles of different ministers, must have been factors. The decision to alter the original was a difficult one, and there was real trepidation of altering, even subtly, the ministers' intended meaning, but after completing the typed version of each sermon, it became clear that readability mattered, and

[6] See the bibliography for a selection of printed sermons from the seventeenth century.

I accept all responsibility for errors in syntax or meaning that may result.

Finally, the notebook may have been assembled by binding together separate sheets of paper, rather than a blank notebook bound and ready for use. This conclusion stems from the dates of the sermons, especially the sermon dated November 21, 1678, which is located between several sermons dated in the year 1680. Strangely, this sermon begins on the same sheet as the previous sermon dated November 17, 1680. It is possible that the notebook's author simply forgot what year it was, but it seems unlikely that this churchgoer would be off the mark by two full years. It seems more likely that the sheet containing the 1678 sermon simply had space left to write on, and that chronology mattered less than the availability of paper.

Since the transcription exactly follows the order of the sermons as they appear in the notebook, I mention these dates to avoid confusion when they appear in the transcription. In other words, I have maintained the pagination of the notebook exactly as it is bound in the original. Based upon the almanacs of John Danforth and John Foster, I have also inserted the day of the week when each sermon was delivered.[7] This is important because of the nature of weekday "occasional," and Sunday "regular," sermons, both of which are contained in the notebook.[8]

---

[7] John Foster, *An Almanack.* Boston, for Henry Phillips, 1680. Also, John Danforth, An *Almanack.* Cambridge, 1679.

[8] For more on regular and occasional sermons see Harry Stout, *The New England Soul.*

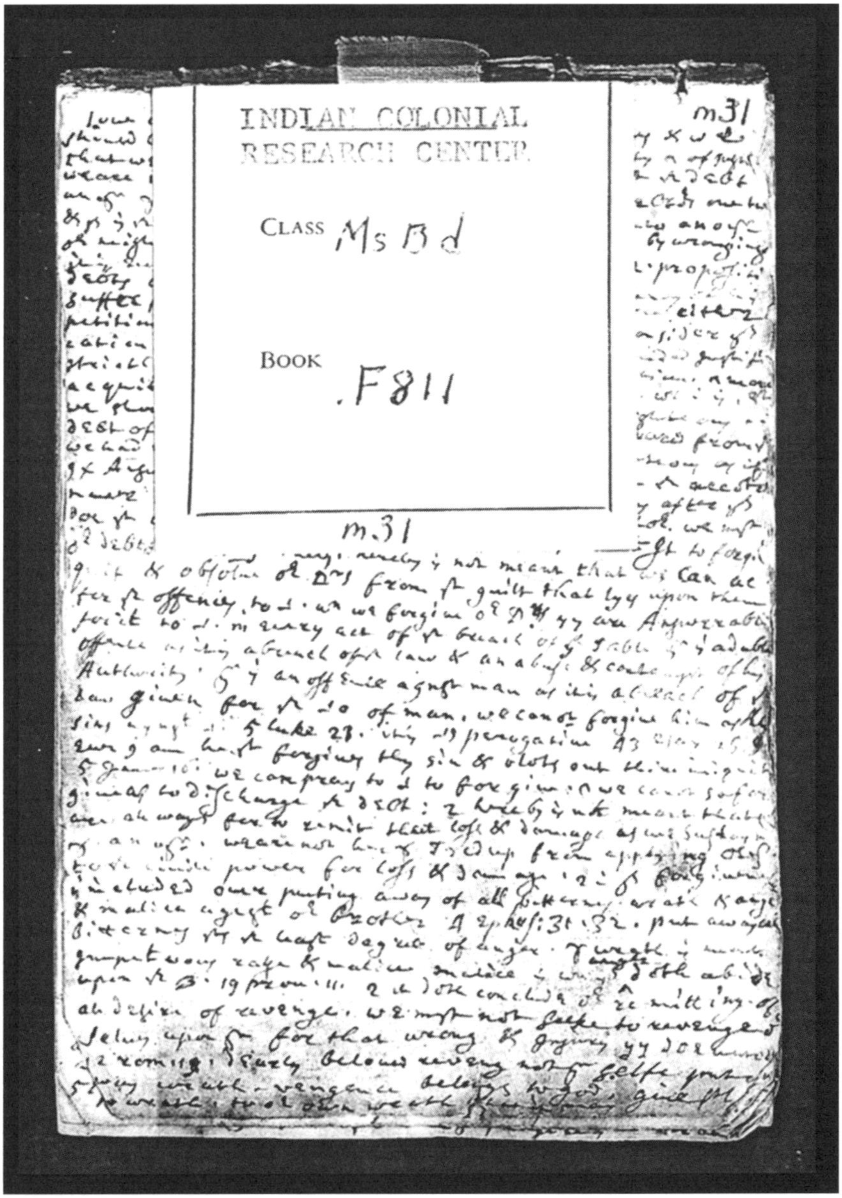

Figure 7. Facsimile of Hartford Sermon Notebook showing actual size.

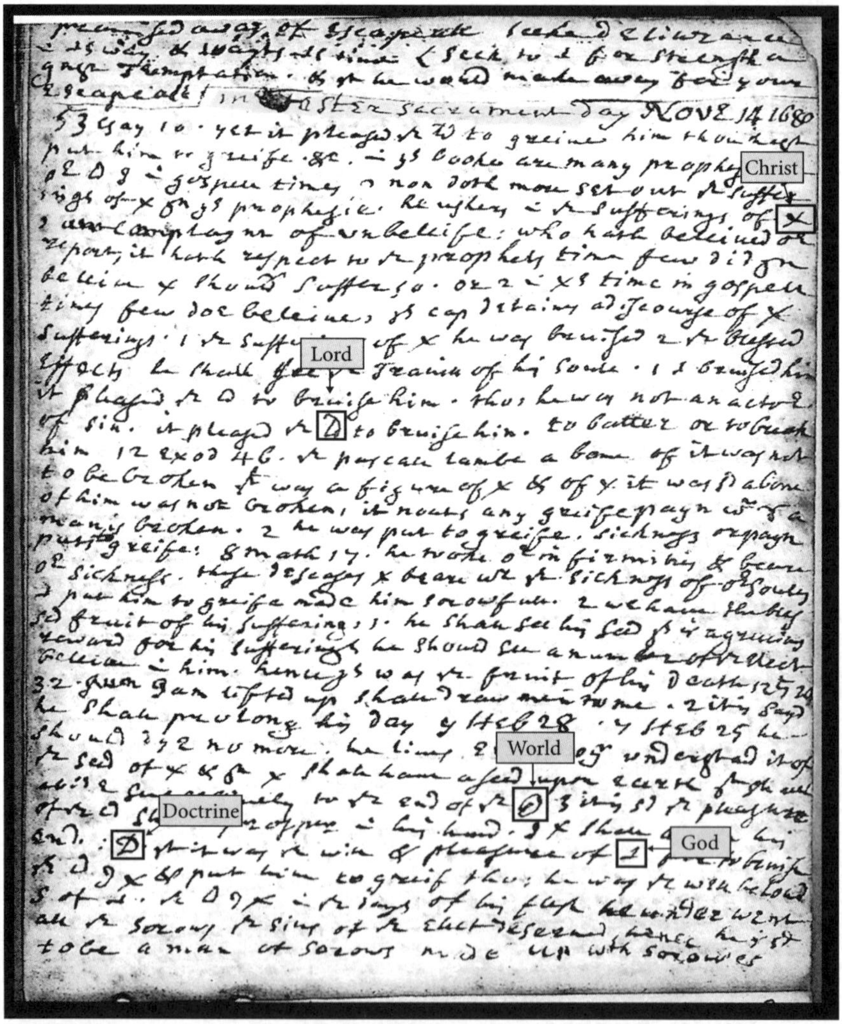

Figure 8. Page 1 of Isaac Foster's November 14, 1680 Sacrament Day sermon.

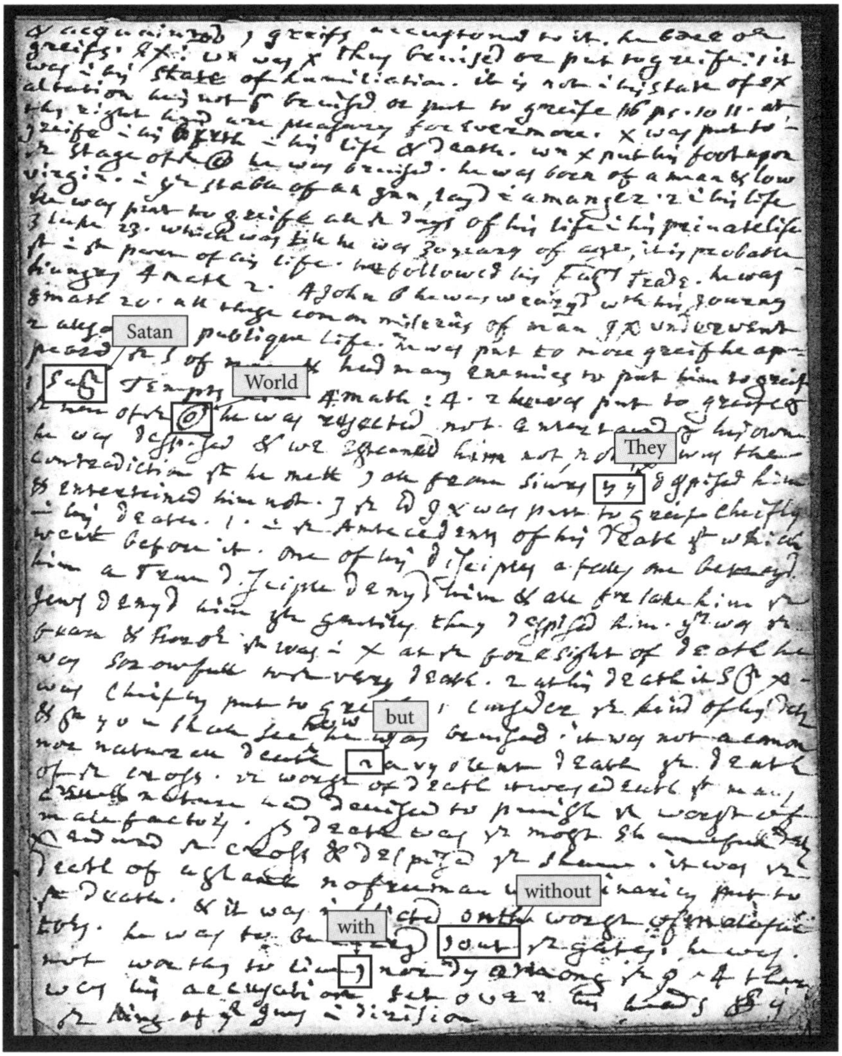

Figure 9. Page 2 of Isaac Foster's November 14, 1680 Sacrament Day sermon.

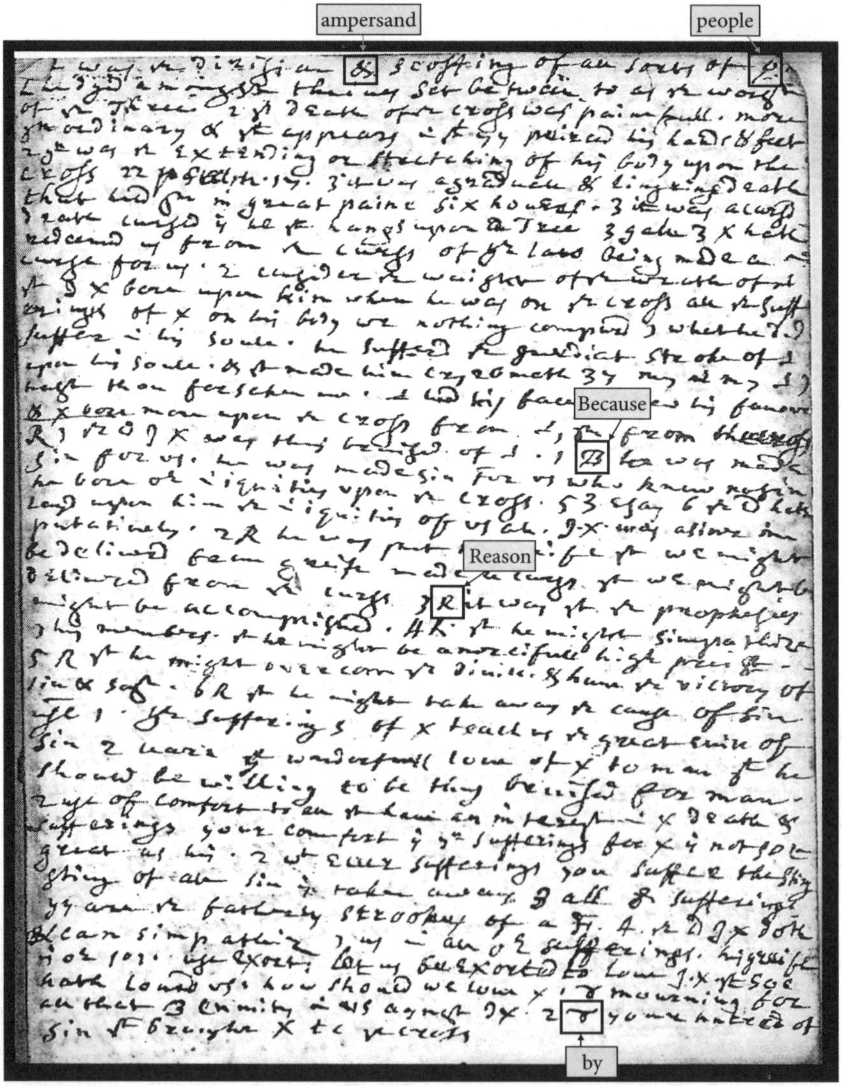

Figure 10. Page 3 of Isaac Foster's November 14, 1680 Sacrament Day sermon.

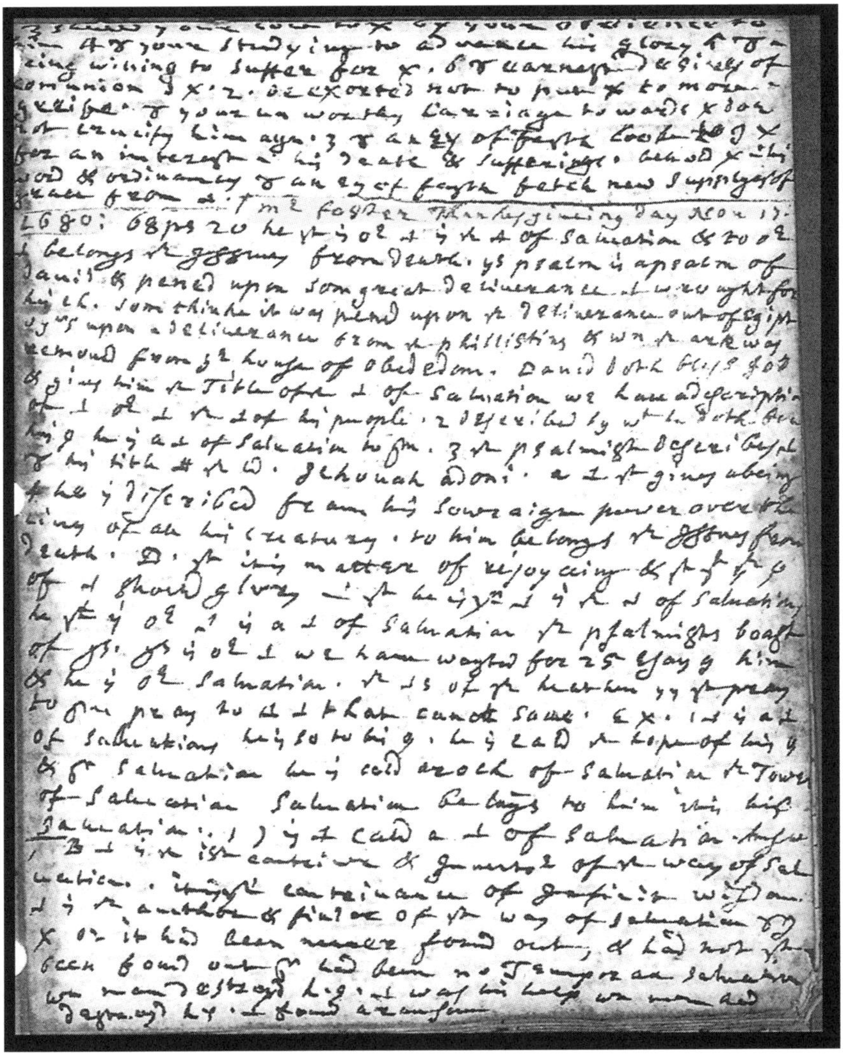

Figure 11. The final page of Isaac Foster's November 14, 1680 Sacrament Day sermon, and page 1 of his November 17, 1680 Thanksgiving sermon.

PART THREE

THE SERMONS

CHAPTER FOUR

A CHURCH SEEKS ITS SHEPHERD

Perhaps more than any other source, Harry Stout's The New England Soul *offers the best evaluation of the importance of the sermon in the lives of the people of colonial New England. In his exploration of the wide-ranging public reach of the sermon in seventeenth and eighteenth century New England, he writes that "The New England sermon—whose topical range and social influence were so powerful in shaping cultural values, meanings, and a sense of corporate purpose that even television pales in comparison."*[1] *Stout's research deals with a wide variety of themes in Puritan religious culture, all stemming from the impact of the sermons people heard. "The average weekly churchgoer in New England (and there were far more churchgoers than church members) listened to something like seven thousand sermons in a lifetime, totaling somewhere around fifteen thousand hours of concentrated listening."*[2]

Stout frames the importance of the sermon in New England by examining the importance of unpublished sermons, rather than the more commonly studied published sermons, especially unpublished regular sermons, whose contents were rarely put to the press in contrast to occasional, election day, and other "public" sermons. Stout's new approach emphasizes the study of unpublished sermons as the best way to understand the entire spectrum of New England preaching.[3] The Hartford Sermon Notebook *contains 62 unpublished "occasional" and "regular" sermons. These sermons are a window into the Puritan religious and communal culture of Hartford circa 1679–1680, and are an important addition to a fuller range of understanding.*

The chapters in Part three are built around the sermon series arrangements of Isaac Foster. I have organized the Hartford Sermon Notebook's *62 sermons into fifteen chapters. The chapters vary in length depending on how many weeks a particular sermon series lasted, and the actual length of the individual sermons. Chapters 4 and 10 are the*

---

[1] Stout, *The New England Soul*, 3.
[2] Ibid., 4.
[3] Ibid.

only exceptions to this pattern since they do not contain any sermon series arrangements. Interestingly, these two chapters contain only two sermons by Isaac Foster, which accounts for the absence of a sermon series pattern.

The themes of the covenant, conversion/regeneration, justification, redemption, and election or visible sainthood, are present in varying degrees throughout the notebook's sermons. The prevalence, meaning, and relative importance of these terms appear throughout the narrative and notes, and are summarized along with some interesting statistics in the conclusion.

Isaac Foster's Ordination Day sermon appears approximately at the halfway point of the notebook, on July 14, 1680. Prior to that date Foster's sermons might be considered a personal trial under the watchful eye of the brethren of Hartford's First Church, a church that had not had an official pastor of its own since the death of Joseph Haynes in May of 1679. Other than Caleb Watson's two part sermon series from Malachi regarding the immutability of God, the remainder of the notebook's sermons cite unique biblical texts, and are not arranged in series.

Three Bibles were used as aids to transcription, and for interpretation of the meaning of scripture: the New Geneva Study Bible, the Oxford World's Classics 1611 King James, and the Geneva Bible, 1560 Edition. The New Geneva Study Bible is a 1995 edition, and was used primarily as a tool to explain the meaning of each sermon or sermon series' opening text. The facsimile 1560 Geneva Bible, and 1611 King James were primarily used as aids in transcription, and to accompany each sermon's opening text. This was important because the opening text of the Puritan sermon introduced the minister's primary theme for the sermon, and in many cases, the notebook's opening texts are incomplete or difficult to transcribe. Therefore, since the Geneva Bible of 1560, and the 1611 King James were the primary Bibles used by New England's ministers, both were essential as transcription and interpretation tools.

The Hartford Sermon Notebook begins with a Mr. Woodbridge sermon that could be titled "The Mercy of God," based upon its overriding theme. In the second book of Samuel, David has become a king, and it is in Second Samuel that David commits adultery with Bathsheba, the wife of Uriah the Hittite. She becomes pregnant, and upon Uriah's death in battle, ultimately becomes David's wife. Fortunately, for David and his people, they have a covenant with God, so that Jerusalem is only nearly wiped out by an angel of the lord. Complete destruction is avoided when

David repents.[4] *Second Samuel 24:14 relates to the Woodbridge sermon because, even though David's sin is great, the mercies of God are greater. 2 Samuel 24:14 translates as follows: "And David said unto Gad, I am in a wonderful straite: let us fall now into the hand of the Lord, (for his mercies are great)* and let me not fall into the hand of man."[5]

Mr. Woodbridge: (Sunday) September 21: 1679. (2 Samuel 24:14) For his mercys are great. The [capt][6] presents to us the sin of David in numbering the people. His sin was his [inclinations] to glory in a multitude and to put trust in an arm of flesh. Joab was against it but David's words prevayle. When God [leaves] a person to sin he will be very violent and act against reason. What followes David's sin? David was softend after his sin, and he confesseth I have don very foolishly. We may also see the means of David's awakening. The ministry of the word that is a speciall and notable means to give a person sight of his sin. The Lord gave David a choys of 3 calamatys by that way God will not spare his own if they sin. The sins of those in publique place have an influence to awaken a judgement upon the land. We have David's reasoning with himself. He was in a great straight. Sin when it is awakened it will bring into great straights. Sin will bring a person in to such difficulty and involve him in to such intricacies that he will not know what to choose. Let me fall into the hands of God. A grieved a troubled sinner may generally find better dealing at the hands of God than of men. The grounds of David choyse for his mercys are great. The Bowels of God are towards siners great. Great in quantity and great in quality.

Doctrine: that the mercys of God are exceeding great: This David affirmes. This every beleiver may affirm. The mercys of God are very great. He is gracious and mercifull. (34 Exodus 6) Abundance in goodness and truth. He is called the father of mercy and the God of all comfort. (1 John 4:16) It is sayed to be love. It is allso acknowledged

---

[4] R.C. Sproul, General Ed. *New Geneva Study Bible: Bringing the Light of the Reformation to Scripture*, (Nashville: Thomas Nelson Publishers, 1995), 424.

[5] All biblical translations are taken from *The Geneva Bible: A Facsimile of the 1560 Edition*, (Peabody Massachusetts: Hendrickson Publishers, 2007), and *The Oxford World's Classics* King James Bible 1611. This initial translation is from page 148 of the Geneva Bible. All subsequent direct biblical translations of the sermon's opening text are placed at the beginning of the sermon and are taken from these editions. They are italicized and cited as *The Geneva Bible, 1560 Edition, and King James 1611.* I have done this because in many cases the minister's opening text is incomplete.

[6] Capt clearly refers to the opening text and may translate as caption. Capt appears throughout the *Hartford Sermon Notebook.*

by the people of God. God hath [multitude] (52 Psalm 1) mercy for poor siners some we may consider the mercifull and gracious [n] of God. Mercy is one of his glorious attributes. He was so in the dayes of eternity before there were vessells of mercy. He hath an infinite stocke of mercys. His mercy is no way diminished. (145 Psalm 8.9) The Lord is gracious and full of mercy. His mercy is over all his workes. The mercys God showes to men are great mercys. If you consider it comparatively by comparing the mercys of God with the creature,[7] they are greater mercys than the mercys of men. (11 Hosea 9.23) (Matthew 27) I will not destroy them. I am God and not man. There is want to be the strongest mercy of parents to the children but God's mercys doe exceed. As a parent doth pity his (103 Psalm 13) child so doth God pitty those that feare him. I will spare them as a father spares his son that serves him. (12 Zechariah verse 10) A mother's affections to her child are noted to be great and to a sucking child, but God's are greater.[8] (49 Isaiah 15) They may forget but I will not forget. 2 The mercy of God is great if you compare it with the justice of God. Indeed all God's attributes are equall, yet in a sence, it may be sayed to be above justice as in the (2 James 13) and mercy rejoyceth against judgment. Mercy is above judgement in regard of its naturalnes and dearness to God.[9] (5 Ezekiel 13) (7 Micah 18) (3 Lamentations 33) He doth not afflict willingly nor greive the children of men. The mercy of God is dear to him. 2 The mercy of God is above the justice of God in his frequent exercise. He is sayed to be a God plentious in mercy and slow to anger. (103 Psalm 18) They are new every morning: but his judgements they are called God's strong worke. (28 Isaiah 21) God is stretching out his hands of love to a people all the day long but when God brings his judgements it is because there is no remedy. In respect

[7] The term "creature" appears throughout the *Hartford Sermon Notebook*. *The Holman Bible Dictionary* defines the term creature as a Hebrew translation of nephesh chayah, which means, "living soul," and that the term is often used interchangeably to denote humankind and other creatures based upon similar physical makeup rather than a higher relationship with God. The word "creature" in the *Hartford Sermon Notebook* is interchangeable with "natural" or unregenerate man.

[8] To the Puritans, God's love to his children far exceeded any temporal love between parents and their offspring, and Puritan sermons frequently refer to human beings as the children of God. Were it possible to construct a Puritan hierarchy of love, God would always occupy the upper tier, with all temporal love at subordinate levels.

[9] By comparing mercy and justice, Woodbridge is comparing the Old and New Testament God. Typological comparisons are present throughout the sermon notebook, and were clearly an important element of Puritan theology.

of the occasions of drawing forth, it must be a great occasion that draws forth the judgment of God. God saw that the wickedness of man was great before he destroyed the old world. The cry of Sodom went up to heaven before God destroyed them. It is sayed of the Amorits that their iniquity was not yet full. God scatters mercy because it doth please him. If there be but ten righteous in Sodom I will spare it sayeth God for their sake. (5 Jeremiah 1) If there be a man I will spare it. Consider the mercy of God absolutely. His mercys to the sons of men are great and manifold. God is rich in mercy. His love is without heigth or length or depth. (3 Ephesians 19) The love of God is so great and wonderful that it doth pass knowledge. (6 Luke 35) He is kind to the unthankefull and to the evill. He causeth the rain to fall upon the evill and good. It is great in that in the midst of judgement God doth remember mercy. The mercy of God appears in his graciousnes and forgivenes of siners. The Lord doth give his gifts as a king and above a king. God doth give lif itselfe. He gives to all life and breath and all things. How shall he not with his son give us all things? 2 God doth forgive. We ow God 10 thousand tallents.[10] We are indebted to God but God forgives sin, and God doth this freely and fully. He doth bestow it upon such as have nothing to give in way of requitall. Thus he gives freely. The Lord is many a [suitor] to men to receive grace at his hands. (65 Isaiah) God doth forgive fully. He doth remit all their sin. The whole debt is forgiven the believer.

Use 1. Hence then learn that those that perish in sin doe perish under the hands of mercy. This is fearfull perishing. They are great siners, despisers of the grace of God. 2 It doth show us the hopefullnes of the condition of a lost and perishing siner. There is no hope in our selves but yet there is hope upon the account of the great mercy of God:

2 Use: It is of encouragement and councill to siners. Draw neer to God in Jesus Christ, for the mercy of God is exceeding great to siners. (55 Isaiah 7) Here is their Incouragement. There is mercy with God that he may be feared. You that are scandalous siners here is Incouragement. The mercys of God are great very great. This may encourage scandalous siners. 2 Destitute and forlorn siners consider

[10] The Old Testament book of Exodus chapter 38, verse 25–26 defines the shekel as the basic unit of weight in Hebrew. The talent was equivalent to 3,000 shekels. *Holman Bible Dictionary*, 1665.

this that the mercy of God is great if you confess your sin. God is ready to forgive it. Let the wicked forsake his way and I will abundantly pardon. The good news is set before you not to angells. They are reserved to the judgment of the great day. It is not sent to the dead but it is sent to you. 2 Consider who Speakes it. It is the Lord that doth it. It is God against whom you have sind. That God that you have no need of it. Consider your condition. You are great siners, and be incouraged by the great mercys of God to turn to God that he may abundantly pardon.

Isaac Foster also delivered a sermon on September 21, 1679, and like Woodbridge, Foster's sermon centers on God's forgiveness and mercy. Woodbridge took his text from the Old Testament, while Foster's text came from the Gospel of Matthew. It is very likely that this was a conscious decision that would furnish the congregation with a kind of typological treatment of the subject of God's mercy. Foster briefly discusses justification as it pertains to the partial perfection that only Christ can deliver. Many secondary sources define justification in Puritan theology. In her fascinating book Opening Scripture, *Lisa Gordis refers to justification as the imputation of Christ's righteousness to the convert."*[11] *Perry Miller defines justification as "the first act of regeneration" and that it is a stage in which God is fully satisfied that the criteria of his justice and law have been met; hence, the individual is absolved of their sins.*[12] *Of course, these definitions do not shield the justified individual from subsequent sin, since, for the Puritan, the perpetual warfare of the soul meant that the process of regeneration never ended in a single battle.*[13]

---

[11] Lisa Gordis. *Opening Scripture: Bible Reading and Interpretive Authority in Puritan New England* (The University of Chicago Press, 2003), 147.

[12] Perry Miller. *The Puritan Mind, the Seventeenth Century*, 27.

[13] Isaac Foster's July 11, 1680 and July 18, 1680 sermons are both excellent examples of conversion renewal, or, regeneration. Many sources discuss at length the process of conversion and regeneration. Murry G. Murphey's 1979 paper "The Psychodynamics of Puritan Conversion." *American Quarterly* 31, no. 2 (Summer 1979) is interesting because his explanations are so thorough and well developed. Murphey explains the process of conversion renewal as a kind of side effect of sanctification, and he does so within the construct of Edmund Morgan's conversion morphology. Murray states that "Sanctification (The leading of a holy life. Morgan. *Visible Saints*, 67) was a temporally extended process and one that was never completed in this life, so even the saints continued to sin and had constantly to struggle against the corruption lingering within them." 140. But as Perry Miller explains in *The New England Mind, Vol. 1*, the recognition of regeneration was no easy thing for the Puritan: "Those who have it, or

Mr. Foster. (Sunday) September 21, 1679. (6 Matthew 12) *6 Matthew 12: "And forgive us our dettes, as we also forgive our deters".*[14] And forgive us our debts as we forgive our debtors.

Doctrine: that it is our duty to pray after this manor. Forgive us our debts as we forgive our Debtors. 1 Every man is a debtor to God to His neighbour. 2 We ought to pray for forgiveness of our debts. We have no other way. 3 We must pray for forgiveness of our debts [ ].

Use 1. Hence, learn that there is no man perfect in this Life. Those that dream of perfection are imperfect. Were we not guilty we need not pray for forgiveness. We are not perfect but only in parts and in Justification. Righteous by the righteousness of perfect in stead there is sincerity.[15] Perfect in Christ. And in regard of your desire and wishes they may sayed to be perfect, but there is no perfection or freedom from sin in this life. 2 Learn we hence the great evill of sin in that Christ calls it debts. Every sin doth make us debtors to God, and lays us under an obligation to give sattisfaction for it. 3 We learn the riches of God's grace that doth teach us to com to him and ask forgiveness of him.

2 Use: of reproofe to those that doe not forgive their debtors. That will pray the first part but neglect the second. Did we consider the debts God forgives us, we should be inclined to forgive our debtors, els we doe hinder ourselves of that forgiveness that God other wise would bestow others. Whoe are they that doe not forgive their Debtors. 1 Those that doe [re a] bitterness rath and malice against their debtors they doe not forgive their debtors. (3 Mark 5) 2 Those that seeke reveng they do not forgive their debtors. (24 Proverbs 29) 3 Those that doe not love their debtors and manifest their forgiveness as there is occasion doe not forgive their debtors. 4 Those that doe not pray for their debtors doe not forgive them. (32 Job 10) (21 Numbers 5.7) They spoke against Moses Yet Moses prayed for them. 5 They that doe

---

think they have it, cannot tell exactly how it was wrought or precisely what happened, and those who do not have it cannot conceive what it might be; furthermore, there are some who are never quite sure whether they have it or not…" 26.

[14] *The Geneva Bible, 1560 Edition*. 5.

[15] According to Perry Miller, justification is the first act of regeneration in which God initially absolves the individual of their sins, which cannot happen unless at the outset God's grace is working within that individual, thus making them a likely candidate for the regeneration. "In the new covenant those who will believe in the redeemer have His righteousness ascribed to them and so are "justified" according to the new terms. *The New England Mind, Vol. 1*, vol. 1, 377.

speake evil of their debtors they doe not forgive them. They that speake evil of their debtors show that they have evill in their hearts against their neighbour: We must speake of the evill of others for reproofe but not of reproach. Let such as are guilty accept this reproofe.

3 Use: exhortation. Let us be exorted to aske forgiveness of God. We have great reason to aske forgiveness because we are debtors. Consider that you are debtors. Men are so secure in their debts and fear not danger there by, because they doe not believe they are debtors. We are debtors upon the account of original sin and actuall sin.[16] 2 Consider the nature of those debts. They are not like other debts. In these debts you have to doe more immediately with God. He hath all ways you in your hand. You have to doe with the great God you cannot flee from his presence. He hath you all ways at his mercy.

2 Consider you have no estate to make payment of those debts. You canot satisfy God's justice for those debts. Other debts you may pay but these canot be payed by any thing you have. (1 Peter 1.19) (6 Micah 6.7) 3 Consider those debts doe indanger the soule. The soule is lyable to be arrested and to suffer for those debts. Now we ought to be more carefull of our souls than of the body. The spirit of a man may sustain itselfe. 5 Consider those debts will ruin you to all eternity if they be not forgiven. (3 Job 17.18) (20 Job 11) Those debts if not forgiven you in this world they will follow you to the other world.

3 Consider how great a mercy it is to be forgiven. It is our greatest happyness. Blessed is the man whose Transgression is forgiven and whose iniquity is coverd. Forgiveness is a great mercy because it proceeds from special mercy and from speciall grace and special love. 2 It costs the greatest price. It cost the blood of Jesus Christ. It makes way for all other mercys and brings a blessing upon all other Injoyments and gives freedom from evill. (33 Isaiah 24) You have more need of this than of your dayly bread. 4 Consider the miserable estate of those

---

16 The distinctions Foster makes regarding sin are straightforward. Original sin is humankind's fall from grace in the Garden of Eden, which from birth is inescapable. Actual sin consists of those things committed after one is born which are violations of God's laws as specified in scripture, such as adultery or idolatry. The struggle for Hartford's Puritans was the same as that of all Puritans, to live a sanctified life to honor God. Actual sins were commonplace enough, or Hartford's ministers would not have been inclined to preach so frequently about the dangers of sin. Of course, the real hope was that God would forgive the Puritan for his or her debts, since eternal life mattered far more than temporal life. The temporal world was merely a proving ground for demonstrating the sanctified righteousness God was surely looking for in his visible saints.

that are not forgiven, they are in the gale of bitterness, and in the Bond of iniquity. (109 Psalm 14) David when he denounceth the great judgments against a siner it let not his iniquity be forgiven. 5 Consider the many Incouragments you have to seeke forgiveness, you hath to doe with a merciful creditor. A mercifull gracious and a sin pardoning creditor. (18 Matthew 27) Then the Lord had compassion and forgave him his debt. God hath encouraged us many ways. God hath commanded us to aske forgiveness of him. (Hosea 14) Take away all iniquity. God bids com and take without mercy (55 Isaiah 1.2) and without price. 2 Consider the promises God hath made. He hath promised to forgive you [c]. 3 Consider how many have been forgiven that have come to him. (1 Timothy 1:15.16) 4 Consider the greatness of your debts is noe hinderance of forgiveness. Pardon my iniquity for thy name sake for it is great. (18 Matthew) We have examples of those that have been forgiven of the greatest debts. 5 Consider all your debts are paid by Jesus Christ. 2 Let us be exorted to forgive our debtors. For [motive] here be willing to forgive: 1 Consider the debts you ow. You are debtors. You are indebted to God and to man. There for let us be merciful to our debtors. (3 Titus 1.2) (7 Ecclesiastes 21) 2 Consider if you do not forgive you cannot be forgiven of God. Except you show mercy you never will receive mercy. 3 Consider if you forgive your debtors you will be like to God. (5 Ephesians 1.4) Consider the great sin and danger of not forgiving your debtors. Without you doe forgive you canot be forgiven. 5 Except you forgive, all your prayers and sacrifices they all will be in vayn. You canot without this lift up holy hands in love with faith to God in prayer. It is in vayn without this to pray.[17] 6 Consider how earnest Jesus Christ is in pressing this great duty upon his Disciples of covering [pr] [ ] [ ] consider of the neer relation we stand one unto another not only as creatures but as people believing in the same Christ expecting the same reward in heaven. (50 Genesis 17) Consider how Good and pleasant it is for people to forgive one another and to live together in unity then God will command the blessing.

---

[17] Foster revisits the subject of vanity throughout the notebook. His message is essentially one of warning that all things of the world are in vain, and should not be substituted for the spiritual gift of God's grace and the salvation of Christ. Many studies of the Puritans accurately point to the harsh realities of life that New England's Puritans lived with. Their theology was a complex design that showed them how to use the things of the world as tools to help them achieve the all-important regeneration that was their life's aim.

The September 28, 1679 sermons of John Whiting also follow a typological theme. The text of his first sermon comes from the New Testament Epistle of Paul to the Romans while the second sermon's text is from Genesis. The first sermon deals with the surety of damnation that comes from unbelief, although faith alone "sola fide" will save. The theme of faith alone ties neatly into Whiting's second sermon on God's promise of salvation for his chosen people. Whiting's sermons are the first in the notebook to discuss the covenant, and the Devil.[18]

Later sermons by Isaac Foster, especially his September, 1680 sermons, are exhortations to Hartford's laymen to be wary of the God of the world. The Whiting sermons also introduce the concept of the natural or unregenerate man. The natural man is a concept prevalent in virtually all of the notebook's sermons, and should be recognized within the framework of conversion. There were far more unregenerate listeners at the sermons than visible saints, which explains the Hartford minister's frequent evangelical message.[19]

The Epistle of Paul to the Romans is considered Paul's most important contribution to understanding the message of the Gospel because in it, "Paul brings together all the Bible's greatest themes—sin, law, judg-

---

[18] The Puritans were a covenanted people, and it is important to understand the nature of their covenant principles. The most current and extensive source to begin with is David A. Weir's "Early New England: A Covenanted Society." (Grand Rapids, MI: William B. Eerdmans Publishing Company, 2005). Also see Perry Miller's *The New England Mind, Vol. 1*, in addition to the works of Edmund Morgan, David Hall, Harry Stout, and Charles E. Hambrick-Stowe. A number of essays are available on a wide range of topics concerning Puritan covenant theology. See: Jordan B. Barkalow, "Changing Patterns of Obligation and the emergence of Individualism in American Political Thought." *Political Research Quarterly* 57, no. 3 (September 2004), 491–500; E. Clinton Gardner, "Justice in the Puritan Covenantal Tradition." *Journal of Law and Religion* 6, no. 1 (1988), 39–60; Alan Heimert, "Puritanism, the Wilderness, and the Frontier.' *The New England Quarterly* 26, no. 3 (September 1953), 361–382; Robin W. Lovin, "Equality and Covenant Theology." *Journal of Law and Religion* 2, no. 2 (1984), 241–262; Perry Miller, "The Half-Way Covenant." *The New England Quarterly* 6, no. 4 (December 1933), 676–715; Perry Gilbert Miller, "Thomas Hooker and the Democracy of Early Connecticut." The *New England Quarterly* 4, no. 4 (October 1931), 663–712 and, David M. Robinson, "The Cultural Dynamics of American Puritanism." *American Literary History* 6, no. 4 (Winter 1994), 738–755.

[19] For detailed studies of church membership percentages in the Connecticut River Valley during the seventeenth century see Gerald F. Moran, "Religious Renewal, Puritan Tribalism, and the Family in Seventeenth-Century Milford, Connecticut." *The William and Mary Quarterly, 3rd ser.* 36, no. 2 (April 1979): 236–254. And for an exhaustive study on church membership and other elements of Puritan religious culture in seventeenth century Connecticut see Moran's PhD dissertation "The Puritan Saint: Religious Experience, Church Membership, and Piety in Connecticut," Rutgers University, 1973.

ment, human destiny, faith, works, grace, justification, sanctification, election, the plan of salvation, the work of Christ and of the spirit, the nature and life of the church, the place of the Jew and non-Jew in the purposes of God... in Romans, the whole landscape of the Bible is open to view."[20]

This sermon also begins the recurrent theme in the notebook that internal faith must accompany the word, that the word on its own is of no value unless combined with the Holy Spirit.

Mr. Whitting. (Sunday) September 28, 1679. (3 Romans 3.4) *3 Romans 3: "For what, thogh some did not believe? Shall their unbelief make the faith of God without effect?"*[21] *3 Romans 4: "God forbid: yea, let god be true, and everie man a liar, as it is writte, That thou mightiest be justified in thy words, and overcome, when thou art judged."*[22] For what if som did not believe. Shall that unbelief make the faith of God without effect? God forbid and [ ]. 1 That men may be and yet many are betrusted with the word of God that do not believe. 2 That unbelievers are not bettered by the word of God. Of the first, many live under the discoveries of the word of God and yet do not believe. Fayth is not so common as the word of God. (53 Isaiah 1) Who hath believed our report? Many have the preaching of the gospel that doe not believe.[23] (12 John 37.38) Tho: he did so many miracles yet that it might be full filled what was spoken by Esias the prophet who hath believed our report. Whence comes it to pass that men doe not believe the word of God? It is fear. The sinfulness of man the [subtilty] of Sathen and the righteous judgement of God. 1 It is from the sinfulness of man. (6 John 4) He that doth see the Son and believe shall be saved, but sin hath darkened the eyes of men that they cannot see and believe. (10 Psalm 5) The misteries of faith and the gospell are beyond the [ ] of a naturall Ey[24] and the reason is because they are spiritually to be discerned. There is a resisting hardnes and obstinancy in the

---

[20] R.C. Sproul, General Ed. *New Geneva Study Bible*, 1764–1765.

[21] *The Geneva Bible, 1560 Edition*. 71.

[22] Ibid.

[23] This passage may be a reference to atheism. The presence of atheism in colonial Hartford, and more generally, in colonial New England is interesting. It must have been a difficult personal philosophy for someone to adhere to in the midst of so much orthodoxy.

[24] By natural eye, Whiting means an unregenerate eye, that the eyes of the natural man are incapable of discerning God's message of hope in the Gospel.

hearts of men that doth resist the power of the word and believing. (35 [ ] 26) I will take away the heart of flint and give a heart of Fayth. You will not come to me that you may [h alife]. Our Lord doth lay the fault upon the will. (3 Hebrews 12) There is an evill heart of unbeleife that doth [move] to depart from God. 2 It is from the subtilty of Saytn. He is setting himself against the fayth of God's people. He workes all the ways he can to wound the faith of God's people. Sathen can bear that the light of the gospell should shine about men but he canot abide it should shine in men. (8 Luke 12) Sathen comes Immediatly and takes away the word out of the hearts lest they should believe and be saved. 3 That men doe not believe by the word is from the righteous justice of God. What he doth do to some he might righteously doe to all. The Lord he doth blind men's eyes, that is doth leave them to that blindness and hardness of heart that is in them.

Use 1: By way of instruction: hence see the insufficiency of means of the word of God as ministered by men to give faith and rest [ ] therein. Many hear the word of God all their dayes and yet never doe believe. (1 Titus 2) Many are outwardly called that did not beleive. (1 Corinthians 3.7) There is no resting in means. If you have the word and means and nothing more there can be no faith.[25] The [mortall] alone will [never] [de id] the matters our gospel [sayeth] the apostle cam not to you alone but it was accompanied with the [H g][26] and with power and then it is efectuall. The word shall work effectually when it comes with the [H g] sent down from heaven. That is the greatest mercy when the converting power of the spirit doth accompany the word of God. Then it doth sinck deep. The hand of man is to weake to turn men to Jesus Christ. If the hand of the Lord be with them they shall believe: 2 Hence see to whom the honor belongs if we believe. Not to our selves by grace are you saved not of themselves. It is the gift of God. A siner may as well [ ] himself as of his. Goe to

[25] Perry Miller frames his picture of the Puritan use of means as a sequence of cause and affect. 'God does all things, He creates the fire and the heat...the fire is a "means" to the heat; it does not, properly speaking, give to heat its being, yet only in a miracle would God permit of heat without the proper antecedent." In other words, the idea of means "prevented believers from being lured into the heresy of natural autonomy; it was an eternal safeguard against atheism. It encouraged humility and patience under affliction, since all the mediate or second causes of our grief must be God's instruments." *The New England Mind, Vol. 1*, 234. Miller's dissection of means is especially helpful regarding affliction, since in the *Hartford Sermon Notebook*, the subject of God's afflictions is a regular theme.

[26] Holy Ghost.

Christ to save him. We have no power to worke fayth of ourselves. No price to purchase faith. [ ] Christ hath purchased [for] you it is given to believe on the behalfe of Christ. 2 They that have faith they are not [debt] to [means] for it. It is not means that gives faith tho Fayth comes by means. (28 Acts 23.24) 3 They that have faith are debtors to God for it. God is the worker of it. It is the gift of God. (2 Colossians 12) (1 Corinthians 4:7) Who hath made the to differ from any other? He that doth what he will by his own [doles] out the unspeakable gift of fayth to whom as he wills and when he wills.

2 Doctrine: that unbelievers are not bettered by the word of God. Some they doe abide under that state of unbeleife. The word preached doth not profit men because it is not mingled with fayth. (5 Mark 26 verse) Men are awakened and suffer many things by the word of God and yet are not the bettered because of unbeleife: and it is so because the saveing advantage of the word of God comes only to those that do believe. The word of God makes men wise to salvation thru faith. The word of God doth lead men to Christ. (1 Thessalonians 1:13) The word of God hath no [further] saving influence In it then it doth bring men to and build them up in Christ. What will it profit that word we have if we be not profited by it? They that have the word while they want fayth they have no hope.

Use 1. Hence, see that unbelief is an exceeding dangerous sin. The dangerousness of this sin appears in that it is very provoking to God. God [p nds] and presents a saviour to siners and they would not accept it so that the wrath of God doth abide upon the siner and God will not be at peace with him. God never was [will] nor can be a friend to unbelievers. Without fayth you canot please God. 2 [s] [w t] Bring condemnation without unbeleife. He that believes not is condemned allready.[27] The sentance is past upon him. He is condemned and abideing as he is he shall be damned. Unbelief shuts men out of heaven. They could not enter because of unbelief. 2 Unbeleife shuts men in to hell. The fearfull and unbelieving shall be cast in to hell. 2 Let us fear unbeleife and [beg] deliverance from it. Fear all sin but

[27] This sounds a bit like predestination, although this sermon also indicates that a person can be delivered from unbelief, which suggests the possibility that one's damnation or salvation may not be predetermined. This is complicated. The Puritans acknowledged free will, but salvation was always predetermined in the sense that it was known to God and determined by God alone. Essentially, a person may be delivered of unbelief if he searches his soul to discover whether he is saved.

most Especially fear unbeliefe. As non sin so non shall suffer as unbelievers under the word of God. Possitive unbelievers shall wonder and perish. 2 Beg freedom from unbeliefe. This unbeleife will [b e] you Forever if you doe abide in it. There is no beleife without the word of God and yet how many [long] [Eno.] heare of Jesus Christ and yet not believe in him. No man can com except the (6 John 44. 45) Father do draw him.

Whiting's second sermon reinforces the nature of God's love to his chosen people, the Elect of Hartford and New England. It is also a lesson from Whiting regarding the covenant of Grace.

Mr. Whitting. (Sunday) September 28, 1679.[28] (15 Genesis 1) *"After these things, the word of the Lord came unto Abram in a visio, saying, Feare not, Abram, I am thy buckler, and thine exceeding great reward."*[29] After those things the word of the Lord came to Abram in a vision saying fear not Abram, I am thy shield and exceeding great reward. The God of glory appeared to Abram that called him and caused to wander after him and made a covenant with him for Abram's Incouragement.[30]

---

[28] Throughout the *Hartford Sermon Notebook*, there are several examples where two sermons are preached on the same day. This was a common occurrence as discussed in several sources. In *The Practice of Piety*, Charles E. Hambricke-Stowe recounts the Puritan's schedule on the Sabbath. "New Englander's worshipped publicly in both the morning and the afternoon of the Lord's Day. Services were long, about three hours each, so in effect the day was spent in church…By granting six hours on the first day of every week for the clergy to rehearse the drama of sin and salvation before the people, New England put the Sabbath at the center of its temporall existence." 99. Alice Morse Earle's *The Sabbath in Puritan New England* is a late nineteenth-century history of Puritan New England. Earle's is a wonderful little book that, while of an outdated mode, should not be overlooked, and in many ways is more enjoyable than much of the modern scholarship. "Time was marked by a strong brass-bound hour-glass, which stood on a desk below or beside the pulpit…so that all the members of the congregation could easily watch 'the sands that ran i' the clock's behalf.' By the side of the desk sat…a tithingman, whose duty it was to turn the hour-glass as often as the sands ran out. This was a very ostentatious way of reminding the clergyman how long he had preached…77.

[29] *The Geneva Bible, 1560 Edition*. 7.

[30] Many secondary sources that deal with Puritan covenant theology include some analysis of Abraham's covenant with God, also known as the Covenant of Grace. David Scobey's ideas concerning this covenant are particularly interesting within the context of typology. Scobey suggests that the Puritans were gospelizing Abraham in order "to use him as a measure for their own work of reformation. In his image they become idol smashers, heroes who had built an altar to God in exile, founders of a holy commonwealth that they explicitly identified with Israel." David M. Scobey, "Revising the Errand: New England's Ways and the Puritan Sence of the Past." *The William and Mary Quarterly*, 3rd ser., 41, no. 1 (January 1984): 16. David A. Weir's

Whilest he was under discouragements appeared to him, renewed His promise, and makes incouragment for him by engaging himself to him in his all sufficiency. Abram tho infinitly pleased with what God had don for him yet he complaines he wants a child. Children were much in Abram's eye all other blessings being little in his eyes. 2 That a child of promise and therein the promised seed was much in his eys. 3 God's answer where in God ratifys the promise of a numerous seed. (Verse 4.5) 2 The Lord repeats and confirms the promise of his seed possessing the land of Canan. (Verse 7) The ground with God confirms it. (Verse 7) The maner of its confirmation from Verse 9 to 17. 2 That promise confirmed the time of the discovery after those things. After Lot was taken and recovered and after the discourses he had with Malchizideck. God did this. God [times] his dispensations. 2 The maner of God's discourses of himself to Abram. God had discourses of [himselfe] to his people of old. (12 Numbers 6.7.8) By vision in a dream and mouth to mouth God manifests himself to Abram in a playn way. 3 The matter of the [discovery] I am [ ] shield and exceeding reward. [ ] eminent duty fear not: 2 Taken from the consideration of what God was and would be to him [ied] to defend a God [t re].

Doctrine: That it is the duty of the people of God not to fear whatever difficultys or dangers they meet with. All they need not fear. Many were his difficulties when he was a stranger in the land. Few in number and the inhabitants of the Land envyed him and they [strove] with him. [ ] (7 Acts 5) Abram had a pleasant [seed][31] in the promise yet he possessed not one foot. To this Abram thus [circumstanced] God says fear not the sam thing, the Lord speakes to all in his [case] (12 Hosea 4) The Lord found Jacob in Bethell and there he speaks with us. (41 Isaiah 14) Fear not worm Jacob. How or what shall fear If not a worm that is subject to all violence. (2 Luke 32) Fear not little flock it is your Father's pleasure to give you a kingdom. 3 Things may be lookt into: who they are that should not fear: Those that are in like

---

"Early New England: A Covenanted Society" is the most in depth study to date on the subject of the covenant in Puritan theology and civil society. In it, Weir writes that "The theme of covenant is found throughout the Old and New Testaments of the Bible, and it is well established that the covenant was a motif that provided cohesion to the nascent New England communities of the seventeenth century...New Englander's...worked to some degree within a covenantal vision that had as its source the Bible and reformed Protestant theology." 221.

[31] 1611, King James Bible, 155.

state with faythfull Abram they should not fear: those that are not only his by creation and covenant with God. Many such ought to fear but those are his by a peculyer right. By election he hath chosen them to be his.[32] The Father's by election the son's by donation. (20 Acts 28) Glorify God in your bodys and spirits which are God's. 3 They are his by effectuall vocation. His by their souls consent gained to be to him and for him. (110 Psalm 3) They are made willing in the day of thy power. They are his own they are new creatures. The workmanship created in Christ Jesus in good workes. (Ephesians 4.21) God is good to Isreell to them that are of a clean heart. His peculyer people his portion.[33] The Lord's people is his portion. The Lord is their portion the portion if Jacob is not like [yours] they are his jewels. 2 Why is that fear forbidden the people of God? Answer. There is a doble fear a sinfull and satisfying feare. This last is a feare every where cald for. It shall be well with them that fear God. There is a groundless fear. Satisfy the Lord of hosts and let him be your fear and dread the matter of this fear, and [so] [the] people of God should not fear the wayt of any evill nor the want of any good. The people of God may have heard things shown them. The people of God may be sore broken by great and grevious suffering. Ye they may Fare the worss from man for keeping close to God. (44 Psalm 2) For thy sake are we kild all the day long. Yet there is no cause of fear: God will support and secure his people. God is faythfull and will not suffer you to be tempted above what you are able to beare. The burthen may be to heavy for you to beare. It may be out of measure and above strength. Your strength. But yet then the Lord's grace is sufficient for you then. 2 Look upon the maner of this feare. The people of God shall want noe good. They that have the fountain shall not want the streams. There is no want to those that fear the Lord. They that seek the Lord shall want no good things. (37 Psalm 25) David sayth I never saw the righteous forsaken.

---

32 Edmund Morgan's *Visible Saints* defines what it meant to be a member of the Elect, or, a visible saint. His book details the method used by New England's Puritans for determining whether one was an Elect of God by way of an examination, in which the members of the church listened to a potential members "relation" of an experience of saving grace. This process was quite complicated. Morgan says that "nonseparating English Puritan divines had been teaching their readers and listeners how to recognize the movements of grace within the soul and thus to determine whether one was a saint or not." *Visible Saints*, 113. If a person was able to demonstrate a convincing "experience," they were considered one of God's Elect or chosen people, and so were allowed membership in the church.

33 "Peculyer people" are God's Elect or chosen people.

(2 Timothy 4:17.18) The people of God may be persecuted by men but not forsaken of God. (84 Psalm 11) No good thing will God with hold from those that do fear Him. Looke to the maner of this fear. The people of God should not fear with a Tormenting fear: by faith Noah being warnd of God built an arke: perfect love casts out fear. What fear? Not fear of offending God, (2 Peter 2:4) but fear of being cast out of the favour of God. (8 Romans 15) 2 The people of God should not feare with a disttrustfull troubling feare: fear and dismayed are put together often: fear not be not dismayed. There is a feare and trembling to be of missing salvation of falling short of it, but a heart troubling fear of what may befall us ought not to be. Christ leaves it as His dyeing counsell. You believe in God believe also in me. Let not your hearts be troubled. In the world you will have trouble, but let all be quiet within. 3 The people of God should not fear with duty hindering fear or [h d] weakening Fear that drives from or discourages in duty. 3 But whence is it a duty to the people of God not to fear? 1 There is the command of God that binds to duty. The command of God is the Bond of duty and that should make us wholly Fearless. 2 There is the promise of God to encourage in it. I am thy exceeding great reward. As the promise bids us not to fear so the promise tells us we need not fear. (4 Romans 12) (13 Hebrews 5.6).

The opening text for Benjamin Woodbridge's sermon comes from Acts. The Acts of the Apostles is a history of the early Christian church as chronicled by Luke, who describes the general theme of Acts as follows: "The Lord is going to expand his work in Jerusalem, and in all Judea and Samaria, and to the end of the earth... Acts is a map of the progress of the church into the ancient world, showing how the present age began."[34] *For the Puritans, New England must have seemed very much like the end of the earth.*

This was one of the more difficult sermons in the notebook to transcribe because of the paleography. The general theme of the sermon is salvation versus damnation. Salvation awaits the converted, damnation awaits the unconverted, and Woodbridge uses this sermon to contrast the differences between the converted and unconverted man. It also contains the interesting theme of the inward and outward man, which appears often in the notebook, and is a fascinating example of the richness in Puritan religious thinking and philosophy.

[34] *New Geneva Study Bible*, 1708–1709.

(Sunday) October 5, 1679. Mr. Ben Woodbridge (8 Acts 39) "*And assone as they were come up out of the water, the spirit of the Lord caught away Phillipe, that the Eunuche sawe him no more: so he went on his way rejoicing.*"[35] And he went on his way rejoyceing. The beginning of the [capt] sets before us a great persecution that cam upon the people of God by the persecution of Steven and that they were scattered yet went about and preached the Gospel: It is with God to enlarg His [ch][36] where men doe endeavourer to straighten. This [capt]: doth make special [i] of Phillips preaching the Gospel and of his goeing into the wilderness to meet with the Ethiopian eunuch.[37] It is with God to find out his elect and chosen tho they are hidden in the world. When God hath worke and arrand to doe he will find a messenger: the conversion of a soule is a great worke in God's account that he will send a messenger to doe. Phillip found him reading a part of the prophesi of [Zefi] when God will inlighten [h] a person serious in reading the word of God. Phillip's reason dost thou understand that thou readest to understand the word is the way to prophet. Now can I except som men shall [guide] see the need of the ministry of the word: (35 Philippians) preacheth I to him. We read of his fayth baptism and [ ] that was in the text he went on rejoicing. He was converted. He found the lambe of God and then he goes on rejoycing.

[35] *The Geneva Bible, 1560 Edition*. 59.

[36] Probably shorthand for "church," [ch] appears throughout the notebook.

[37] New England's Puritans envisioned their journey into the wilderness of New England as a historical progression of the Israelite's wilderness journey as chronicled in the Old Testament. The story is told in (Deut. 1:19) of the Hebrews wandering in the wilderness following their escape from Egypt. The wilderness was a pilgrimage of renewal for the Israelites, and it reappears throughout the Bible with the experiences of John the Baptist in the wilderness of Judea, and Christ's resistance to the temptations of Satan in the deserts east of Galilee. *Holman Bible Dictionary*, 1672. Charles E. Hambrick-Stowe says, "For New Englanders in the seventeenth century the idea of wilderness was irresistible whenever a pen touched paper... Also, the satisfaction and overturning of wilderness deprivation, hardship, and violence commonly formed part of the vision of biblical prophets." *The Practice of Piety*, 17. Perry Miller explores the importance of the wilderness to Puritan theology in *Errand Into the Wilderness*. For the Puritans, the errand into New England's wilderness "was being run for the sake of Reformed Christianity; and while the first aim was indeed to realize in America the due form of government, both civil and ecclesiastical, the aim behind the aim was to vindicate the most rigorous ideal of the reformation, so that ultimately all Europe would imitate New England." *Errand in the Wilderness*, 12. For the Puritans, the errand to New England's wilderness was an opportunity to complete the work of the reformation with a free hand, unfettered by the opposition of the Anglican and Roman Catholic forces of Europe.

Doctrine: a converted life is the most joy fullest life. The most pleasant peaceable joyous and most happyest life. Example: what is understood by a converted Life? We shall not [trade] of conversion. Now there are 2 souls converted and unconverted. Such as are in Christ out of Christ siners and satisfyed persons such as walked with God. Eunuch walked with God and Noah a just man walked with God. So it was of old in the gospell they had conscience in all things to live honestly without offense. These as apposed to those that know not the rule, know not the Lord, estranged from God walke in Sin.

2 Example: what is to be understood by a joyfull life? 1 Negatively. We doe not understand that mirth and [jollyty] that some empty and [frothy] persons may be addicted to: (2 Ecclesiastes 2) I said of laughter it is mad and what doest it. It is not this. But a joyfull lif doth consist in 1 being secured from those evills that are want to afflict or annoy or oppress soule or body. These when they ly long they doe afflict the soule or body. Some of those Evills that doe afflict soule and body and make it not comfortable, as fears that doe respect evill to com. When we See evills coming in and no way to escape it these doe affright man, and make man live uncomfortable. (17 Job 15) The doubts the soule is subject when it is in susspens between hope and fears so the cares which a person is subject which is anxious. There are spirituall evills [judicially] afflicted of God, as an amazing sight of sin that God some times gives to a siner. God doth reprove men and set their sin in order before them that it appears Terible to them. (37 Matthew 4) I have sind and betrayd innocent blood sayeth Judas. So a dreadfull thoughtfulness and expecting of a fearfull dome from the judg of the world, so divin [dirilection]. Those are fearfull and afflicting evills. So being under disgrace and reproach and tryalls of reproach and [b ds]. All those doe make a life uncomfortable: now to be secured from these doe express a joyfull life: 2 A joyfull life is that we are interested in and made [p] of some good that can administer to us rest delight and comfort and [co p ec y] to us. (16 Psalm 6) The lines are fallen to me. I have a goodly heritage [hencfor] with the Lord is my portion. A person will be weary unless he can as the psalmist say return to thy [cast]. Oh my soule there will be new desires and without this there canot be a fullness of joy.

3 When there is a [re ness] and lightness of spirit consisting in inward revivings and refreshings which doe infuse it selfe into that outward man and make his actions more lively. Thus Jacob's spirit revived and sayd it is eno: Jos is alive. So the Ch (126 Psalm 9) when

the Lord did turn against the captivity of Jacob we were as those that dreame, then was our mouths with laughter and rejoicing. 3 The evidences of these things that a converted life is the most choysest pleasant life, but there is an objection. [P ts] in which is layd partly from persons observation. Those that are most conscious walke closest with God. Live as dull a life as another's [th s] Job a pattern of patience and of affliction too. So the Ch. ([ ] Lamentations 12)[38] is there any sorrow like [om]. So the wicked have joyfull lives as other men as the scripture speakes. The wicked ar (73 Psalm 5) [not] in trouble as other men: the objection is to be Answered. In generall the Lord doth hide his [o]. In an evill time the wicked are sought out for and punished. Fayth hath delivered som from temporall judgments when as sin doth many times hasten and bring them. The adversity of the righteous is better than the prosperity of the wicked. 1 The afflictions of the righteous, they are moderated and made easy to them In that the everlasting armes of God are near to them.[39] Yet they are sweetened to them. They rejoice in their afflictions because they are sweetend to them. We glory in tribulation (5 Acts: 41) (5 Job 22) 3 They are not only moderated, swetend, but satisfied and made beneficiall to them and there by comfortable and beneficial and usefull to them, but the prosperity of the wicked that is but short. It is but for a season. Their life is but short. 2 It is a cursed prosperity curst in the inward and in the outward man. [j sure] waxed fatt and quickly forget God. 3 It is an uncomfortable prosperity their sinn is unpardoned. They are subject to wrath so that in the midst of their laughter the heart is sad.

The Reason of the Doctrine is: 1 in that they have the best foundation of true joy and comfort. That joy is best that hath the surest foundation. Som there are that doe built without foundation and when the wind riseth they Fall. There is no Foundation of joy to the wicked. They are condemned all ready. But the righteous have a foundation of joy

---

[38] (1 Lamentations 12) in 1611 King James, 898.

[39] New England's Puritans experienced their share of affliction, especially regarding epidemics and Indian wars, but there is a theological precedent for affliction that engenders hope, as long as one is a believer. The supreme nature of God is founded in affliction, and affliction exists throughout the Bible. Of importance to the Puritan was the knowledge that God was aware of afflictions, in fact God had created them, so that the manner in which one dealt with affliction reflected one's relationship to God. "The purpose of affliction is to show the power of Christ. The discipline of affliction produces strong faith. The end of affliction is the salvation of God's people." *Holman Bible Dictionary*, 32.

being justified by faith.[40] We have peace with God. (8 Romans 1) There is no condemnation to those that are justified by Fayth. Who shall lay anything to the charge of God's elect? It is God that justifyeth. Blessed is the man whose transgression is Foregiven, whose sin is [concred].[41] They are mostly free and best secured from those evills that render our lives uncomfortable as from feares. The wicked doe Flee when no man persues, and feare where no feare is. (26 Leviticus 36) But he that has made his peace with God feares not. (112 Psalm) The righteous is not afrayed of evill tideings. I will not be afrayed of 10000s of the people that compass me (3 Psalm 6) about. (1 Peter 3) 6 So if disappointments, who are so subject to it as the wicked? (11 Proverbs 7) The hope of the righteous makes not ashamed, it shall be gladness. So for inward troubles the righteous are under the promise of support. My grace (2 Corinthians 12) is sufficient for the. Their troubles are not so dureable as the wicked. Weaping may endure for a night (30 Psalm 5) but joy comes in morning. But the wicked are full of trouble. Looke to the externall affliction they are troubled with. They are bowed down and held down under them. (2 Corinthians 4:17) 2 Consider that they are interest in the best good they can afoard most good to the soules. (14 Jeremiah 3) But it is not so with the wicked. The world fayles them, but the righteous have an all sufficient God to goe unto: (66 Isaiah 11) God can create joy and comfort for his people. 3 Look into the exaltenes of spirit is ther in the godly, but who should administer this to the wicked? The lord can give such an evidence of life to a soule that he shall rejoice with joy unspeakeable and glorious.

Use: it doth [c i ness] of that Eror that is taken up in the world, that righteous life is the most saddest and uncomfortable Life when indeed it is the most joyous life: the believer hath it upon the most surest foundations. Their joyes are best most spirituall most firm and soled and more holy and pure more perminent and durable than the joyes of the wicked. Consider the godly can finde more joy and comfort than you can in what you doe enjoy. As within riches that is so right after for delight and they may be as well given to the righteous

[40] The theologian James White, a contributing editor to the Holman Bible Dictionary, defines justification by faith using the letters of the apostle Paul. "Paul insists on justification by faith in opposition to justification by any work of righteousness, for faith, by nature, places all men on the same level and allows for no gradation." *Holman Bible Dictionary*, 971.

[41] [concred] is probably "conquered."

as to the wicked tho thou hast a larger portion of riches yet they doe injoy more comfort with it than you. They have a litle and no sorrow with it. (16 Proverbs 8) Better is a little[42] with righteousness than great reverence without it. 3 Consider they have spiritual riches that thou art destitute of. Rich in fayth. Heires of a kingdom. They have the [p] of [p]. (1 Corinthians 3) Last, all is yours and ye are Christ's and Christ is God's. (2 Corinthians 6:10) [ ] the believer when he seems to have nothing he doth posses all. The Lord is my shepherd. I shall not want. He is the living water he hath robes of righteouness to closeth us with. We have an eternal house in the heavens to honouer delight and comfort, but the Lord doth confer the most honor upon those that honor him. Those that honor me I will honor but the name of the wicked shall rott. 2 There is more honor and comfort that comes by our reconciliation to God than can by any wordly honor or advancement: rejoyce (10 Luke 19.20) Rather that their names are written in heaven. They can find joy in God in thoughts of God In drawing nigh to God, but the wicked dred the thought and presence of God. 2 They rejoice in your afflictions but the wicked they cannot. 3 They can rejoice in Temptation. (James 1.2) 4 They may rejoice in death they may lift up their heads. Their redemption draws nigh they may have peace in death, and victory over death. 2 It is often profe to those that doe forsake God their [own] mercys and comforts. 3 It should perswad all to break their sins and com in and live to God. You should then have joyfull Lives. It will be better with you then now. You will never find comfort. Without God all creatures will be empty when you com to dy, but with the Lord there is fullness of joy. You may receive life and more abundantly, is fullness of (16 Psalm 11) joy and At his right hand are pleasures for ever more.

"Psalm" means song, and the theology of the psalms is as large as the Old Testament. "The Psalms looked forward to Christ's coming, His suffering, and His glory."[43] In the New Geneva Study Bible Psalm 19 is subtitled "The Perfect Revelation of the Lord." It is a Psalm that "praises the Lord for his two great gifts to humanity: creation and the law."[44] This is also a sermon about the excellency of the word of God, and Foster

[42] There is no word between little and with, in the notebook.
[43] *New Geneva Study Bible*, 754.
[44] Ibid., 772.

exhorts his congregation in Hartford to embrace the importance of hearing the word of God, and of reading it and meditating on it.

Mr. Foster. (Sunday) October 12, 1679 (19 Psalm 10) "*And more to be desired than golde, yea, then muche fine golde: sweter also the honie and the honie combe.*"[45] More to be desired are they then gold. Yea than much fine gold. Sweeter than honey and Honey combe. The designe is to prayse God for and set forth the excellencys of those things by which we come neer God. He sets forth the excelencys of the workes of God where by we come to know God. From v: 1 to 6 the heavens they doe declare the glory of God. God by his workes doth show some thing of himself to pore man. (1 Romans 20): 2 David sets forth the excelency of the word of God. The booke of nature showes that there is a God, but the word of God shows what this God is.[46] From verse 7 to the 13. David useth many titles to set forth the word of God the law of God the Testimonies the Statuts of God. (1 Kings 2:1) The law of God is perfect. The whole word of God is perfect: it is sure. More to be desired are they than fine gold. The Excelency of the word in the text is set forth comparitivly by comparing it with and prefering it above all precious things— more precious than gold more sweeter than honey.

Doctrine: that the word of God is more precious and more pleasant to a child of God than the more excelent things in the world. More to be desired are they than gold than much fine gold. More precious than gold, more sweeter than honey. The word of God is more precious than the finest gold and more sweeter than the sweetest honey. David doth frequently express his delight in the word of God. I rejoice in the word (119 Psalm 152) as they rejoice in their great spoyle. More than [h] necessary Food. As the body cannot live without food so the soule cannot live with out the word of God. Example: 1 Consider the

---

[45] *The Geneva Bible, 1560 Edition*. 239.

[46] "Early Christian doctrine held that God was the author of two texts, the Book of God, or the Bible, and the Book of Nature. The two were co-extensive: given the right interpretative tools, one could read the eternal verities of God's design from Nature back to the Bible, and *vice versa*. The medieval world was thoroughly semiotic, the stars in the sky and the leaves on the trees were shot through with semantic meaning, signifiers of the Creator's absolute authorship. Writing in the twelfth century C.E., Hugh of St. Victor reminded his contemporaries that the true Christian is an unflagging hermeneut, who in reading the Book of Nature seeks to penetrate the outward appearance of things in order to recover their God-sent meaning." Christopher Keep, Tim McGlaughlin, and Robin Parmer. *The Electronic Labyrinth*, University of Victoria. http://elab.eserver.org/elab.html (accessed February 19, 2008).

children of God have had a longing desire more after the word of God than after anything in the world. They desire it more than anything. I opened my mouth and [p nt d] for I longed for they commandment. (84 Psalm 1.2) My soule longeth even faints for the tabernackles of God.[47] 2 The children of God have been wont to take more delight and contentment in the word and ordinances of God than in anything in the world besides. (119 Psalm 72) The law of they mouth is better to me than thousands of gold. (103 verse 174 verse) I have longed for they salvation for they law is my delight (14 verse) I have rejoiced in the way of they testimony, more than in all riches. 3 This is evident from the bitter lamentation the people of God doe make in the want of it. (Lamentations 2: 6.7) And he hath violently taken away his Tabernackle. (119 Psalm 82) Mine eys [fayle] for thy word saying when wilt though comfort me: 4 The children of God have been willing to part with these injoyments for the sake of the word of God. 5 This is evident from the constant and sincer desires and endevoures after the injoyment of the word of God above all.

1 Reason: is from the excelency of the word. It is more excelent than gold. 2 By the great benefit they receive by it. 3 From the vanity of all those things considered [favored] of God. From the excelency of the word, it hath more real worth in it than gold. The word is excelent. 1 It is excelent in its author. The excelency of the Booke of the scriptures is the author. It is the word of the great God. (2 Timothy 3:16) All scripture is given by divine Inspiration of God. Men were the writters but not the Indicters of it. Holy men of God spake as they were moved by the [ ] [ ]. 2 The word of God is Excelent in the matter. There are more excelent things contained in the book of God than in any other booke what ever. The booke of God doth speak of excelent things and wonderfull things. The word of God doth discover God to us in his nature, Essence, and in his attributes. [There is] the clear and [fine] [discourse] God to [behold]. Herein is the excelency of the book of God. 2 Herein is a discovery and revelation of the Lord Jesus Christ unto us. There fore it is excellent in his matter. (5 John 39) Search the scriptures for they doe testify of me. What he is, his nature, works, offices, and benefits. 3 Here it is discoverd to us the state of man. It is

[47] In Hebrew, tabernackle means "to dwell", and the Old Testament specified three kinds of tabernackles or dwelling places, provisional, Sinaitic and Davidic. The wilderness narratives (Num. 2 and 3), which were especially important to the Puritans, describe the tabernackle as a portable sanctuary. *Holman Bible Dictionary*, 1552.

not known any other way. Man's first estate, what he was when created, this discovered to us in the word of God. 2 His fallen estate in to sin and misery subjecting to the curs by sin is revealed in the word of God. 3 Man's renewed estate and recovery out of sin is revealed in the word of God. Man's finall state, a state of glory or misery, is discovered in the word of God. 4 The word of God doth contayn all the precious promises we have to trust unto, they are all in the word of God. 5 As to the way and means of salvation it is excellent. [Here] is the way to life and happyness revealed and the way of death how to be avoyded: 3 The word of God is excelent in its properties. 1 It is most sure and certain. It is a word of truth. (119 Psalm 160): Yi word is true from the beginning. (2 Peter 1:19) We have allso a more sure word of prophesie to which you doe well to give heed to: 2 It is a pure and holy word. (7 Romans 12) It is a holy word, a just word, and a true word. (12 Psalm 63) The word of God is a most powerfull and efficatious word. (1 Romans 6) It is called the power of God unto salvation. It is powerfull to humble the proud lift up the humble to convince convert and humble. It inlightens the minde and doth convert the will. It doth not only inform but conform. 4 It is most excelent in his end. The end for which it was given for to man as in [the]. (2 Timothy 3:16) It is to teach, to reprove, correct, perfect us for all good works, to lead man to God. (2 Titus 11) It is called the grace of God that brings salvation.

2 Reason from the benefit they receive by the word of God. They price it because they receive most benefit by it. 1 It is the word of God that hath inlightened them. (19 Psalm 7.8) They have been made wise by it even to salvation. (3 Proverbs 14.15) The merchandiz of it is better than silver or choyse gold—(119 Psalm 98.130 verse). 2 It is the word that doth guide and direct them. It is said to be a light to thy feet and a lamp to the steps. It is the word of God that keeps them from wandering. 3 It is the word of God that hath convinced them of their sins. (7 Romans 7) I had not known sin but by the Law. It is the word of God that doth affect the heart with remorss for sin. (2 Acts 37) The ministry of the word did prick them at the heart. It is the word of God that doth convert also from [sin]. The law as the Lord is perfect converting the soule. It is by the word of God that siners are cleansed. (17 John) [itify][48] them by thy truth thy word is truth. It is the word of God that doth worke Grace in their hearts. (10 Romans 17) Fayth comes

[48] (17 John 17) "Sanctify them"...1611 King James, 140.

by hearing the word. Every grace is wrought in the heart by the hearing of the word. (4 Acts 4) Not only the beginnings but the Increase of grace is by the word. They are edifyed by the word and built up. The Increase of grace is by the word of God. (4 Ephesians 11) The word is for the edifying of the saints and the perfecting of them.[49] (1 Peter 2:2) We should desire the sincer milke of the word to grow there by. It is the word of God by which they do resist Temptation. The word of God is that sword by which men over come the Temporal. Againe the word of God doth comfort in afflictions. (19 Psalm 8) (119 Psalm 54) It is the word of God that doth stablish the soule in the wayes and truths of God and saves from apostacy and Eror. The God of all grace stablish you by his word.

3 Reason: is from the vanity of the most excelent things in this world compared with the word of God. They are vanity compared with the word of God in Two respects. 1 In that they will not afford that satisfaction and contentment to the soule that the word of God doth. The word of God that will comfort, revive a dyeing soule, but there is nothing in the creature can do it. It canot [convey] that comfort to the soule that the word of God doth. 2 They are vanity compared with the word in regard of their fadeing perishing nature. They are things that are not. They are therefore called uncertain riches. (119 Psalm 136) I have seen an end of all perfection but thy law is exceeding broade—

Use 1: Of instruction hence, learn how great a mercy for God to give his word unto a people. It is a greater mercy than to have gold and Treasure. (147 Psalm 2) Last verses. God hath done much for his people if he gives you his word. It is matter of great Thankfulness that we have the word of God that great advantage that the [ ] hath much every way cheifly that they have the oracles of God committed to them. 2 Hence learn it is one of the greatest and Sorest Judgements of God that can befall us for God to take away his word from us. (8 Amos 11) Behold the days com that I will send a famin not of bread nor thirst for water but a famin of hearing the word of God. This is the greatest because it brings spirituall death. When there is no vission the people perish. 3 Se the great [ ] of most in the world that doe preferr

---

[49] This is the first direct reference to the word "saint" in the *Hartford Sermon Notebook*. Saint appears many times in the notebook, and was one of the most important elements in Puritan theology.

gold and the honey combe above the word of God. (10 Luke 41.42) Mary Martha like they trouble themselves about many things. But [few a Mary] like sit to heare the word of God:

2 Use: of reproofe: to those that doe not prize and esteem the word of God, that are not like David and Jobe doe not price and Esteem the word of God. It is a sad signe they have not received good by the word that many are ded in sin and not quickend by the word of God. (1 Corinthians 2:14) It is a sign that there are many naturall men that doe not discern sweetness in the word of God.[50] 2 It reproofs those that are not thankfull for the word of God that is better than the best riches [t]. 3 It reproves those that doe not Improve all opportunities to heare the word of God. Few would loose an opportunity of getting gold and yet loose the word of God. It reproves those that com to heare the word of God without an apetite, that tast no sweetness in it. It reproves those that doe not meditate on the word of God, that doe not price it read of it and meditate on it. (119 Psalm 97) Oh how I love they law. I meditate on it all the day. [L] It reproves those that are content to loose advantages of hearing of the word for outward accomadations. This is not David's spirit.

3 Exortation: be exorted to price the word of God that is so precious. 2 Be thankfull for it. 3 Pitty those that want the word of God, 4 and pray for the continuance of the word of God among you. 5 Be we exorted to improve the word of God. 1 Be much in reading of the word of God. (17 Deuteronomy 19) Be much in searching in to it. 2 Meditate on the word of God and pray over what you read [is].[51] 3 Hear it when God gives you opportunity, do not loos it. 4 Practice the word of God and doe it: for motive doe you consider the excelency of the word of God? 2 Consider how proffitably the word of God will

---

[50] A natural man is an unconverted, unregenerate man, in other words, a person who has not been born again.

[51] The word meditation appears often in the *Hartford Sermon Notebook* and is worth exploring in some detail. Charles E. Hambrick-Stowe offers much of the best secondary analysis on the subject of meditation. Hambrick-Stowe defines Puritan meditation as part of what he refers to as the practice of secret devotion. "In the practice of secret devotion—especially in the early morning, at night just prior to sleep, at midday on the sabbath or days of fasting, and on Saturday in preparation for the sabbath—individuals ideally meditated after reading and before prayer. Meditation was the natural outcome of reading in that the substance of the exercise often emerged from the pattern read. In meditation the believer applied the written text to the soul." *Practice of Piety*, 161.

be. 3 Consider the danger of neglecting the word of God. It will bring outward Judgements on the. It is dangerous for thy soules. Heare and your soules shall live. If you doe not heare your soules shall dye. Those that doe not heare and believe the word of God God will give them [eys] to [strong] or [tions] to believe [ ] that they may be [ia].

CHAPTER FIVE

MEDIATION

Chapter 5 begins with a short sermon series from Isaac Foster based on First Timothy chapter 6 verse 6. The preface to First Timothy in the Geneva Study Bible *is entitled Christ the Mediator. "The saving ministry of Jesus Christ is summed up in the statement that He is the 'Mediator between God and men' (1 Tim. 2:5)... The mediator must have links with both sides so as to identify with and maintain the interests of both, and represent each to the other on the basis of goodwill."*[1] *The reformer Zacharius Ursinus describes the mediator within the framework of the covenant, that Christ mediates between fallen man and God: "God gives assurance to men that he will be merciful to them, remit their sins, grant unto them a new righteousness, the Holy Spirit, and eternal life by and for the sake of his Son, our Mediator... We were the enemies of God, and hence there could be no way of access to him, unless by the intercession of Christ, the Mediator..."*[2]

Based on the sermon dated 5 October by Ben Woodbridge, who had recently been dismissed by the disaffected congregation in Windsor, Foster's source of inspiration for this series may have been the plight of his fellow preacher. Chapter 5 also contains two sermons whose opening text comes from the Book of Psalms. The theology contained in the Psalms so impressed Martin Luther that he called the Psalms "a little Bible, and the summary of the Old Testament."[3]

Mr. Foster. (Sunday) October 19, 1679. (1 Timothy 6:6) *"But godliness is great gaine, if a man be content with that he hathe."*[4] But godlyness with contentment is great gaine: It is naturall for man to seeke after gain. Man's covetous heart carrys them after that who will show us good is the great [ ] but such is the great darknes of man that he doth not know what [ ] is. But the text doth tell us what it is. It is godliness that is the greatest gaine. Tho men may thinke themselves loosers there by. Yet

[1] *New Geneva Study Bible,* 1910.

[2] William Stacy Johnson ed., *Reformed Reader: A Sourcebook in Christian Theology* (Louisville, Kentucky: Westminster/John Knox Press, 1993), 100.

[3] Ibid., 745.

[4] *The Geneva Bible, 1560 Edition.* 99.

in the end it will be the greatest gayne. In this [cap], he shows the duty of servants to their master both to the believing and unbelieving man in the first and second verse. 2 The apostle doth Illustrate and confirm this Doctrine by comparing it with the Doctrine of the Fals teachers, and he tells who they are in the third and fourth. Here is the reason that these teachers content about matter of words. 3 The effect of this in the fourth and fifth verse. Hence cometh strife and [ ]. 4 A description of those that are seduced by falls teachers. Verse 5 in having reproved those he shows godliness is great gaine [and] contentment, that is If a man be contented with the state and relation they are in whether rich or poore. Yet godliness is great gaine.

Doctrine: that godliness with contentment is great gaine.[5] The greatest and the truest gaine. The whole world is not so great gaine to man. Many there are that seeke for contentment other ways but their gaine is nothing to this. (13 Proverbs 7) A poor godly man that hath nothing in the world hath great riches. The gain that is in godlyness is durable and abideing. They that love me sayth wisdom shall in [r] substance. It is durable. Durable riches and righteousness they goe together. Godlyness is proffitable to all things. Bodily exercise profits Little. If you take it for labour this profits Little. (1 Ecclesiastes 3) (2 [cap] 22) 2 If you take it for those exercises of runing and wrestleing where in they strove for a corruptible crown that profits little. 3 If you take it for the external act of mortification, of subdueing the body, this proffits little, but now godliness is profitable to all things and hath the promises of this life and that which is to com. It is gayn great gaine tho it brings nothing with it. Seeke first the kingdom of heaven and the righteousness there of and all those things shall [be] [aded]. (3 Proverbs 9.10) Honor the Lord with they substance then barnes shall be filled with plenty and your presses shall brake forth with new wine. (22 Job 23.24) Then you shall lay up gold as dust and have plenty of silver and God shall keep the. Here is gayn in this life (33 Isaiah 5.6) The feare of the lord is his Treasure. It is this as doth Inrich Him. It is a great treasure in that it [bri t] in Treasure (112 Psalm 1.2.3) (128 Psalm 1.2.3) Outward blessings shall be to them. Example: what is meant by godliness? 1 The word may be taken more strictly. And then it noates the feare

[5] In this doctrine, Foster stresses two important ideas. First, that it is not only important to be godly, but a person must be content with himself or herself, and second, that the gains of the world are nothing compared to godliness.

and worship of God and so it doth hold forth the dutys of the first table. And so godliness is set against righteousness which (1 Timothy 2:2) 2 doth contayne the dutys of the second table. (2 Titus 12) Godlyness doth respect man's duty to God and the outward act and forme of worship but sometimes it noates the Inward part of worship. What maner of persons ought you to be in all godliness? (2 Peter 1:6) 2 Godlyness is sometimes taken for the Doctrine of [ ] religion. (1 Timothy 3:16) Grat is the mistery of godliness that is the Doctrine and fayth of the gospel. God manifest in the flesh. 3 It doth noate our whole duty and obedience to the law of God. 2 What is meant by contentment? Is it the soul's rest in that condition and with that portion that is allotted to it by God—it is that inward quiet spirit freely submitting to God's disspos. It may be taken and consider it as it consists in the moderating and Bounding of the soule in its desires after the things of this world and so it is the positive (13 Hebrews 4) duty commanded in the 10 commandments. It may be considered as it doth consist in the quietnes and stillnes of the mind in all conditions what so ever. In whatever state (4 Phillipians 11) I am I have learned to be content. 3 [When] doth the apostle Joyne godlyness with contentment? 1 Those two they doe ever goe together. They ever meete in the same subject. It is true Every godly man hath not always the act of contentment but he hath the habbet of it. But there is no wicked man that hath this contentment. 2 Contentment without godliness is not gayned. To be content in an ungodly estate is not gayne, but it is the greatest loss to be content in a way of sin a way of ungodlyness. (3 Revelations [ ]) 3 Godlyness and contentment together doe include our obedience to the whole will of God and then they doe [complement] a [ ] for in godlyness there is obedience to the [perceptive] will of God. In contentment there is obedience to the providenciall will of God. 4 Contentment is gayne as well as godliness, therefore both together may be sayed to be great gaine. Tho the state of godly man may be secure as to another [world] yet it canot be comfortable to him here without contentment. 5 Contentment doth flow from godliness and it is a [f it] and effect of godlyness. When there is godlyness there is rest and peace and sattisfaction and quiet the soule. Every grace of the spirit of God hath a tendency to contentment as faith love selfe deniall they doth all teach contentment. The understanding is inlightened and the will and affections they are rectifyd and all teach contentment: 5 What is this gayn that comes by godliness with contentment? It is a reverent, a great gaine. 1 It is Temporall. There is gaine in this life. It is gaine to his name. (112 Psalm 6) The righteous they shall all [d] in everlasting remembrance. But the name of the wicked shall rott. It is a greater gaine to be said a man is a godly man than to be said he is rich or honourable. 2 It is gaine to that [ ]. (3 Proverbs 7.8) Fear 3 it is gayn to thy estate. His state is increased and blessed. Fear God and all those things shall be [added]. (112 Psalm 1.2.3) (22 Job 23) This gaine is spirituall. The image of God is renewed to the soule. Here is everlasting gaine, that reward of their workes doe follow them in to another world. How may it be proved and demonstrated that godliness is so great gaine? 1 This may be proved by the great misery of ungodly one and the great loss in ungodlyness. The wrath of God is revealed from heaven against ungodlyness and unrighteousness of men. (73 Psalm 12) Not withstanding all the gaine that is in ungodlyness there is the curss that followes. (28 Deuteronomy 15) An ungodly man is curst in his basket and store (101 Psalm 16). He gave them their request and [gentleness] in to their soules. 2 Because it hath the promises godliness is great gaine: the promise is gaine. It is the greatest gain to get an Interest in [then]. (2 Peter 4) Where by he hath given unto us exceeding precious promise. Life and heaven and happyness are given in the promises. Christ is the greatest gain and he is made over in the promise. David priced his interest in the promise above all he had in the world. (2 Samuel 23:5.6) This is all my salvation and all my desire. (2 Samuel 7:20) 2 Godlyness hath the promise there fore it is great gaine. The promises are either first of grace or to grace off grace and that is indefinatly. 2 To grace God will bestow this upon this or that man that hath grace. They only can claim the good promised. The ungodly are strangers from the covenant of promise. Godlyness hath the promise of the life that now is. (6 Matthew 31). Seeke the kingdom of heaven and the righteousness there of and all those things shall be added. 1 Godlyness hath the promise of long life belonging to it. (91 Psalm 14.15) With long life will I sattisfy him and show him my [s l at d n] (34 Psalm 11) Com ye children, hearken to me and I will give you long dayes. Life is great gaine. [Skin] for [skin] all that a man hath he will give for his life. Long life in this Life is a great blessing: long life doth not always prove a blessing and God may allso shorten life in mercy. 2 Godlyness hath the promise of all the good things of this life. [t] For the lord is a [s] and shield will give grace and glory and no good thing will be withheld from those that feare him. 1 Godlyness hath the promise of [provission] in this life: a rich man may loose his riches but a godly man shall not loose his promise.[6] Take no thought for tomorrow (111 Psalm 5) He hath given [t] to them that feare him. He will be ever mindfull of his covenant. (33 Psalm 18) Gods ey is upon them that feare him to keep them alive. (37 Psalm 25) (22 Job 23) 2 Godlyness hath the promise of honour in this life. (91 Psalm15) He shall call upon me in trouble. I will be with him and honour him. (3 Proverbs) Riches and honor are in his hands. 3 It hath the promise of pleasure, her ways are pleasantnes and her paths are peace. 3 Godlyness hath the promise of being delivered from all the evills of this life. (34 Psalm 20) (91 Psalm 10.11) 4 Godlyness hath the promise that all shall worke together for the good of the godly. All things worke together for the (8 Romans 28) good of the godly, for them that are called according to his purpose. There is and must needs be great gaine that turns everything to gaine. (3 Isaiah 10.11) It is well with the godly men in every condition say to the righteous. It shall be well with them as godliness hath the promise of God's guidance and protection throught this life, (32 Psalm 8) for this God is our God and will be our guide unto death. It hath the promise of peace. In death the end of the (37 Psalm 7) perfect man is peace. 2 Godlyness hath the promise of the life that is to com and there in is the gaine of godliness. (10 Hebrews 36) The greatest gaine is that godlyness hath the promise of deliverance from death and condemnation. Upon such as these the second death hath no power.[7] 2 He hath the promise of everlasting life [ ] 2.25 This is the promise, that he hath promised us ever eternall life. 3 Reason: by godliness we come to have union and communion with God it doth bring:

Use 1. Hence, learn that there is no gain in ungodlyness—(5 Ephesians 11) They are called unfruitfull workes of darkness. There is no gain in them. What fruit had you then in those things where of you are ashamed? There is no fruit nor gaine, but there is unspeakable loss in wayes of sin. (33 Job 27)

---

[6] By "Godly," Foster was referring to those people of Hartford who were actual members of the church, or visible saints. Much of this sermon is an exhortation to the people of Hartford who were not yet full members, hence not godly.

[7] Second death denotes eternal separation from God and includes being "thrown into the lake of fire." *Holman Bible Dictionary*, 1456.

This sermon is a continuation in the series from First Timothy and is another exhortation to the ungodly or unconverted to convert, but it is also a message to the converted to be thankfull for their blessings.

Mr. Foster. (Sunday) October 26, 1679. (1 Timothy 6:6) But godlyness with contentment is great gaine. 3 Godlyness is great gain because godlyness it doth bring us to the injoyment of God who is the greatest good, the fountayn of all good without whom there is no good to be injoyed. 1 The injoyment of God is great gaine, the greatest gain on earth and in heaven. The greatest gaine of heaven is the fruition of God. Creatures are but streams God is the Fountayn. David more priced this than the creatures. (4 Psalm 6) Lord lift up the light of thy countenance upon us. The misery of [di ias] and David doth ly in their separation from God. This Cain takes notice of. Thou hast hid me from they face. (144 Psalm 15) Happy is that people whoe is such [in] [case]. The happy is that person whose God is the Lord. It is greater gain to enjoy God than all the creatures in the world. Thus Jacob I have eno I have all [ ] the children of God thus find it so the injoyment of God to be more than all the world besides. The people of God have found it by their experience that he is blessed, that God causeth to approach to him. There is a 3 fold experience that a child of God hath of the worth of communion with God in the sence and sight of that last estate he was in before conversion. Every child of God hath been brought to see his lost Estate that [is] no hope is without God in the world. He then saw this to be the greatest gain to be neer to God, to have communion with him. When God doth depart and leave the soule after conversion at such [ ] they see the gaine of being with God and having communion with God. (88 Psalm 15) Tho God hath a love to his people that is everlasting love yet they may want the sight and sence of God's love. God hath ever a love for his people, but yet they must not see the [kings] face. In this [season] the people of God they doe see the worth of and can price communion with God as David. (63 Psalm 1.2.3) They that have seen the power and glory of God in his [s uary][8]—3 when God doth in an exterordinary way manifest his love to them how then doe they price communion with God when God hugs and embraceth them? (5 [ ] 4) 2 Godlyness brings us to this enjoyment of God and it is in the way of godlyness that we have this communion with God. The lord hath set apart the godly man for him self that he may have injoyment of God

[8] "Sanctuary" Geneva Bible, 1560 edition, 248.

and communion with him. (25 Psalm 14) The secret of the Lord is with them that fear him and he will show them his covenant. (19 Job 8) God makes known his secrets to them that fear him, the secrets of his love and favoure. (29 Job 3) They shall have neer and intimate communion with God. (12 Hebrews 14) Without holyness no man shall see God: but blessed are the pure in heart, they shall see God. The godly see God and injoy God in this life in his ordinances. (24 Psalm 3.4) Whoe shall assend into the hill of God injoy God in his ordinances?[9] He that is of clean hands and pure heart. They shall injoy God in the Life to come. Then they shall see God as he is in himself Face to face in the other world. 4 Godlyness is profitable to all things and therefore it is great gaine. It is proffitable (1 Timothy 4:8) to all things therefore it must needs be the greatest gaine. It is profitable to all persons at all times in all things. It is profitable to ourselves. (9 Proverbs 12) If thou be wise, thou shall be wise to thy selfe. Thou shalt have the proffit of it to thy selfe: (2 Ecclesiastes 18) It is proffitable to a man in Every respect: 1 to his outward Estate. (8 Proverbs 18.21) Riches and honor are with me. The durable riches and righteousness that I may cause them that love me to inherit substance. (1 Psalm 3) They that fear God shall inherit substance. (2 Chronicles 31.10) It is profitable to a man in respect of his name and credit it gets and Everlasting remembrance, a name better than that of sons and daughters. I will give them an everlasting name that shall be not cut off—3 It is profitable to the soule. It is profitable in every condition a man is brought to. In generall, calamity it was profitable to Noah to Lott. 5 It is profitable in Every relation that a man stands in. It is that which doth fit him for his place and for the duty of his relation. 2 It is profitable to another's godliness. The ungodly fare the better for the godliness of the godly. Thy righteousness (35 Job 8) proffits the [sons] of men. The wicked injoy many good things for the sake of the godly. The world would be destroyed were it not for the godly. Godlyness brings peace and plenty upon a people.[10] Oh that thou hadst harkend unto my (48 Isaiah 18) godly commands thus peace should have been as the river and they righteousnes as the waves of the sea.

[9] In the King James version, the reference is to a hill, while in the Geneva Bible, it is to mountaine. This is a good indication that Foster relied on texts from both versions of the Bible.

[10] Foster is telling the congregation that the world cannot survive without the presence of the godly, converted members of the church. This is another exhortation for conversion.

5 Godlyness is great gaine because it brings contentment with. It is the greatest portion to have contentment with our portion. The comfort of a man's life lyeth not in having much but in being contented with what a man hath. The being of a man's Life doth not consist in those things nor the continuance of it nor the comfort of it neither, but in contentedness, and this is found in godliness. It is not to be found in any creature injoyment.[11] Those things are compared to the wind. They may puff up, but that they canot sattisfy. (29 Isaiah 8) It shall be as a hungry man that sleepeth and thinkes he eats but he awaketh and is not sattisfyed. This contentment is not to be found in anything under the sun. They are so far from bringing contentment that they do rather hinder it. They are vexation of spirit. (20 Job 22) In the fullness of his sufficiency he shall be in straights. (2 Ecclesiastes 1 to 12) 2 Contentment is to be gained in godliness. (12 Ecclesiastes 13) Fear God and keep his commands, For this is the Whole duty of man: the greatest gain is godlynes. Godlynes is everlasting gaine and therefore the greatest gain. Here is the gain that no moth nor rust can corupt. It is the gaine that will carry you to the other world. (2 Ecclesiastes 18 verse) The gain of this world is but a winged vanity, but godliness that will abid by you.

Use 1. Hence, learn the great folly that is in men in that they seeke after gaine in ungodlyness. Men naturally seeke after gaine, but they mistake, they seeke after evill instead of good. They seeke gain, but it is not true gain. All the pleasure will end In bitterness, and the gain will end in loss. (20 Proverbs 17) The workes of darkness they are unfruitfull: the end of them is deth. (20 Job 12.14) Men may gaine the world but loose their soules. 2 Learn what is the best course that we can take to be the greatest gaine. It is to take godly courses. 3 See the Reason God doth [bl st] the designes of men in the world. This may be one reason [ ] [ ] is so like godliness in the world. (6 [H i]) 4 It reproves those that doe seek after gain, but not godliness. [ ] they seeke after the world, but not godliness. 5 It reproves those that account ungodlyness gayne and godliness. There be such as these. (73 Psalm 13) Many count the worship of God a burdensom thing. (4 Amos 5) They are weary of the Sabbaths and New moones.[12] It reproves such as aime at nothing but gain in godliness.

[11] Creature injoyments is a reference to the pursuits of the unconverted.

[12] This reference to new moons may denote a kind of cyclical weariness whereby the ungodly are simply tired of the cycle of the weekly Sabbath.

[ ]: Use: is of comfort to the people of God. If godliness be a great gaine then [ ] is a gainer how ever it be. It is of Teror to ungodly men what ever their state be they are loosers.

Use: Exortation. Be exorted for to rejoyce in and be thankfull for the portion. Hath God given you grace. It is more than he had given you the world. 2 Do not enjoy the prosperity of the wicked. (73 Psalm [31.3]) Labour to Encrease in godliness that so thou must be a great gainer. (1 Timothy 4:7) 4 Let every godly man be content with his portion. Consider the soveranty of God, he dissposeth of us as he will. Consider the justice of God, he doth nothing with us but what is right. Consider the mercy of God and the wisdom of God. God doth order all things in wisdom. The wisdom of God is seen in the chooseing of the best end. God orders all things for his glory the best end. 2 God makes the use of the best meanes and uses those meanes the fittest time. A godly man may be persuaded to be content because God hath done more for you than he hath done for others. 2 God hath promised more to you than he hath done others. 3 You have assured hope of more in the life to come. 4 All things worke together for the end to make you happy here and forever. Let us all be exorted unto godliness. Let us [Excuse] ourselves here in. (2 Timothy 2:22)

Ecclesiastes is primarily about its author's argument (the author may have been Solomon) that "God is the only avenue to satisfaction in this life."[13] *For Puritans seeking a church of the Elect, Ecclesiastes might have been understood to be "addressed to God's people, rather than to those who are ignorant of God or in rebellion against Him."*[14] *This sermon also echoes the first chapter of the* Immitation of Christ, *which was a widely read book in the seventeenth century.*[15]

It is an interesting exercise in logic to suggest that all things of the world are vain; thereby suggesting that God their creator is vain. Foster suggests that the vanity inherent in the Earth is the creation of God, and that God created the physical world so that he would be exalted by his people. Ultimately, this sermon argues that all things are vanity next to

[13] *New Geneva Study Bible*, 986.

[14] Ibid.

[15] Thomas A. Kempis, translated by Rev. William Benham. "The Immitation of Christ," *Harvard Classics* vol. 7, (New York: P.F. Collier, 1937), 206. In, *Worlds of Wonder, Days of Judgment*, David Hall refers to dozens of books and tracks that were important to the Puritans, including *The Immitation of Christ.*

God, which is a logical argument since God created the world to serve his own ends.

Mr. Foster. (Saturday) November 1, 1679. (1 Ecclesiastes 2) "*Vanitie of vanities, saith the Preacher: vanitie of vanities, all is vanitie.*"[16] Vanity of vanity sayeth the preacher all is vanity. The scope of Solomon in this book is to guid men to it teach happyness and to that end he takes them [ ] from all things besides, and shows them that happyness is only to be had in the fearing of God and keeping his commands. Happyness is only to be had and injoyed in God. In the 21st verses of the [cap]: we have account of the Author of the booke. verse1. It was Solomon described by a 3 fold relation which agrees to Solomon only as he stood related to the [ch]. He is called the preacher. His natural relation, son of David, his civill relation, King of Iserell. 2 The subject of the booke verse 2. Vanity of vanity and the whole booke may be said to be a sermon upon this text. In the text here is the subject and that is all things. 2 The adjunct that is predicated upon them they are vanity. 3 Here is the Illustration of this vanity. By dubleing of it all is vanity. 4 The confirmation of this by the Test of the preacher. The subject is all things. All things are vanity. All things colectively and together they are vanity. By all things may be taken every creature. Every creature is vanity. As to man's happyness, the angells are vanity and [saints] are vanity. As to the happiness of man, all but God is vanity. All things besides Christ is dung and vanity. 2 All things may be taken in a limited sence. Those things discoursed of in this booke. All things under the sunn is vanaty. (1 [Cap] 14) All creatures and creature Injoyments that God hath made and given to man upon the earth they are vaine as to happyness. The creatures are vayne: 2 All the workes of man with all that a man can doe and atayne by his labour, paynes, and study are vayne: (1 Ecclesiastes 3:11 verse) 3 All those things where in wordly men place happyness or seek happyness In is vayne. As with naturall and morall wisdome it is the best thing a naturall man can enjoy, and it is next to grace, but yet this is vanity. It is so far from making man happy that it makes him more miserable. He that Increaseth knowledge doth Increase sorrow. 2 All worldly delights and pleasures are vaine as to happynes. (2 Ecclesiastes 1.2.3) In the midst of laughter the heart is sad and the end of it is heaviness. 3 Honour and power and grandeur is vanity. (2 Ecclesiastes from 9 to 12) 4 Riches and great possessions

---

[16] *The Geneva Bible*, 1560 Edition. 277.

in this world are vanity. 5 Freinds and relations and whatever may be Injoyed of that nature is vanity. (62 Psalm 9) Men of high degree they are vanity. 2 The adjunct or what is predicated on this subject all is vanity. That is vanity that is light, Empty, and unprofitable, that doth not seeke the end we aym at. Vanity is that which is unprofitable. (3 Malachi 14 verse) That which brings no profit is vain. Serve the Lord with all your hearts and doe not follow after things which will not profit. (11 Proverbs 4) Riches doe not profit in the day of wrath. (16 Matthew 26) A man may be a happy man and loose the world, but if he gaines the world he may be miserable for all that. 2 Those things are said to be vanity that have no solidity and substance in them, (41 Isaiah 29) no reall worth in them, they are said to be vanity. (8 Proverbs 21) Wisdom sayth those that Love me shall Inherit substance. (5 Ecclesiastes 16) What proffit hath that labours for the winde? (12 Hosea 1) Ephraim feedeth upon the winde when a man is following the delights of the word. (29 Isaiah 28) 3 That which is called fals and deceptfull is vanity. That which is (32 Deuteronomy 29) fals and deceiptfull that is vaine. Falls and deceitfull men they are called vaine men within the (12 Psalm 2) because they doe deceive the hopes and expectations of those that trust in them. They are vanity and are called lying vanitys. (2 [Jonah] 8) 4 Marke you read of the deceiptfullnes of riches. 4 That is called vanity that doth frustrat men of their hopes and expectations and aymes and ends, and upon this account all those things are vayne. (23 Proverbs 4.5) 5 That is sayd to be vanity which is uncertayne, unstable, unsettled, weake, and frayle, and feeble. This is vaine all things are uncertain Riches. (8 Romans 12.21) (40 Isaiah 6.7.8) All things are like grass fadeing and perishing soone gone and soone lost. 3 Here is the amplification and Illustration of this vanity by the [In ination] and the doubling of it. All is vanity, and 1 this repetition and doubling of it it doth noat the greatness of it. It is a great vanity the greatest vanity. 2 It noates the certainty of this vanity. (8 Isaiah 9) We often repeat what we would confirme. [41 Genesis 32] The thing is doubled: to show that it is Established. 3 It noates the multitude and the variety of vanaties that are in the creature. 4 It doth noat man's backwardness and [p ptnes] to believe this, and therefore it is doubled. 5 It noates the consequence of the matters of wayte they are doubled. 6 It noates the earnest affection of Solomon. His heart was deeply affected with this vanity, and he doth Endeavour to Effect others with it. 7: It is a noat of admiration, Solomon doth admire at the vanity of these things. 4 There is the confirmation of this by the preacher and [there] is a great deale of Force in this. The preacher doth tell us this tho our hearts doe not believe it. (2 Corinthians 10) 1 All is vanity. If we consider the condition and quality of the preacher, and there is more force in the Testimony. He was a prophet: what he spoke he spoke by in the Inspiration of the spirit of God and therefore it is true. 2 The preacher he had experience of all those vanities. He had set himself to make the exactest search of the creatures and then he passeth the sentence of them. They are vanity. 2 He was as a great and mighty king. He had what he calls vanity. He doth not slight them because he could not [get] them. Againe he was the wisest of all that were before him and that should come after him. The preacher now was an aged convert, thus he doth speake in the wisest part of his life. (1 Kings 11) 4 He had known soe much as ever any man shall know of the creature which he passeth this sentence all is vanity. (2 Ecclesiastes 12) (1 Kings 3:12) Doctrine: that all things under the sun as to any happyness and sattisfaction that we seek after in them they are extreme and exsessively vanity. Tho they may comfort the life of man yet they cannot make it happy. God did never make the creature for man to rest in. We may wander from mountaine to hill but there is no happyness but in God. (3 Ecclesiastes) All the world cannot fill the heart and make a man happy. (8 Genesis 9) We are like the [o][17] there is no rest to be had till we do return to God. The things of the world are like the [shs], they will not satisfy. If we will have bread we must return to our Father's house. There only our soules can be satisfied. All things in the world were vanity before the fall of man. The creature was made subject to vanity. How or in what respect are all things under the sun said to be vanity? 1 Negatively how they are not vanity, and by way of caution that we may not slight or despise the workes of God. They are blessings of God tho not the choysest blessing. (11 Numbers 5.6) Consider the creatures are not vanity in themselves as they are the workes of God. Nor as to the end wherefore God made them. (14 Romans 14) When God Looked upon what he had made behold it was good. (1 Timothy 4:3) Every creature of God is good and it is to be [reced][18] with thanksgiving. (111 Psalm 2.3) (4 Deuteronomy) (143 Psalm [ ] 6) The saints are want to admire the workes of God. (8 Psalm) The workes of God are not vaine. They are all for an end. (45 Isaiah 18) Speaking of the Earth, he created

[17] "dove" in King James Bible, 9, and Geneva Bible, 4.
[18] "received" King James Bible, 261.

it not in vaine. He made it to be Inhabited. They are not vanity in regard of Last end. (16 Proverbs 4) He hath made all things for himself, the wicked for the day of evill. (43 Isaiah 7) (1 Romans 20 verse) The eternall power and Godhead is seen by the creation of the world. The greatness of God's power is declared in creation. His goodness wisdom and glory is seen in the creature, therefore they are not in vayne. 2 Creatures are not [made] vanity in regard of their next end and that is the good of man, and as to this end they are not vanity. (115 Psalm 16) The [heavens] are the Lord. All those they are given to the children of men. They are Service 2 able to men and so doe Answer [rend]. There fore they are not to be slighted but to be used with thanksgiving. These things are vanity affirmatively. 1 They are vaine comparatively, compared with other things that are better. 2 They are vaine as to happynes. They will not bring to heven nor yet keep from hell. All those creatures they are vaine if you compare them with other and better things. The earth is vanity compared with heaven, and all the creatures they are vanity now if you compare it with what it was when God made it. 1 All those things they are vanity compared with God. The best the brightest the most glorious creatures are nothing to God. (6 Canticles 4) (4 Job 8) He charges his angels with foly. All nations they are as a drop of the Bucket in comparison of God, they are vanity and nothing. (62 Psalm 8.9) The goodness of the creature is vanity in comparison of God. There is none good but God. So the wisdom, strength of the creature is vanity to the wisdom of God.

Mr. Foster. (Wednesday) November: 5, 1679. Thanksgiving day.[19] (103 Psalm 2) *"My soule, praise thou the Lord, and forget not all his benefits."*[20] Bless the Lord oh my soule and forget not all his benefits. This psalm is a psalm of thanksgiving pened by David where in he doth bless God

[19] During its October session of 1679, the General Court of the Colony of Connecticut ordered a day of thanksgiving. It reads: "This court appoynts the first Wednesday in November next (November 5) to be solemnly kept a day of publique Thankesgiveing throughout this colony, to prays God for his mercy to us the year past, in granting to us the continuance of our priviledges civill and ecclesiastical, with such peace and health as we have injoyed, and in giving such a comfortable harvest as we have received, and more especially for the goodness of God in protecting and saveing our Lord the King and his people in England, as well as ourselves, notwithstanding the plotts and machinations of evill-minded men against the interest and kingdom of Christ there and heere." *Public Records of the Colony of Connecticut*, October 1679, 45–46.

[20] *The Geneva Bible*, 1560 Edition. 257.

for his benefits. We may take notice of David's call and exortation of his soule to this worke of thanksgiving. He would not bless God with part but with his whole soule all that is within him. 2 The ground of matter of his prays (verse 3.4) how pardoneth all thy sin, healeth all thy deseases, redemeth [yi] life. 2 He prayseth God for his goodness to all mankind. (verse 6) In the text you have David's desire [wh] he calls upon his soule. 1 To bless God. 2 To [revere] for his benefits. To bless God for his benefits and not himself. Bless the Lord. This word of blessing is 1 attributed to man. Man is sayd to bless man and that is when they wish good one unto another and pray one for another. [Thus] David blest his house. 2 God blesseth man and that is when he doth bestow good upon man. Man's blessing is a wishing blessing but God's blessing is opperative. He blesseth and they shall be blessed that God doth bless. 3 Man is said to bless God and that is when we doe prays and magnify God for his blessings. Not that we ad anything to God's [blessedness], but when we doe exalt and speake highly of God, then we doe bless God and speake well of him. 2 Forget not all his benefits but remember them.

Doctrine: that it is our duty for to bless God in the remembrance of his benefits. It is our duty to remember the benefits God hath bestowed upon us and to bless God for them. Keep them in our minds that God may [have] the prays of them. We are more ready to remember our afflictions to pine at God for them than to remember his benefits to prays God for them. 1 It is our duty to remember all God's benefits, and this appears from the command of God. The will of God is the command, is the rule of our obedience to the commands of God. (4 Deuteronomy 9) (78 Psalm 5.6) They were to remember what God did for them and teach their children. 2 God was want to put his people in minde of the benefits he bestowed (32 Deuteronomy 7) on them when they had forgot it. God mindes David of what he had done for him. (2 Samuel 2.7) (6 Deuteronomy 15 verse 12) 3 This appears from the example of the people of God that thus doe. (78 Psalm 1.2.3) They show unto their children the workes of God. I will meditate of all thy workes and talke of thy doeings. 4 God hath been want to reprove his people when they have forgot (78 Psalm 42.43) his wonders that he hath don them. (32 Deuteronomy 18) When they forgot what God had don for them God saw it and obhord them. (106 Psalm 6.7)

Reason 1: is from the great benefit we shall have by remembering God's benefits for this will teach us to price them and esteem them. 2 This will put us upon thankefullnes to God for them (102 Psalm 18) when we do remember them, but if we forget them then God Doth loose the prayse of them. 3 The rememberance of God's benefits it will serve to keep us humble. We shall see that we have nothing of our selves. All is of God's grace. (8 Deuteronomy 10.17.18) Thou shalt remember the Lord thy God. 4 This will teach us to pitty those that want the benefits we have. 5 This will comfort under afflictions. (143 Psalm 4.5) (77 Psalm 10.12) 6 This remembrance of God's benefits will engage us to trust and hope in God for the future.

2 Reason: from the evill effects and consequences that will arise from our forgetfulness of God's benefits. We shall forget God If we forget his benefits. Iserell forgot God's benefits and were unmindfull of the rocke of their salvation. 2 If we forget God's benefits we shall forget what they cost: they were dear bought. They cost the blood of Christ: 3 If we forget God's benefits we shall forget to prays God for them. 4 If we forget them God will take them from us. Those that slight them they shall loose them. (106 Psalm 21.27)

3 Reason: is because God remembers them there fore we should remember God's benefits. God knows and will call us to account for what we [have] of him. 2 It is our duty in the remembrance of God's blessings to prays God for them. We are not to remember them for to slight them, under value them, to set our hearts on them, or that our hearts should be drawn from God by them. We must not remember them to make a bad use of them, but to bless God for them. (115 Psalm 1) The Reason why we are to bless God in the remembrance of his benefits is because God is the author of them. All we enjoy comes from God there fore we are to bless God for them. 2 This is the end why God bestowes his blessings upon us. It is that our soules may blesse the Lord. (50 Psalm 23) He that offers prays doth glorify God. (8 Deuteronomy 6.10 verse) 3 God doth delight in being blessed. He delights in the prayses of his people. (69 Psalm 30.31) (50 Psalm 9.14) 4 Bless God he deserves it. He is worthy to be praysed and magnifyed by us. (4 Revelations 11) 5 We can do no more but bless God. This is all the requitall that we can make to God: 6 We stand in need of new benefits every day.

Use 1: Se we hence great Reason to keep such a day as this is a day to bless God for his benefits. We must remember what God doth for us so as we may bless God for him. 2 Here is ground of reproofe to those that are backward to this great duty. How many forget God's benefits but remember their afflictions? 3 Let us be Exorted to remember and not forget the benefits of God and so to remember them as to prays him for them. (100 Psalm 4) Set our selves to call to mind the benefits that God hath done for us. They are more than can be minded by us. Let us remember God's benefits bestowed upon his [ch][21] and people in the world and bless God for them. (137 Psalm 5:6) That the [gats] of [hell] hath not prevailed against it. That God hath [kept] his little flock. We have cause to bless God for what he hath done for our own nation (147 Psalm Last verse) but one. He hath not so dealt with every nation. He gives you his words. God hath once againe preserved that land from the [t] and yoke that God hath preserved our Lord the king. 2 Bless God for his blessings to us. God hath kept us and lead us. Remember the benefits God hath bestowed on his people, those most common. We enjoy our priviledges civill and ecclesiasiticall. That our rulers are [continued] to us and our church priviledges that our feet may stand in Jerusalem. That we have the ordinances of God. 2 That we have our peace restored and [continued] to us.[22] (4 Lamentations 12) (106 Psalm 43) 3 We have allsoe health in our dwellings.[23] This ought to be remembered this day. 4 God hath blest the labours of his people and crownd the years with his goodness. (8 Deuteronomy 7 verse) There are speciall particular personall blessings that God hath bestowed upon us which we should call to mind and bless God for. God hath taken care of us, fred us from our mothers belly he hath freed us with food and gladness, carryd thru many dangers and as in (6 & 7) troubles, delivered us from sickness and from dangers by sea and land.[24] Remember all these and bless God for them especially soule blessings. Pardon of sin hath God given you Light out of darkness bless God for them. (2 Samuel 22:42)

The December 7 Woodbridge sermon is concerned with the works of God, and the proper consideration that must be given to them. It is also a sermon about the providential nature of God.

<u>Mr. Woodbridg. (Sunday) December 7, 1679.</u> (64 Psalm 9) *"And all men shall se it, and declare the worke of God, and thei shal understand, what he hathe wroght."*[25] For they shall wisely consider of his doeing. The psalmist prays to God to secure him From his enemies. The Lord

---

21 "Ch" appears throughout the notebook and is shorthand for the word church.

22 Possibly a reference to King Phillips War.

23 It is ironic and regrettable that less than two years later, Foster died in anepidemic.

24 If we accept the history that Isaac Foster was held captive b y Turks, along with his merchant father William, then we must agree that Isaac was qualified to preach regarding dangers by sea.

25 *The Geneva Bible*, 1560 Edition. 248.

is the great preserver of man from his Enemies. A description of those Enemies (verse 3) and the persons they [B d][26] against the perfect. 4 Their confidence described (verse 4) they fear not. They encourage themselves. They shall go on unpunished because non sees. We have God's taking notice of their doeings. Retaliating their evills after their own heads. We have also layd down the fruit of God's doings. They shall wisely consider it. The persons they[27] the wise hearted and the serious what they doe. They shall consider of God's doeings, they shall wisely doe this. It is not always the Effect of God's doeings. The workes of God do many times stick [neer] to siners then the word.

Doctrine: it is a suitable [ ] and becoming thing for all persons to consider of God's doeing. This duty is often called upon in the word of God. (37 Job 14) Hearken [t][28] this oh Job stand still and consider workes of God, in your day of adversity consider. But what doth this wise considering importe? It is the bringing of the object neer to the understanding in that it be not a transient act, and here it is requisit that the minde be free and prepared there to. (22 Matthew 5) It is said that they [might][29] Light of it and went one to his farme. Some are so full of the world that they regard not the worke of the lord nor consider the operation of his hands. Those doe not wisely. 2 It is necessary that our mindes be intens and fixed upon the workes of God if we would consider wisely, so consider the workes of God that we doe wisely deduce God's Instructions for ourselves that we do learn to no more of God and more of ourselves. 2 What doeings of the Lord it is that we are to consider? In generall all the Lord's doeings are wisely to be considered. (28 Isaiah 9) This allso coms forth from the Lord of hoasts who is wonderfull in counsell. Our God is a rock and all his workes are perfect. The works of creation discover much of God. (1 Romans 20) The power and God head of is seen [ ][30] the creation of the world. (139 Psalm 14) I will prays the for I am fearfully and wonderfully made. 2 The works of God's providence are wisely to be considered. ([19] Psalm 2) Day unto day uttereth speech, and night to night doth give knowledge. The doeings of God to [ ] reasonable creatures should be by us considered. He

[26] In the King James text the word is "bend," p. 673, but the Geneva bible does not contain the word bend in these passages.

[27] There is no space or unreadable word between "they" and "the" in the notebook. Whoever was taking the notes may have missed what Foster said and simply continued to write.

[28] "unto" King James Bible, 635, and Geneva Bible, 233.

[29] "made" King James Bible, 31, and Geneva Bible, 13.

[30] "by" Geneva Bible, 71.

provides for the [fou] cloathes the [Li ies]. (8 Psalm 3) The saints doe use to consider God's workes. God doth exercise a special providence over his reasonable creatures, angels, and men. The doeings of God to the angells may be wisely considered. The establishing that good angells showes som what of goodnes to them. His punishing of the evill angels [restraining] them in chaynes of darkness doth show the Justice of God in God's dealings to man, towards others, towards our selves, and with his doeings to the wicked. How he doth bring their divills to their own heads. He brings to nought all their wicked [desires]. The [coun i s] of the [Frow d] they are caryd head long but the doeings of God to the righteous God doth hide them in a day of [fr b] and keeps them. Stand still and see thee salvation of God. Sometimes God doth take them away from the evill to com 3 the doeings of God to our fore Fathers. (44 Psalm 1) We have heard with our ears oh God our Fathers tould us how thou didst drive out the [heathen]. Consider the doeings of God to our selves the psalmist the (22 Psalm 9) thou takest care of me from the beginning. Consider God's doeings in refference to the outward man. God Feeds and cloathseth us, but especially the doeing of God to the inward man. The warning God gives the counsell we have had to fly from wrath [ec] that we [live] in a [land] of light. That the misterys of grace [ ] yet continued to us and If we be brought Home to God this is to be considered of by us.

2 The Reason: [ ] we must consider God's doeings, 1 that we may there by come to know more of God. We are miserable darke and ignorant of God and the things of God and hence we sin agaynst God. We know not God and therefore depart from God. We doe not the workes of God and so do not close with him.[31] There is much of God to be known by his doeings. We had need know more that we may be kept from sin. 2 Consider God's doeing for there is a great mistery and wisdom in they are full of wisdom and wonders and therefore they are

[31] The Covenant of Works is Adam's original covenant with God. According to Perry Miller, God "promised that if Adam would perform certain things, Adam and his posterity should be rewarded with eternal life, and He laid down the specific conditions in the moral law, which he implanted in Adam's heart. Hence, the first terms of the first covenant, the Covenant of Works… Perry Miller, *The New England Mind, Vol. 1*, 377. Unfortunately, for humankind, Adam was unable to uphold his part of the covenant when he ate of the forbidden fruit. When Miller talks about the implantation of the moral law in Adam's heart it is suggestive of Adam's, and more broadly, humankind's understanding of right and wrong, or their awareness of right and wrong. Adam knew he had failed God, which is why he tried to hide from God after eating the forbidden fruit.

much to be considered. There is a depth of wisdom in all God's ways. His wayes are in [your] [deeps]. God doth bring forth glorious Effects out of all the [wildeings] and Intricasys of providences. So it is if you consider Joseph when he was sould it looked dark but when he is the [s d] [ ] kingdom and preserves the land it is glorious. 2 Consider God's doeings because of the many advantages that doe come to our selves there by. 1 He may here by come to be confirmed in the beliefe of the word. There is a great correspondency between God and his workes. It may [pres ll] us from fretting agaynst divine dispensations. (71 Psalm 1) Asaph was Like to fall. I was envious at the prosperity of the wicked. 3 It may be a means to keep us from Fainting under soule exercises. (40 Psalm 12) He was ready to faint in prayer but the considering of God's doeings doth uphold him. When I consider the days of old 4 it is a means to strengthen our Fayth wisely to consider God's doeings. We had need to [greten] our Fayth. We know not what Evill is before us.

Use 1: It shows us the danger and disadvantage of being inconsiderat: (39 Psalm 3) My heart was hot within me while I mused my heart burned. 2 The workes and doeings of God are remarkeable for us to be considered—3 Hence how large a field of meditation a [creature] hath before him all the workes of God. 4 We see the need we have to beg divin skill and understanding and that the Lord would inlighten us that we may consider wisely. 2 It reproves those that doe not consider what God is doeing. 3 It is of conselation that doe consider of God's doeings. God takes notice of such and will [re i] them to glory where they [shall] contemplate God's works.

CHAPTER SIX

SALVATION AND COVENANT

With the exception of Caleb Watson's sermon on January 17, and the Woodbridge sermon of February 1, chapter 6 is built around Isaac Foster's sermon series taken from Hebrews: chapter 2 verse 3. The first sermon in this chapter is also the first in the notebook from Hartford's schoolmaster Caleb Watson. Watson's sermon is included in this chapter because he and Foster preached on the same day.

The opening text for the Caleb Watson sermon that follows is from Malachi, which played an important role in Puritan theology because of its prominent covenant themes. It is also an interesting text within the framework of late seventeenth century New England, and the declension of the Puritan spirit that prevailed. According to the Geneva Study Bible, Malachi spoke to people whose "vision of the coming messianic age did not materialize. Instead, they experienced poverty, drought, and economic adversity, and they became disillusioned with God and their faith. Malachi's word confronts a people skeptical of the promises and therefore indifferent in their commitment to live in the light of those promises and to worship and serve the Lord with all their hearts."[1]

Six months later, Watson revisited the same opening text in a sermon that also echoes declension. Increase Mather's Reforming Synod was held only one month prior to that sermon, in May of 1680. It was a Synod that took New England's ministers to task regarding New England's declining spiritual state. Caleb Watson's sermon is the first in the notebook to implore Hartford to resist the declension of New England.

Mr. Watson. (Saturday) January 17, 1679. (3 Malachi 6) *"For I am the Lord: I change not, and ye sonnes of Jaakob are not consumed."*[2] For I am the Lord. I change not therefore you sons of Jacob are not consumed. We have a prophesy of John baptist to prepare the way for Jesus Christ. 2 A prophesy of Christ who forth with comes as soon as John had prepared the way. 3 The manor of his coming is terible to the wicked comfortable to the godly. (43 Isaiah 4) The powerful Effects of Christ's coming upon

---

[1] *New Geneva Study Bible*, 1485.
[2] *The Geneva Bible, 1560 Edition*. 385.

the godly and wicked: to the godly he makes their offerings acceptable to God, 2 to the wicked to consume and to destroy them. In the text we have a description that God gives of him self. I am Jehovah I chang not. 2 A conclusion therefore you chang not. I am Jehovah God that an Eternall. It noats his existance and giveing being [to] all. It noates God's giveing rest, there is no rest to be had but in God. It allso God's imutabillity in his being and decree. He is unchangable. The conclusion yet you sons of Jacob are not consumed though I am a God of justice. Yet I am a God of mercy.

Doctrine: that God is an imutable and unchangable being.[3] All other beings are changeable. Commonwealth, kingdom, nations, [ch s], Famalys and persons are subject to changes. Our Fathers [r] are they and our prophets doe they live Forever? So riches, honor, they do fade, but Jehovah is the same. Without change. With him there is no variableness nor shadows of change. You oh Lord shalt endure for ever, and thy remembrance to all generations. (1 Hebrews 10.11)

1 Example. How is God Immutable and unchangeable? 1: in his Essence and in his nature. Unchangableness and his being is the sam according to his name. So he is I am that I am. (8 [ ] 58) Before Abram was I am. God is immutable in his attributes properties and divine perfections. His mercy and loving kindness is unchangable and shall Endure Forever. Let Isrell say his mercy Endureth forever. (103 Psalm 15.16.17) His power and strength is imutable and so a fit object for to rest on. (26 Isaiah 4) His love is unchangeable, he loves to the end. His faythfulness, goodness, wisdom, holyness, and righteousness is unchangeable: 3 God's decres, counsells and purposes are imutable: the councells of the Lord (33 Psalm 11) they do stand for Ever, (8 Isaiah 10) and the thoughts of his heart to all generations. Men's thoughts perish but God's doe stand. (14 Isaiah 23 Verse) As I heard purposed so it shall stand. (5 Job 12) The Lord doth disapoynt the devices of the crafty. Nothing can hinder what he hath determined. God is of one minde and who can turn him? (19 Proverbs 20) The councill of the Lord shall

[3] The *Westminster Shorter Catechism* is a document that New England's late seventeenth century preachers would have been familiar with. It contains a definition of God that is quite similar to that of Caleb Watson. "Question: What is God? Answer: God is a Spirit, infinite, eternal, and unchangeable, in his being, wisdom, power, holiness, justice, goodness, and truth." William Stacy Johnson ed., *Reformed Reader: A Sourcebook in Christian Theology* (Louisville, Kentucky: Westminster/John Knox Press, 1993), 82. Whether the Westminster Shorter Catechism directly influenced Hartford's preachers is difficult to say, but many Reformed documents spoke with a similar voice.

stand whatever our [de ders] be. 4 God is Imutable and unchangable in his word for ever. Oh Lord thy word is [setled] in heaven. The word of the Lord is more firme and abideing than the heavens: the grasses withereth the Flower fadeth but the word of the Lord Endures forever. (55 Isaiah 10) (1 Zachariah 5.6) Their fathers where are they and their prophets doe they live forever? Did not my words take hold of you? God is unchangable in his prophesies hence God is carefull to set a star upon the fulfillment of them. Hence the [ca ing] of the [Juts] the destruction misticall Babilon they shall certainly be Fulfild. Therefor we should wayt with patience for the accomplishment of them. 2 God is unchangable in his promise. Take your bible and gather altogether the many sweet and precious promises and they shall all be accomplished. Hath he said and shall he not doe it? Hath he spoken and shall he not fullfill it? There shall not [Fa] one thing of all the good that God hath promis us. (1 Kings 8:56) 3 God is imutable in his Threatenings. (23 Josiah 15) God Is imuteable and unchangable in his covenant of grace and mercys.[4] (54 Isaiah 10) The covenant of mercy shall not be removed. (2 Samuel 23:5)

Reason is taken from the absolute perfection of God. God is a perfect being and therefore not subject to change.

2 Reason is taken from the simplicity of God. It is a property of God whereby he is without all mixture and composition. God is one thing.

3 Reason is taken from the Eternity of God. He is unchangeable because he is eternall, without beginning, succession, or end. He hath all his being at once.

Use 1: This showes us God is a better good than the world can afoarde. There is an [autome] put upon all other comforts. The world is a flying comfort. All Earthly things are vaine and Transitory. They are but shaddowes. But in Jehovah there is no chang. He is the same yesterday and today. (18 Psalm 46) My God liveth and blessed be my rock. Friends, relation dy, but God liveth. (73 Psalm 26) God is a portion forever and that is worth a Looking after. This God is our God and guide forever.

[4] Perry Miller writes at length on all Puritan covenants making it somewhat challenging to share his best examples. In *The New England Mind, Vol. 1*, Miller describes the Covenant of Grace as "A true contract of mutual obligation," but unlike Adam's failed Covenant of Works, the covenant of Grace depends on faith rather than earthly deeds. *The New England Mind, Vol. 1*, 377. For a more recent and exhaustive treatment of Puritan covenant theology see David A. Weir, *Early New England: A Covenanted Society*.

2 Use: is a sad word to all inpenetent sinners that go on in sin. All the threatenings in the word of God they shall be made good against them. Hath God said he will raine snares on the wicked and wound the hairy scalps of the wicked? That the wicked shall be turn to hell, that he will come in Flaming fire rendering vengeance. It is said that the Fearfull and unbelieving and [c] shall have their part in the lake that burns with fire. Hath God said it whose threatenings are unchangeable? Then woe to the wicked: Unless we chang God will not change. Unless we chang our wayes he will not turn.[5] (7 Psalm 11.12) (30 Isaiah [ ]) (32 Deuteronomy 41 .42) Doe we not tremble at these threatenings we are worse than Felix. Worse than the devills who beleive and tremble at the threatenings. Consider this you that forget God least he come against you and tare you in peices. (5 Jeremiah 12) Take heed of saying as they did then his words are but wind. But looke Verse 14. My word in they mouth shall be fire and the people shall be [his][ ][6] consumed by it. Be counseled to breake of your sins by righteousness. This God doth affectionatly call siners because he doth not de- (33 Ezekiel 11) light in your death.

The book of Hebrews is referred to as a "'word of exhortation'... to persevere in the pilgrimage of faith is grounded in the author's proof that the Old Testament itself testified to the imperfection of the covenant at Sinai and its sacrificial system, thereby pointing ahead to a new High Priest—Jesus Christ, Jesus is better than the mediators, sanctuary, and sacrifices of the old order... Unlike the earthly and external aspects of the Old Testament sanctuary, Jesus sanctifies us for the true worship of God, so that we draw near to heaven itself with clean consciences. He is the guarantee of this better covenant bond, for He links us inseparably with the God of grace."[7]

---

[5] These passages represent the second generation's much celebrated sermon form known as the Jeremiad. Much of Perry Miller's academic reputation stems from his thorough dissection of the Puritan Jeremiad, a sermon style that David Scobey calls a "combination of self-castigation and filial piety." According to Scobey, the Jeremiad was a renewing of a rhetorical form "which English preachers had of anxiety and accusation that testified to their increasing conviction that New England had failed its world-historical mission." Scobey, *Revising the Errand*, 21. See also Sacvan Bercovitch, *The American Jeremiad*.

[6] "wood" King James Bible, 833, and Geneva Bible, 308.

[7] *New Geneva Study Bible*, 1933.

The covenant is an especially important aspect of this sermon series. The subject of the covenant remains subdued in Foster's sermons until it returns in the chapter 14 sermon series from Micah. In addition, this series from Hebrews marks the beginning of Isaac Foster's discursive treatment of the Devil, which reaches its climax in his September sermons the following year. This sermon speaks directly to the salvation that comes from Jesus Christ, and the great punishment awaiting those that neglect the gospel.

Mr. Foster. (Saturday) January 17, 1679. (2 Hebrews 3) "*How shal we escape, if we neglect so great salvation, which at the first began to be preached by the Lord, and afterwarde was confirmed unto us by them that heard him.*"[8] How Shall we escape if we neglect so great salvation which was first spoken to us by the Lord and then confirmed by those that heard them? He exorts them to attend the excellent Doctrine of the gospell by Reason of the excelency of the discovery of this Doctrine. The son of God the brightness of His Father's glory. The author is not only a man or angell but the Son of God the king of His [Ch]. 2 The consideration of the great punishment of those that shall neglect the gospel, set forth by the punishment of those that breake the law. (verse 1.2) If those that broke that were to be punished than how shall we excape? In the text, 1 here is the subject spoken of salvation. The neglect. Supposed if we neglect the punishment of this neglect of the word preached by Christ. The subject is salvation. Noe subject should be more welcome to siners then salvation so great. This salvation is first meant the gospel; called by the name of the effect it doth produce: salvation. The salvation is Ilustrated by its greatness. It is worthy of the greatest respect above our thoughts and words all though it doth presuppose that this great salvation is often neglected if we have little care about it. Doe not labour to be interested in it. It is a neglecting of it and then the punishment follows. If we neglect how shall we escape? 1 This expression doth noate the certainty of the punishment of such. How can they, by what way shall they escape? They that breake the covenant of workes may escape, but they that neglect the gospel there is no way for them to be saved, they cannot excape. 2 It noates the justice of God in the punishment of them 3 It noates the greatness of the punishment. It is in expressible. 4 The Reason why they shall not escape unpunished is Because this salvation was first spoken by Jesus Christ himself. He was the purchaser and the preacher of this gospell.

---

[8] *The Geneva Bible, 1560 Edition.* 103.

Doctrine: that they that doe neglect that salvation that was purchased by Jesus Christ and in [ ] by the gospell is revealed unto us and bestowed upon us shall suffer the greatest punishment of all Siners. They are the greatest sinners that neglect the gospel: 1 There is salvation purchased by Jesus Christ for fallen man. 2 The salvation is revealed to us and bestowed upon us in and by the gospell. 3 This salvation is exceeding great [there is] none like [to ys]. 4 This salvation though it be so great yet it may and often is neglected. Men being so careful about other things forget this. 5 This neglect it shall be punished with the greatest punishment. Their punishment is certain and exceding great. 1 There is salvation for siners man's condition since the fall though it be [ ] yet it is not desperate. God hath found a way by which he may be saved. Man hath destroyed himselfe but in me is their help. (33 Job 24) God hath found a ransome for men (1 Luke 68.69) God hath raysed up a horn of salvation for man to save him from all his enemies. Man that was a man of death condemned may say as Simion my eyes have seen thy salvation. As all men dyed in Adam so they are alive in Christ.

Reason: Is from the soveraigne good pleasure of God that is the ground of this salvation. (9 Romans 18) Therefore hath he mercy on whom he will and whom He will He hardens. There was nothing in man to merit their salvation. 2 God hath ordered it that there is salvation for man that His mercy may be glorified. God doth seeke the advancement of His glory and mercy and here by it is advanced. 3 It is from the love of God to mankind that is the Reason God saves man and not angells. (3 John 16) For God so loved the world that whoever believes in Him might not perish but have Everlasting life.[9] 2 This salvation is revealed to us and bestowed upon us in and by the gospell and therefore the gospell is cald salvation Because it is the cause of it and it doth declare it to us. This salvation is declared to us in the gospel. This good newes is in the gospel. (2 Titus 11) For the grace of God that brings salvation hath appeared to all men. (2 Timothy 1:10) Life and immortality is brought to us by the gospell. 1 It is not to be known by the light of nature. (1 [ ] 5:9) Christ doth inlighten every man, but it doth not bring light and immortality. The light of nature shows nothing of Christ. It is not to be knowne in the Booke of nature. (1 Corinthians 1:23) The world by wisdom knew not God. This salvation is discovered by the ministry

[9] John 3:16 is the passage that revealed the meaning of the shorthand symbol for "world", a smaller circle within a larger circle. See Figure 9.

of the gospel, but by the workes of God. We canot see the salvation tho: the eternall power of God may be seen by the workes of God. God as a creator may be known, but not God as a redeemer. It is not revealed in the Law of God. It speakes nothing but death to sinners. (2 Corinthians 3:6.7) (3 Galatians 8) 2 The gospel is bestowed upon us by the gospell. It is a powerfull effectuall means appointed by God to worke this.

Use. Learn what great incouragement there is for all sinners to looke to Christ for salvation. Here is a posibility of salvation for fallen man. There then is a probability this salvation is presented to you and this salvation is great salvation that is offered unto you in the gospell.

It is interesting to note that the second installment in Foster's series from Second Hebrews may be an attempt to clarify the previous week's sermon. The second installment appears to be somewhat more detailed as a lesson, as if he had to preach it again because the first time did not achieve the desired effect.

In this sermon, Foster is discussing the greater importance of salvation through the gospel, and that God's deliverance of his people from bondage in Egypt was far less important than a sinner's deliverance from sin through the gospel of Jesus Christ. Foster is making an interesting comparison between God's temporal salvation of the wicked, and His eternal salvation of believers. In other words, God can and does save both, but the eternal salvation is the one that counts. This sermon series also clarifies the difference between God's Old Testament law and New Testament salvation. The Hartford Sermon Notebook contains many comparisons between Old Testament law and New Testament salvation.

<u>Mr. Foster. (Sunday) January 25, 1679:</u> (2 Hebrews 3) How shall we escape if we neglect so great salvation? The subject spoken of salvation. Great salvation 2 a neglect of this [supposed].

Doctrine: that they that neglected so great salvation as is purchased by Jesus Christ and in the gospell [h d] forth to siners canot Escape great punishment: 1 There is salvation purchased for siners that is from God's soveranty of his grace. He hath mercy [ ] [om] he [I]. 2 It is from the love of God to mankind. 3 It is for the glory of God. 2 This salvation is revealed to us and bestowed upon us in and by the gospell. It is revealed in the gospell. It is the grace of God that doth bring salvation. Nature doth not reveale it, nor the booke of the creatures, nor doth the law reveal it. It is conferred upon us by the gospell. (1 Romans 16) I am not ashamed of the gospell for it is the power of God to salvation. God hath ordayned it for this end. It is the power of

God to salvation. The spirit of God doth Improve the word for that end. (1 James 21) It is able to save your soules. (2 Thessalonians 2:14) Where unto He called you by the gospell. (1 Corinthians 4:15) For in Christ Jesus I have begotten you thro the gospell. The law is also of use in this great worke. (3 Galatians 2) The law is called [ ] in [Ester] to bring us to Christ. To lead us to Him. All the shaddows of the ceremoniall law did lead to Jesus Christ. God makes use of the law in convincing of the siner and bringing him to looke to Christ. And yet the law is the ministration of death, but it is the spirit that doth give life. The gospell is a spirituall word and is accomanyd by the spirit to confer spirituall and eternall life upon the siner.

3 Proposition: This salvation is exceeding great. So great salvation inexpressibly and superlative great. It is beyond our Expression. It is great salvation comparativly compared with all other salvation, and it is exceeding great. There is no savour like to this saviour nor no salvation wrought out like this. It is great compared with the salvation of Isrelle out of Egiptiann Bondage. If they could not escap that did neglect that great salvation [than] much more those that doe despise this. (9 Exodus 16) God showed his great power and got a great name by that salvation, but this deliverance is far greater the saving of siners from bondage to sin and Sathen. God doth [ ] to bring siners to heaven than to bring the children of Isrell out of Egipt. God gave men for their [rau s] but God gave his son for this salvation. 2 This salvation is great compared with the salvation of wicked men. (1 Timothy 4.10 verse) He is the saviour of all men but Especially of those that doe believe. The wicked of the world by the [bounty] of God are many times saved from many deaths. (2 Corinthians 1.10) Whom hath freed us from great death? 1 The salvation that God doth bestowe on the wicked is Temporall, but there is Eternall salvation. God saves the wicked but for a little time, but [ ] will save those for Ever. This salvation will certainly end their destruction. (5 Hebrews 9) But God is the author of Eternall salvation to all that doe obey him. 2 That salvation is of the body only, but this is salvation of the soule. Saved from spirituall death. Both soule and body they are both redeemed from it. 3 The salvation of the wicked is in sin, but this salvation is from sin. (2 Corinthians 15:56) (1 Matthew [ ]) You shall call his name Jesus. He shall save his people from sin, from the guilt of sin and from the filth of it, and from the power of it. It doth not reighn in them nor over them. (2 Corinthians 5:21) Christ was made sin for us and we thereby were raysed from sin. 4 This salvation is from Saythen allso. Jesus Christ hath purchased salvation for our

soules. [ ] This salvation is perfect, but the salvation of the wicked is not so. Saved but not from hell, delivered but not put into heaven. Some were saved out of Egipt but they perished in the wilderness. Jesus Christ hath perfected them that beleive. 3 It is great compared with that salvation that was in the law in old Testament times. (1 Corinthians 10:1.2.3.4) They dranke of the same rock and that rock was Christ. (30 Revelations 8) Jesus Christ is the lamb that was slaine before the foundation of the world. The greatnes of this salvation appears in the [clernes] of the discovery and manifestation of it to us above that in the law. They had Christ, but in [tipes] and shadowes, that which was then vayled is now revealed. That that then was in [Tipes] we have in the [Antitipe]. 2 It is great in regard of the greater pouerings out of the spirit of God now, above what it was then. (44 Isaiah 3) For I will pouer water on him that is thirsty and my spirit upon all flesh. (2 Acts 16) (11 Matthew 11) It is great salvation if you compare it with the extent of that in old Testament time. Salvation was of the Jue, but now it is of the Gentile as well as to the Jue. (1 Romans 16) The gospell is the power of God to salvation to the Jue first and also to the Gentiles. God now doth pouer out his spirit upon all flesh. 2 This salvation is great also [L tly] and considered in itselfe upon many accounts. 1 In regard of the love of God which is the first and principle Impuls of it. The free favoure and love of God. This salvation is an effect of the love of God: God so loved the world that whosoever beleives in Him should not perish but have eternall life. This salvation is an Effect of the love of God. 1 Of his bounty and unlimited love. (15 [ ] 13) Greater love no man can show. 2 It was the freest love. Free as to any merit in the creature. Here was love. God loved us not when we loved God, but when we were unworthy and lay defiled in sins. God [c a ded] his love to us that he dyed for us when we were siners. God gave his son only son: 3 This love of God is unchangeable love. (1 John 3:1) Behold what maner of love he hath bestowed on us. 2 This salvation is great in the contrivance of it, the wisdom of God contrived. All his workes are wisely don. (104 Psalm 24) Oh Lord how many fold are they workes, in wisdom thou hast made them all. (1 Timothy 3.16) Great is the mistery of godlynes. God manifested in the flesh. (3 Ephesians 10 verse) It is called the manifold wisdom of God. (11 Romans 33) Oh the depths of the riches both of the wisdome and knowledge of God. None but the wisdom of God could find out this way that man should escape the threatening without wrong to the truth of God. (85 Psalm 9.10) It is contrived by great wisdom. (1 Peter 1:12) There is such wisdom that the angells doe bow down to looke into it. 3 This salvation was purchased by a great person and therefore may be called great salvation. Christ was the first preacher of it and the purchaser of it, therefore it must be great salvation. (9 Isaiah 3) His name shall be called wonderfull. He purchased it 4 in regard of the great price payd for it. It is great salvation. It cost the greatest price. What this price was you may see in that of the (1 Peter 1:18) not redeemed. With coruptible things as silver and gold are you not redeemed, but with the precious blood of the son of God. (10 Ecclesiastes 19) Non of these coruptible things are of worth to redeem your [soules]. (20 Acts 28) The flocke of God is purchased with the blood of God, and therefore of infinite value: (43 Isaiah 3.4) That purchase was great when God gave Egipt and Ethophia for then it was a great price, but this was far greater when the life of Christ must be given a ransom for many. 4 This salvation if we consider the subject of it. Whoever they that are saved what are they? They are greate siners. Man had destroyed himself, was in a lost [u d] condition. 6 This salvation is great also in regard of the evill we are delivered from by it. We are delivered from sin. The greatest of all evills. They that know the nature of sin, the guilt of it, they will account salvation from it. The greatest salvation he shall save his people from their sin. He saves the polution of sin, the defilement that sin hath brought upon the soule. Jesus Christ doth wash and purify the soule from all sin by his blood. Here is salvation from the power of sin, from the condemning power of it. 2 Here is allso salvation from the condemning power of sin from Bondage to it. It doth not reine over them. 2 Whereby we are delivered from our greatest enemies, from Saythen and his instruments so as Saythen shall not over com them. Saythen shall not pluck them out of his hands. (1 Luke 69.71) 3 In this salvation we are delivered from all the fruits and the Effects of sin, from the wrath of God that sin hath kindled. Jesus doth deliver from the wrath which is to come. It is great in regard of the great good that is bestowed upon us by this salvation. We are intitled to and shall be put in posession of the greatest good not only delivered from sin but brought to heaven. He gives grace and glory. (8 Romans) We are sons and if sons then heires. It is great in regard to the duration and continuance of it. It is not only Temporall but it is spiritual, Eternal and perfect: It is great in regard of the great honor and glory that he brings to God by it. The mercy and justice of God and all the glorious attributes of God are hereby glorified by this salvation. (17 [ ] 4).

4 Proposition: This salvation may be and is often neglected. The supposition doth show that it is possible. (1 [ ] 13) Christ came to his own and they received him not. When He came to bring this gospell this Doctrine of salvation, it was neglected by them. The Reason that this salvation is neglected is from Saythen. He labours to destroy them. It is contrary to his design and therefore he labours to hinder our imbracing this Doctrine: 2 From the world they hinder our acceptance of the invitation of this salvation. 3 It is from our [i s]. They will have non of me.

Use 1. Hence learn how great a Treasure the gospell is and [ly t] in this because this great salvation is brought to us by it. The greatnes appears if you consider the want (4 Matthew 6) of it. Those that have not the gospell sit in darknes and the shadow of death. 2 Se the wonderfull love of God to man kind. 3 See hence how in Excuseable all such are as they perish under the gospel. Their condemnation is most just. Their damnation is because they despise salvation. 4 Their punishment shall be most dredfull. This is the condemnation. Light is come in to the world but men love darkness.

The First Epistle of Peter is a letter of hope to bewildered Christians. In it, Peter instructs Christians about proper behavior in the midst of unjust suffering. The cause of Christian suffering was the Roman Empire, which ultimately had Peter executed. "The central exhortation of the entire epistle can be summed up in the phrase 'trust and obey.'"[10]

Based on the sacramental theme of this sermon, it is very likely the work of Ben Woodbridge, who had spent over a decade preaching in the contentious climate of Windsor. Baptism and the Eucharist were essentially the only sacraments officially sponsored by Puritans, and Windsor's church had fallen apart because of them. It is true that Hartford's church also endured the sacramental strains of Half-Way membership, but Hartford appears to have resolved its conflict somewhat more peaceably than its neighbor to the north. The presence of John Whiting's sermons in the notebook demonstrates at least a degree of amicability among Hartford's factions.

This Woodbridge sermon also refers to the "sad and bloody times that Hartford and New England have seen." This is most likely a reference to

[10] *New Geneva Study Bible*, 1967–1968.

King Phillip's War, which, three years earlier, had devastated many of New England's towns. There are other references in the Hartford Sermon Notebook *that point to the memory of this war's destruction.*

Mr. Woodbridge. (Sunday) February 1, 1679 (1 Peter 1:19) *"But with the precious blood of Christ, as of a lambe undefiled, & without spot."*[11] But with the precious blood of Christ as of a lamb without blemish and without spot. The apostole writes this Epistle to the [Jues] scattered abroad. He exorts them to walk worthy of their calling as obedient children: (verse 15.16) By the holiness of God He doth exort them be holy as God is holy. 3 From the Justice of God: 4 He [presses] it from the costlyness of the price whereby they were bought they were deare bought. Exprest negatively, it is not silver and gold you are bought with, but that which is farr more precious. 2 It is the precious blood of Christ. Therefor serve God with holynes. The price it selfe layd down for siners it is blood. The subject of it the blood of Christ, the costlynes. It is precious as a Lambe without spot.

Doctrine: the blood of Christ is precious. It is precious in respect of the fountayn from whence it flowes, the love of Jesus Christ. He loved us and gave himselfe for us. Death comes sometime from nature is spent, but it was not so hear. Death comes by Justice. Sometime men forfeit their Lives and that is dreadful, but it did not com from this, but from love. Sometime death comes from violence but that is not Christ dyed it came from the fountaine of love. And most costly for men to spend their blood for love. It is the heigth of love. Greater love than this hath no man. Nothing can ly deeper than love and rise higher in death: 2 It is precious in regard of the subject of it. It is Christ's blood: It is precious because it is human blood. In sacrifice of old, God did not require human blood but blood of bulls and goats. The [murterer] is to dye because there is no sattisfaction suitable to it. 2 The blood of Christ was inocent blood. Guilty blood is most vile but innocent blood is precious. Christ had done no sin neither was guile found in his mouth. (1 Peter 3:18) There was no [grain] in the blood of Christ. 3 It is precious blood it is the blood of God as well as man. Feed the [ch] which God hath purchased with His own blood. Jesus Christ offered himself through the Eternall spirit. The blood of Christ is infinite of infinite value because it was an infinite person that offerd himselfe. There is infinit distance between the power of God and man, between

[11] *The Geneva Bible, 1560 Edition.* 109.

the blood of God and blood of man. 3 The blood of Christ is precious in regard of the efficacy of it and so precious, but the blood of Christ is reconciled to man. Through the blood of Christ God reconciled to man and showes mercy. God was in Christ reconcileing the world to himself. The blood of Christ takes away sin and that is the presence of God. If a person be under the applycation of Christ's blood we may say thy sins are forgiven. Behold the lambe of God that doth take away the sins of the world: The blood of Christ cleanseth from all sin. The blood of Christ doth save from death and condemnation. God sayth when he seeth the blood of Christ applyd I have found a ransom and [i] be gracious. The blood of Christ doth cut of the Execution of the sentence: furthermore, the blood of Christ doth passify the conscience, and makes a calme in the Earthe. All is quiet. [Ryn] Joy and gladness is in the Earth. The blood of Christ doth clens from a guilty conscience. The whole world is not so good as an interest in this blood. There is nothing in the world can quiet the soule but this blood. Nothing can reconcile God and the siner but this blood, therefore it is precious.

Use 1. This is for the deep reprehension of those that doe despise and profane the blood of Christ. Those that profane it are exceeding vile. (10 Hebrews 29) They tread under foot the blood of the covenant and count it a prophane thing. Such are they that hear of the blood of Christ and doe no price the mercy of God the Father, admire the love of Christ. They that doe not receive this mercy and love of God that is Tendered to them, it is a grevious despiseing of the love of Christ. So those that doe make use of the blood of Christ to save them from trouble and misery, that they may live more quietly in their sins. When they are in trouble for sin then they need the blood of Christ, but when they are in peace they have no need of it. 1 Some profane the blood of Christ that is outwardly applied in baptism. Christ's blood is sprinkled upon them and yet they live in sin, in all unholyness. Parents take no care to bring up their children in the fear of God. Herein they doe despise the blood of Christ. Unbaptized persons doe not take care of their wayes but run into sin. They doe greviousley offend God and prophane the blood of Christ. Baptized persons should Inquire what God requires of them. What shall I doe? Men doe not consider that they are in covenant with God. Sealed with the blood the precious blood of Christ. Men walke as if they were under no engagement to God. This profaning of Christ's blood will be [required] of you. Of how much [souer] punishment is that man worthy of that Treads underfoot the blood of the covenant? 2 It reprehends those that sin under the inward application of Christ's blood in the sacrament off the Lord's supper: men despise the blood of Christ by not preparing of themselves duely for that ordinance. He that doth not examine himselfe for the ordinance: so that fall into sin after the ordinance by worldliness [ ] [ ] siners doe profane the blood of Christ 2 times. He that names the name of Christ let him depart from iniquity. (4 Revelations 6) Before the throne was a sea of glass like to cristall. There is sea of the blood of Christ to wash away all sins where God is to be worshiped. The sea of glass is the blood of Christ. It is [Esy] [Injured] and the least [yl] is discovered. Therefore despise it not: Live not in sin. Alow not thy selfe in any sin.

2 Use: of incouragement to those that laboure in the guilt of sin. They see so much vileness in sin that they see not the Excelency and fullness of the love of God, blood of Christ. Take incouragement. The blood of Christ is precious. Thy sin cannot be so vile, but there is more preciousnes in the blood of Christ. Remember to bring your sin to this precious blood. But my sins are greater than others so and so aggravated. I say mourn over thy great sins and remember to com to this precious blood. But I have repeated my sins. Be not discouraged. Christ's blood is precious. But my sins [cleane][12] close to me. Mourn over close [cleaning][13] sins the more and yet come to the precious blood of Christ. It will take it away.4 But I canot mourn for sin [ ] [cam] to that blood of Christ, it will take away hard hearts. The blood of Christ will cleanse the from all sin and make the whiter than snow. The blood of Christ is of glorious Efficacy.

3 Use: instruction. 1 Hence observe the great vanity and folly of those that build upon themselves and there own priviledges in order to [life]: for men to boast they are [ ] members there is a great confidence in this. It is a wonder when there is such light men should be left to rest in [se] things and neglect the precious blood of Jesus Christ. If you had tasted how precious the blood of Christ is you wod have cast off those things [r ged] righteousness. [That is not that as will cloath themselves]. 2 Is the blood of Christ precious than we see need of [ch] discipline. It must be kept from profanation: Christ hath Established discipline for this end:[14]

---

[12] Possibly the word "cling".

[13] "Clinging."

[14] Does this mean do not baptize the children of half-way members? It is difficult to infer from the passage, but there is a feeling in the language of this sermon that would indicate such a view.

4 Use: of Exortation. It calls upon us to Esteem and looke upon the blood of Christ as precious, conceive it so and carry it so towards it. Many have cause to say they cannot se Christ's blood precious. Looke upon the necessity of Christ's death and it will make it precious, for there is not, shall not, be one sin forgiven without the blood of Christ. Tho a man should hide his sin and use all the words he can to take it away and all will not doe. If he should repent and bewayle it and devote himself to a religious life if there be no more, if nothing of Christ's blood be washed on him yet his sins still ly upon him, this should make Christ's blood precious. 2 Nothing can save us from death and hell but the application of Christ's death. There is no other name by which we can be saved. Every siner under sin he into hell without the blood of Christ. 2 Learn we to [cary] it to the blood of Christ as precious. 1 We should inwardly adore and admire of the love of the Father that appears unto us in Christ Jesus. Everyone that is an humble broken hearted siner is an adorer and admirer of Jesus Christ. (5 Revelations 9) Thou art worthy to receive the booke because thou hast been slayn and saved. (Verse 11). The despiser of Christ should be ashamed to see the thousands of those that prays God. But you will say I can not price Jesus Christ. How is it possible if you [say] our [s]. 2 We are to be unsattisfyd in our hearts we [ ] [ ] partakers of the blood of Christ, for all you have is nothing without Jesus Christ therefore be unsatisfied without it. (10 Hebrews 3) When Christ is come there is no more sacrifice. 3 Is the blood of Christ then we should leave all things for the blood of Christ. It is worth the parting of all for it. Our own wisdom, whatever we have to rest in and boast of. 4 We must come for the blood of Christ if we count it precious. Come to it. Use all [means] that you may attayne it, have part in it. Siners are not sprinkled of the blood of Christ at a distance. You must come to Christ if you will partake of it. You must be united to Christ if you will have any benefit by it. 5 You must get the blood of Christ applyd to you. Rest not in prayer for it: but be sure you be interested in it. 6 Walke worthy of Christ in holiness. This is accounted as carrying towards the blood of Christ as precious when you walke in all holiness. [Esteem] the blood of Christ as precious and perfect holyness in the fear of God: beware of carnality, pride, and hardness, they hinder us of priceing Christ. Carnality men are so supported with comforts and creatures that they see no need of Jesus Christ. They will not come to the supper Christ prepared because of the oxen [farmes]: so pride stiffens in the necke whereby they canot bow nor stoop to the righteousness of another. So hardness which is that

whereby a person knows he must be saved of and by the righteousness of another, yet there is such hardness of heart that it can [relish] with him to quicken you [here].[15] There is a [g] in the world to whome the blood of Christ is precious. They doe want it and price it. (41 Isaiah 1) Others there are that have felt comfort in Christ and they doe price Christ and all other things are vanity to them. 2 God accounts the death of Christ precious. The Father was well pleased with it. It is that for which the Father gives heaven, life, happiness through Christ he gives every good thing for it. Whatever we want: We should leave all for it. The love of Christ to us in death should make us price it. 3 This only will heale the great evill that is upon every siner. Those that are under the gospel guilt of sin the rath of God makes them afraid, but the blood of Christ applied makes the sinner sit down in quiet. 4 In bloody times the blood of Christ will be precious. There are sad and bloody times to com upon siners sometimes when men dy [ ]. We have seen such days.[16] Now the blood of Christ will be precious. An interest in the blood of Christ then is precious. 5 We are in a good or a bad Estate [ ] [ ] doe esteem but despise the death of Christ. A beleiver doth price Jesus Christ. 6 They will despise everything that despise the blood of Christ and esteem nothing. The siners doe brake the law of God destroy themselves, spill their own blood. It is no wonder they do despise the blood of Christ. 7 The blood of Christ will cry aloud against man. At last the divils will say you had life Tendered, the blood of Christ shed for you but you would have none of it. The blood of Abell cryd for vengeance. So will Christ's blood at last cry louder than that of Abell.[17]

Foster's third installment in this series is yet an even more developed argument exhorting the need for salvation.

[15] In this passage, Woodbridge may be calling to task those residents of early Hartford in need of regeneration, some of whom were probably listening to his sermon. It must have been difficult for an unconverted churchgoer to sit among the righteous members of the congregation, but this passage also suggests that some of Hartford's residents did not attend the service at all. Many seventeenth century New England histories indicate that attending the service was a requirement, possibly not the case in Hartford.

[16] This is very likely a reference to King Philip's War.

[17] Another typological reference, this time between the Old Testament's Abel, and the New Testament Christ.

Mr. Foster. (Sunday) February 8, 1679. (2 Hebrews 3) How shall we escape if we neglect so great salvation and Doctrine: that they that neglect so great salvation as is purchased by Christ for siners, and revealed to them and bestowed upon them in the gospell, canot escape great punishment. There is great salvation purchased by Christ. 2 This salvation is revealed and bestowed by the gospell: 3 It is great salvation. 4 This salvation is often [time] and may be neglected. Many perish not only under the law but under the gospell. (2 Thessalonians) All men have not fayth. Some willfully neglect the salvation of the gospell. This neglect of this salvation is not because we have no need of it. No we need of it. 2 It is not because it is not worthy of our acceptance. 3 It is not because there is any other way of salvation, for there is no other saviour. 4 It is not because men are not Invited. No the Invitation is to all and God is in Earnest in offering. 4 It is not because it is not our interest, no it is our great Interest: but when is it we neglect it it is from [Saythen]. He is the great enemy of man and he doth endeavoure to destroy the worke of God. 2 It is from the world and 3 from ourselves. You will not come to me that you may live: (10 Romans 1) 4 It is from love to the world. 5 It is from the presumption that is in the hearts of men. They presume upon the mercy of God. 6 It is from the personall judgment of God. He gives men over to believe lyes.

4 Proposition: Of those that neglect this salvation canot escape: this noates the punishment is inavoydable. There is no escapeing of it. It is unavoydable because there is no other saviour but this. 2 The condemnation of those that neglect this salvation shall be most dredfull, greater suffering there can be exprest. (1 Peter 4:17) Their punishment shall be most dredfull. What shall be the end of those that obey not the gospell of God? (3 Lamentations 2.3.4) The judgment of God upon his own people is sometime dredfull, but then much sorer punishment they shall have that despise the gospell. They shall perish without mercy.[18] (11 Romans 22) Behold the severity of God: (13 Acts 40) The apostle gives this solemn warning Behold you despisers and wander and perish. 1 In respect of temporal judgements, the greatest Judgement fall on men in this life for contempt of thy gospell: Christ wept over Jerusalem and now sayth he your house is left into you desolate for that contempt of

[18] God's judgment on the Elect of Hartford is often harsh, but his judgments on the unconverted, unregenerate, will be far worse. "They shall perish without mercy." This must have been a troubling revelation for those listeners who had not yet become members of Hartford's church.

their salvation. (21 Matthew 41) He shall miserably destroy those wicked men that did not reverence His son. 2 As to spiritual judgements, the greatest spiritual judgements are brought upon them that doe despise: God gives them up to strong delusions, to Believe lyes that they may be damned. God punisheth them by other sins by [a ing] them to fall in to great sins. (11 Romans 22). Behold the severity of God. They were cut of. 3 Eternall judgements, the greatest damnation shall be to those that doe despise the gospell. Those mine enemies (19 Luke 27) that will not that I should raine over them bring them to me destroye them. 1 Those that despise the gospell their condemnation shall be greater than the hethen. (2 Romans 9.10) Tribulation and anguish to every soule that obeys not to God. To the Jue first: it shall be more to [breath] for Sodem than for you in that day that doe not accept of this message of salvation. 2 They shall suffer more in the day of Judgement than those that willfully rejected the law of Moses.[19]

Reason 1: They shall be thus punished. It is from the author of thy salvation Jesus Christ. Now Christ is the author of it as he is the preacher of it and 2 as he is the preacher of it they then neglect this salvation. They neglect the word of Jesus Christ. (3 John 13) He that speakes from heaven, he it is whom we ought to heare. In all things God doth conclude we will reverence his son, but they that doe neglect this salvation doe despise Christ. 2 Christ did purchase this salvation and that by his own blood.

2 Reason: Is taken from the great aggravation of this sin of neglect. As the sin is aggravated so is the punishment: they that neglect this salvation they neglect a treaty of peace: God offers reconcilement and peace to those that are offenders. 2 It is a sin agaynst the greatest light. Light and knowledge doth agravate sin. (5 John 22) If I had not spoken to you, you had had no sin comparatively. (4 Matthew 16) When the gospell was preached there came light to those that did sit in darknes and the shaddow of death. The gospell is light. 2 They sin agaynst the greatest love. (2 Romans)[20] despisest thou the riches of goodnes. You receive the grace of God in vaine and despise his love, and greatest

[19] Though Old Testament prophecy foretold the coming of the gospel, it did not yet exist in the time of Moses. Foster's proposition is a warning. Those that despise the gospel will be condemned worse than the heathen (Indians) because Indians did not know any better, they had not been shown the gospel and were therefore somewhat innocent. To have been shown the gospel and still despise it was a surety of damnation.

[20] (2 Romans 4) in the King James and Geneva Bible.

love. The greatest love of God the Father is in this, in that he gave his son was manifested his greatest love in giving his son his only son. It is agaynst the greatest love of Christ who gave himself for us. 3 They that neglect [this] salvation do rob God of his greatest glory and rob themselves of the greatest good.

Use 1. We see how great a Treasure the gospell is, we ought to price it. 2 The wonderful love of God to man that hath provided salvation. 3 The danger of those that neglect this salvation. 4 This encourageth great siners because this is great salvation.

4 Exortation: 1 To those that have an interest in this salvation that thru: the infinite love of God are brought out of a state of nature,[21] and be Exorted to admire the riches of God's grace to you that man is saved and not angells, and you and not other men. Say as David (2 Samuel 7:18) Who am I or what am I that I am brought hither to admire the grace of God? (9 Romans 18.16) (11 Matthew 25) I thanke thee oh Father. Even so Father because it seemeth good unto thee. Consider how unworthy you have been of this grace of God. (1 Timothy 1:13.14) 2 Be humbled for your former neglects of this salvation (53 Isaiah 2) when Christ was despised, rejected by you. 3 Be exceeding thankful unto God for this: that God hath not suffered you to perish in this neglect but hath enabled you to believe. Be thankfull unto God for his son that he hath given his son to purchase this salvation. (1 Luke 68 V) God raysed a horn of salvation for you. 2 Be thankfull for the gospell that doth reveall this salvation to you. 3 Bles God for your interest in this salvation. For this our soules should magnify the Lord. Doe you exalt Him and Glorify his name? 4 Let such as have an Interest in this salvation rejoice in it. (1 Luke 46) My soul doth magnify the Lord. I will rejoice in the God of my salvation. This shud be matter of joy to you in every condition. Rejoyce in the Lord always and again I say rejoyce. Rejoyce that you know God that their names are ritten in heaven that you have an interest in this Saviour. 5 Be exorted to rejoice in the Lord Jesus Christ and love him that hath been the purchaser of it. He hath layed down his life that you may have yours. You can never love him to much that hath loved you. 1 lov his person love his offices love his [bers]. 6 Be exorted that you doe not neglect this salvation for the Future. You are in danger still to neglect it therefore be not high minded.

[21] Brought out of a state of nature means to be born again or regenerated, which was the goal of the pious Puritan.

(11 Romans 20) but feare. 7 Be Exorted to walke worthy of this salvation, walk worthy of your vocation whereby you are called. Walke worthy of the Lord Jesus Christ whoe hath called us. Walke so that you may adorn the gospell. Walke worthy of the Lord who hath called us to his kingdom and glory. All mercys oblidge to duty. This is the greatest blessing. You are bought with a price glory by God (2 Titus 14) who gave himselfe for us that he might redeem to himself a peculyer people zealous of good workes. Take heed of living & lying in that Christ came to save you from. (9 Ezra 13) After God hath given you so great salvation shall you again sin against him? 8 Be exorted to pitty and pray for those that live in neglect of their salvation. Pitty those that canot pity themselves. Pray for those that cannot pray for themselves. Let you heart's desire be for them that may be saved. When thou art converted, strengthen thy bretheren: 9 Labour after an assurance of your interest in their salvation. ([2 Galatians 10.20])[22] That life which in now live in the flesh is by fayth in Christ who loved me and gave himself for me. (1 John 2.3) Hereby we know that we know him if we keep his commands. 2 It is of Exortation to those that hither to have neglected and live in the neglect of their salvation and they are such as were never yet truly convinced of sin. They that have not a sight of sin never had a sight of Christ. God doth first convince of sin before he gives a saviour. There is a naturall conviction of sin. Natural conscience doth convince of sin. (2 Romans 15) 2 There are spirituall convictions wrought in the heart by Jesus Christ. (16 John 8) When he is come he will reprove the world of sin of righteousness and judgment. (2 Acts 37) The siner is pricked in his heart for his sin. 2 They that were never thoroughly humbled by their convictions of sin the law convinceth of sin then humbles, and then the siner condemneth himself for his sins. Doth the sight of sin worke contrition and brokenness of heart in you? 3 Did you ever see the need of a savioure? The law is our scholemaster to lead us to Christ. Whoe is represented to us by the sacrifices as [Tipes] of him? Have you bin brought to inquire after a saviour? If not you have neglected Christ. 4 Those that did never see Christ to be an able and fitt person to be a saviour, they never have accepted Jesus Christ to this day. 6 Have you ever [rowled] your soule upon him and closed with him as your only

[22] There is no second Galatians in the Bible, and it only contains six chapters, so it is difficult to determine the accuracy of this reference. It may be referring to 1 Galatians 12: "For I neither received it of man, nor was I taught it, but by the revelation of Jesus Christ." King James Bible, 233.

saviour? Have you given up yourself to Christ to be ruled, governed and taught as well as saved by him or Els you have neglected Christ. Are the fruits of this fayth to be seen in your lives and conversation? Our obedience to Christ doe declare our faith in Christ. Good workes are the fruits of our closeing with and believing on Christ.[23] Let such as thos be awakened under the sin of their neglect of Christ, and 1 consider what your state and condition is so long as you live in this neglect. Did you see your condition you would not be content to live one day without Christ. You are without Christ, without God, and without hope in the world, and you doe ly in sin and in wickedness so long as you are without Christ. You are in your sins an unclean [leapor]. You ly in your blood, ly under the guilt and power and dominion of it. 2 You are under the power of Sathen allso: you ly in sin. You are of your Father the Devill. You are in subjection to sin. Your soule is the dwelling place of wrath under dispensation of rath, under the sentence of condemnation. You are condemned allready if you believe not in the Son of God. 2 Consider what it is that you are neglecting. It is salvation. You are ready to dye and you doe refuse to be saved. You neglect that which you should be first seeking after. It is the voyce of him that sayes looke unto me and be you saved. It is he that doth delight to be about that worke of saving. 3 Consider what you hazard by this neglect. Not your Estate the life of your body, but it is the life of your soule. 5 Consider how often you have been warned of this neglect and yet you live in it. 6 Consider how often Christ and salvation hath been often offered you how often hath Christ been offered and you neglect: 6 Consider the danger of this neglect, of rejecting Christ. They are nigh to cursing and their end is burning. 7 Consider what will be the Issue of their finall neglect of their salvation. It will be great and everlasting destruction. It will be easier for Sodom than for you.[24] I may say to you as Christ to Judas. It had been good for them they had not been [borne]. 2 Such allso should be Exorted to neglect their salvation no longer. (19 Luke 9) This day salvation is still offered to you. Christ tells you If you com to him there is safety. Be encouraged to looke to Christ and consider for your encouragement what good news it is you hear. It is salvation and offer of life that Christ is now makeing to you. 2 Consider that there is

[23] Foster's definition of works sounds very much like sanctification.

[24] In the Old Testament, God wiped out Sodom, so this was very strong language for Foster's congregants. Foster often describes the threatening nature of the world after Christ's death, for those who remain unregenerate.

yet hope for you tho: you have neglected because you have the offer of it, and Christ is yet able to save you perfectly. 2 Consider you are yet under the call of the gospell and therefore there is yet hope. (10 Mark 49) Consider you are yet under the promise of salvation if you come to Him. 4 Those that have neglected salvation as long as you have upon the coming (2 Matthew 6) to Christ [be] [then] saved.

The fourth installment in this sermon series continues Foster's warning to the reprobate. It is also a sermon that defines the Elect. What began as an exhortation for salvation develops into a dire warning for those that neglect their salvation. Foster was adept at building a theme over many weeks, which presumably left a more lasting impression on his listeners, who by week four of the series must have clearly understood Foster's application of the text. Considering that it was generally illegal not to attend church on the Sabbath, this sermon series seems geared toward those in attendance who had not yet been converted, the unregenerate of Hartford.

Mr. Foster. (Wednesday) February 18, 1679.[25] (2 Hebrews 3) Doctrine: that they neglect so great salvation as is purchased by Jesus Christ for siners and is revealled to them and bestowed upon them in and by the gospel. They canot escape great punishment.

Use: of exortation to those that have neglect this salvation be awakened not to live in this neglect. 2 Be Exorted to live in this neglect no longer. Consider how good news God sends to you goodness. It is salvation. It is a message of life and offer of salvation: 2 consider there is yet hope for you. Jesus Christ is able to save [t] at most: 2 You are yet under the call of the gospell. 3 You are yet under a promise not to be rejected. 4 Others that have neglected as long as you have been saved. [ ] motive: Consider God is most reall heart [ ] and good, earnest in his call of the gospell to every siner to com to him for salvation. (16 Mark 15.16) Go preach the gospell to every creature. He that beleives shall be saved, but he that beleives not shall be damned. (22 Revelations 17) Whoever will let him take of the waters of life freely God is most serious [heart] reall and in good Earnest in this call. God doth not dissemble in this matter. The call of the gospell is reall.

[25] The appearance of a sermon from a series on a weekday occasional slot does not seem to indicate anything particularly unusual. Perhaps Foster simply did not have a Wednesday sermon prepared, so it may have been appropriate to continue preaching his series from Hebrews. Harry Stout discusses the details of the sermon series in *The New England Soul.*

tho: men doe dissemble yet God doth not, but some may say how can this be? How is God reall in his offer and call to the reprobate? For Answer. Consider and [premise] that our Imperfect reason is not the measure of divine truth. There is some times the greatest verity In that we canot se clearly into in the Doctrine of the Trinity and personall union. We are to beleive what is to be warranted by divine truth though our Imperfect reason canot understand it.[26] 2 It is as hard to reconcile God's reality and [seriousnes] in the offer of the gospell with his foreknowledge as with his [decre] of reprobation. There is the like difficulty with the one as with the other. God calls to those to beleive that he knows will not beleive, so that we may as well [ ] the [sinian] deny God's foreknowledg as with the Arminians denye God's decre of reprobation.[27] 3 We may as well say God was not reall in the first covenant with Adam as well as in the second covenant if this argument were of force, for God knew Adam should fall. Shall we say God was not reall when he said [doe] and [e]? 4 Consider there is no [disimulation] with God in this matter. [ ] God is reall [heart] for if God be not so it must be because he revealls that to be his will which he hath not willed. Or els because he promist that which will not [perf] but [wither] of those are so with God in the offer of the gospell doth reveall His will. 1 God doth in the gospell doth not reveall his will that everyone shall be saved, that this his purpose that you shall be saved. 2 God hath revealed in his will of command to men that they should believe, and his will is that they shall be saved, but his will of purpose is not reveallled. 2 It is not because God doth promise that which he will not perform, for God doth promise salvation upon the condition of faith. He that doth beleive shall be saved God hath promised and shall be made good: 1 God hath nott declared nor intended that all to whom the gospell is preached shall be saved. The call of the gospell is larger than election. (22 Matthew 14) The externall call of the gospell is to all, but effectuall to those only that are called according to his purpose. 2 Consider that the word of the gospell is principally intended for and presented to the elect of God.[28] (18 Acts 9.10) Speake and hold not thy

[26] The doctrine of the trinity is a difficult concept to grasp in any period of history, so it is not surprising to see Foster attempting its explication.

[27] Here Foster is showing his more Calvinist roots with this reference to the Arminians denial of predestination, or Gods foreknowledge of the reprobate.

[28] Again, the exclusivity of Puritan doctrine regarding election is staggering. This doctrine is known as limited atonement, that Christ died only for the sins of the Elect.

peace for I have much [people] here and hence (2 Timothy 1:10).[29] I Labour and Endure all things for the elect sake. [ ] Thou [gavest] me them and I have made known thy word to them. The reighn is upon the rocks as well as good ground, so is the word for the elect. 3 There is no siner can say in truth that lives under the gospell that can say God doth not intend salvation for him. He is not elected of God. A man may know he is a wicked man and is in a state of condemnation, but not that he shall be rejected of God, except he hath sined the unpardonable sin against the [ ] [G]. Tho a man have not faith yet he canot say he doth not beleive. A man may be sure of his election by his calling, but not of his reprobation. We ought not to beleive it. 4 Consider it is the good pleasure, will and command of God that all where the gospell is be called upon to beleive that they may be saved. (1 John 3:23) This is His commandment that we should beleive on his son Jesus Christ. Now God commands all Every were to Repent, but this time of their ignorance God [wincked] at. God doth will the fayth and repentance of all [ ] the will of comand that they doe believe. 5 Hence it is the indispensable duty of everyone that doth live under the gospell to beleive that they may be saved. It is God's will that is the rule of our duty, his reveall will. God's will is our law. 6 Hence it followes God is reall in calling men to believe, and Justly punish us If we disobey his command. 7 Consider that all tho: God doth not declare what his secret purpose is concerning everyone that lives under the Gospell yet God doth leave sufficient encouragement to every such one to looke after their salvation. There is not one word in the booke of God to discourage a siner from lookeing after their salvation, because God hath granted salvation to all conditionally upon the condition of their believing. Then it was doe and live, and now it is beleive and live: 2 God hath absolutely promised salvation to some: [ ] of the he that beleives shall be saved and he that beleives not he shall be damned. God hath made an infaliable conextion between Fayth and salvation, all that do beleive they shall be saved. 2 There are many absolute [Indeffinat] promises that God will bestow faith and salvation upon them. Though the Gospell call to many be effectual yet some God will call. All that my Father giveth to me shall com to me. (10 John 16) And other sheep I have that

One wonders what might have been the outcome of this kind of preaching on non-church members. Was Foster's intention to worry them into regeneration?

[29] (2 Timothy 2:10) in King James, 263.

are not of my fold and they shall hear my voice. (30 Deuteronomy 6) The lord thy God will circumcise thy heart. (36 Ezekiel 26 and 27) I will put my spirit in you and they shall love me. (53 Isaiah) All those promises are conditionall in respect of the obedience of Christ and indefinite because the number of their names is not defined. This is ground of encouragement to siners to looke after their salvation. Here is salvation offered to siners, that some shall be saved. 8 Whatever may object, yet there is none of those miserable reprobate that shall perish under the gospel, that shall have anything to say in the day of judgment. He shall then see it was not because God was not reall in making the offer of salvation but because God was reall in the neglect of it.[30] (23 Matthew) He that had not the weading garment it was sayed him how comes thou here and he was speechlesse, had nothing to say when God cam to call him to account. 4 Motive. Consider how joyfull glad and welcome will the day of Christ coming to judgment be to all those that have an Interest in their salvation, and that should encourage you to get an Interest in it. It is Christ com and se you be ready. Watch. If you want this salvation you will not be ready, but if prepared that day will be the day of [refreshing]. It is the day when Christ will appear for your salvation, to compleat and perfect it both body and soule, and you shall appear with him in glory and be made glorious like to him. How joyfull a day this will be. 5 How dreadfull will that day of judgment be to you If you continue to the end to neglect that salvation? Christ will come then to take vengeance on them. (1 Thessalonians 7:8) Christ coming will be to take vengeance and to punish with Eternall destruction. (28 Matthew 3) How Terible was the appearance of one angel? How Terible will it be when Christ comes in Flaming fire with all His holy angels to those that do reject Him? Those that neglect Christ now are his enemies and Christ will slay them. Consider how Terible a day it will be: it will be a day of perdition unto ungodly men. It will be a day of rath, and a Terible day. Let this persuad siners not to neglect their salvation. The consideration of the Teror of the Lord. Knowing the Teror of the Lord we persuade you: 6 Consider that there is joy in heaven at the salvation of a siner. This should affect the heart of a siner

[30] It would have been more difficult to reconcile predestination with a congregation than to simply preach salvation through faith in Christ. Foster seems very shrewd for such a young preacher. Rather than leave his congregation feeling helpless regarding their salvation, he gives them hope that faith in Christ will save them, and he further reassures them with the applicable Biblical text.

to lay hold of salvation. (16 Luke 7.20) You neglect that which the angels would rejoyce to see you Embrace. The Lord Jesus doth rejoice to see you believe. The day of his [Espousalls] is the day of the gladness of His heart. If all siners should neglect their salvation as you doe Christ had dyed in vayne.[31] 7 There are many salvation in this one. It doth comprehend in it salvation from all evill and comunication of all good. If you neglect this salvation you will never be saved from sin. They that have an interest in this are saved from guilt of sin. There is no condemnation to them from the power of it. Sin hath no dominion over them saved from the filth of it, delivered from Saytn. The Divill canot overcome you. 3 Here is salvation from death, from the second death, from the sting of death. You have a victory over death. Saved from the conquest of death. You are saved from the curss and from wrath to come. 8 The neglect of this salvation is a signe of reprobation. This should awaken every siner. Would you have the signe of reprobation on you? It is a signe if there be a [totall] and Finall neglect of this salvation. (38 Isaiah) 9 Consider how sad the remembrance of this salvation will be to you when it is past. It will aggravate your misery that you have had an offer of salvation and that you have neglected: and there is no [recalling] of it when it is past. 10 Is that in (2 Corinthians 6:2) Behold now is the accepted time this is the day of salvation. When should you looke after it but now in the accepted time: now is an accepted time. A well pleasing time or a time liked of: now is a time chosen of God. Wel pleasing to God. Liked of by God. God doth approve of it and says now to siners looke to me and be saved. God likes it. Do you like it? It is well pleasing to God so let it be to us. (24 Acts 25) Do not say to Jesus Christ go away at this time. Maybe God may not accept of another time. 2 Now is a time of [acceptation] for us. Siners may be accepted if they goe to God. (8 Ecclesiastes 5) A wise man's heart discerns time and judgement.

Throughout this series, Foster had been exhorting his congregation on the need for salvation. Now he is exhorting them to make haste in achieving it, so as not to die without it. He is imploring his congregation to convert now, before it is too late.

[31] Foster uses the word "you" in this passage. He was talking to the people sitting directly in front of him, and he was calling them out. This must have been stirring for many of his congregants.

Mr. Foster. (Sunday) February 22, 1679. (2 Hebrews 3) Doctrine: that those that do neglect so great salvation as is purchased by Jesus Christ and declared and given to us by the gospell shall be punished with great punishment.

Use of Exortation: to receive the Lord Jesus Christ. God is reall and [heart] in receiving siners. Motive. Consider now is the accepted time the day of salvation. 1 It is the time God likes God approves to offer salvation to you. 2 A time wherein you may be accepted. 2 It is the day of salvation. When should you looke for salvation but in the day of it. Now is the day of salvation. God the Father sayth to Christ in an acceptable day will I heare the. Now is the day of salvation. (1 Samuel 25:8) Siners may go to God and plead for salvation for they come to God in a good day. It is a day of salvation and let us not neglect. 1 This is such a day as Is had from others and bestowed upon you. It proceeds from special grace to you that you have such a day. The [divills] never had a day of salvation as you have. There is a day of judgment for them but not a day of salvation. 2 This is such a day as the most of the world have not. The greatest part of the world they sit in darkness and they have no light. (19 Acts 2) What is sayd of the third person may be said concerning the second. They never heard of a savior. 2 There is no day of salvation but this. Loose the day and you will never have another. There are other days will follow this but they are not dayes of salvation. They are dayes of darkeness. (11 Ecclesiastes 8) The grave is the house of darkness. (38 Isaiah 18) They that goe down to the pit they canot hope for thy truth. There is no time to repent believe to worke out our salvation. (11 John 43) When siners are layd in the grave Christ will not call them forth to a day of salvation. Christ will then say to them sleap on: when the soule is in hell, in that dark pit, there is no salvation there.[32] (1 Peter 3:19) 2 There is a day of judgment [ ] follow this that will not be a day of salvation but of condemnation. 3 Consider this is a special season of salvation called a day of salvation, therefore doe not neglect it. (8 Jeremiah 7.3) Now is the season now is the appointed time. Let us know our time and season and Improve it. 4 Consider this time wherein salvation is offered to us, it is but a short time, a little time, not a year, a month, but a day. A short time that will soon have an evening and be

[32] The language in this part of the sermon is particularly wrathful and even frightening. Based on the other sermons in the notebook, this type of sermon was not common in Hartford, and must have evoked strong reactions from those in attendance.

past. By day of salvation may be meant the day of the life. Death putts a period to this day, but take it so and the time is but short. It noates the time we have the gospell amongst us and this may be shorter. God may take away the gospell from us. It may also noate the time wherein God by his spirit is striveing with us and that is or may be short. The Divill doth increase his rage because his time is but short. We should improve our time because it is but short: we are not sure of forty days for repentance: Be awakend not to delay. 5 This day of salvation when it is past it shall not be recalled. (10 Joshua) It is not like the day of Joshua that stood still or a [ ] that came back againe to guid and help siners to get salvation. What shall I doe to be saved? (16 Acts 30) Beleive in the Lord Jesus Christ and you shall be saved and they house. God hath made an infaliable conextion between faith and salvation. Would you be saved then beleive in Christ for help here. Laboure for a clear and right understanding of your naturall state and condition. If you would have help from the phasisian then know your desease. And 1 know you doe live under the guilt of sin. By Adam's sin you are guilty by [Imp tation] and participation. As you participate with him in the act so is the guilt: we eat the forbidden fruit in Adam. Labour to see this and be affected with it. Naturall [conscience] doth not accuse of this sin therefore it is litle minded. 2 In this state you are in by nature you are deprived of originall righteousness holynes. You lost in Adam. You are not naturally [conformed] to the law of God, be convinced of this. 3 You are depraved with sin as you are deprived of righteousness. And in the [rome] of it there is originall coruption. There is the roote of all sins in your natures. 4 Consider you are hence under the curs of God, the wrath of God, a child of rath condemned all ready by virtue of that old [sentance] surely those shalt dy. 5 You have lost all power of [writin]. Life by your [own] obedience and by the workes of the law. Would [You] ever come to Jesus Christ? You must begin there. Labour after this conviction of [ ] labour to see your absolute need of a savior, one to scare you out of this sinfull estate, or else you will perish in it. 3 Labour to see the Lord Jesus Christ to be an able and fit person to do this worke to redeem man. He is able as he is God to serve you and as man he is a fit person to save. He was by God designed for the worke and he cam into the world for this end. 4 Labour to be convinced that it is God's command and your duty to beleive in Jesus Christ that you may be saved and you are obliged as much to yeild obedience to this command as any command in the morall law. 5 Be sensible of your own inabillity to yeild obedience to this command. You [are as unable to obey] this gospel command as any command of the law. Be sensible of your own unworthynes of this grace of God. Renounce all righteousness of [their] own. 8 Be diligent and constant in the use of [means]. God will save the siner though not for his own doeing, yet he will save in the way of doeing: we must be found in a way of duty.[33] Pray unto God for to draw you unto Christ. Pray for fayth and pray fervently: 2 Be diligent and constant in reading and hearing the word of God.[34] Fayth comes by hearings in a way of duty. Cast them selfe at the foote of the mercy of Christ. (1 Corinthians 16.26)[35] If any man love not the Lord I let him be another Maranatha. 1 He [tra ts] of the colection for the saints. The 4th part is the apostles [valediction] where in he denounceth a curss upon all that love not Christ, a blessing upon all that believe. The text doth containe a most dreadfull curss against all those that love not Jesus Christ. He doth conclude this epistle where in he had been preaching Christ that they may be stird up to imbrace a supposission. If any man love not Jesus Christ thoe Christ be lovely, yet some see [borne] nor comlyness. Jesus Christ tho lovely is not loved. (3 Galatians 1) In the text there is the [Exe zation] Let him be accursed. The Lord cometh. (1 Galatians 8) [This is] the same word. Maranatha signifies the lord cometh.[36] These words hold forth that everyone that loves not the Lord Jesus are in a cursed state. (3 Galatians 13) Christ hath redeemed us from the curss being made a curss for us, but those that love not Christ are acursed. 2 They noat that those that love not Christ ought to be excomunecated and separate from the church of Christ. 3 It noats that they that doe persevere and continue in enmity against Christ and doe

[33] In other words, works are not what you do but rather the way you do it.

[34] David Hall's *Worlds of Wonder, Days of Judgment* provides many fascinating details about Puritan literacy and erudition. In addition to Hall's fascinating study, there is an economic historical perspective that supports his conclusions entitled *Economic Growth and the Standard of Living in Southern New England, 1640–1774*, by Gloria and Jackson Main. In addition to providing a variety of tables detailing the wide variety of living standards in Colonial Connecticut, the paper contains a table showing a variety of amenities owned by Connecticut households across the entire spectrum of income levels, from the poorest third to the richest third. Consistently, among all income levels, religious books are among the most common amenities owned, and the percentages are nearly equal at every income level. In other words, the importance of religious knowledge transcended class lines, and was more important to most people than fine foods or quality earthenware.

[35] 24 in the *New Geneva Study Bible*.

[36] Marantha is an Aramaic expression that was used by Paul in a letter to the church at Corinth. Marantha actually means, "Our Lord has come." It is an expression implying the imminent return of Christ. *Holman Bible Dictionary*, 1076.

not love Christ, they shall be acursed forever. Christ comes then to make those cursed that his word hath pronounced cursed.

Doctrine: Those that love not the lord Jesus Christ are in a cursed Estate and so shall continue to be cursed when Christ comes to judgment. All Christ's enemies shall be slayn when Christ comes to judgment They that love not Christ in his person, in his offices, they shall be acursed. They that are enemies to Christ appose Christ and his gospell, let them be accursed. 1 There are many that love not Jesus Christ. Many profess love to him but there are but few that doe really love him. Some follow and love him for Honor, but doe not love him. There are many that doe not receive Jesus Christ cam to his own, but they received him not in their hearts and affections. They doe not love Christ. (15 John 18) The world doth hate Christ. It doth not love him. tho: Jesus Christ be beloved of God yet he is not beloved of man, tho God doth delight in Christ and love him. He is the Father's beloved son, (1 Colossians 13) his dear son. Yet to many he is not beloved nor dear to them. Jesus Christ is chosen of God and precious but disalowed of men. Jesus Christ is to the Jews a stumbling block.[37] 1 Who are they that love not Jesus Christ? They that do not beleive on him they doe not love him. They do not set their affections Christ. Unto you that beleive Jesus Christ is precious. 2 They that do not yeild obedience to Jesus Christ they doe not love Christ. Herein our love is perfected. (1 John 2:5) He that beleiveth his word in them the love of God is perfected. It is to be understood that their love is to perfection, but that it is sincer, for this is the love of God that we keep his commandments. (15 John) You are my friends if you doe what I command you. 3 They that doe not hate sin they doe not love Jesus Christ. They that love the lord hate evill. Their affections agreeable to Christ. 4 They that doe not love the word and ordinance of Christ doe not love Christ. ([ ] [ ] 6) His mouth is most sweet. 5 They that doe not love the name and honour of Christ, the advancement of his kingdom, they doe not love Christ. (5 John 23) They will Honor him that love him. 6 They that doe not love the disciples of Christ love not Christ. They that doe not love whole Christ love nothing of Christ. They that doe not love the members love not the head. 7 They that doe not rejoice in Christ doe

[37] The *Holman Bible Dictionary* describes the metaphorical aspects of this phrase and highlights passages where it appears in the Bible. It also suggests that "stumbling block" may have been used as a warning for the disobedient that Christ himself was a stumbling block, which may indicate its meaning here.

not love Christ. (6 Galatians 14) They will rejoice and glory in Christ. 9 They that love anything in the world more than Christ doe not love him at all. Jesus Christ hath no compettator in the hearts of those that love him. You must hate all for Jesus Christ. They that love the world more than Christ love not Christ. I count all things but as dung in comparasen of Christ.[38] (2 Corinthians 8:9) 2 They that love relations more than Christ doe not love him. The strongest love in the world is between Christ and the beleiver. 3 Those that love their lives more than Christ doe not love him. Love is strong as death. (12 Revelations) They loved not their lives to the death if a man's love to Christ be not more than to the world. 2 Why is it men doe not love Christ? It is not because he is lovely. It is not because he desires it not. It is not because he doth not deserve it, but it is because we doe.

[38] There are several examples in the notebook where Foster refers to himself in the first person. It is a style avoided by the other ministers in the notebook.

CHAPTER SEVEN

DECLENSION, PAST AND PRESENT

The text for Isaac Foster's chapter 7 sermon series is First Corinthians, chapter 16, verse 22. Paul's letter to the Corinthians: "reveals that the Corinthian church,... had developed a remarkable number of serious problems, such as division, abuse of sacraments, disorder during worship services, theological problems, and the extremes of moral laxity and unhealthy asceticism..."[1] *Some of the residents of Corinth even believed "that association with sinners was permissible and necessary..."*[2] *In dealing with the historical problems of the church in Corinth, especially the problems of division and theological interpretation, Foster may again be alluding to the difficulties in Windsor, where he was nearly ordained. This new sermon series begins with Foster's exhortation to love Christ above all else.*

(Monday) March the 1, 1679. Mr. Foster. (1 Corinthians 16:22) "*If any man love not the Lord Jesus Christ, let him be had in execration, yea excommunicate to death.*"[3] If any man love not the word Jesus Christ let him be [another] Maranatha.

Doctrine: those that love not the Lord Jesus Christ they are in a cursed state and so continuing not to love him they shall be accursed at his coming. 1 There are many that do not love the Lord Jesus Christ. The world it hates Christ altho: Jesus Christ be lovely in himself and the beloved son of God his dear son, yet he is not dear to men. Of many it may be said they doe not love him. Who they are that doe not love Christ have been declared. 2 What is the ground or Reason men doe not love the Lord Jesus Christ? Answer negatively. What is not the Reason men doe not love the Lord Jesus Christ? It is not because Christ is not lovely men do not love him. No, Jesus Christ is altogether lovely. He is white and [rudy] the cheifest of ten Thousands. Jesus Christ is all together desirable. What soever is lovely is in Christ. He is altogether lovely. Noat the perfections that doe attend the excelencys of Jesus

[1] *New Geneva Study Bible*, 1797.
[2] Ibid.
[3] *The Geneva Bible, 1560 Edition*. 83.

Christ. They are not attended [with] no Imperfection. 2 It noats the Transendency of those perfections. He is perfect in the highest degree. There is none so lovely as Christ. He is the desire of all nations. He is most lovely. Lovely as God is the express image of his person and the brightness of His glory. (52 Isaiah 13.14.15) 2 The Reason why Jesus Christ is not beloved of man. It is not because Jesus Christ doth not desire our love. Jesus Christ doth desire it earnestly. He is an earnest suitor for our love. He offers his love and Tenders a marriag relation to us and he rejoices in our love.[4] It is the day of the gladness of our hearts. 3 It is not because Jesus Christ doth not deserve our love that we doe not love him. There is no such discerning object of our love as Jesus Christ. 1 For what he is in himself he is worthy of our love. Consider his nature. As God he is the cheifest good and worthy of our love. 2 Consider what Christ hath done for us. He hath merited our love. (15 John 13) He dyed for us and therein he hath manifested the greatest love can be. He layed down his life for us. 1 Consider what our condition was when Christ loved us. We were most unlovely. We deserved no love. 2 Consider how Christ manifested his love not only by wishing well to us, praying for us, but dyeing for us. 4 It is not because there is any better object in the world for us to set our love upon. It is not because there is something better than Christ that men doe not love Christ. (3 Philippians 8) Doubtless I count all things as loss for Christ. They are but dung for Christ. Without Christ and in comparison of Christ there is nothing in the world to be loved by us. 5 The Reason is not because of the unprofitablenes of this love that men doe not love Jesus Christ, tho Jesus Christ love us freely. Yet in our love to Christ there is the greatest gain and the greatest proffit. I love them that love me those love me. They that seeke me Early shall find me. Those that love me I will cause to Inherit substance. They that love the world love lyes and things that are vaine and cannot proffit. 2 Affirmative the reason why men doe not love Christ is from their ingnorance of Christ. The Lord Jesus is [T t] known and therefore men doe not love him. Men doe not see the lord Jesus Christ and therefore they doe not love Him. Jesus Christ tho he be lovely yet men doe not see it and therefore are not taken with it. Paull was ignorant of the Lord Jesus Christ, hence he persecuted Him.

[4] The metaphor of marriage to Christ is quite common in the *Hartford Sermon Notebook* and is probably related to the covenantal/contractual belief that dominates Puritan theology.

(1 Corinthians 2:8) They know not Christ and therefore they persecuted him. (1 Corinthians 2.14) The things of God they are not discerned by carnall men because they are spiritually discerned. (20 John 25.28) Men cannot love Christ till they see him and doe know him.

2 The Reason men love not the Lord Jesus Christ is from their love to other things. Other things are the objects of man's love and hence Christ is not loved. and: 1 It is love to sin. Men love to sin and so canot love Jesus Christ. Herod Loved a [st] and that hindered his love to Christ. 2 It is from love to the world. (3 Ecclesiastes 17) The heart of man is full of the world and hence they forsake Christ. This love to the world causeth alienation of heart from Christ and apostacy. [Demas] hath forsaken us. He [embraced] the present world. We canot love the world and Christ too. They are contrarys. 3 Men love not Christ by Reason of that cross that followes the profession of love to Christ. (5 Matthew 11.12) Blessed are you when men persecute you and speake all evill of you for my sake. (5 John 18.19) There is a 3 fold cross. A cross of probation and of tryall whereby Jesus Christ will try those that love him, of corection where by he will corect those that love him, and a cross of [ ].[5]

4: Reason is from that natural enmity and hatred that is in the children of men against Jesus Christ. (1 Romans 30) Man is an enemy of God and a hater of God. Man is a hater of God and of his son Jesus Christ.

5 Reason. It is by Reason of the [c tr riety] that is in the [s] Nature and [ ] of Jesus Christ to the hearts and lives of man. Contrarys are Enemies to another. The world canot hate you but me it hates because I testify of it, that the workes of it are evill: Jesus Christ is light and men hate him because their workes are darkness. They com not to the light lest their workes should be reproved.

2 Proposition: They that doe not love Christ are in a cursed Estate and so continuing they shall be accursed of Christ at his coming: The apostle declares their present state, what it is and what it shall be for the future: this cursing doth imply a separation from Christ and of communion with him. (2 Corinthians 6:14) They that love not Christ are separate from communion with him. 2 It implyes separation to destruction. (1 Galatians 8) They that love not the lord Jesus are at present under the curss and shall be separated from Christ. (49 Psalm 16) There is the curs of God upon their soules, bodyes tho: they prosper and have

[5] The third part of the threefold cross metaphor is missing.

outward blessings yet they are cursed.[6] 1 The Law doth pronounce every siner accursed (3 Galatians 10) Cursed is every one that continueth not in the booke of the law to them. He that beleiveth not is condemened already. 2 There is no other way for man to be free from this curs but only by Jesus Christ. He hath delivered us from the curss being made a curss for us. For it is written, cursed is everyone that Hangeth on a Tree. Jesus Christ suffered the Esensiall torments of hell. The whole cursse of the law. 3 They that love not the lord Jesus Christ have no interest in the deth and sufferings of Christ and are not redeemed from the curs, but live under the curs. Hence it followes they are in a cursed Estate: sin lyeth at the dore. The punishment of sin, vengeance of God doth ly at the dore to seiz them, and when Christ comes to judgment he will then make them to be accursed. (Jude 14)[7] Christ will come as a Judg to execute vengeance on them that know him not. Christ will then say to them depart you cursed. They shall then be sepperated from God, from angels, and saints and from the communion with God. 2 They shall be separated in to all miserie. To everlasting destruction. Their miserie shall be hoples helpless and without end.

The Reason they shall be so accursed that love not Jesus Christ. 1 Because they are gilty of the breach of the first and great command, that is first in order. (23 Matthew 37) God is first and to be loved above all. The morall law requires us to love Jesus Christ.

2 Reason because they are guilty of the breach of the great command of the gospel, therefore are accursed. (1 John 3.23) This is His command. That we should believe on him and that faith on Christ doth Imply love to him. The law requires love to Christ as God. The Gospell loves to him as mediator.

3 Because they that love not the lord Jesus Christ they despise the love and grace of God the Father in the guift of his son. Jesus Christ is the greatest gift of the Father's love and this was the greatest grace manifiested therein. (22 Genesis 12) Here was great love and it was not given to be despised by us.

4 Reason because they despise the love of our Lord Jesus Christ in giving of himself for us and in laying down his life for us. (15 [ ] 13) Jesus Christ hath manifested great love and that is despised by those that doe not love Christ:

[6] Outward blessings appears to be a reference to the physical elements of the world.

[7] (Jude 15) in the King James Bible, 299, and in the Geneva Bible, 114.

5 Those that do not love Jesus Christ they hate Christ with a possitive hatred. There are no [ters] in the gospel. Those that doe not embrace and love Christ they doe resist and appose and hate Christ.

6 They shall be accursed because they do reject the means where by they should be delivered from the curss.

Use: Hence learn the great folly and wickedness in the hearts of men that they doe not love Jesus Christ that is so lovely, that they should not love Jesus Christ that is [ing] of our love. 2 It greatly concerns everyone to whom the lord Jesus Christ is preached that they see that they love Him with their hearts and affections for they that doe not love Jesus Christ they are accursed.

3 Use: of Tryall, [whether we do or no in deed] love the Lord Jesus Christ. This is a Reason of greatest weight for every one of us. Doe we love Jesus Christ? [Put] that 2 to your hearts as Christ to Peter. Dost thou love me more than [thoss]? Doe you love Christ more than the world, more than these or those? Let us examin ourselves and try our hearts whether there be any love in our hearts to Christ. 1 Doe you delight in the company of Christ or doe you desire communion with Christ? Doe you delit in Christ's presence, to be with him and [injoy] communion with him. Can you say concerning the Lord Jesus that he is the cheifest good that you looke after? Lord lift up they countenance upon us. Doe you mourn and groane after Jesus Christ. Is this world and all the [injoyments] of it [ ] a dry and Thirsty land. Doe you delight in Jesus Christ and [after] more communion with him? He put his finger in the whole of the dore and his [bowels] yerned towards him. If nothing can sattisfy you but Christ, if you be inquiring after Christ, it is a signe there is true love in the heart to Christ. Doe you long for the second coming of Christ when you shall have a full and perfect fruition of Christ? (8 Canticles 14) Make hast my beloved. Com quickly. Jesus Christ for his love to us hath prayed that we might be with him where he is. They that have any love to Christ will say amen to that prayer and with Paul say it is best of all to be with Christ. They that love Christ doe love his appearing. They that love Christ in deed and truely at sometimes, may be affrayd of Christ's coming to Judgement. 2 Try your self by this. Are you affrayd of that as doth offend Christ? Doe you hate all sin and all lust? Would you part with all sin rather than greive the lord Jesus? 3 Doe you love the commands of Christ? Try your love to Christ by that. (1 John 5:3) For [this] is the love of God that we keep his commands and that they are not grievous. Try your selfes by this. (5 Canticles 16) Doe you love the word of Christ? (19 Psalm 10) (1 John 2:5) Doe you

love Jesus Christ as your lord to govern you as well as your saviour to save you? 4 Are you concerned for the name and honor and interest of Jesus Christ? If our hearts be set on Jesus Christ the least wrong and Injury done to Jesus Christ it will touch our hearts. Doe you so love Jesus Christ that you are greieved to see his name blasphemed, his enemies prosper? Doe you love the disciples of Christ? Everyone that does love Christ love the disciple. They that love him that begets beloves the begotten. They that love Christ they doe love the pictures of Christ. They that love the [head] love the members. (2 Samuel 9) First: David Enquires were any of the house of Jerusalem left? What love have we showen to Christ in his members? (25 Matthew 35 verse) Let us try ourselves by this. Are we willing to suffer for Christ do we love the cross for Christ? (6 Galatians 14) God forbid I should glory in any thing save the cross of Christ. 7 Doe you love nothing more than Jesus Christ? Is He preferred above all? He will be loved above all or not at all. Doe you love Jesus Christ more than all Injoyment, more than [r s] pleasures proffits? Could you part with all for Jesus Christ or rather than Jesus Christ? (4 Matthew 8) (8 Canticles 6.7) 2 Doe we love the lord Jesus more than our dearest of nearest relations? (14 Luke 26) He must hate mother, brother, and sister if he wilt love Jesus Christ, that is he must love them less than Christ. (12 Matthew 58) (19 John 26) 3 Doe you love the lord Jesus Christ moor than your own life?[8] You must love Jesus Christ more than your life. Your love to Jesus Christ must be strong as death.

The second sermon of this series is the famed jeremiad of New England's second generation, although some scholars have insisted that the jeremiad continued in America through the close of the Civil War and beyond.[9] In this sermon, Foster implores his Hartford congregation to change its evil ways. Perhaps Foster was using the opportunity to sharpen his oratory on the subject of New England's decline prior to attending the Reforming Synod in May. The absence of sermons in the notebook during the time of the Synod is proof of nothing, but it would be interesting to learn whether Foster made the trip to Boston.

[8] The rhetorical question upon question catechism style of this sermon is interesting and occurs nowhere else in the notebook to this extent.

[9] See: Sacvan Bercovich, *The American Jeremiad.*

Mr. Foster. (Sunday) March 7, 1680 (1 Corinthians 16:22) If any man love not the lord Jesus let him be.

Doctrine: That they that love not Christ are in a cursed Estate and persevering and continuing so they shall be accursed when Christ comes. 1 Many doe not love Jesus Christ. 2 They that love not Christ are accursed and continuing so shall be so when Christ comes.

Use: See the great folly of those that love not the Lord Jesus.

2 Use: Hence learn that it is of great concernment that we see that we doe love the Lord Jesus for if we do not we are accurssed.

3 Use: Is of tryall. [ ] we be of the Number of those that love Christ.

4 Use: is of Lamentation. That there are so few that love Jesus Christ and so many hate him, that he hath so many Enemies and so few friends. The apostle (3 Philippians 8) [weapes] that there were so many Enemies. Love the cross of Christ and [might] not the apostle lament amongst [us] [ ] so love [ ] Christ. Men are lovers of themselves and lovers of pleasures more than of God tho: many pretend love to Jesus Christ yet their hearts do not love Jesus Christ. Our love we should show to Christ is not in word and with the Tongue, but in deed and in truth. We should love Christ for Christ's sake, for his owne sake, and not for outward advantage. When Christ is held forth to poore siners they are not taken with him, but turn aside from him and hide their faces from him, that is they loath and hate Jesus Christ and turn away from him their faces. They looke upon Christ as an unlovely object: Jesus Christ is observed and despised of men. Christ is hated in the state of his Exaltation.

4 Use: of conselation. To all those that do [inoffed] love the Lord Jesus Christ they are blessed. If they are accursed that love him not then by the consequence of contrarys they are blessed that love him. The grace of God, the blessing of God, will come upon all those that love the lord Jesus. (5 Ephesians) The grace of our Lord Jesus be with all those that love him with sincerity. They that doe not love Jesus Christ they shall perish in the way. (9 Romans 33) Whoever believes on the lord Jesus he shall not be ashamed. He shall be blessed. [ ] To as many as receive him he gave power to [best] sons of God. A crowne of righteousness shall he give to all that love his appearing. There are these grounds of comfort arise hence if you love the Lord Jesus. You may be assured he loves you. (14 John 21) He that loves me shall be loved of the Father and I will love him. Your love to Christ is an evidence of Christ's love to you, for our love is a fruit of Christ's love to us. We love him because

he loved us first, by the knowledge of the Effect we know the curse. To have Christ love us is more than if all the world loves us. 2 If you love Christ you may be assured that he will manifest himselfe to you. (14 John 21) He that loveth me I will love him and manifest myself to him. (23 verse) If a man love me, my Father loves him and I will love him, and we will take up our aboad with him, and what ground of comfort is this. 3 They are sure of the acceptance of [this] [person] and [services] Jesus Christ. That there are persons are accepted and sins are pardoned not withstanding all our infirmities. (91 Psalm 14 verse) Because he hath set his love upon me I will deliver him. He shall call and I will Answer him, but especially to the glory of God. We are humbled for it and turn from it.

Use: Exortation. To turn from sin: It is everyone's worke to turn all. Everyone, rich, poore, high, and low all are to turn from sin. (5 James) Lost soule salvation depends upon turning from sin. Everyone should put away sin. Let not wickedness rest in the house. Everyone must turn from all sin, Especialy his own, return from all iniquity and so it shall not be your [raine]. (18 Jeremiah 11) Turn everyone from his evill way. Put away the strang Gods and [Ashtorch] from you. Put away all sin any security the [ ] put away all sin any [deedness] 3 This turning it must be reall. Pictures will not pass with God. They are of no Esteem with God. (7 Jeremiah 5) Doe not padle with repentance but turn in deed 4 for the time of this returning it must be present and continued. Turn you now everyone from his evill way. Today is God's time.[10]

3 Use: Is matter of deep humiliation that there is no more done at this great duty. We seem to be a people that are not [moulded] to a turning frame of spirit. The people turn not to him that smites it. We had need to be greatly humbled before God because we have been, are afflicted. We doe forget ourselves except we doe remember we have been afflicted the worm wood and the [gall] tho: God hath not dealt with us as we have deserved, yet we have been afflicted more Eminently. We have had our 7 or 7 times 7 more afflictions. God hath smitten us with blessings [ild es] our young men have fallen by the sword, our horses have

[10] The voice of the jeremiad resounded in Hartford as well as Massachusetts Bay. New England's churches may have been experiencing difficulties regarding baptism and church politics, but the ministers were clearly on the same page regarding the moral decay of the people. See Sacvan Bercovitch, *The American Jeremiad* (Madison Wisconsin: The University of Wisconsin Press, 1978).

been taken from us, and the [stinck][11] of our [lamp] hath com into our Nostrils. The Lord's poore [ ] have fled and fallen before the Enemie many times. Many lives lost and habatations left desolate. If we looke back to the solemnity of that day we may say the Lord afflicted us sore: We are afflicted at this day. God is renewing his witnesses against us. The lord's hand is stretched out still against us. Difficulties at Home and abroad. The heavens grow cloudy as if a storm were at hand. That noysome sickness now com again amongst us.[12] That heavy blow that God hath given us by taking away that [prince] and a great man is fallen in our Isrell. (31 Job 14) A rebuker in the gate that such a man should be taken away at such a juncture it bodes ill. 2 Have we turned or are we indeed Turned from our evill ways? That is our worke, but have we done it? Doe we doe it? For is there not Idolatry, a provoaking sin amongst us? How comon is it for professors to Idolize the world to set it above all in their hearts? For what Ever it is that hath more roome in thy heart than God that you makest thy God. When the minds of men are busyd then they doe minde Earthly things. Favoure with God is of no waight and worth with them. Hence it is said that God is not in all their thoughts. It is the caracter of the godly they feare God and thought upon his name, but most their mindes are so stuft with the world that there is no roome for God in their hearts. It is a fearful thing for men to have their faces set to God and their backes turn to God: They have no will for God, for Jesus Christ. They will not come to me that they may have life. (2 Amos 7 verse) How many ar well contented without seeing the face of God, that spend dayes and years without heart reachings after God. 2 Is there not pride amongst us still? Pride against God when we canot fall before God and bow and bend to the will of God.

---

[11] Alice Morse Earle's nineteenth-century history *Home Life in Colonial Days* contains many interesting details of life in colonial New England. Conveniently, she describes in detail the physical characteristics of many tools and implements used by colonial New Englanders, including lamps. Earle says that for many years lamps were not extensively used in America, but the most commonly used lamps were called "Betty-lamps." These lamps "were small, shallow receptacles, two or three inches in diameter and about an inch in depth… They usually had a hook and chain by which they could be hung on a nail in the wall… They were filled with tallow, grease, or oil, while a piece of cotton rag or coarse wick was so placed that, when lighted, the end hung out on the nose. From this wick, dripping dirty grease, rose a dull, smoky, ill-smelling flame." Alice Morse Earle, *Home Life in Colonial Days* (Stockbridge Massachusetts: Berkshire House Publishers, American Classics Edition, 1993), 43.

[12] Epidemics were common in colonial New England, but it can be difficult to locate specific documented instances of outbreaks.

(13 Jeremiah 9.10 verse) Men are too stately to be at God's beck and at the command of the word of God: (Jeremiah 30.15) Heare and give Eare and be not proud for the to speaketh. There is allso pride against man. (3 Isaiah 5) The child to behave himself against the ancient [proudly] and the [base] against the honourable pride in this sence workes the ruine of a people. There is pride under priviledges, therefor the apostle [puts] in that [caveat] be not high minded but fear. (25 Acts 23) Se pride in apparel. (3 Isaiah 3) Is there not sensuality among us, uncleaness and Intemperance, a payre of evills that doe go often together? Whordom and New wine go together. (5 Jeremiah 7) Thy children when I fed them at the fall they committed adultery. In Zion thy children they forsake me. How shall I pardon the for this intemperance? There is to much cause to fear tho down right druncкeness doth not yet, excessive drinking is to common amongst the. Scripture gives a woe to those that are strong to drinck strong drinke. Woe to the drunkards of Ephraim, woe to those that sell the poore heathen drinke. I speek it in the name of God. Woe to them. If an Effectuall course be not taken to suppress this raigning Evill we shall suffer a great deal more from the heathen than we have done for our teaching them that great sin.[13] Is there not unrighteousness amongst us? Great defects in commutative justice. (22 Ezekiel 12) When there is a gredines of gaine, of dishonest gaine for the people of God to oppres one another, this is sad. Is there not too much contention among the people of God? Little differences make great disstances. There are some that doe but seemingly turn from sin. Judah dealt but Treacherously with God. (3 Jeremiah 6)

(2 Chronicles 34:35) They wer not sincere and [r wnd] in what they did hence it comes to nothing. They are like the morning cloud and early due. 2 Som there are that turn not at all but doe but looke as if they would turn. (2 Jeremiah 34) 3 Some there are that they are so farr from turning from sin that they turn to it, draw iniquity with cart roopes and sin, with cords of vanity. 3 Ground of humiliation: is that for an afflicted people not to turn from the Christ. Evill ways is Exceeding dangerous. 1 Because affliction is a means Eminently [bitt] by God for that End to turn us from sin. We have got nothing by wandering from God. We have Evidently and undeniably worstend ourselves by goeing from God. (4 Amos 9) (7 Hosea 9.10) 2 A peoples not turning from sin after affliction it argues great haughtiness and hardness of spirit. God

[13] This is very likely another reference to King Philip's War.

smites but non refuse to return but harden their hearts against God. They are not humbled to this day tho afflicted many times. Such a cours as not turning from sin it makes way for greater anger to be left to sin the greatest and sorest judgment. Ephraim is joined to his Idols let him alone. Not turning from sin is the way to be turned out of all our comforts. Mans Impenitency continued In will make God weary of us. I will destroy my people [sith] they turn not their way. (4 Amos 12)

As in Watson's January 17, 1679 sermon, the opening text is Malachi, and the lesson remains the constancy and unchangeableness of God. This lesson must have been a welcome one for the people of Hartford, who had experienced many temporal changes, such as warfare, epidemic disease, and church strife. God was a constant in a world full of ever changing experiences.

Mr. Watson. (Sunday) June 20, 1680: (3 Malachi 6) For I am the Lord I change not.

Doctrine: Jehovah is imutable and unchangeable. All other things are changable. (102 Psalm 25.26) The Lord changes not what ever changes pass upon second beings. How God is unchangable is his essence, nature and being. (3 Exodus 14) 2 He is imutable in his desires attributes and divine perfection. He is unchangeable in them all. 3 He is unchangeable in his counsels and eternall purposes. 4 In his word he is unchangeable, in his prophesies promises and Threatenings and in his covenants.

Reason: 1 From the perfection. He is a most absolut and perfect being. 2 From the simplicity of God. He is a pure act: 3 His Eternity. He is unchangeable being.

Use 1: This showes Jehovah is a better good than the world can affoard. He is imutable and unchangeable. All other comforts have their autumn, but God is an unchangeable being and good.

2 Use: is of Teror to all siners [Impenitant] because of those dreadfull threatenings that are in the booke of God against impenitent siners. Woe unto the wicked. Unless we chang God will not chang, not turn except we turn:

3 Use: is of comfort and conselation to the godly is God unchangeable in his word and promises. It is of strong conselation to the godly that all those promises that God hath made unto his people they shall all be fullfilled in due time. Hath God said it shall goe well with the righteous here and hereafter? Hath he said all things shall worke together for the best whatever motions and commotions? Hath he said he will never leave nor forsake them, but be with them in the face of persecution?

(5 Job 19) Hath God promised grace love and glory here after and withhold no good thing from those that walke up rightly. Be these the promises of an unchangeable God. With them they shall certainly be accomplished. (89 Psalm 31) God will not suffer his faythfullnes to faile, the strength of Isrell will not ly. [ah] he canot ly. God may brake our colonys, [ch], Townes, familys, persons, but he will not breake his word. It is for Ever settled in heaven.[14] Whatever changes there be the children of God should live upon the unchangeableness of God in the promises in the midst of fears and difficulties. (32 Genesis 10.11) Com along with us and we will doe the good for the lord hath spoken good concerning Iserell. God will be as good as his word. (66 Psalm 1.2.6) (27 Psalm 13) The more we believe the more we trust in God, the more conselation. 2 The immutability of God's word holds forth conselation to the people of God in generall. How many gracious promises hath God [uited] to that low Estate of his people? It is the day of Jacob's trouble but [ ] will free them out of them all. God hath promised that the kingdoms of the world shall become the kingdom of Jesus Christ. That [bub] shall fall, that they shall hate the whore and burn her flesh with fire. (16 Matthew 8) He hath promised that the gates of hell shall not prevayle against his church and people. Let the enemies of God's people associat themselves and they shall be broken to pieces. (12 Zachariah 1 verse) 2 The [ch] is said to be a cup of Trembling and burthensom stone to the enemies. The Enemies of the people of God they are said to show their strength by taking up a burthensom stone that is to heavy for them. The enemies of God's people may [strive] who shall lift most against the people of God, but they shall be able to [do] no hurt to her. 3 The immutability of God is of comfort to the godly, it doth asure them of their Eternall salvation. 1 Consider that the Eternall decree and purpose of God concerning your salvation is imutable and eternall. (6 Zachariah 1) (2 Timothy 2:19) The foundation of the lord stands sure. (10 Luke 20) Rejoyce [you] then that your names are written in heaven. Other things they are but pore things to rejoice in, rather rejoice in this, that your names are written in heaven. (18 Matthew 14) It is their Father's will and pleasure that these shall not perish. (28 Romans 29 verse) (11 Romans 17) But the Election hath attayned it. 2 The free and eternall love of God towards you it is immutable and unchangable. It is the

[14] Clearly, the physical world was transient compared to the everlasting word of God, and Hartford's preachers exhorted this point in many of their sermons.

free love of God, it is sure, constant, and abideing, an everlasting love, therefore with loving kindness will I [draw] the. (8 Romans 38.39) Outward afflictions doe not change this love of God. I will visit them with a rod, yet my loving kindness I will not utterly take from them. Inward desertions Doe not withdraw his love from a people. For a moment I hide my face (54 Isaiah 7.8.9.10) from the, but with everlasting kindness I will draw the. 3 Consider that the infinit power of God that is engaged for the salvation of his people is Imutable and unchangeable. Trust constantly and for ever in the lord. All that are his shall be kept by the power of God through faith unto salvation. 4 For your comfort consider that the covenant of grace and mercy the lord hath made with his people it is imutable and unchangeable. Ordered in all things and sure in this covenant God gives his [son] grace here and glory here after, so that all things are sure in this sure covenant the sure mercys of David. God is sure, Christ is sure, the spirit is sure, and eternall life and glory is sure. It is imutable and unchangable. Jesus Christ is the surety of the better covenant that canot be broken. 5 Consider that the gifts and callings of God they are without repentance. (11 Romans 27) They are imutable unchangeable. Consider that to the immutability of his word and promises he hath added the immutability of his acts that thereby the heirs (6 Hebrews 17) of the promise might have strong conselation. Had God only promised salvation that is enough, but such is the riches of God's goodnes that to the immutability of his word he added his acts.

CHAPTER EIGHT

THE GLORY OF THE ELECT

Ecclesiastes is primarily about its author's argument (the author may have been Solomon) that "God is the only avenue to satisfaction in this life."[1] *For Puritans seeking a church of the Elect, Ecclesiastes might have been understood to be "addressed to God's people, rather than to those who are ignorant of God or in rebellion against Him."*[2] *Finally, Ecclesiastes teaches how God's Elect, pilgrims in this world 'under the sun' (1 Pet. 1:1), but also citizens of heaven (Phil. 3:20), should live amid the profound frustrations and tensions of the present age (Rom. 8:18–23).*[3] *Based on this interpretation, it is not difficult to see the appeal of this Old Testament book to New England's Puritans.*

This sermon series is about the glory of a godly man's (a saint's) death, that it should be glorified as freedom from the influence of Satan. The first installment sounds especially like a funeral sermon, and it probably was. In his Colonial History of Hartford, *the historian William De Loss Love writes about a prominent early resident of Hartford named Major James Richards. Loves' history was originally published in 1914 and his research was based on original sources. According to Love, James Richards was a highly respected man who served as a magistrate for sixteen years.*[4] *Richards died on June 11, 1680, exactly when Foster was preaching his sermon series on the death of a godly man.*

It is interesting to note that at the time of his death, Major James Richards' estate was valued at nearly 8,000 pounds, making him the wealthiest resident in Hartford, so it is plausible to suspect that he was at least partially the subject of Foster's sermon. Moreover, if Richards is in any way the subject of Foster's preaching, what does this say about the relationship between Hartford's First and Second Churches? At the time of his death, Richards was a full communion member of Hartford's Second

---

1 *New Geneva Study Bible*, 986.
2 Ibid.
3 Ibid., 987.
4 DeLoss Love, The Colonial History of Hartford. 333.

church, under the pastor John Whiting, while three weeks later Isaac Foster would be ordained the minister of Hartford's First church.[5]

Mr. Foster. (Sunday) June 20, 1680. (7 Ecclesiastes 1) "*A good name is better then a good ointment, and the day of death, then the day that one is born.*"[6] A good name is better than precious ointment, and the day of deth than the day of one's Birth. Here is a comparasen between a good name and precious ointment, and prefers a good name above it. A name that is gotten by good workes, by precious ointment is all treasure, and their good name is better than all riches. It is better for to be a good man than a rich man, it is better because it gets more love than riches. 2 A man will be more honoured for his good name. It will allso long. A good name will last when his Estat perishes. (112 Psalm 6) His good name he inherits when others inherit his Estate and riches. 2 Solomon prefers the day of death before the Birth and this is contrary to the opinon of the world. (40 Genesis 20) The day of birth is often a Festival day, so Pharoh and Heris kept their birth dayes, and the day of death is a mournfull day. Some men doe Expound these generally of all men good and bad the good and wicked. The sooner they dy the wicked the less evill they doe to themselves and others. When the wicked perish there is shouting. (11 Proverbs 11) (2 Peter 2:20) It is not true of all but of the godly it is true.

Doctrine: that the day of a godly man's death is better than his birth. Unto a godly man the day of death is better than the day of birth. They receive and Injoy more happyness by death. A day is said to be good in regard of the good we enjoy in that day. (1 Phillipians 21) To me to live is Christ and to dye is gayne. When a godly man departs out of the world it is best for him to be with Christ. It is better to be absent from the body and to be present with the Lord. The servant of God in times of Temptation and trouble prefer death before life and so allso in the best times. Solomon in his repentance and Paule when he was in [after ight] and deliberated the matter he prefers deathe before life.

Reason 1: is taken from the great evill that doth accompany and follow men's death. 2 Fear the vanity of all men injoy in this life [ ] from the sorows death freed from. 4 From the happyness men enjoy at death.

[5] Hartford, Connecticut: *Records of the Second Church of Christ, 1669–1731.* Hartford: Connecticut State Library, 1914.

[6] *The Geneva Bible, 1560 Edition.* 83. In the Geneva Bible, this verse is numbered 7 Ecclesiastes 3, but the notebook clearly indicates a 1, and this holds true for each sermon in this series.

1 of the. 1 From the evill that accompanys and follows man's birth. The evill of sin doth accompany and follow the birth. Every man is born in sin, he hath a sinfull being. He comes into the world a poluted defiled sinfull creature. The [g toin] is unclean and all that proceeds from him is lik him polluted and defiled creature. The fountain is unclean and all that proceeds from him is lik him, poluted and unclean. Every man is born with the sin of Adam. He is poluted with the birth of sin, dead in sin. He is born a siner but he doth not dye a siner, and therefore the day of his death is best. As he is born a siner so he lives in actuall sin. He is sold under sin and sin continues in them. 2 Therein is the evill of sorow and affliction that doth follow man's birth. Man is born to trouble as the sparkes fly upward. Death is the end of trouble to a godly man but the day of birth is but the beginning of it: (3 Job 2.7) Job curseth the day of his birth because it did not hide sorow from him. (14 Job 1) It is a part of the curs that man's dayes are full, but that they are full of trouble is the greater part of the curss. (2 Ecclesiastes) All his dayes are sorow and full of greife. An account of these sorows. They are 1 Externall, 2 internall. 1 Externall: those outwards sorows are such as light upon the body, those sicknesses, aches, and paines that fall upon the body. The sorows that com upon his name by reproche and shame. It was a great part of the suffering of Christ the reproach of his name. 3 There is sorow in regard of losses in a man's Estate. Sorow in getting of it in keeping and in parting with it. 4 Sorows in respect of our relations. There is sorow and trouble men meet with upon account of relation in this world. There is sorow from the sins of relations. There is sorow in the sorows of relations and there is sorow in the deth of relations. 2 There is allso internall sorows and they are farr more than these. Those troubles that light upon the soule, a wounded consciens who can beare.

2 Reason: is taken from the vanity of all that is to be injoyed in the world while we live. (1 Ecclesiastes 2)[7] All is vanity (verse 14) and vexation of spirit. Here is a great deal will increase his misery. Were man to live as Adam did it were better, but now there is the curss upon the world.[8]

---

[7] Foster dedicated his November 1, 1679 sermon to this text, the vanity of wordly pursuits.

[8] This is a reference to original sin. The *Hartford Sermon Notebook* makes several references to God's curse upon the world, the result of man's original fall from grace in the Garden of Eden.

3 Reason: is taken from the Evill man is delivered from in the day of death. A godly man is freed from all evill. 1. A godly man is at the day of his death delivered from in dweling sin, from the power of it, the filth of it and being of it. They are then made perfect. Death separates the soule from the body and sin from the soule. (20 Job 11) The wicked man lys down with his sin in the dust, but the godly are freed from it. It shall have no home and dominion over them. They are then freed from Sathen. Jesus Christ is the seed of the woman that hath bruised the head of the serpent. A godly man at his death is absolutely freed from the Divill. 3 The day of death it doe free the godly from the company of wicked men. Lott's righteous soule was vexed for the wicked conversation and David wo is me I dwell in [Keder].[9] Then the chaffe and wheat shall be separated. The godly they are by death gathered to their people and the wicked they are gathered to their people. They shall com no more to the people of God to vex them. The day of death it frees them from all that hard labour and travel. They are exercised with in this world they rest from their Labour:

Use 1: Hence, we have no reason for to Lament the condition of a godly man at his death. His condition is not lamentable: There may be cause to bewayle the condition of the wicked as David Absolom. Tho: there be no cause to lament their condition yet we ought to mourn for their death because every godly man is an instrument of God's glory. When a godly man dyes there is [ ] dead that is an instrument of God's glory. 2 We have cause to mourn for such because it is a sign of evill coming upon us and therefore we have cause to mourne. (57 Isaiah 23.1.2.3) (3 Isaiah 1.28) 3 There is cause of mourning because such as these are a common good to the places where they dwell. Again we stand in special need of such men. We need their prayers we need their advice counsel and admonition and we need their example and their very presence. It is a blessing to a people. Therefore there is great cause to lament the death of a good man.

<u>(Sunday) June 27, 1680: Mr. Foster:</u> (7 Ecclesiastes 1) Doctrine: that the day of a godly man's death is better than the day of his birth. A godly man by death is delivered from sin from the evill of sin. He

[9] Kedar is a reference to a lesser-known tribe that took its name from the grandson of Abraham. They were renowned for skilled archers and were of importance during the time of Isaiah. *Holman Bible Dictionary*, 977.

is born of sin but he doth not dye in sin. (30 Job 23) For I know thou wilt bring me to the grave to the house of all living [s] is. Sorrows will follow them to the grave but [then] there is an end. He will not stretch out his hand to the grave. Then there is an end of all sorrows, then they shall be delivered from all evill. They shall be redeemed then by death from present evill, the evill that he suffers here: By death he is at once freed from it. At the day of death the godly man is freed from all sin, from dwelling sin, the remaynder of sin that dwell in the best of men, but now sin dwells no more in them. The day of death is the day of deliverance from the body of death, the old man that shall dye when they dye there shall be perfect deliverance from sin. The being of it shall then no more remaine. When the Earthly Tabernackless dissolved their sin is allso dissolved and taken from the body. (20 Job 11) It is not so with the wicked, their sins follow them to the grave and go down to hell with them, but it is not so with the godly they are made perfect. 2 He is freed allso from actuall sin, tho the habbit doth remain yet then the act is allso destroyed. (38 Psalm 17) The godly they doe hate sin but yet they doe it in this world, but then they are freed from the act of sin. (7 Revelations 9) They stand before the lambe in white robes. They goe to the spirits of Just men. Made perfect they are then freed from temptation to sin, freed from Saytn. A godly man at the day of death is freed from Temptation. The God of the world canot tempt in this world.[10] The prince of this world hath no power in the world to come.[11] (1 Peter 5.8) (9 Zachariah 1) Saytn was at the right hand to resist them. 3 At the day of death a godly man is freed from the company of Saytn and his evill instruments. He is freed from the company of the wicked. (2 [Cant] 1.2) David laments that he dwelt in [Keder] [ ] that godly [ ] death are delivered from the company of the wicked. (1 Acts 26) Every wicked man at death goes to his place and is gathered to his people. They goe to their own place.

4 Reason: The day of death freed the godly man from and puts an end to all the difficulty of his labours. Christ puts and end to all the sore Travells and afflicitive labor. (14 Revelations 13) They rest from the their labours and their workes follow them.

---

[10] Satan.

[11] Prince of the world is yet another name for the Devil. The variety of naming conventions used for Satan in *the Hartford Sermon Notebook* is interesting. If nothing else, it may have simply been a way to diversify the language employed in the sermon.

(26 Matthew 24 verse) The body of man in this life is consumed with sore trouble and sorrow, but then they shall hunger and thirst no more. God shall then wipe away all Tears from them. (3 Job 17.18.19) 5: The godly man at the day of his death is freed from all spiritual dissertions. Here the very heirs of heaven feel the Teror of hell when God doth hide his face and withdraw his presence from them. He will not let them se his face but lets his Terors fall upon them that is ready to disstruct them, but at death then they shall have a full sight of God. They shall se God without Interuption. They shall see him face to face. (33 Exodus 11) That is the happynes of every godly man. He shall then have a full tast of the love of God without any Interruption. Death doth not separate a man from the love of God. (23 Genesis 4) It brings to the full fruition of this love. Then shall we be ever with the Lord. 6 Death doth deliver the godly man from all afflictions whatsoever. (21 Revelations 4) Death doth wipe away all tears from their eyes from all sorrow and greife that they are Lyable to meet with also. 7: Death frees the godly man from all Imperfections of nature and [grat] darkness is removed and the understanding is Inlightened. 2 The day of death doth deliver the godly man from all future evils, from the evill that is to com in this life, from the evill that is to come upon an evill world. (57 Isaiah 1) The righteous is gathered from the [fall] of evill. God takes away good Josiah from the evill to com. God provides an arke for Noah to keep him from the Flood and [ag] for [n s] before the flood. The godly man is by death freed from the evill of the world to come.

4 Reason: is taken from the good the godly men at the death are made partakers of. It is of the greatest good and that is possitive happiness. By death the godly man is brought into a glorious state. He is not onely delivered from all evill, but he is made partaker of all good. 1 Death brings him into a glorious place. The day of a man's birth brings him into a cursed place, but death carrys him to paradice. (2 Revelations 5.6.7) Death takes them hence and carrys them into their Father's house. 2 Death doth bring the godly man into a glorious state, a state of rest and bliss. The soule is stript of the body, but is clothed upon with Imortall and Eternall glory. The godly then do receive a crown of glory. Deth 3 brings him to glorious company tho: it leaves its company (12 Hebrews 22) here upon Earth yet it comes to better company. 1 They are caryd to God to the presence of God. They are present with the lord. 2 There is Jesus the mediatior of the New covenant. (1 Phillipians 23) They go to Jesus Christ and they are with him (17 John 24) as Christ prayed

that those that God had given them might be [where is]. 3 They are caryd to an inumerable company of angells that are ministering spirits to the elect here and companions with them forever. 4 They goe to the godly, to the spirits of just men glorifyd in heaven.

Use 1: No cause to lament the case of the godly deceased. We may lament their loss because they are taken from the evill to com. We stand in need of them. We need their prayer, advice, and counsel and their example and their presence we need for their sake the world stands. 2 Hence learn that the godly they must dye as well as others. They that have done most for God his glory, they must dye as sure as there is life they must dy. It is apoynted for men to dye. They must all dye. God will bring them to the house appoynted for all Living. (13 Acts 36) They that have served their generation according to the will of God must se corruption. 1 The godly man must dye for he is made of coruptable principles as well as others. The best of men are dust and Ashes. 2 The godly as well as the wicked are under the sentence of death as well as others. They sined in Adam and as sin passed over them so death passes over them. All men were included in that one sin and so death passed over them all. They are all dust and shall return to death. The lord Jesus Christ freed the godly from the second death 2 not from the first. He hath taken away the sting of deth, the curss, but yet he must dye. 3 The godly man must dye that he may pass into eternall life. 4 He must dye that he may be conformable to Christ in his sufferings, 5 that God may have the greater glory in the resurection of their bodys. 3 Hence the godly man hath great reason to be patient under all his sufferings in this life because death will be an end of all his suffering. Be patient in life for you shall be freed from all evill in death. (30 Job 24): 4 Hence learn a speakeable [ground] of comfort to all that are mourners for godly relations, all tears are wiped from their eyes. Why should they stand in our eyes? We should mourn for all men. The house of the dead is called the house of mourning. Especially the death of the godly is to be lamented, yet their consideration doth give comfort in mourning. (1 Thessalonians 4:13) Mourn not for those that are asleep in Jesus as for those that have no hope. Their death is gaine to them. They are taken from you, but they go to their Father's house. (3 Malachi 17) God is [bindeing] up [ ] when they dye. (2 Samuel 18:31) (2 Samuel 12:21.23) 5 Hence learn unspeakable [ground] of comfort to the godly in respect of their own death. He need not fear death he may rejoice over death. Death canot hurt them. (1 Corinthians 3.22) All is yours, all thing is yours. Death itselfe is yours. It is ordained for your advantage and is a meanes and passage to Eternall life. Death is Terrible to nature it is [ ] of Terors. It is terible to nature. (55 Psalm 4) The Terors of death doe compass me about. Several considerations are ground of comfort. 1 The names God gives it in the scripture. God hath given it such names as are familyer to us. It is cald a sleep. The death of the godly is cald asleep to them. The godly they doe sleep in Jesus. The grave is compard to a bed. (57 Isaiah 2) They shall rest in their beds. 2 Death is cald an unclothing of man. It is also called a departure the death of the godly. (1 Philippians 23) It is called a goeing to our Father's, a being gained to our people. It is called a putting off of the Tabernackel. (1 Peter 14 verse) (2 Corinthians 5:1) 2 Death canot breake the covenant that is between God and him, and that is a ground of comfort to the godly man in death. When you dye God is [your] God and the God of your seed after. (48 Genesis 21) Behold I dye but shall be with you and bring you to the land of your Fathers. 3 Death canot dissolve the union between a godly man and Christ and that is a ground of comfort. It canot separate you from the love of God. The lord Jesus that is your redeemer he hath the key of death and of the grave. (1 Revelations 18 verse) 6 Hence learn the difference that is between the death of the godly and the wicked. The day of the godly man's death is a good day, a happy day, but the day of the wicked man's death is the day of his Execution. 1 For a wicked man doth dye in sin. 2 He dyes under the curss. 3 The sentence of condemnation is past upon them and it is allso Executed.

The Ecclesiastes series is also about preparedness within the Puritan's journey toward salvation. These sermons are a warning to Hartford's congregation concerning the hazards of living in an unregenerate state.

Mr. Foster: (Sunday) July 4, 1680. (7 Ecclesiastes 1) And the day of death [then] the day of one's birth.

Doctrine: that the day of a godly man's death is better than the day of his birth: The godly and the wicked are born alike but they dye not alike. Indead as to what is outward there is no difference. Who so dyes the wise man as the foole dyeth. As to the main they are both forgotten, their names are covered with darkness both. Both are turned to dust: The (3 Ecclesiastes 9) Not only the godly but the wicked dye alike and so doth man and beast they dye alike: yet not withstanding all this there is a vast difference in the death. 1 Respect of the consequences of it and it lyeth in these 3 perticulers: 1 The wicked man doth dye in sin. All that sin he brings into the world with him he doth carry it out of the world with him. The godly cary no sin with them, they are delivered from the power of death. The lord Jesus Christ Hath removed them from death taken away the sting of it. (8 John 21). You shall dye in your sins a wicked man. First of all dyeth under the guilt of sin. The guilt of sin doth ly upon him. A wicked man tho he hath dyed yet he hath not satisfied the law. 2 The filth of sin, the staine, blot and pollution of sin lyeth upon him. His soule is still defiled with sin. (4 Ezekiel 13) In they filthyness is lewdness because I purged the and thou wouldst not be purged after death. He shall not be purged from his filthyness anymore. 2 Every wicked man at death his soule is in the power of Saytn. As he tempted them while they live so he will Torment them when they are dead. That portion of a wicked man is with the Divill and his angells. 3 The wicked man at death goes to hell. The godly they goe in to Abram's boosome. (12 Ecclesiastes 7) The spirit of the wicked as well as the godly they goe to God that gave it. The godly God absolves and rewards them, but the wicked they goe to God to receive the sentance of condemnation. The spirits of the wicked they goe to hell, to the spirits in [prison]. The godly they goe to the spirits of just men made perfect. The soule of the godly man is made happy and the soule of the wicked is made miserable, and the miserie stands within their separation from God. 2 In separation to misery to death and darkness. Depart from God into darkness. This misery is increased by their company to the Divill and his angels, amplyfyd by the duration Eternall fire. 7 Hence learn we abundant cause for to admire and wonder at the grace of God with respect unto the death of the godly: 1 Admire grace in the moderation of the curss. Every man deserved to dye as same as he came into the world that God but should delay and defer and give time to prepare for it, that God doth not take away in sin but gives repentance for sin. This is caus of admiration: 2 that this curss should not only be moderated but turned into a blessing, that death it should bring to life, and that it should make us most happy so that death is better for us than to live. This is the great goodness of God. If our hope were only in this life than we were of all men the most miserable. 3 That all this should be done by the death of Christ, that God should send his son to dye for us that our death might be our way to live, this is from the death of our Lord Jesus: Christ dyes that the [worm d] and [a e] might be taken out of our deth.

2 Use: of Exortation: Let us be exorted to prepare for death that the day of our death may be better to us than the day of birth. It is not so to Everyone but it is so to the godly. Let us seriously labor after that which [Balam] vainly desired. (23 Numbers 10) Let me dye the death of the righteous and let my last End be like theirs. For motives 1 consider that to be fit for death is the end of life. Not only as it is the Term of life but as it is the worke and business of life, that you may be prepared and fitted for death. This is the great worke that God calls to. Oh that my people were wise that they would consider their latter end. 2 Consider it is a great part of man's wisdom to prepare for death. Wisdom doth ly in this, it lookes at the end of things. (4 Job 21) They dye without wisdom. There is no wisdom in their death. (49 Psalm 20) It is a signe of foly not to be prepared for death. 3 Consider it is a very hard and difficult thing to dye well and to be fitted for death. There is a great deall of worke to dy. Sin must dye in you and spirituall life must be in you before you are fit to dye. Christ must be united in you before you are fitt to be disunited. You must be Twice born before you are fitt to dye once. There must be a resurrection in the soule before you are fit for the death of the body.[12] Every godly man is not actually fit to dye as that good king. Hazikiea was afrayd to receive the message of death at the time. David (30 Psalm 10.13) a good man was afraid of death. Oh spare me give me space to gather strength before I go hence and be no more. The wise virgins had oyle in their lamps and yet they slept. 4 Consider that life is Exceeding short. Let this move and stir up everyone to be prepared for death. Man's dayes they are hastening as [post]. (4 Job 5) 5 Consider also the uncertainty of life. We are not sure of a day, month, a week, or an hour. No man knows the uncertainty of them. (14 Job 5) Thou hast appoynted the bounds which he shall not pass. (21 Job 23) The most of mankind dye in infancy and some dye in their full strength. Death doth observe no seniority.

6 Consider there is no returning to life again, to such a state of life as man injoyes now in the world. A state of life 7 Job to prepare for death. Therefore now is the time to prepare for death. You shall have

[12] This passage is perhaps Foster's best explanation for the structure of regeneration. Foster is clearly very concerned about stressing the importance of preparing for death. Considering the common occurrence of sickness and disease, these sermons may have been addressing a real need, although I have been unable to find any evidence to support an epidemic in Hartford at the time of this sermon. There had been a smallpox epidemic in Boston in 1677/78, as recorded in Cotton Mather's diary, and it is possible Hartford was experiencing a similar outbreak.

no time besides. An eror in death is not be corrected. Man that dyeth shall com up no more. (14 Job 7): It is not with man in this respect as it is with other things. 7 Consider of how great concernment it is to be prepared for death. You that enter into an unchangeable Estate: The eternall concerns of our soules depend upon it: consider that there are but few that dye well. There are many whose death is miserable: There are many are weary of life and yet they are not fit for death. If Christ should come their lamps would not be [trimmed].[13] How many have been unready for it. 9 Death is the [k][14] of Terors to those that are not prepared for it. (18 Job 13) To the godly, death is their cheife of comforts because it is a passage to glory, but to others it is Terible upon the account of the Antecedents of it, Sicknes and paynes and deseases. 2 It is Terible upon account of what it deprives him of and separates him from, all friends and relations, his state wealth and honor. 3 It is Terible in its own nature which is the separation of soule and body. 4 It is Terible upon the account of the future Estate of the soule. How Terible will death be to those that have no Interest in Christ? There is nothing will be so terible to them. 10 Consider the day of death will be no season to prepare for death in. 1 God doth ordinarily [and] often deny his grace to such. Tho: he hath offered it to them before, that hour of salvation is past and the day of [gr] is then over. (1 Proverbs 24) Because I have called and ye refused and I will mock at your calamity and laugh, when your fear comes you shall call and I will not Answer. 2 Consider upon account of bodily sickness you are unfit then to prepare for death. (6 Matthew v [ ]): Sufficicent for the day is the Evill of it. You canot attend the great work you are now called to. (1, 2 Ecclesiastes) Remember thy creator in the dayes of thy youth before the evill dayes came. 3 Consider Saytn with his Tempatations will then be most [busy] with you. When his time is but short his rage will be most against you: 4 Consider death is many times [s da] before you are aware of it. (24 Matthew 37.38) As the flood did it comes suddain, so is the coming of the [s] of man. 11 Consider how comfortable it will be when we com to dye if we be prepared for death. It will be more joy and comfort than anything in the world could be: it is the day of that confirmation of the marriage between Christ and their soules. Some directions to help us in this great worke. 1 Let us often meditate

[13] In other words, they would not be ready for Christ's arrival.
[14] "K" possibly shorthand for King.

upon and let us be confirmed in faith of this that we must dy. It is a proverbiall speech as sure as death. Live in the beleife of this. This is the appointment of God. It is appointed for all men once to dye and you may be assured of it. All flesh shall turn to dust againe:

(5 Genesis 24) We read of those that do not dye of Enoch. It is sayde God tooke him, that is translated him that he did not see death, and so Elijah. So there are some that shall not see death as those that are alive when Christ comes. (1 Corinthians 15.1) All shall not sleep but they shall be changed. There change is equivalent to death. Let not this make us doubt in the great article of fayth. It remaynes a truth all men are under the leave of mortality. (30 Job 23) I know the wilt bring me to death the house of all living. (49 Psalm 11) 3 Things that should confirm us in the faith of this. 1 The consideration of sin. Remember you are a siner and be assured the soule that sins must dye. 2 The consideration of the Examples we dayly see: There is the house of mourning with us. You se man dyeth and goeth to his [lay] home. 3 The beginnings of death that are upon men while they live should persuade us that man must dye. Sickness, weakness, they are the beginnings of death. (1 Corinthians 15:3) 1 The apostle sayth I dye dayly: (103 Psalm 14) Consider our own frame and remember you are but dust. 2 Doe not looke on death as being afar off but looke upon it as neer to you. Doe not put away the evill day far from you that will not keep it farr from you. Do not defer your preparation. Till tomorow you know not what a day may bring forth. Be confirmed in the belief of this truth that there is a life to come. Tho: death a separation of parts yet it is not an anhiolation of either part, but be assured there is another state of life. (1 Corinthians 15:32) Consider death it doth not end your being. It is the end of man. It doth separate soule and body yet it doth not anhiolat soule or body. 2 The soule immediately after death is Judged of God. It is brought to God's Tribuniall. 3 The soule must continue in that state to which it is sentanced till the resurection of the body. 4 At the day of Judgment the soule and body shall continue united forever. 4 Let us labour to get our hearts [weaned] from the world. 1 And consider your chief good is not in this life. 2 All injoyments in this life are under the same law of Imortality with [themselves]. 3 The more their hearts are set upon the things of this life the more sorow you will have in parting with it: 4 The use and end of all these Injoyments under the sun they are only for our lives. (2 Ecclesiastes 18) You canot carry them out of the world with you. 5 They that make the world their end their end will be destruction. (3 Philippians 19) 5 Labour to be sure of the death

of sin. Labour after the mortification of it. Looke to it that you dye to sin before you dye for sin. 6 Make sure of an Interest in Christ or else you canot be prepard for death. 7 See that there be a principle of life in you. 8 Ever keep a godly conscience. If you would dye in peace, exercise you selfe therein in having a conscience towards God and towards men. (2 Corinthians 1:12) 9: Live in the exercise of grace. You must have oyle in your lamps and they must be burning. 10 Be ever diligent in your worke before that when ever death finds you it.[15]

[15] This sermon is incomplete.

CHAPTER NINE

ORDINATION

Among this chapter's important ordination sermons is a short series from Isaac Foster based on the Gospel of Matthew, chapter 18, verse 3. The New Geneva Study Bible frames the Gospel of Matthew within the context of the other Synoptic Gospels of Mark and Luke, and states that together with John, "they offer Jesus Christ, the incarnate Word, to all generations."[1] *Indeed, the significance of the Word to the Puritans has been discussed at length in this book, but the New Geneva Study Bible offers another interesting interpretation in its comparison of Matthew's five principle discourses, and the way in which they compare to the Old Testament books of Moses. The relationship of the Old and New Testaments was critical to the Puritans since they based so much of their mission to New England on New Testament fulfillment of Old Testament covenant principles and prophecy. The July 11 Sabbath is another occurrence in the notebook where two different ministers preached on the same day.*

Mr. Woodbridg. (Sunday) July 11:1680. (8 John 34) *"Jesus answered them, Verely, verily I say unto you, that whosoever committeth sinne, is the servant of sinne."*[2] And Jesus answered them verily I say unto you who so Ever committeth sin is the servant of sin. In the 30 verse you have an account given of some success the word had. Tho: Christ spent much of his labour in vayn yea he had som success. Many believed [in] him. He Exorts them to continue in his word. He Encourages them. Then you shall be my disciples Indead. There be som do believe in Christ that are not disciples indeed. 2 Another encouragement Christ givest them. You shall know the truth and the truth shall make you free. Som stomacked the word of Christ. What are we such slaves that we had need of the word to make us free? In the text Christ explains his meaning. Though you are not literally slaves, yet you that comit sin you are in a state of bondage and slavery.

---

[1] *New Geneva Study Bible*, 1503.

[2] *The Geneva Bible, 1560 Edition*. 47.

Doctrine: siners are in bondage under the power of sin. Where sin is committed there ariseth a power in sin and slavery to it. (2 Peter 2:19) They themselves are the servants of corruption for of whome a person is overcome he is brought into bondage. What is that power sin hath over the soule? 1 A power to hold siners that they shall not return. 2 To set them on work sin holds those that are transgressors and keeps them from returning to God and from coming in to Christ's kingdom of liberty and peace. A siner is held fast that he canot return. They are in the Bond of iniquity. They are held with cords of (5 Proverbs 22) sin. Sin holds sin by its wisdom. When conversion is proposed sin doth present and object against and dasheth such motions. 2 By its will the siner is held In sin till God turns the [stream] of the will Godward and Christward. Thus [m s] when all objections was Answer send by whom you wilt send, his will was not gaynd. The siner is held 2 by being Imployd in the acting of sin and in the doeing of wickedness. The motions of sin (7 Romans 5) worke in the heart to make it comitt sin. Sin is always breaking forth into the soule. The wickedness of men's hearts were great and Evill and onely Evill and that continually. (7 Proverbs 21) The strong woman with her flattering lips overcome her. Sin doth over com the siner to comit great sin against their own resolutions and purposes. Sin drives them on. I will hedg up their way with [thornes] and she shall follow after her Lovers whence this doth arise. 1 From the law of God. The strength of sin is the holy and righteous law of God. The law is the strength of sin as it curseth and condemneth the siner to be out of the [service] and favour of God and to ly under the power and pollution of sin. 2 The power of sin ariseth from this that all the faculties are under the command of sin. Sin hath the possession of Every strong hold. The mind is dead and under the power of sin. The will is the fountain of corruption and the conscience is dead, so that there is nothing can begin a good work in the soule. He canot deliver the soule nor can he say there is a ly in my right hand. 3 The strength of sin ariseth in that sin has the possession of the wholl soule and of all the Faculties of man are full of Evill. 4 Sin rules and governes in the soule by love and that is the greatest and strongest rule. Sin rules as Husband in the soule hence sin is sweet to the soule. It is a sweet bit to the soule. There is power aded to sin. There is strength in sin from the world, the credit of the world and profits of the world. The world [promiseth] to the siner and if he forsakes the world there is the [frow] of the world and the example of others. They doe [so they] do strengthen sin. The siner by sin doth increase the power of sin [ag] a [custom] in sin strengthens sin.

Use 1: Hence, siners canot save themselves. They are servants, they canot doe as they like. They canot do it. If they would, Christ would not be needed. Siners unless God looke upon them and help them that they perish not or els they will assuredly perish. God will see you as a drowning man, struggling to be freed before he will deliver you.

2 Use: We see the great miserie of siners to be under the power of sin. It is hard worke it is a hard taske and burthen that lyes upon the soule. Sin makes a man to labour and Toyle but it is to destroy themselves. Thou art wearyd in the greatness of thy ways. Sin doth give but poore supports. Ephraim feeds upon ashes. (44 Isaiah) [listen] the East [wind]. Sin is a bitter enemy to the soule. It watcheth to bring him into ever lasting destruction, and the wages of sin is death. Oh that the siner might be awakened.

3 Use: of Exortation. Learn we to try. When we are under the power of sin doe we ly under it or are we layd by the power of the spirit of God? The stillness, the quietness of sin is not the deth of sin. If the power of sin be broken in [this] soule then there is a strugling in thy soule against sin. [Thou] beleiver is a continuall strength against sin. 2 Be exorted to get from the power of sin, we all ought to be shaking off the power of sin. We are under the bondage of sin both by [pride] and power. If the son shall you make free then you shall be free Indeed. 2 Cry out unto God to save and deliver: So Paule, oh wretched man whoe shall deliver us. (22 Deuteronomy 31) He is able to save: 3 Seeke we reconciliation unto God and get your sins forgiven to you in the blood of Christ. He shall turn to us have mercy upon us and subdue our iniquities. Sin shall not have dominion. You are not under the law but grace. You must mourn for sin past and then you will be able to put away future sin.

Foster's July eleventh offering is mainly concerned with the Puritan's day to day struggle against the power of sin and the vital importance of a daily renewal of conversion.

Mr. Foster. (Sunday) July 11, 1680. (18 Matthew 3) "*And said, Verely I say unto you, except ye be converted, & become as little children, ye shal not enter into the kingdome of heaven.*"[3] And said verily I say unto you unless you be converted and become as little children you shall not enter into the kingdom of heaven. [ ] [ ] who was greatest Christ tells them except they becom less they shall not com [ ] not as children

[3] *The Geneva Bible, 1560 Edition.* 11.

in ignorance, but in respect of malice and inocens and humility be as children. They must becom converted. But they were converted before, but you must be converted from your pride and ambition and be made humble. You cannot enter into the kingdom of Christ. That is the kingdom of glory.

Doctrine: that conversion must be renewed by them that are all ready converted or els they canot enter into the kingdom of heaven. (3 Acts 19) Repent that your sins may be blotted out as the time of refreshing. Conversion is a worke we must always be doeing. It is not finished at once. We must goe forward and continue in it. They that are converted had need be converted again & againe.[4] [(22 Luke 31) Peter] When thou art converted strengthan thy bretheren. That is when [you] art converted from that sin then strengthen and C. They that are converted must turn from sin mor and more and turn to God more (8 Romans 13) and more. 1 What is conversion? 2 When is conversion to be renewed?

3 The Reason 4 [their] Use. [ ] What is conversion hereby is meant the great worke of repentance, a siner's unfained repentance for sin and turning to God. Hence they are put together, repent and be converted. Then siners shall be brought to repentance and to turn from the evill of their way. A siner is goeing in a wrong way. By conversion he turns in to the right way the siner doth turn from. 1 From sin. Every True converts turn from sin, Satan, selfe & the world. 1 From sin (26 Jeremiah 3 verse) If they will turn from the evil of the their ways. They must turn from sin in heart and affection and in life and conversation. He turns from sin. 2 In conversion there is a turning from Saytn. (26 Acts 8) To open their eyes and to turn them from the power of Saytn to God, From the kingdom of Sathen to the kingdom of God. (2 Ephesians) In conversion there is a turning from Saytn, from the power of Saytn. 3 In conversion there is a turning from the world, from the lusts of the world and from the injoyments of the world from all, from all Inordinate love and affection to the world. The world is crucified to him and he to the world. 4 He is turned from his good that he doth not love him self more than God, but can deny himself: [part] with himself. There is a naturall selfe, sinfull selfe, and righteous selfe. He turns from them all. He hath no confidence in his owne righteous-

[4] Conversion renewal was extremely important in Puritan theology. It was never enough to simply be saved or converted. Daily existence was a continuous process of regeneration and renewal.

ness. 2 In conversion there is a Terme to which he is turned and that is God in Christ Jesus. He doth not turn from one sin to another but from sin he turns to God by unfayed lov, unfained faith, and sincere obedience. 2 When is conversion to be renewed? Answer 1. Every day. It is every dayes worke. We should turn to God every day, but Especially upon our apostacy or falling in to sin. Then we are to convert and turn to God again. (10 Ezra 1) (2 Samuel 24:10) (51 Psalm) David renewes his repentance and turning to God. 2 When we come to worship God there should be a renewal of conversion. We should then turn from sin and turn to God. (1 James 21) Then we should lay aside all superfluity of haughtiness. Would you draw night O God clens their hands and purify their hearts. (19 Exodus 10)

(6 Ecclesiastes 1) [Kep] your feet and clens your heart when you appeare before God. You must put away your sin an resolve never to com to them more. 3 A time of affliction, when God is afflicting us for sin. Then is our time to turn from sin. I have afflicted them, but they have not turned to me sayeth the lord. Sin doth cause affliction and bring it to us, but then is our duty to return from sin. God's end in bringing affliction upon us is to turn us from sin, that was the end God brought Jacob's children to affliction. This is a speciall season and that doth appear [because], by repentance the sting of affliction is removed and taken out. 2 This will support us in our affliction and comfort us this repentance of sin. Innocence is a comfort to the soule. This will be a means for the removall affliction. Sin doth cause God to send affliction. When we turn from sin God turns from affliction, so times of speciall mercy.

Use: Learn hence the sad condition of those that were never converted to enter in to the kingdom of God. If the (2 Peter 4:18) righteous shall scarcely be saved where shall the siner appear.

The Second Epistle of Paul the Apostle to the Corinthians is described by the New Geneva Study Bible as an intensely personal letter, filled with "expressions of deep emotion...it affords us an extraordinary insight into the gospel ministry as carried out by Paul. Two chief themes reveal the nature of Paul's apostolic ministry, service of divine comfort and encouragement in the midst of suffering and troubles, and God's strength manifested in human weakness."[5] *Additionally, the glory of the*

[5] *New Geneva Study Bible*, 1826.

ministry of the new covenant and the principles of Christian stewardship are important elements in Paul's letter.

The applicability of the text to Isaac Foster's most important day of ordination is not difficult to see. Paul may be the greatest apostolic minister of all, so it is likely that Foster held him in high regard. In his ordination sermon, Foster implores his congregation for their love and support in much the same way that Paul implored his listeners, but Foster makes it very clear that while his ministry is nothing without Christ's presence, so Hartford's congregation is nothing without Foster's presence, in a kind of spiritually symbiotic relationship.

Finally, second Corinthians chapter twelve deals with the problem of false apostles, and considering the difficulties surrounding the Half-Way Covenant and the Connecticut Valley's general ecclesiastical woes, Foster may have needed to establish his own authenticity to the people of Hartford.

<u>Mr. Foster Ordination. (Wednesday) July 14, 1680:</u> (2 Corinthians 12:11) *"I was a foole to boast my self: ye have compelled me: for I oght to have bene commended of you: for in nothing was I inferior unto the verie chief Apostles, thogh I be nothing."*[6] Tho: I be nothing. The conclusion of all his glory [is] that I am nothing. I am become a foole in glorying yet it is you that have compelled me. You have forced me to it. Tho I be nothing in your eyes, yet I am not less than the cheife of apostles in the cause of Christ. Christ would not be beat down by those that had Esteemed him as nothing.

Doctrine: That the best and ablest ministers of the gospell are nothing. This Paull acknowledgeth that was the cheife of the apostles. (6 Galatians 13) They that thinke them something deceive themselves. (1 Corinthians 15:10) 2 How and in what respect are they said to be nothing. 1 Negatively they are not nothing as being in [sh ts] in the hand of God by which he doth convey salvation to the soules of men. (11 Romans 14) (1 Corinthians 3:5) They are not to be despised and slighted as if they were nothing. 2 Affirmative. They are said to be nothing in respect of God. Nothing compard with God and nothing without God. 1 Their being and preservation is of God. They depend upon God for that only they depend upon God for all. (1 Colossians 17) By him all things consist for [ ] pleasure, they are and were created. 2 All ministeriall qualification they are given them of God. Without

---

[6] *The Geneva Bible, 1560 Edition*. 87.

them they are nothing and these gifts are given unto them by God. The spirit God is the author of those gifts that are given to them by the [ch] of God. These ministeriall gifts are Natural ability of learning and grace. 3 That continuall supply of grace is given to us of God. (15 John 1) Without me you can do nothing. (2 Chronicles 32:31) 4 That power and authority which they have as ministers to act [these] gifts is of God. (4 Colossians 17) There is a call of God by man but receive their authority of Christ. 5 All the success that they have in their laboure and worke it is of the lord. (1 Corinthians 3.6.7) (1 John 13) 6 Their acceptance in their worke and reward God gives them is all of free grace. (17 Luke 10 verse)

Use: Hence, lern the [h b] pride and foley is in the hearts of men in regard of that oppinion they have themselves. They thinke themselves to be somebodys wheras they are nothing. 2 Learn the best of men have still need of grace. 3 Learn not to trust man for he is nothing. (15 Job 21) (6 Job 21) 4 Learn the wonderfull grace of God that he hath any regard to man. 4 Lern the power of God that he is pleased and able to such improve [such nothing] to see good purpose in this world by those that are nothing. 6 Lern to acknowledge God in all that is don by man.

2 Exortation: to thos called to Christ imployed in that work labor after more of Paul's spirit when we have don all see nothing. 2 In the sence of [you own] be nothing. Seeke to God to enable you to you [ ] God. (2 Corinthians 3) But be nothing in your self and see your sufficiency in God. 3 Be Exorted to give unto the glory of God all the good you have don. 4 Admire God's grace for calling such nothing within the worke of the ministry. 5 Emprove that grace you have received from God for God the worke of the ministry let not the grace of God be in it. 6 Be Exorted to looke to God for his blessing upon you in your labors. 7 Be not discouraged but incouraged in your worke tho you are nothing. 2 The [ch s] and people of God to whom they are sent be Exorted not to Idolize in their ministry for they are nothing. 2 Be exorted not to dispise your ministers tho they are nothing of themselves yet they are something by Christ. (1 Corinthians 4:1) They are the ministers of Christ. 1 Be Exorted to love them. It is a duty you ow them. 2 Honor them. They are to be honored and esteemed in lov for their worke sake, that is their due. 3 Give maintenance. 4 They are nothing without grace. Pray for grace for them. 5 Obey them. 6 Stand by and assist them.

3 Exortation. to this [ch]: 1 Let not the nothingness of that instrument you have called to this worke cause you too neglect your duty to him. Let my weakness and Fayling quicken your prayers to God for me to strengthen me in that worke. Doe not cease to pray for me, the benefit will be your owne.[7]

Mr. Woodbridge was present at the ordination of Isaac Foster because the practice of imposing hands was part of the ordination rite (see note 13, page 28), and it is appropriate that Woodbridge selected Second Timothy as his opening text since Timothy was Paul's young protégé. The New Geneva Study Bible points to a number of different themes in second Timothy including: the nature and function of scripture, the faithfulness of Christ, salvation by grace, and election. Second Timothy was Paul's last letter, and his ministry was on the decline. Most of his friends had left him, and the outlook was quite grim, but Paul remained confident because he knew that he had been faithful to Christ.[8]

Mr. Woodbridge. (Wednesday) July 14, 1680: (2 Timothy 3:1) *"This knowe also, that in the last days shal come perilous times."*[9] This know also, in the last dayes perilous times shall com.

Doctrine: that it is a truth, gospel days will prove difficult dayes to the ministers of Jesus Christ and they ought to be warned of it. The last dayes (1 Timothy 4) are Infamous days (2 John 3:18) 1 From [wence] these difficulties arise. 1 There are 3 things the apostle grounds as the Reson of this. 1 From the erors and falls oppinions of men. 2 From prophaness, wickedness in practice. 3 From malaty among professors. Wherein will ministers meet with difficulty? Answer. In their whole worke. 1 In speaking the word in the [publi ly] the times will com wherein men will not bear sound doctrin. 2 In private speaking of the word. [2] Difficulties lyes in admission to sacraments, Especially to the lord's supper. 3 Is difficult in disspensing of sensures. 4 Difficulties in his conversation. 3 The Reason [why] the ministers in gospell dayes times are so difficult to [e]. The Reason is from the abuse [ ] [ ] face, abuse of divine light and love.

---

[7] Foster concludes his ordination sermon by directly imploring the congregation to support him. This is one of the best sermons in the Hartford Sermon Notebook in terms of hearing the ministers voice, where we can almost feel Foster's presence.

[8] *New Geneva Study Bible*, 1917.

[9] *The Geneva Bible, 1560 Edition*. 100.

Use 1: It confuts the oppinion of those that are enemies to the ministers, that they lead to easy lives.[10] 2 Hence observe that the worke of the minister doth not only [a ma] godliness to guide, lead, and Feed them it is to easy an life. 3 Hence ministers should prepare for difficulties in their place. 4 Ministers should be wise to heale, prevent the difficulties they meet with in their places. 1 Ministers should in the first place get the presence of Jesus Christ with them. 2 Ministers should get and Exercise wisdom to prevent difficulties that they may meet with in their places. 3 Ministers should have and show philanthropy to man. It is a love to man made in the image of God. Pitty to him in his fallen state and care to him In respect of help by Jesus Christ. 4 The dispensation of the word ought to be with all faythfullness. (58 Isaiah 1) The gift of utterance is a speciall gift. 5 There should be strictness in discipline. Negligence [in] it is that as will cutt of and keep out sin. 6 Beware [where] of arbitrary government in the church, that is that will breed division in the churches. It will let in profaners, confustion and destruction at last.[11]

Use: Every [ch] should see they make their minister's worke and place as easy to them as may be: remember faythfull minister meet with discouragements from within. How shall we carry ourselves? Be converted and thrive in grace. 2 You should love and honor the servants of Jesus Christ. Esteem them and love them. If you despise your ministers they will doe you no good. 3 Due recompence them for their labours. Be not deceived. God is not mocked. 4 Submit to their government and management of things in humility and meekness. 5 Submit to private reproofs. Doe not let thy spirit riss against.

---

[10] It is not difficult to imagine a sentiment of hostility towards the life of a minister if we imagine the difficulties of the labor-intensive life experienced by most colonial New Englanders. For laymen, day-to-day life was physically demanding, whereas the town minister seemingly lived a life of ease. Of course, demands on the minister's time were quite numerous, from births and deaths, preparing sermons, dealing with discontented church members, and the latter especially considering the nature of church schisms in the Connecticut Valley during the time of the *Hartford Sermon Notebook*. Even though ministers may not have lived a life of physical toil, they clearly had a busy existence. For discussions of a minister's duties see: David D. Hall, *The Faithful Shepherd: A History of the New England Ministry in the Seventeenth Century* (Cambridge Massachusetts: Harvard University Press for Harvard Theological Studies, 2006). See also: Alice Morse Earle *The Sabbath in Puritan New England*. New York: Charles Scribner's Sons, 1891.

[11] "Arbitrary government in the church", "division in the church", these passages are probably the work of Benjamin Woodbridge.

Foster's July 18 sermon is his greatest exhortation for conversion, and in it he uses the word conversion 51 times.[12] *I consider Foster's pattern of word usage to be a kind of verbal literary device that he employs throughout the notebook. Another excellent example can be found in his September 12, 1680 sermon in which he directly refers to Satan or the Devil 49 times. Clearly, this was a conscious style Foster employed to impart the focus of his sermon into the congregation's mind. It is critical to bear in mind that oral delivery gives the sermon its power and not written text.*

Mr. Foster. (Sunday) July 18, 1680. (18 Matthew 3) And said unless you be converted and becom as little children and [c].

Doctrine: that they that are converted must be converted again or they cannot enter into the kingdom of God. What is a season of renewall of conversion? When God bestowes any speciall [n r s] or favoure upon us. When God doth turn to us we should turn to God. (11 Isaiah 8) When God's repentings are kindled to us, our repentings should be kindled towards God: The love and kindness of God should turn us from sin and Sayten to God. The kindness and love of God to us should breake our hearts for sin (1 [ron] 22.18.19) and kindle love in our hearts to God. God expects that when he hath wrought good for us that we should turn to God. The love of God should draw us to God. 2 When we seek to God for any special mercy we should then renew our conversion and return to God in [t] seperat between your God and you and sin keeps off good things from you. This hath been the practice of the [ch] and people of God in all ages. 6 When God is in

[12] The importance of conversion and regeneration in Puritan theology is one of the concepts explored here. The words conversion and regeneration appear multiple times in 11 of the sermons, and individually in nearly all of them, so it was clearly an important subject to Hartford's ministers and their congregations. The principle scholars used in my analysis all devote considerable attention to the subject, especially Perry Miller, Edmund Morgan, Charles E. Hambrick-Stowe, Harry Stout, and David Hall. Many essays include discussions of conversion and regeneration. The following list is not exhaustive, but includes essays that have helped shape my understanding of the importance of conversion to New England's Puritans: Francis T. Butts, "The Myth of Perry Miller." *The American Historical Review* 87, no. 3 (June 1982), 665–694; Charles L. Cohen, "The Post Puritan Paradigm of Early American Religious History." *The William and Mary Quarterly*, 3rd ser., 54, no. 4 (October 1997), 695–722; E. Brooks Holifield, "Peace, Conflict, and Ritual in Puritan Congregations." *Journal of Interdisciplinary History* 23, no. 3 (Winter 1993), 551–570; David M. Robinson, "The Cultural Dynamics of American Puritanism." *American Literary History* 6, no. 4 (Winter 1994), 738–755; David E. Stannard, "Death and Dying in Puritan New England." *The American Historical Review* 78, no. 5 (December 1973), 1305–1330, and Michael P. Winship, "Were There any Puritans in New England?" *The New England Quarterly* 74, no. 1 (March 2001), 118–138.

a speciall [maner] striveing with us we should renew our repentings and turnings to God. The times of ignorance God [win th] (14 Hosea 1.6) When God stands at the door and knocks we should turn to God and let God in. [ ] When we renew our covenant with God there is a speciall time of renewal conversion. Then we should turn more from sin and turn more to God.[13]

Reason 1. Conversion is to be renewed. It is taken from the reminders of sin that are in the best of men after they are converted. Sin doth remain in the best converts and there fore there is need of conversion. Sin dwelles in them and remaynes in them to this day. If we say we have no sin we deceive ourselves and the truth of God is not in us. Sin doth remaine after the first conversion therefore there must be a second.

2 Reason: Is taken from the weakness and Imperfection of grace in new converts and there fore they must yet be turned to God tho: they love Christ yet they should love him more. Though they are holy yet they should labour to be more holy.

3 Reason: Is taken from the many sad falls of true converts into many greate sins. There is sin in the hearts and in their lives and conversations. This is so because God doth leave them to themselves. Themselves they fall into sin and so need convertion againe. In the matters of the Embasador God left Hezikiah, God suffers Saytn to overcome true converts and to perswad them to sin. Saytn stird up David's to number the people. 3 It is from the alurements of the world that they are [many] [times] from God to sin so that they must be converted again. Soloman fell into many gross sins. (7 Ecclesiastes 26) (51 Psalm) David falls into sin and renews his repentance so Hezikiah it is sayd of himselfe that he humbled them [ ] for the pride of their hearts.

4 Reason: Because [mel t] thing can enter in to the kingdom of God can [c y]. (21 Revelations 7): There shall in [e f] [t r ay] thing that [defileth] or [h th] a [l e].

Use: Lern we the sad condition of those that never were converted at all. If the righteous shall scarcily be saved where shall the ungodly appeare?

2 Use: Hence lern the Erors of those that do assert perfecsion in this life. If we had perfectly turnd from sin we need not turn from it againe. (3 Philippians 12.13) There is a Two fold perfection, 1 of parts, 2 of degrees in parts, and so every true convert is perfect in the whole man.

[13] This sermon is an exhortation to conversion, as well as the renewal of conversion.

The whole man and every part of it is satisfyed. I pray God satisfy you in body and spirit throughout.[14] There is perfection in respect of the seed of all grace that God gives unto the soules. All is infused into one. 2 There is perfection allso as to degrees and so there is non all perfect in this life there is something lacking to love to [fear] to every grace. There is want of growth in grace. There is no perfection in this life. (1 John 3:2) Beloved now we are the [sons][15] of God, but it doth not yet appear what we shall be. 3 Hence lern we ground of unspeakeable comfort to every true convert that doth renew their conversion. You shall enter into the kingdom of God. It is yours. (5 Matthew 8) 4 Hence learn the foly and Eror of those that doe flatter themselves with hopes they shall enter into the kingdom of heaven though they doe not turn from sin, but follow their own wayes. (119 Psalm 155) Salvation is far from the wicked. They seeke not thy statutes. 5 Hence learn that those that are true converts should not be [to] secure. Rest not in what you have don: 6 Hence see the difficulty to get into the kingdom of heaven. A man must be converted first. A man must becom a new man. He must be turned from darkness to light, from the kingdom of Saytn to God. This conversion must be renewed dayly. 7 Hence it is of great concernment for Every one to looke to this that he be converted and that he renew his conversion dayly, For without this you will loose the kingdom of heaven.

2 Use: Is of Examination and tryall. When we are converted and [whether] we have renewed this worke of conversion ye or no: 1 Have you laid a sight of sin? Every true convert that hath been brought to turn from sin hath seen the evill of it. Have you been convinced of the evill of sin? Conviction goeth before conversion. 2 Have you had a sight of your absolute need of Jesus Christ and in the sence of that need have you lookt after Jesus Christ? The spirit convinceth the world of sin and reighteousness. 3 Are you made like God? (8 Romans 29) They that are converted they are Transformed into the image of God. In knowledge, holiness, and righteousness. 4 Doe you delight in the obedience to the will of God as formerly you did to sin and Saythen? Do you delight to do the will of God? (40 Psalm 8) I delight to doe they will oh God. (84 Psalm 1) 5 Have you new affection and aymes and ends in all your wayes and action where your conversion is. All

---

[14] Another instance of Foster's use of the first person in his preaching.

[15] "sons" in King James Bible, 294, and Geneva Bible, 112.

things that are old are past away all things are become new. 6 Doe you grow in grace. If you are a True convert you have encreased with the Increasing of God and doe grow in grace.[16] (1 Peter 2:2) You may try when you are converted, doe you make progress in your obedience? 7 Are you as little children? Is there a spirit of a child in you that you have no malice nor envy in your heart? Have you the humility of a child? (131 Psalm 1.2) 8 Is your conversion generall, are you turned from [all] and every sin? They that love any [one] sin have parted with no sin. 9 Doe you persevere and continue against all sin? 10 Doe you love those that are converted? (1 John 3:14)

3 Use Exortation: 1 To those that are not converted the exortation is to you. Be converted that your sins may be blotted out at the time of Refreshing from the presence of the Lord. Labour that this great chang be wrought in your heart. By motive consider what you are exorted to turn from. If it were any good thing it were difficult, but it is sin, the greatest Evill, the only Evill, the greatest Evill to your [w le] and happiness. 2 Consider what you are exorted to and that is to turn unto God. The fountayne of all good the fountayn of liveing watters. All [the] springs were in him. (32 Deuteronomy 6) Doe you thus requit the lord oh foolish people and unwise. Turn unto God that is the [father] of the [fatherless] that is the God of your lives and the length of your days, that hath power to destroy you and power to show you mercy. 3 Consider the benefit you are made partakers, hereby you have heaven and happiness and all good. 4 Without this your condition is most miserable your sin is not blotted out and that is to have the wrath of God kindled against you. 5 Consider how long you have remayned in an unconverted state. Let that quicken and awaken you to loose no more time:[17] (30 Jeremiah 20) 6 Consider how ready and willing God is to Embrace poore repenting siners. (15 Luke 20) Poore siners are a great way off, yet God is looking upon them: 7 Doe not live in an unconverted state. God hath given you the means of conversion.

[16] Hypocrisy was a grave concern of the Puritans, as revealed by Edmund Morgan in *Visible Saints.* "In England and Holland, anyone who wished to join a Separatist church could qualify himself to do so by actions that lay within his own power. In New England, membership required an experience that was beyond the power of a man to attain by his own efforts. Hypocrites might dissemble it and the New Englanders were the first to admit that their churches contained hypocrites…But they held it a duty to exclude from the church everyone who failed to persuade them in speech or writing that he possessed saving grace." Morgan, *Visible Saints*, 93.

[17] Another plea for the urgency of conversion.

(24 Ezekiel 13) 8 Consider the danger of neglecting deferring this great worke. There is danger in 5 respects. 1 God may take away your life and what will become of you. 2 God may take away the means of grace from you. 3 God may deny his spirit to strive and accompany his word for that good. 4 The longer you defer this worke the Harder and more difficult it will be. 5 If ever you be converted after ward yet it will be a matter of greife as long as you live that you were not converted no sooner. 2 Those that are converted be Exorted to renew you conversion and turn from sin to God more and more. 1 For motive the renewal of your conversion it will renew your peace. 2 It will make the ordinances of God more profitable to you. Wash your hand in [inocens] and so com before. 3 You will hereby have that greater assurance of your entering into the kingdom of heaven and for help to go forward in this conversion. 1 Renew the meditation and the consideration of your sin. Oft thinke of your heart and of your wayes and turn your feet into the way of God's testimonies. 2 Watch against all Temptations to sin. 3 Have a care of evill companions that will draw to sin. 4 [Wayth] upon God in His ordinances. (19 Psalm 7) The word of God is perfect, it converts the soule. 5 Convers with those that are true converts, be a companion of all that fear God. 6 Be much in selfe Examination. 7 In the sence of your own unability to be converted look to God to convert you. Looke to God for converting grace.

CHAPTER TEN

A VISITOR FROM THE BAY

Chapter 10 is similar to chapter 4 in its absence of a sermon series, and this chapter also contains the only sermon by Thomas Cheever of Malden, Massachusetts. His sermon is particularly interesting since it contains a large number of the terms explored in this book. With the exception of Caleb Watson's opening text from First Samuel, all other opening texts in chapter 9 have been previously discussed.

Foster's July 25 sermon sounds a bit like a sales pitch, where Foster seems to be selling himself to the congregation. An important question then becomes whether or not Hartford's church was experiencing conflict between the brethren and Foster. Was Foster experiencing rejection, or was he simply preaching the next text on his list. Harry Stout confirms that New England ministers often planned out an entire years worth of sermons in advance, but this may not explain Foster's apparent need to clarify his function and purpose to his congregation.

Mr. Foster: (Sunday) 25 July, 1680: (2 Timothy 4:1.2) *"I charge thee therefore before God, & before the Lord Jesus Christ, which shal judge the quicke and dead at his appearing, and in his kingdome," "Preache the worde: be instant, in season and out of season: improve, rebuke, exhorte with all long suffering and doctrine."*[1] I charg the before God and Jesus Christ. These words contain the solemn charg that he gives Timothy: before his departure to be faythfull in the worke of the lord there is 1 the solemnity of this charge, 2 the duty or worke preach the word in season and [c] I charg the for God's sake and Christ sake that thou be faythfull, or I call God to witness that I solemly charge the, or as you will Answer it unto God and Jesus Christ at the great day, to preach the word in this solem charge. 4 Things are implyd. 1 It is a matter of great weight and of absolute necessity that a minister be faythfull in his place. The Honor of God and welfare of people is concerned in it. 2 It implys that the best and ablest ministers of the gospell are in great danger of being negligent in their work or els Timothy would not have

[1] *The Geneva Bible, 1560 Edition*. 100.

had such a charg Except it be your need. 3 It implys the fearfull judgment of God that will befall all unfaythfull ministers. Every minister must give account and as the worke is waighty so the punishment will be fearfull to those that are unfaythfull in it. Knowing the Teror of the lord we perswad men. (1 Corinthians 9:16) 4 It implies the gracious reward that the lord Jesus Christ at his coming will give to those that are faythfull at that day. 2 Heer is the duty containd in the charge set down in the second verse. 1 More largly to preach the word: This tho [ ] be the whole yet it is a principle part of their work and duty, and it may include the whole, because in all his administrations the word is his rule, and this is amplyfyed by the maner of the performance. It be instant, be constant, and it must be with all long suffering the maner, reprove, rebuke, exort, and teach. The maner of the performance of this duty it must be instant and that implies earnestness and diligence. There must be zeale and affection in it. Labour and paines must be used in it. 2 It must be in season and out of season constant. Improve all seasons. He must preach the word in season, a fitt time or oppertunety. The word may be sayd to be preacht in season, 1 in respect of the time. The Sabboth is a fitt time to preach the word. It is satisfied for that end. So weeke dayes that are by man appoynted for this worke is in season. 2 The word is sayd to be in season in respect of the hearers, when they are prepared to receive the word. When there is a doer open for to receive the word. [ ] Isrell was prepared (8 Nehemiah 1) to heare the word, they desired to heare it, and they were attentive in hearing. 3 The word may be sayd to be in season in respect of the subject matter that is preached. When it is a word fitly spoken and suitable to the occasion of hearers. (25 Proverbs 11) Words fitly spoken are like aples of gold. The word is to be preacht upon the Saboth, upon week dayes, and when people are willing to heare, and it must be fit to the time and season. 2 The word must be preached out of season also, that is in respect of man's carnall reason, and not out of God's institution. The word of God may be out of season to carnall reason, 1 in regard of the time. (24 Acts 25) Thus Paule preacht the word to Paule out of season to Felix. Go thy way, when it is a fit season I will call for thee. 2 It may be out of season in the oppinion of men in regard of the subject handled. Some doe not love to hear such dutys prased and such Doctrine handled. Herod loved to hear John preach but not that he should have his bro: Philip's wife: 3 It may be out of season in regard of mans not being prepared for the word of God. Their unpreparedness should not hinder ministers in duty. 4 Ministers should preach the word out of season tho: they hazard their lives and all by preaching of the word of God. 3 It must be with all long suffering. That implies meaknes, patience, and long tarrying. (2 Peter 2:24) The minister of the word must not strive but be patient. 2 The severall parts of this duty set down reprove a minister of the word. In preaching of the word he must reprove it is profitable for this end, and the word is [convince]. The word must convince the Eronious and [cons te] the Eror. 2 Rebuke. And this hath respect to coruptions in maners. Those that are vicious in life must be rebuked.

3 Exortation: Some render this word comfort if it be understood to Exort it is to all [people/creatures] dutys and graces that they may shine in their lives and conversations. If we render it comfort then all that are weake and infirm, the word of God is to be improved for their comfort. 4 Teach. Men must be Instructed from the word of God after the principles of the [Christian] faith.

Doctrine: that it is the most solemn charg that the lord Jesus Christ gives to all that he calls to and [Imploys] in the ministery of the word that they do preach and apply the word with all diligence and long suffering. This is the solemn charge that Jesus Christ doth call them too. (6 Acts 4) [Whereas] we will give ourselves continualy to the ministry of the word and prayer. (1 Corinthians 117) There must be diligence in preaching the word. They must take paynes herein and labour. They are called labourers in Christ's harvest. (1 Timothy 5:17) They must doe it with dilligence and with Long suffering, making applycation of it to the hearts and consciences of men. (1 Corinthians 14:3)

Reason 1 is taken from the perfection of the word of God. It is a pure holy word, a convincing a comforting a powerfull a profitable word, there fore preach the word.

2 Reason is taken from the account every minister must give to Christ. 1 What is it to preach the word? It signifyes to publish and make known the will of God and the duty of man from the word. In the preaching of the word there is necessary Two things. First, the Explication of the word, it must be rightly Expounded and divided. This is one maine part of the worke of the minister of the gospel, it is of greater use to expound the word than to rays Doctrinall notions from it. (8 Nehemiah 6) He gave them the sence and meaning of the word.[2] (24 Luke 27.32) So Christ opened the word to them that in

[2] Beyond Perry Miller's exhaustive treatment of the "Plain Style" in The New England Mind, Vol. 1, there are a number of good sources that describe the mechanics and purpose of this mode of preaching. See Mary Morrisey's excellent analysis in "Scripture, Style and Persuasion in Seventeenth-Century English Theories of

preaching of the word there is the faythfull application to be made of to the hearts and consciences of men. (4 Luke 7) Thus Christ did and the text reprove, rebuke, Exort and this is to be done by the lawfull ministers of the word. It was Timothy's work and not every [creature/person/Christian's] worke.

Now for the Reason 2 Is taken from the account every minister must give to Jesus Christ of his ministry when Christ shall com in glory to Judg the world. Every man must be judged. (1 Corinthians 5:10) Therefore Every one should be faythfull in their duty because they must all give account to God. (13 Hebrews 17) They watch for their soules as those that must give an account. The ministers of the gospell they are but stewards of the ministry of Christ and they must give account. 1 They must give account of their gifts and parts God hath bestowed upon them for the worke of the ministry. (1 Corinthians 12.7) 4 There are diversity of gifts but the [s] spirit. They must give account how they [h sed] and improved them. 2 They must give an account of their time and seasons of preaching of the word. They must give account of the soules of hearers. (13 Hebrews 13)[3] They watch for their soules as those that must give account that is for their soules, that if they perish through their negligence they must give account for it. (33 Ezekiel 7) His blood will I require at thy hand if you give not warning. By being faythfull they save themselves and their hearers, but unfaythfullness destroys both.

3 Reason is from the great Interest of Jesus Christ in his [ch] and from the great price that he hath payed for your redemption. (20 Acts 8)[4] They are his church he hath purchased them with his own blood,

---

Preaching." *The Journal of Ecclesiastical History* 53, no. 4 (October 2002) in which she quotes the influential English Reformer William Perkins: "So the words that the preacher delivers are not plain and powerful because they are the voice of God unmediated by the preacher, but because they show the preacher's attempt to interpret and explain the truths contained in Scripture in a way that all hearers can understand and that most powerfully demonstrates his conviction of that truth" 4. See also Morrisey's "Interdisciplinarity and the Study of Early Modern Sermons." *The Historical Journal* 42, no. 4 (December 1999), 1111–1123; and Alfred Habegger, "Preparing the Soul for Christ: The Contrasting Sermon Forms of John Cotton and Thomas Hooker." *American Literature* 41, no. 3 (November 1969), 342–354. See also Lisa M. Gordis, *Opening Scripture: Bible Reading and Interpretive Authority in Puritan New England.* (Chicago: The University of Chicago Press, 2003).

[3] (13 Hebrews 17) in King James Bible, 280.

[4] (20 Acts 28) King James Bible, 177.

therefore feed the flock over which that [ ][5] hath made the overseer. (5 Ephesians 25) He satisfys them by his word. (21 John 15)

4 Reason is taken from the great concernment that their faythfullness and diligence hath to the soules of men. The life of the soule doth depend upon this, and the Eternall concerns of the soule. It is of great concernment to his own soule that he be faythfull. (43 Ezekiel 7) (1 Timothy 4:6) They doe hazard their own soules by their unfaythfullness. 2 It is of concernment to those that hear them. Their unfaythfullness and slowness in their workes doth prejudice the soules of men.

5 Reason is taken from the great good that is conveyed to and conferred upon men by the ministry of the word. The greatest good comes thereby. Siners are thereby converted and that is a great worke. (26 Acts 16) To open their eyes to turn them from darkness to light, from the power of faith to God. Conviction of sin and conversion from sin is by the ministry of the word. Faith comes by hearing and we are born again by the word of God. (Corinthians 2.14) It is by the ministry of the word that siners are turned to God. Grace and glory is conveyd by the ministry of the word, and where there is no [vision] the people perish. 2 The ministry of the word is for the perfecting of the [saints]. It is the seed by which we are born and the milke by which are nourished. (20 Acts 22)[6] I [command][7] you to God who is able to build you up.

6 Reason ministers should be diligent because of the many Erors, and [ifis], and fals teachers that shall rise up in the [ch] and among the people of God.

7 Reason is taken from the departure of the faythfull ministers of Jesus Christ. They are gon and goeing, therefore those that succeed them they should be faythfull.

8 Reason from the great glory is brought to God thereby, and the great reward every faythfull minister shall have of God. I have Finished my course, I have fought the good fight,[8] hence forth is layed up for me a crown of glory.

Use 1: Learn hence that a faythfull preacher is a great blessing to his people. God reckons it as a great blessing that God raysd up prophets

---

[5] Holy Ghost in King James Bible, 177, and Geneva Bible, 65.

[6] (20 Acts 32) King James Bible, 177.

[7] King James Bible, 177.

[8] Fight the good fight is from (1 Timothy 6:12): "Fight the good fight of faith: laye holde of eternal life, whereunto thou art also called, & hast professed a good profesio before many witnesses." Geneva Bible, 99.

and [n ts] and a great curss when it is threatened that the sun should set upon their prophets. 2 Hence learn it is the great duty and the interest of a people to pray for their ministers that they may be such. 3 It is a duty of people to submit to their reproves. 4 Learn hence that the office of a minister is paynfull and difficult: 5 Be Exorted then to hear the word of God in season and out of season, and to accept of reproves and rebukes when they are administered to us by the ministers of word to persuade here unto. 1 This hath been the practice of the servants of God in all ages. 7 Consider these are ordinary wayes and meanes whereby God workes grace in the soule. 3 Consider the gaine you will receive thereby God will comand the blessing then for direction com with an awfull dread of the [make] of God when you com to heare the word of God. 2 See that your hearts be prepared when you com to hear the word of God. 3 Receive the word with faith and love com Hungering for it. Pray for God's blessing on it and practice it in your lives.

Mr. Wattson. (Sunday) August 15, 1680: (119 Psalm 71) *"It is good for me that I have been afflicted, that I maie learne thy statutes."*[9] It is good for me that I have been afflicted that I might learn they statuts. This psalm was pened by David in his Excile. In the text the psalmist declares the good he got by his afflictions. The [position] layd down, it is good for me I have been afflicted. (42 Psalm 2) All thy [wa s] and [Billowes] goe over me. 2 Ther is the reson in forcing the conclusion that I might learn they statutes. David was a good scholer in the schole of affliction. When we gaine that lesson God would teach us by afflictions then we are blessed. When we are taught out of God's law by them then they are for our good.

Doctrine: That satisfied afflictions are for spirituall good, profit, and advantage for God's people. It is good sayeth David for me that I have been afflicted. Times of afflictions usualy are our best times. God doth afflict his people to doe them good and not hurt: (8 Romans 28) We know that all things shall work together for the good of them that feare the. Then all outward afflictions, Inward [desertions] worke for that good. God doth afflict his people for their proffit.

1 Example: How are afflictions for God's people for their profit? Answer: In themselves they are grevious Evill, part of the curs due unto sin. Hence, they are not to be desired nor prayed for, for though

---

[9] *The Geneva Bible, 1560 Edition.* 262.

they be evill in themselves, yet by God they are adored for their good and spirituall advantage. 1 Satisfyed afflictions are fruits of God's love. As many as I love I rebuke. God doth not afflict his people because he hates them, but because he loves them. (3 Proverbs 12) God showes his love to his children by afflictions, whome he loves he chastens. (89 Psalm 32.33 verse) 1 Read it. No surer signe of God's reprobateing anger than letting his people alone in sin. 2 Afflictions they are for the good of God's people because they bring more of the gracious presence and blessing of God with them in to our soules, to bless and keep, guid and direct, save and deliver, to satisfy and too sweeten our afflictions. If the [ch] be all in a fire the angell of the covenant will be in the midst of it, and it shall not be consumed.[10] God is never nearer his people than when they are under firy tryalls. If Joseph be cast in to prison God will be with him there. IF David walke thro the valley of the shadow of death God will be with him with his rod and staff to comfort. If you have more of afflicitions you shall have more of God's presence with you. 3 Satisfyed afflictions are for good to God's people because they do seale up instruction to their soules. They doe teach and instruct them. A schoole of afflictions is a schole of instruction. (74 Psalm) That which doth seale up afflictions is for the good of God's people. It is an evill and bitter thing that we are departed from God. It teacheth God's people to fear him, stand in aw of him, to Fly unto the lord for help. God doth teach them to obey him by their afflictions. (94 Psalm 12) Blessed is the man whom you chasten and teacheth out of thy law. 4: Afflictions worke for the good of God's people because they worke out their sin. By this the iniquity of Jacob shall be purged and their sin taken away. The people of God loose nothing by the furnace of affliction, but what they can well spare. The best of God's people have their sin about them and therefore need afflictions to purify them by. Afflicitions satisfied doth break our hearts from and for sin. Satisfyed afflictions they doe open and inlighten our understandings to see the evill of sin. When Joseph's Brothers wer in distress then they saw the evill of selling of their Brother. (36 Job 9.10) 2 Satisfyed afflictions they bring us to a free ingenious hearty confession of sin with the great-

[10] The *Valley of Discord* by Paul Lucas is a good place to begin an exploration of the church strife of the Connecticut River Valley in the seventeenth century. There are many references in the *Hartford Sermon Notebook* that can be attributed to the contention between Presbyterians and Congregationalists, as well as backlash from the Half-Way Covenant.

est detestation. Thy hand lay heavily upon me day and night. I sayd I would confess my sin and thou forgavest my iniquity. (10 Judges 10) Then they cryed unto God and sayed we have sined against thee in that we have forsaken the lord and served Balan. 3 Satisfyed afflictions they command us to depart from iniquity. Afflictions they open men's Eares unto discipline and command us to depart from iniquity. 4 God afflicts his people that so he may humble them and make them low in their own Eyes and that is for their good. (2 Hosea 6) Afflictions are compared to thorns, they are to prick the [bladders] and let out corruptions. Afflictions when they humble us they doe us good, for God's doth dwell with the humble. Christ Jesus delights in an humble soule. 6 God afflicts his people to take [after] their hearts [affe d s] from the word and the things thereof, and that they might be set upon heavenly things. God doth take away our comforts that we may not set our hearts upon them, that so we may love and live more upon Jesus Christ. The God of all our comforts and Injoyments [on] the streams faith we should goe to the fountayn and lay [fast] [hand] upon Jesus Christ. 7 Afflictions are for the good of God's people because they doe exercise and increase grace. They doe draw [ ] forth in a godly man. The wise as well as Foolish virgins they all sleap, but God by afflictions doth awaken, quicken, and draw forth their graces in to worke that they may not be idle.

(2 Habakkuk 4) The just live by faith. They doe increas grace. They blow up the graces of God's afflictions into a flame. (5 Romans 3.4) 8 Afflictions worke for the good of God's people because they worke for them a far more eternall [wayte] (2 Corinthians 4:17) of glory.

Use 1: It shows what cause the people of God hav to bless God for satisfyed affliction Because they bring with them certificates of God's love and are signes of God's favoure. (7 Job 17.18) Job calls afflictions God's magnifying of men. [People/Christians/Creatures] should not pore to much upon the evill of afflictions, but upon the good of it. [12 Hebrews 11] 2 It is a sad word to those that get no good by afflictions, that remayne impenatent under afflictions, and are not bettered thereby returned to God. (4 Amos 9.10) May not God [complayne] of us and of them, yet you have not returned to me sayth the Lord. (5 Jeremiah 3) Doe not som grow worss by their afflictions like what in the time of their distress he yet sind more and more against the Lord. (1 Isaiah 5)

God hath Two furnaces, of affliction and hellfire. If the first doe not purg the last will consume us.[11]

Preaching on the same day as Caleb Watson, this sermon is John Whiting's offering on the role of the minister, and again one wonders why the role and function of the minister needed so much explanation. Additionally, what was Caleb Watson's role as schoolmaster in Hartford regarding John Whiting's Second Church? Did Watson function as schoolmaster for both congregations?

<u>(Sunday) August 15, 1680: Mr. Whitting.</u> (14 Acts 22) *"Confirming the disciples hearts, & exhorting them to continue in the faith, affirming that we must through many afflictions entre into the kingdome of God."*[12] Confirming the soules of the [disciples] and Exorting them to continue in the faith, and that we must through many Tribulation Enter the kingdom of God. In the booke we have a record of the acts of the apostles. In generall and of Paule and Peter in perticular. We have Paul's Journey by imediat call of God. (13 [Cap.] 1.2) The Imediat preparation for their worke verse 3 their success in the work and their return where in we have the places where they went.

(14 [Cap.] 1.2) 2 The work they did in their return wattered what they planted. In their return they gave the [ch] an account of what they did. In the text we are informed how they did with those they had carryd the gospel, gave them holy counsell wherein we have 1 their confirming the disciple, those that they had brought to believe in the lord. It was their soules were confirmed.

1 Doctrine: The lord hath a true care of disciples. Minister's work is about men's soules. 3 [hei] have need of confirmation.

Doctrine: is the lord hath a great care of his true disciples. He looks after them that they be supplyd. Who are these true disciples? 1 They are those that [doe] learn and are the disciples of Jesus Christ. You read of the disciples of John and of Moses and of false teachers and of Christ. Those disciples are so in profession name or show only and of those there be many that do looke at the sayings of Christ to be hard things. Christ [ ] will not go down with them. They leave Christ will

[11] This language is very powerful and must have had a dramatic impact on the congregation.

[12] *The Geneva Bible, 1560 Edition.* 62.

Follow him no longer. Such believers of Christ will not believe them, but 2 then are disciples in sincerity and truth that are disciples indead, realy and truly so, and they ar such as have so learned Christ or are taught by him to beleive him in earnest. 1 The lord Jesus himself he is their teacher, they are taught by him. (6 John 4.5) They shall all be taught of God. God teacheth inwardly by his spirit. God teacheth not onely the eares, the head, but the heart allso: If God be your teacher then you shall be taught to purposs ministers may teach in vayn. It is too no purposs unless God teach by and with them. (2 Corinthians 10:4.5) The weapons of our warfare are not carnall but mighty thro God to cast down strongholds of sin. 2 How they are taught the matter of it is to believe in and obey Jesus Christ. They deserve not the name of a disciple of Christ that have not learnd those Two lessons to believe and obey. (18 Acts 27) Fayth complexly taken is the first saving lesson that God teacheth the soules of men. They shall all be taught of God, Everyone that hath heard and learnd of the father that comes to [men]. Hence those that have not true faith they are not taught of Christ. (10 Matthew 24): You yourselves are taught of God to love one another. Faith and obedience are the true markes of Christ's disciples. Now the maner how they are taught it is to believe and obey Jesus Christ in good Earnestness. (9 Luke 6.7) Many disciples will follow Christ as long as it [b es] well with them, but true disciples have not so learned Christ. 2 [Why] is it that Christ hath such a regard to true disciples? 1 It is from their neer relation to Christ, they are his Friends. I say unto you my friends, Abram was cald the friend of God. All the sincere obedient are Christ's friends. You are my friends if you doe all that I command you. 2 It is from the dear love Christ bears to them. They are his own by the father's gift. All that the Father gives [to] shall com to me. They are Christ's own by purchases. You are bought with a price. They are his purchassed possession, his own by their consent they are made willing in the day of his power [ ] and thus his own and so he loves them and that to the end. Jesus Christ is a friend that loves at all times. What shall separate us from the love of Christ? Christ loves his people at all times in sickness as in health. In reproach he loves them as well as when they are praysed. He loves them never the worss for that the world hates them. They ly neer Jesus Christ. His heart they have a deep interest there.

Use 1: hence Let us all be counseld and exorted to see that we be found and to prove ourselves the true Disciples of Jesus Christ, to be so indeed is rare. That we may not mistake here take the text. (16 Matthew 34)

As we would approve ourselves to be the disciples of Jesus Christ. Let us deny ourselves and take up our cross and follow Christ. It is the worke of a disciple to deny himself. There is a three fold self. 1 Sinfull self is always to be absoulutely denyed. (7 Romans 18) In me remaynes no good thing. There is an ey of grace in every godly man that is to be nourished and an ey of sin that is to be denied. The grace of God hath appeared to all men to teach them to deny all ungodlyness and wordly Lusts. All maner of sin is to be denyd by us. We should give sin a flat denyall. The old man is an impudent begger. Let sin make its profesers. It is allways to be refused. By faith Moses denyd to be calld the son of [th ro s][13] daughter. 2 Religious selfe is to be denyed as to any dependence thereon for Justification in the sight of God. (10 Romans 3.4) They that have no better clothing to appeare before God in than their own [sp] righteousnesse, they canot will not be accepted of God. All our righteousnesse is as Filthy rags. 3 Lawfull selfe is to be denyd as it stands in competition with the will and command of God. Thus Christ If it be possible let this cup pass yet not my will, but thy will bee done. (14 Luke 26) The best of our injoyments they must be forsaken For Christ. Are you ready to forsake all to follow the lambe? [ ] The worke of a disciple is to take up his cross, his own crosse not another's. Where it be a suffering from God or for God how shall a man know it is my crosse? When God lays affliction before a man that he canot [shift] without sin that is yi cross. He must take it up. There is a submission from and freeness of spirit that is to be acted in it. They should bid the cross welcome that looke for salvation by a crucafyed Christ. 3 The work of a disciple is to follow Christ, 1 to Imatate his example. It is Christ onely that without exception is to be followed. It is the work of the scholer to write after his master's coppy. Following Christ may be taken for conforming to his will. (1 John 3.13) A carefull constant [clea ing] to and falling in with the will of God is the guise of a disciple of Christ.

In this sermon from Thomas Cheever of Malden, Massachusetts, the main theme is regeneration, which Cheever defines. He also discusses the role of the ministry. In the wake of Boston's Reforming Synods, New England's ministers, lead by Increase Mather, were attempting

[13] The Pharoes.

to reestablish their dominance over the spiritual declension populace.[14] *What does Cheever's presence in Hartford suggest about New England's ministry in the waning years of the seventeenth century? Perhaps nothing. Foster and Cheever were classmates at Harvard, so he may have simply been visiting as a friend. Alternatively, perhaps he was sent by the powerful ministers of the Bay Colony, especially Mather, who was probably curious about the state of church politics in the Connecticut River Valley.*

(Sunday) August 22, 1680. Mr. [Chevers] [Mauldin] (3 John 3) *"Jesus answered, and said unto him, Verely, verily I say unto thee, except a man be borne againe, he can not se the kingdome of God."*[15] Except a man be born agn he canot see the kingdom of God. The scripture may be called evagelicke prophet: In this [cap] 2 parts. 1 A discourss between Jesus Christ and Nicodemas. 2 John's profession of [ ] and his Doctrine: The text is Christ's setting Nicodemas a lesson to learn that great fundamentall article of regeneration. There is a strong affirmation Except a man be born agn. It is universall. 2 The thing affirmed is regeneration. A man must be new made not mended. Sin hath so spoyled the house that repareing will not doe. 2 There is the confirmation of that affirmation. Verily I say unto thee the author Jesus Christ the God of truth, he it is that doth affirm without regeneration there is no salvation. It is a supernaturall worke. [ ] things must be don away and all becom New. (34 Psalm 12), (27 Psalm 14) Without regeneration there is no Enjoying God. By the kingdom of God is meant the kingdom of grace and kingdom of glory.

Doctrine 1: The lord Jesus Christ is willing to teach all those that com to him to be instructed in the things of the kingdom of heaven.

2 Doctrine: that a man my be [o] and very knowing in externall things and yet ignorant of the soule matters.

---

[14] According to the historian David M. Robinson in his review of the work of the historian Stephen Foster, Increase Mather was America's "first master politician." In the reforming Synods was Mather's "program for revitalization, ideologically expressed in the jeremiad's call for a return to abandoned first principles... The Reforming Synod of 1679–80, engineered by Mather, ratified covenant renewal as New England's principal weapon against any besetting cultural evils and thus reestablished the church and its ministers as the fundamental unit of cultural identity and social cohesion." "The Cultural Dynamics of American Puritanism." *American Literary History* 6, no. 4 (Winter 1994), 744.

[15] *The Geneva Bible, 1560 Edition*. 44.

3 Doctrine: regeneration and salvation by Jesus Christ is the great article that the teachers of God's people ought to be teaching and Instructing their hearers dayly in.[16]

Doctrine: that with out regeneration there is no man or woman shall obtayn salvation. (18 Matthew 3) Without you be converted you shall in no ways Enter in to the kingdom of heaven. They are kept through fayth to salvation. Be you what you will, Except born agn you shall not enter the kingdom of heaven. Regeneration is absolutly necessy to the Inheriting of Eternall life.

1 Example: What is regeneration? It is a worke of God's spirit whereby out of his good will and pleasure, for his own glory and salvation of his Elect, doth renew the whole man after the image of God. The Efficient cause is God's good spirit. It is the over shadowing of the [h.g.] that is the cause of it. Regeneration is cald a worke of creation created (2 Corinthians 5.17) anew. Nothing but an almighty [ar e] can doe it. It is the power of God that must rayse up the soule from the grave of sin. It is a worke of the spirit of God. The gospel is the power of God through faith unto salvation. (2 Acts 32) When we were dead in sins hath he quickened us. 2 We have the [moveing] cause and that is the good will and pleasure of God by grace are ye saved. (9 Romans 16) It is not in Him that willeth or runeth but in God that shews mercy. (11 Matthew 25.26) 2 [Ver] So Father Doctrine it is thy good will and pleasure. God hath mercy on whome he will and whome he will he hardens. By grace are you saved that of your self. It is the gift of God. Regeneration is the worke of God. (11 Acts 18) (2 Timothy 2:25) [3] The instrumentall cause of this worke is the ministry of the word. It [pleased] God by the foolishness of preaching to save those that shall believe. God doth [ ] ty himself to [means], but God bindes us to the use of meanes and the ordinary means is the word. By his own will hath he begot us with the word of truth. The ministry is the power of God to those that doe believe. 4 The finall cause is the glory of God and the salvation of the Elect: (47 Isaiah) These people have I Formed For my self. They shall show forth thy prayse. The saints, the regenerate, shall prays God and bless God. They are sayed to be to the prays of the glory of his grace thro the beloved and it is that the Elect may receive

[16] Cheever seems to be telling the congregation what they should be learning from their minister. While the nature of Cheever's presence in Hartford might never be certain, he may simply have been there to support the new ministry of an old classmate.

Eternall salvation. 5 The subject of the worke is the whole man. Every part, every faculty of the soule, [member] of the body is renewed. The apostle prays that God would justify them throughout, soule body and spirit. (2 Corinthians 5.17) He that is in Christ all old things are done away and all is become new. The whole man must be changed. 1 The understanding must be renewed that men may see and understand in what case they are that they may see what need they stand in of Christ. (1 Corinthians 2:14) The naturall man understands not the things of God. The body and soule are not destroyed but renewed. God gives new light to the darke understandings of men. 2 The heart is renewed and made new. The old heart must be changed or els it will bring men to the place of the old serpent. The heart of stone must be taken away and a heart of Flesh given them. They are not so as they were before. 3 The conscience is allso renewed in this worke, (20 Proverbs) and when this worke is wrought, conscience doth then discharge his duty and men are at peace with it. They comply and obey the dictates of their conscience. 4 The will is allso renewed by this worke. Men's wills are set upon their own destruction. Men are not made willing. They shall be so in the day of God's [power]. God doth not force man's wills but he workes sweetly and powerfully upon their wills. If the saints had power of their will they would be as perfect here as they shall be in heaven. (73 Psalm 25 verse) (63 Psalm 1) [ ] Man's memory is renewed that retaynes the knowledge of God and the things of God so the members of the body ar renewed. His [feet] run the ways of God's commands. All members they are imployed for God's service and glory. The time of this [w] God. Regeneration is a specificall chang from nature to grace. [Sntification] is a growing of grace in the soule till grace shall be perfected in glory.[17] [L] the pattern in which this image is renewed and that pattern is the image of God. (45 Psalm 13) 2 Without this regeneration there can be no salvation.

1 Reason: Because men must be prepared for before they shall be admitted to heaven, the vessells of [ey] are prepared unto glory. A siners eys in this world run so with the [ume] of corruption that they canot see glory.

---

[17] Cheever's definition of sanctification is interesting because it is an inward or spiritual definition, rather than an explanation of how a sanctified person appears outwardly. A Puritans outward behavior might appear sanctified, but it was the inner, spiritual sanctification that mattered.

2 Reason: Persons must be united to Christ before they can be partakers of the benifits that com by Christ. They must be marryd to Christ before they shall partake of the benefits that com by Christ.

Use 1: Information. 1 Hence we may be informed of the miserable delusion and foley of those that thinke to have salvation while they remayn in an unregenerate stat: If you thinke to get to heaven in such a state as this you must quite destroy the condition of salvation. Be not deceived. God is not mocked with such. As you sow you (1 Corinthians 6.9.10) shall reap: they that doe such things shall not enter in to the kingdom of God. (2 Thessalonians 2:11) Those that com to salvation it is thro sanctification of the spirit in beleife of the truth. For those Christ hath obtained salvation. He hath obtained freedom from the power of sin. Those who are Elected to life are predestenated to holyness. (3 Colossians 11) Christ is all and in all. What ever men may think of it God hath set his seale to it. Verily I say unto thee, Except a man be born againe he canot see the kingdom of God. Heaven is a father's house and it is onely provided for saints, and no other shall be admitted to it.[18] 2 Hence be informed of the insufficiency of severall things to give us a right and title to salvation. There are many [s d] foundations. Mere civility is no syne of salvation. (18 Luke 11) 2 A glorious profession is not sufficient to make a man happy. Profession doth becom the greatest man, Even profession of religion, but that is not enough: it is not sufficient to take the name of God into our mouth except we doe depart from iniquity. 3 Injoyment in gospell priviledges is not Enough to speake our right to heaven. Men may have great priviledges, but they doe not are not enough to give us an inheritants to heaven, for men may be exalted in priviledges that they may be cast the deeper into hell. (6 Genesis 12.4) 4 Great gifts and [p ts] doe not speake men to be regenerat: Gifts are like the moon may have som borrowed light, but

[18] There are many examples in the notebook of the exclusivity of the elect. Cheever is probably preaching to both the regenerate and the unregenerate. In *Opening Scripture*, Lisa Gordis shows how important both audiences were to the preacher: "Even in New England, where many hoped that the defiantly unregenerate would be few, ministers had to assume that their audiences would be at least in part unregenerate." It would seem likely that most ministers knew exactly who the unregenerate were outwardly; the challenge was reaching the inwardly unregenerate. For Gordis, the expertise of the minister was vital in terms of "opening scripture" for those congregants who lacked the guidance and power of the Holy Spirit, or, Christ's voice. *Opening Scripture*, 34–35.

grace hath light in itselfe.[19] 5 Externall dutys and performances are not enough to bespeake a man in a converted state (6 John 20) (Matthew 13) The stony grownd received the word with joy and yet brought forth nothing. The good opinion of godly men of you is not enough: to speake you in a converted state. (50 Psalm 13) David was deceived in a [chitoph ll] and Peter in Simon [ma us]. (8 Acts 21) The apostles were deceived in Judas. Men's own good opinion of themselves is not enough to make them happy. It is not end to bring men to heaven and happiness the light within them that leads to the dark of chambers of hell. Men must be guided by their consciences. [no far] than that is guided by the light of the word. To have som good affections in a man is not enough: to make happy. The hearers of Christ wondered at the gracious words that proceeded out of his mouth and yet were Enemies to Christ. 3 Hence be informed of the great difficulty of obtayning salvation. It is a hard and difficult worke. (1 Peter 4:18)

2 Use: examine and [try] whether you are regenerate, Yea or no: Except a man have this new birth you had better never been born: 1 All your worth depends upon this. If regenerate you are happy if not you are [undone] forever. 2 Consider God will most certainly try you by mercys or by afflictions. God looks into your hearts. He will try you and discover you, and if God doe not in this life he will certainly doe it in the day of judgment. 3 Consider it is possible to know when you are regenerate: or els God would not bid you worke out your salvation: You must be a converted from sin and 2 you must carefully [prosecute] all good. You must try it by the Effect. A new born babe desires the means of grace. 2 He groweth Every day and 3 he endeavours what in him Lyeth to convert others. Thus Abram oh that Ishmal might liv in thy sight. 3 Exort the unconverted to labor for this blessed work. Take heed to defer it least death surprise you in an unconverted state. Be

---

[19] In Bonnie Lew Strother's Ph.D. dissertation *Imagery in the Sermons of Thomas Shepard* (Shepard, and later his son Thomas Jr., were both ministers of the church in Charlestown, which was Isaac Foster's family church), she devotes a section to the imagery of the cosmos. Cheever's imagery in this passage seems very beautiful, but there is no way of knowing whether he was its originator. As Strother demonstrates in her dissertation, the stars, the moon, the sun and the planets were frequently the subject of Shepard's sermons, and based on Cheever's sermon, the heavens were likely a popular device in the imagery of Puritan sermons more generally. In addition, toward the end of the seventeenth century astronomy had become a new subject in the Harvard curriculum. See: Samuel Eliot Morison. "The Harvard School of Astronomy in the Seventeenth Century." *The New England Quarterly* 7, no. 1 (March 1934), 3–24.

persuaded to a serious consideration with yourself, what your state is. Consider of the endless miserie of the unregenerate and the happiness of the blessed ones. 2 Be persuaded to a diligent use of all the means of grace that God hath provided. Go to the pooles of [Bathesda]. Wayt upon the ministry of the word. It is by the incorruptible seed of the word that you must be begotten. Wayt upon God for this blessing. 2 You that are regenerat acknowledge this goodnes of God to you, be thankefull to God for it, and faythfull to men by praying for them, and charging them to serve the lord.[20]

John Whiting's August 29 sermon is about the glory and righteousness of being a saint, and is a kind of blueprint for Puritan theology on the concept of the visible saint.

Mr. Whiting. (Sunday) August: 29 1680: (146 Psalm 8) "*The Lord giveth sight to the blind: the Lord raileth up the croked: the Lord loveth the righteous.*"[21] The lord loveth the righteous. In this Ps, which is one of the first that begin and end with haleluyu, he prayseth to a duble duty to prayse and trusting in God, urged from the vanity of all other trusts. The best of creatures are vain. 2 The happynes of those that trust in God verse 5. The arguments taken from the power of verse 6. The faythfulnes to his word verse 7, and from his goodnes to the sons of men verse 7, 8, 9 and 10. 4 From his special care of the faythfull the Lord loves them. 5 His rath to the wicked he turns them upside down. 6 From the [sour] [ones] of God. Verse last.

Doctrine: That the lord Loveth the righteous. Jehovah loveth the righteous. Zion's God that raignes forever, he loveth him that followeth after righteousnes. 1 Whoe are the righteous that God loves? They are those that are indeed sincere converts. True, sound godly men. Those that by the power of God are brought out of the state of nature to grace. The lord knows the way of the righteous, but the godly shall [scarcely] be saved. 1 They are righteous [imputatively]. The righteousness of Jesus Christ is reckoned to and set to the account of a believing siner. (23 Jeremiah 26) It is to all intents and purposes set to the account of a believer, and is as avaylable as if they had done and sufferd themselves. Hence he is sayd to be made righteous to them. The believer is perfectly

[20] Cheever is preaching with clarity to both the converted and unconverted churchgoers. This is a style throughout the sermon notebook, initial conversion for some, conversion renewal for others.

[21] *The Geneva Bible, 1560 Edition*. 266.

righteous in Christ. It is such a righteousnes as is Equaley bestowed upon and belonging to all that doe beleive. Fayth is the only [just] and [co yance] of this righteousness, hence all the godly are sayd to be made righteous. By the obedience of one many are made righteous. 2 The righteous are allso righteous inherent, that is a righteousness imparted to and wrought in the believer. (2 Corinthians 5:17) This righteousenes is from that power that is no less than that that made the world of nothing. It is also called the new man. It is that which is exprest by the writing of the law in the heart. It is an inclination of the heart to the law of God to saints, and fall in with the law of God. Grace is predominate in the righteous. They are not siners but saints. 3 They are righteous practically, not only by a principle of grace in the heart but by the actings of that principle. He devotes himself to put the commands of God into Execution. He walketh uprightly and worketh righteousness. The law of God is his way and the will of God is his worke. Now for his conformity to the will of God they are sayed to be righteous. Noah was a righteous man and he is sayed to walk with God, hence Noah was cald a preacher of righteousness. He preacheth it in his conversation. So [Zach] and [Liz] were righteous before God. They walked in all the commands of God blamlesly. (7 Ecclesiastes 20) There is not a righteous man on Earth that doeth good and sineth not: but in heaven they are perfectly righteous and without sin. They are righteous in Christ. 2 In what love is it that God bears to the righteous? Love is put in to the [ ]. 3 [ranke] with Benevolens. God loves the saints with the love of benevolens. God wisheth well to them, wishes good to them all. The good they are capable of that is in his heart to do great things for them. Hence they are sayed to be [ordained] to Eternall life. Their names are written in the booke of life. They are sayed to be chosen and appoynted to salvation. God hath not appoynted us to wrath but to salvation by Jesus Christ. (20 Matthew 16) Fear not, it is the Father's pleasure to give you a kingdom, heaven, and happinesse. 2 The lord Loves the righteous with a love of benifisens. As he wills all good to them so he workes it all for them. God's covenant is he will surely doe them good. I will call upon God most high who performes all good for me. God is the author and the finisher of all good for his people. 3 The lord loves the righteous with the love of [compl nes] and Delight. His holy heart doth take contentment in them, in and through Jesus Christ. Jesus Christ is the only one with whome their hearts may take delight. The faythfull are the darlings of heaven the objects of divine delight. Others are objects of hatred but God takes pleasure in his people. Every godly soule may be cald [Hepzibah][22] for the lord delights in the. They may be sayed that God delights in their holy dutys, but the wicked, what Evil they doe displeases God. Whatever they doe they cannot please God and the reason is because without faith they canot please God. The sacrifice of the wicked is an abomination to God, but the prayer of the upright is his delight. ([Hab.] 1.13) Sin is [never] the [less] loathsome to God. (2 Samuel 11:8) Offer up spirituall [cer ies] acceptable to God. God delights in the prosperity of his people.

Use 1: Hence the righteous saints in Earnest are beyond [mesur] beholding to God. Love lays engagements upon the soule above all. (2 Samuel 4): The love of God to his is passing more than the love of men and angells. 1 Consider who it is that loves the righteous. The text tells you it is Jehovah. He changeth not the blessed God that is [in] and for himself without change or alteration. It is uterly impossible that any alteration should be made in him by anything that we can doe.[23] (22 Job): God doth gaine nothing by the good word or workes of men. (35 Job 6.7) As men canot hurt the lord by their sins so they canot advance him by their good dutys. 2 Consider whome he loves and that is those that in themselves considered are no less mean and merciless than any others. (113 Psalm 5) It is a selfe humbling in God to take notice of his creatures. What is man that God should magnify him, and set his heart upon him, but what then is sinfull fallen man? (42 Isaiah 24.25) This is the [astonishment] of heaven that God loves sinfull man. 3 Consider how God loves that he loves freely, abundantly. 1 Freely God loves them Freely that that [moves] them to it is in and from [H.S.] The love of God to his poore people it doth flow from [H.S.] 2 God loves the righteous abundantly. 3 He loves them always with an Everlasting love. His love is firm constant and inviolable. (32 [ephe] 13) God the father doth love the believer as he loves Jesus Christ with the same love. 2 He loves them allwayes. [Home] he loves he loves to the end.

2 Use: Doth God love the righteous? Then see the happiness of saints and the misery of siners. The saints are happy the lord loves them. They are the lord's delight. They have his heart they have his ey. (33 Psalm

[22] Hephzibah is a symbolic name for Jerusalem. It also means, "my delight is in her." *Holman Bible Dictionary*, 750.

[23] All of Hartford's ministers appear to have been interested in the idea of the immutability of God. It is a recurrent theme throughout the notebook.

18) The ey of the Lord is upon them that feare him. The Eys of the Lord are upon the righteous, but what is that God sees all men his Eyes that are upon the righteous his favoourable and pleasing. Let me see thy face for it is lovely. Hence God is sayd to looke to them, his good will is to them. He sees the lowly. They stand high in his account. God doth so looke upon the godly as to send after them. (24 Jeremiah 60) God withdraws not his Ey from the righteous. 2 They have God's Eare (34 Psalm 15) His eare is to their prayer. (2 [Cant] 14) The prayers of the godly are his delight, God is ready to heare the prayers that are made by them. We know God does not hear siners, that is, such as are in love with sin and walke in it. If I regard iniquity in my heart the Lord will not hear my prayer, but if in anyone be a worshiper of God and doth his will, God hears the Fervent prayers of the righteous. 2 God is very ready to hear prayers for the righteous. As in Abrams prayer for the righteous in Sodom God [c s] [d] from fifty to Ten. Concerning [ty] sons the workes of my hands command me. (15 John 26.27) The Father himself loves you. 3 They love the hand of God. They shall never want help as Long as he can help them. The salvation of the righteous is of the lord. How then comes it to pass that the righteous have so many afflictions? (8 Ecclesiastes 14) Where in doth God's love reveale itself? God's love runs thorow all their afflicitions. It is God's love that he doth send them in to afflictions. Whom the lord loves he sends in to afflictions. God doth love his children and therefore chastens. The wise father knows his children need [phissick] as well as food. All shall worke for their good, purg out sin, fitt them for heaven. It is in love God keeps his children in afflicition in the deep waters. God stands by so that no evill shall befall them. No evill shall happen to the righteous, they are surrounded with divine favoure. Hence is that great sign the bush is in the fire burning, but not consuming. The Bush is never so fruitfull as it is when in the fire, and it is through the good will of him that dwelt in the bush, and it is of the Lord that they are delivered out of affliction: the righteous shall com out of trouble.[24] (24 Proverbs 16) The righteous falls 7 times, but he doth rise again, but the wicked they fall into mischiefe. 2 Hence see the misery of siners. How woefull is

[24] Another recurrent theme in the notebook is the affliction of the righteous. Did the pervasiveness of this theme parallel reality in late seventeenth century Hartford? Did Hartford's people suffer with regularity, thus inspiring the minister's nearly continuous theme of affliction? If, as the Puritans believed, God afflicts because he loves, then there appears to have been a regular amount of suffering in Hartford.

the condition of the wicked. The Lord hates the wicked. God is angry with the wicked. Every day God's anger is never turned away as long as they abide wicked. (10 Job 15) If I be wicked wo to me. How many may take this woe to themselves? (27 Job 2.5.6.7) Let my Enemies be as the wicked. (3 Isaiah 10.11) Woe to the wicked. The reward of his hands shall be given to him. A saint at the lowest hath the upper ground of the wicked in all his height a little that the righteous is better than the riches of many wicked, and the reason is because what the righteous hath coms from the love of God. 3 Hence see the folly of a sinfull world. God and men can seldom agree, they hate [h m] God loves. (29 [p] 27) (23 Psalm 12) God that loves the righteous will not leave the [ ] the hands. The salvation of the righteous is of the Lord. (37 Psalm 8) God will deliver them because they put their trust in him. (36 Psalm 10) God will take his time to make the Enemies of his people to love them.

2 Use: is matter of serious inquirey in a matter of the greatest concernment that can be to inquire whether God loves ye or no. What is the good word of creatures? If God love the this is worth all. Nothing then can com [an ise] you may pass cherfuly throw the greatest tryalls doth God love the. It will not satisfy the soule without a grounded faith that God doth love. Art thou the man the woman [that] God doth love the? Is it so? How shall we know it and not be deceived of it. It is not what befalls man in the world will determine this. Present prosperity is no certain Evidence of God's love. Nor afflictions an evidence of the countrary, but this doth it. Are you righteous? God loves the righteous. Are you sound believers? Have you obtayned like precious faith? Hath God by the hand of his spirit taken hold of thy heart and drawn it to God? Hath God been at worke to make thy soule willing to forsake all sin and to fly to Jesus Christ for righteousness and salvation? True fayth is always accompanyed with love to God Jesus Christ to you that believe he is precious. Those whose hearts are cold to Christ how far are their hearts from Christ? Is Christ altogether lowly to the. Are you sicke of love to Jesus Christ? Happy you if you can make a true affirmative Answer. Is there a [fea our] of love to Christ in the. Doth the puls of they love beat hard of love to Jesus Christ? Can you as Peter thou knowest I love the thou knowest all things thou knowest I love the. Doth Jesus Christ [L e t] thy heart? He loves not Jesus Christ at all that doth not love him best of all, but dost thou love Christ go in peace. I love those that love me. 2 Doth thou love the people of God?

Hereby we know we are translated from death to life because we love the brethren. Doe you love them because they are saints, because they doe belong to Christ, because they are holy, because they doe beare the image of God on them? This love is extencive. It takes in love to all saints and the more Likeness to Christ the more love to Christ.[25] 2 The sincerely obedient are righteous are you so? Sincere obedience it is universall. A faythfull servant will Bawke none of God's commands. He is a David Endeed, a man after God's heart that doth all his will. (9 Acts 5) 2 Sincere obedience it is delightfull. The heart goeth along with the hand. The commands are not greivious to them. (7 Romans 39) They delight to doe the will of God. Thy law is within my heart. 3 Sincere obedience is constant. Fits and starts in duty are not constant. Steadynes in duty is a great matter. The hipocrit will he always call upon God? Noe their goodnes is as early clowd and the morning dew. I have Inclined my heart to keep thy statutes, Even to the End all the days of my life.

Saul's rise to power and subsequent rejection are considered the plot of First and Second Samuel, two books that the New Geneva Study Bible refers to as "masterpieces of literature."[26] The books of Samuel focus on the new concept in Israel of an earthly king. "The key issue is how a human king can be accommodated in the framework of the covenant relationship existing between God and Israel. How can Israel have a king without compromising God's kingship? It is not that Israel is never to have a human monarch, for a king has long been anticipated. What is objectionable is for the people to want a king...because this desire is a rejection of the greatest King, God himself.[27]

Caleb Watson's sermon follows the New Geneva description of First Samuel. In this sermon, Hartford's school master defines the nature of God to the congregation, and his erudition as a schoolmaster is reflected in the language of his sermons.

Mr. Watson. (Monday) November 15, 1680. (1 Samuel 2:2) "*There is none holy as the Lord: yea, there is none besides thee, & there is no God like our God.*"[28] There is none holy as the Lord neither is there any

[25] These passages represent what is perhaps the best description of the visible saint in the *Hartford Sermon Notebook*.

[26] *New Geneva Study Bible*, 374.

[27] Ibid., 375.

[28] *The Geneva Bible, 1560 Edition*. 122.

like the. Neither is there any rock like our God. Hanna begins her song with a description of the greatness of God. 1 From his incomparable holynes there is non holy as the Lord that is superlatively and transendently holy. 2 From the Incomprehensible strength of God there is no rock like our God. He is the rock of ages. A rock is a place of safety where men run and bests run for safety. The lord lives and blessed be my rock. (2 Samuel 22:47)

Doctrine: God's holynes is incomparable. God is infinitly Transcendently holy. The holiness of the creature is but impurity compared with the holynes of God. The holynes of angells is charged with folly. God is glorious in holynes. God is a [Non] such for holyness. The holy one of Isrell is a title ascribed to God in the old testament. (6 Isaiah 3) Hence it is we have that acclemation of the [scrap] [hi][29] crying holy holy holy Lord God of hosts. Thrice holy is most holy. That God is most holy appears 1 His holiness is essentiall and naturall to him and hence there is non holy so but the Lord. Essentiall holynes is God's conformity to himself. Whatever is in God is God himself. God's holynes and his nature are Two things. God is a pure act, and whatever is in God is God himself. God can as well cease to be as to cease to be holy, but holynes in the creature is an [adjunct]. A man may cease to be holy and yet not cease to be. Every atribut of God Is God. God is a holy [eifull] powerfull God. 2 God is originally holy. He is the author, the originall, the fountain of all holiness. There is no holiness to be had but from the holy one of Isrell. It must com from the father of lights whence comes every good and perfect gift. Could holy minister communicat holynes to people, or parents to their children, they should not goe to hell, but God only can doe it. 3 God's holiness is a universall attribute. It runs through all his attributes. His power is a holy power, his wisdom holy, his love holy, his anger holy, his mercy his justice his word is holy. It is pure. Converting the soule and inlightening the eys. His ordinances his sabboths they are all holy. His kingdom is a holy kingdom. His subjects are holy, his angelles are holy. His people are a holy people. So he is righteous in all his wayes and holy in all his workes. (145 Psalm 17) His frownes are holy and his smiles. He is holy in giving and in takeing. 4 The holiness of God is infinit and usearchable and thus there is non holy as God. He is holiness in the abstract. His holynes is infinite and

[29] The King James translation for what resembles two words in the notebook is the single word Seraphims. p. 770.

unsearchable. It canot be Limited, Lessened. (35 Job 6.7) God's holiness is always the same. 5 God's holynes is a most pure perfect and unmixed holynes. He is light. In him is no darkess at all. He is so pure that not the least speck can [c ance] to him [ ] a most pure act there is all light and darkness, but in the saints there is a great deal of mixture of sinfullnes and holynes. 6 God's holynes is constant and unchangeable. He is holy yesterday today and forever. It is naturall to God to be holy. It is his nature as well as his [name]. Our holynes may languish and decay but God's is not so.

Use: is there non holy as the Lord? Then it shows us how unlike the, how contrary all men are naturally to God. There is not the least sparke nor beam of holiness in any naturall man. I know in me in my flesh dwells no good thing. 1 We were made like God in holynes, but this crown is fallen from our heads. Wo unto us that we have sined. (3 Romans 10.11) We are all as [unclean] things all our best [d s]. (15 Job 14.15) Read this text again and again. How much more abominable and filthy is man that drinketh down iniquity as water? How much cause hav we with Job to say behold I am vile, and with Peter to say depart from me for I am a sinfull man? 2 It shows how hatefull and abominable men are to God. Thou art a God that hatest all the workers of iniquity. Sin is the abominable thing God's soul hates. Take heed of sin and when Tempted to it remember it is the thing God's soule hates. His pure eyes canot behold sin without detestation. There is an antipithy against sin in God. God hates us and we hate God. God's soule doth loath us and we abhore God. How unsupportable will this be if you continue in your sins against God. Without holiness the lord will follow you with all the affects of his displeasure forever. 2 It should teach us to give God the glory of his holynes in all his dispensations toward us. God is holy in all his wayes and workes. We should give God the glory of his holynes though he Answer us in Terible things in holiness and righteousness. They doe acknowledge God to be holy in all his workes that glorious Seraphims.[30] (3 Ezekiel 12) When God is departing from his people from Isrell, yet then they give God the glory of his holynes and of his justice. God is holy in deserting a sinfull people. We should give God the glory of his holynes in whatever he brings

[30] Seraphims means "the burning ones." They were winged serpents in Egyptian culture who acted as guardians. The *Holman Bible Dictionary* states "Isaiah envisioned the seraphim as agents of God who prepared him to proclaim the Lord's message to Judah." *Holman Bible Dictionary*, 1463.

upon us though it be [p f mally]. 2 In times of publique calamity, be affected with the holynes of God that doth appeare in the judgments that he doth execute in the world. 3 This should teach us to [sntify] the great and dredful name of God in all our [neere] approaches and [drawings] neer to God. Draw right to God in a holy maner. Clens your hands and purify your hearts. Lift up holy hands when you doe prays God. We should lift up our hands to God in a holy maner. God will be [satisfied] by all that come before him and among all the people will I be glorifyed and [ar held] his peace. (1 Samuel 6.19) Who is able to stand before this holy God? (93 Psalm 5) Holynes becomes his house forever. Ye shall keep my sabboths and reverence my [su t ar y].[31] 6 It shows us the reason of God's severity in punishing his own people his covenant people. A people that is [igh] him when they sin against him. God will not beare with them. (24 Joshua 19.20) The more good God hath done to such a people the more hurt will he doe to them if thy sin against him. God will punish them soarer and soarer and sorer than others. Judgements shall begin at God's house. You only have I known above all, and you will I punish (9 Daniel 12).

[31] Possibly sanctuary.

CHAPTER ELEVEN

DAYS OF JUDGMENT

The New Geneva Study Bible *states, "Proverbs is a collection of wise sayings from a number of authors... also, that Solomon's general influence upon the Book of Proverbs is considerable, and his direct authorship of much of the material need not be doubted."*[1] *The need for wisdom was crucial for New England's Puritans, especially at the end of the seventeenth century, as they sought guidance in the wake of church schisms and full-scale Indian wars. In other words, they were experiencing challenges that the Book of Proverbs may have helped them face.*

Isaac Foster's January 2 sermon is the first in his sermon series from Proverbs, and is mainly concerned with sin and confession, and their relationship to justification. Perry Miller's definition of justification is straightforward. He calls it "the first act of regeneration" and states that it is a stage in which God is fully satisfied that the criteria of his justice and law have been met; hence, the individual is absolved of their sins.[2] *Atheism reappears in this sermon, and there is an interesting segment on the nature of secret sin. Foster also emphasizes the importance of forsaking sin over simply confessing it, since the act itself is the foremost concern.*

<u>Mr. Foster: (Sunday) January 2, 1680.</u> (28 Proverbs 13) *"He that hideth his sinnes, shal not prosper: but he that confesseth, and forsaketh them, shal have mercie."*[3] He that covereth sin shall not prosper, but whoe so confesseth them and forsakes shall find mercy. Since man fell in to sin it hath been his guise to hide it. It is as naturall to men to hide sin as to confess it. Adam had no sooner sined but he thought to cover it as in (31 Job 33). Least I hide sin as Adam. Cain hid his sin by denying of it. Solomon in the text showes the great folly of man in soe doeing. That which man thinkes the way to misery is the way to mercy. The text [discovers] an Impenitent siner. He is [ ] that sins cover sin shall not prosper. A penitent siner he confesseth his sin

---

[1] The *New Geneva Study Bible*, 923.

[2] Perry Miller. *The Puritan Mind, the Seventeenth Century*, 27.

[3] *The Geneva Bible, 1560 Edition*. 276.

forsakes it. He shall prosper. An impenitent siner is one that covers it. He hides it. Covering sin Implyes pardon of sin. It is sayed to be covered when it is pardoned. (32 Psalm 1) Blessed is the man whose iniquity is forgiven and whose sin is covered because God doth put out of his sight. When we forgive sin it is covered. Charaty it doth cover a multitude of sins. Love covers all sins. How so? By forgiving of them. Forgiveness of God forgiveness of man [ ] covering. 1 Concealing of sin, hideing of it, is covering of it. There is a hideing of sin from God: not that man can doe so, but he that doth Indeavoure it doth not confess it and acknowledge it before God. 2 He that covers sin from man shall not prosper. We are not always bound absolutely to confess sin to man as we are to God. We are not bound to confess our sins to man in som cases, but in some cases we are Bound to confess it to man. 2 An impenient siner is discovered by the consequence of his [t] he shall not prosper. 3 Things implied. 1 They shall not attend that end they aime at in covering of sin. That they seeke to hide shall be discovered. Those that hide their sin God will lead them forth with the workers of iniquity. (2 Hebrews 13) At the great day of judgment all sin shall be brought forth (1 Corinthians 4:5) and discovered. (12 Luke 2) There is nothing covered but shall be revealed, and what is hid shall be made known. 2 He shall not prosper Implys God's denying of his blessing to them. A secret curss will follow those that go on in secret sins. He shall not have peace and joy and comfort on his soule. It implies a great and heavy curss upon those that doe hide their sin. He shall not only not be happy but shall not be blessed. 2 In the text there is the description of the truly penitent. He doth confess it, own and acknowledge it. He that truly confess, he doth confess the fact what is done in this or that case. (7 Joshua 19) 2 There is the confession of the fault the evill of the dead. (51 Psalm 4) Against the have I sined and done this evill. (1 Samuel 23) I have done foolishly. 3 There is the confession of the [merit] of the fact. (51 Psalm 4 verse) There is a justifying of God. 2 He doth allso forsake his sin. Bare confessing of sin is not enough to procure mercy, but we allso must forsake it. 3 He that doth thus shall have mercy and that he Implyeth forgivenes of God. He shall be forgiven (1 John 1.9) and clensed. He shall be Justified and satisfied and 2 he shall be graciously accepted of God and Entertained by Him.

Doctrine: As Ever we would prosper and have mercy of God we must confess and allso forsake sin. Must not be covered but confessed if we would Finde mercy. Our confessing is the way to God's covering and obtaining mercy of God. In the Doctrine: 1 He that covers his sin shall not prosper. We canot Expect to prosper as long as we doe hide sin, and this appears by the gracious promises to those that confess sin, (1 John [ ]) and by his threatening those that do hide sin. In (30 Isaiah 1) Wo to those that hide sin, that cover, but not with Christ's righteousness. 2 From the Examples of those that have obtained mercy in the way of confessing of sin. (32 Psalm 5) I sayed I would confess my Transgression and thou forgavest the iniquity of my sin. That is the Trespass of it against God. (15 Luke 20) The prodigal son when he confess his sin had mercy. 3 This is evident from the example of those that have hid and covered their sin, they have not prospered. 1 Looke in to the example of good men. While they have covered sin they have not prospered. (32 Psalm 3) When I kept silent my bones waxed [old]. I confest my iniquity and thou forgavest my sin. (2 Samuel 12:10.11.12) The sword shall not depart from thy [o] thou [dids] it in secret. 2 Wicked men hid sin and shall not prosper. (12 Joshua) [an] confesed not his sin. He hid his sin and was stoned. (7 Joshua 25) (50 [ekal])[4] (2 Kings 5:2) In the 20 verse you have his sin, his covering in the 25. The [p sh] verse 27 the leaprousy of [man][5] shall [c a] to the so [Annonites] and Zaphira. (8 Acts 7) They covered their sin with a Lye. The issue is they both fell down dead at the apostle's feet. Example: whoe are they that cover sin? 1 They that secretly comit sin they hide and cover it, (10 Psalm 8) that choose places and times of secrecy to comit it. (4 Job) The Ey of the adulterer wayts for the twilight. (7 Proverbs 8.9) 2 They that conceal sin after it is comitted are guilty of covering of it. 1 Those that are silent when we doe not confess it. While I kept silent my bones waxed old. When there is not an acknowledgment when called to it, or at any time when we are silent before God, and allso by denying of it we cover sin. A lye is often made a cover for sin. 1 Men cover one sin with another. (2 Kings 5:25) Thus did Cain when God askt where is thy Brother he said I know not. Am I my brother's keeper? 3 Men doe cover sin by extenuateing and leasening of it, makeing of it less than it is when the siner doth call it little. (25 Psalm 11) Pardon my iniquity for it is great. A true penitent makes his sin great. (32 Exodus 22.23. 24 verse) Some make their sin less as Aron let not the anger of the lord wax hott. I cast in the fire and lo cam out this calfe. He lessons his sin tho: it is sayed he made the

[4] Ezekial.
[5] Naaman. King James, p. 454.

calfe. 4 Sin is covered and concealed by laying the fault upon others that we are guilty of ourselves. Adam covered his sin. (Genesis 3) He lay the Blame upon the woman and God and she lays the blame upon the serpent. (1 Samuel 15:21) He charges the people with his [in] in the spareing of Amaleck. 5 Many cover sin by setting others [aw h] as instruments under them. Thus David covers his sin by sending For Uriah and by ordering Joab to place him so as that he might be slayn. 6 Many cover sin by their mayntaining of it. They will confess a fact but not [own] the fault. (5 Isaiah 20) They will call good evill and evill good. 7 Many seeke to cover sin by makeing and multiplying many vaine and frivioulous excuses and apologizes whereby they seek to take it of from themselves. 1 Som will excuse their sin by being Tempted to it. 2 The perswasion of others I did it, but I was persuaded to it inticed to it thus. Saule (1 Samuel 15:9) and Aron excused [t] because of the people they were set on mishceife. 3 Many Excuse their sins by fear. I was in great danger and was afraid: Saule I feared the people and (1 Samuel 15:24) did it. 4 The example of others is an Excuse others did so. 5 Ignorance they did not know it or 6 for a good end as Saule it was to sacrifice to God in [i] you. 2 Why do men hide and cover sin? It is from that Atheism that is within their hearts.[6] They do not beleive there is a God or that he is such a one as he is. They beleive not the omniciensy of God. 2 It is from the desperat pride in the hearts of men. They will not ly low befor God and take shame for it. 3 The feare of punishment doth make men hide sin. 4 From want of a sight of the mercy of God and the faythfulness of God in His promise they doe hide it. 5 From that naturall light that is in the heart of man that doth discover sin to be a loathsom and hatefull thing and their consciences accuseing them for it.

Use 1: It showes us the great Evill that is in sin. It is an evill that no man will own. 2 It shows the folly of those that seek to hide sin. They shall not prosper.

2 Use of Exortation: Be Exorted not to cover sin by adding of one sin to another to cover sin and, 1 know our covering of sin will not hide it. It will not hide it from man allwayes. Every thing that is had it shall be revealed. All the secret workes of darkness shall be revealed.

---

[6] In this passage, atheism should probably be taken literally, as someone who does not believe in God, rather than as a distinct belief system in Puritan New England. In fact, every instance of atheism in the *Hartford Sermon Notebook* can probably be interpreted this way.

2 It will not hid it From God at all. When we goe to hide sin then it is discovered and seen by the lord. (139 Psalm 11) (2 Hebrews 13) 2 Consider hiding of sin Is an agravation of sin. 3 You canot prosper if you hide sin. Your soules canot prosper as long as you hid the desease. 3 You canot have pardon as long as you hide it. Conscience will accuse you and condem you. As long as you hide it your own conscience will condem you and God will not pardon it as long as you doe hide it. It will not be to the horror of God. 5 Consider the gracious promise of God to those that confess sin. God will cover it. [L] It will be greatly to the glory of God if we doe confess our sin. (7 Joshua 19) Joshua to Aran give glory to the God of Isrell and confess what thou hast don. We hereby give glory of the omniciensy of God, the glory of his mercy grace and power. 2 He that doth confess his sin and forsake it shall find mercy—[7]

Mr. Foster (Saturday) January 8, 1680. (28 Proverbs 13) He that doth confess his sin and forsaketh it shall find mercy. In order to obtayning mercy there must be confession. We must confess sin. Every siner's duty is to confess sin. Confession is 3 fold 1 of faith, 2 of prays, 3 of repentance. Confession of sin is absolutely necessary. We must own ourselves guilty before God pardons. We must justify God before God will justify us. Confession of sin is to be made to God and to man so farr as the rule requires. Confession to God is absolutly at all times and for all sin, but to man it is but in som cases. God's name is dishonord, his Law Transgressed, therefore confession must be made to him. (7 [Job] 19) [My] [son] give glory to God and confess to him. This confession of sin to God must be inteligent. We must be convinced of it, know our sin. (69 Isaiah 12) As for our transgressions we know them. 2 This confession it must be voluntary free and willingly. Pharoh when the plaugs were upon him he confest his sin. (27 Matthew) Judas confest his sin when he was under Teror. Men cast away their sins as mariners do their godlynes in a storme.[8] 3 It must be affectionate confession to God of

[7] In the notebook, the terminal punctuation for this sermon consists of three prominent dashed lines, instead of a period or colon. These are called flourishes, and were used for emphasis.

[8] Isaac Foster's father was a sea captain, which might account for references to mariners and the sea, but after a thorough study of many of the best secondary sources on New England's Puritans, I quickly discovered this to be a universally employed image. Many of the books cited here contain some reference to the Puritan minister's fondness for images of the sea.

sin. There must be greife and sorow and shame For our sin. The heart and affection must be in it. (9 [Ezra] 3) The children of Iserell when they made confession to God they drew water and poured it out before the Lord. Some thinke it was a ceromony that they were washed and purified from sin. Others that they were in a lost condition or the abundance of Teares that proceeded from a broken heart. 4 This confession of sin to God must be with abhorance and loathing ourselves before God for it. (9 Daniel 7.8) Unto to us belongs shame. (42 [J])[9] I obhor my selfe in dust and ashes. 4 This confession of sin it must be in fayth in the mercy of God. It must be with fayth in Christ and hope in the mercy of God. 5 This confession of sin unto God it must be particular. A generall confession it may be sound and it may be sincere, yet we must not rest in that, but it must be particular, a confession of those things where in we have sined. (19 Psalm 12) Who can understand his Errors? Our confession of sin it must be particular. 1 In respect of the kind of sins, in that respect we ought to be particular, that thereby we may be humbled both for originall and actuall sin. (43 Isaiah 26) God requires this. Sins against the law and gospel youth ignorance sins of heart and life. 2 Our confession must be particular as to our own sin. That which is our own sin that we are more addicted to it and more over com with it. (32 Psalm) Myne iniquity have not I hid. 3 Those sins that are of a more gross and scandolos nature these ought to be confest. Thus Moses (32 Exodus 31) doth make confession of that great sin. The people have sined a great sin and [ ][10] Gods of gold. (9 Deuteronomy 8) At [h rebor] the law was given they sined against the law. (1 Samuel 12:19) We have added to all our evils the sin in asking of a king. They askt a king in rejecting of God and his government. 4 Our confession must be particular as to the aggravations of it. Great in their nature and great in their number. My sins are more than the haires of my head. They are greatly multiplied. 5 Our confession must be so particular to Every particular act of sin so that there may be no design to hide or cover any one sin. He that hides any one sin doth confess none. A confession may be sincer where every act of sin is not discovered, but it canot be sincere when any one sin is covered. No one act must be hid.

[9] (42 Job 6) King James, p. 640.
[10] "have made them" King James, p. 107.

The reason why there must be this confession of sin to God. Not because God is ignorant of it before we confess it, or because he doth not know it till we tell God of it. No, God hath an ey to see sin though we have no tongue to confess it. God is acquainted with all our follys and sin. (44 Psalm 20) (69 Psalm 5) Oh God thou knowest my foolishnes and my sins are not hid from the, but affirmatively confession of sins are to be made to God that we may give glory to God. By comiting of sin we dishonor God, but by confession we doe give glory God. (13 Jeremiah 15.16) Give glory to God before your feet doe stumble upon the Darke mountains. It is our end to give God glory. God hath the glory of all his attributes and of his holynes. Confession of sin is an acknowledgment that God is a holy God. It gives God the glory of his Justice. We doe ascribe righteousness to God. (51 Psalm 4) Against the only have I sined that thou mayst be Justified when thou speakest and righteous when thou judgest. 3 There is the glory of his patience in bearing with, and forebearing of siners appears in confession. 4 He hath the glory of His mercy in the pardon of sin when the siner confesseth. 5 The glory of His [sovranty], that he is the law giver that can punish and pardon the siner according to his pleasure.

2 Reason: is that we may be affected with it and the more humbled for it. Confession of sin to God is to humble and to abase our selves.

3 Reason: confession is to be made to God because he is the party that is firstly and principly injured by sin.

4 Reason: because he only can pardon sin, and he will only pardon it in this way of confession.

Use 1: Instruction and reproofe to [ ]. 1 It doth reprove the foley of those that do alow themselves willfully to sin. 2 It reproves the foley of those that doe seek to hide sin from God. It is a vayn thing. We [ought] to confess it. 3 It reprofes those that tho they doe not hid sin yet they doe not confess it with shame and greive for it. (3 Isaiah) They do not hide their sin, but declare it as Soddom. 4 It reproves those who instead of confessing of their sins doe justify themselves before God: (18 Luke 11) Let us be Exorted to sincere confession of our sin unto God. There is none so holy, but he hath sin to confess. God expects this and God lookes for it and God takes notice of it.

<u>(Sunday) January 16, 1680. Mr. Foster</u> (28 Proverbs 13) He that covereth his sin shall not prosper but he who confesseth and forsakes them shall find mercy. He that doth confess and forsake his sin shall find mercy.

2 Use of Exortation:[11] If we are [thus] to confess sin to God. 1 Let us learn and be Exorted to have a charitable esteem of those that confess sin and not sencure and upbraid them. They shall have mercy from God and ought to have it from us. Let him not judge him that hath confessed. God hath received him. We should rather love and Esteem such. We should receive penitent confessors of sin considering our selves, what we are and what we have been. 2 Let us labour after conviction of our sin to have a sight and sence of it. (54 Psalm10) We ought not cast our sins out of our sight, but we ought to remember them. 3 Be Exorted Everyone to make this confession of sin to God. It is indispensable necessary at all times for all siners of all sin. Give glory to God and make confession to him. Let there not be a seeking to hid sin from God, but let us confess it before God. It is a great and weighty duty Incumbent upon all. 1 Wicked men they should confess their sins unto God for you want the pardon, and without this you shall never have it. (5 Numbers 6) Are there any guilty siners before God you whose iniquity God hath not covered doe not you cover them but confess them. 2 Saints do you confess sin? The best of men fall into sin. So long as you fall into sin you should confess it and there is reason for it, for tho you have obtayned yet you need more mercy, and there fore ought to confess. There are special aggravations in the sins of the godly, and that in regard of the relation they stand in to God. Their sins are the sins of sons and daughters. Again the sins of the godly are more scandalous. Let us take up David's resolution. I said I will confess my iniquity. (38 Psalm 18) I will declare my iniquity and be sorry for my sin. (15 Job 3) For motive here: 1 Consider God knowes our sins tho we should not confess them. God hath an ey to see tho we have not tongue to confess them. It argues great folly in men to attempt that which is not possible, to keep from God what he knows already. (17 Jeremiah 9.10) The heart is deceiptfull and desperately wicked. Who can know it: but God he searcheth the heart and tryes the [reighnes]. He doth know all the sin of the heart and the life. (2 Kings 5:26) All sin is known to God and darkness doth not hid from him. 2 Consider as your sin is known to God so it shall be known to men and angels in that great day when Every work shall be brought to

[11] Here, Use: 2 follows Use: 1 from the previous week's sermon. Foster may have had to split up his sermon due to time constraints, or he simply intended to preach this sermon as a series over several weeks.

light and Every secret thing shall be brought to judgment. Some [mortal] sins goe before to Judgment and some Follow after. 3 Consider our covering of sin doth Increase sin. Sin is increased while it is not confessed. Sin doth grow upon us and therefore it is dangerous to hide sin. It is increased 1 in the strength of it. It doth grow stronger and we are under the power and dominance of it till we confess it. 2 Sin doth Increase in the guilt of it while we doe not confess it, sin is continuing and the guilt of it Increased, for not to confess sin is to ad sin to sin and that doth increase the guilt. 3 The filth of it is increased. The wound and putrifying sore of sin is increased. 4 Concealing of sin doth increase the teror of sin. As long as sin doth remayn and is not confessed we canot have peace in our consciences. 4 If we doe not confess sin now we shall be brought to confess it in the day of Judgment. Our own Tongues shall accuse us as well as our consciences condemn us. (14 Romans)[12] So then every one of us shall give an account of ourselves to God. It is better to confess sin now while God will pardon it than to confess it then, when God will condemn all those that doe confess it then. 5 Consider how gracious God is in that God requires no more of us than to confess our sins. God might as well require sattisfaction as confession, but God is gracious and requires sattisfaction by Jesus Christ. Consider while we doe conceale and cover sin we doe keep the Divills councill and we joyne with him against God whilest we cover sin. 6 If we doe confess our sin to God we shall have mercy from God. Our confession of sin to God is that we might live that we may be justified. Consider we shall be forgiven of God if we confess sin. 2 We shall be forgiven in the court of conscience that will acquit us. See the great Evill that is in sin and that should move us with loathing and detestation to confess it. [L] Consider the Excelency of this duty and the great proffits that come to us thereby, and in some respects to God himself by the performance of the duty. The glory of God and the good of man is promoated here by. God is hereby glorified. It is for our good. A great deale of good comes to us thereby. For 1: confession of sin to God doth humble the soule. It is a means to take down the pride of our hearts. The siners confessing of sin is a means to abase. 2 It is a means to affect the soule with the Evill of sin and to quicken the soule to godly sorrow. They that never did declare or confess their sin to God were never sorry for it. It doth promote contrition

[12] The text reference is 14 Romans 12 in the *1560 Geneva Bible*.

and godly sorrow for it. 3 It is a means to engage the heart against sin, to alienate our affections from it and to turn us from it. 3 This confession of sin to God will convince us of our need of mercy from God. 4 Our confession of sin will make us to price Christ who hath satisfyed for sin. 5 It will bring peace of conscience and joy in our hearts. David while he kept silent his bones were broken, but when he confest he had joy and gladness of heart. For direction to help us to confess our sin let us be much in the [meditative] of our sin that we may make confession of it to God. (9 Deuteronomy 2.8) We should keep it before us. 2 Often meditate upon the incouragements that are given us to this duty. Often meditate on the word of God. Compare our hearts with the word and that will be a means to bring us to this confession. 2 We ought to confess sin to man so far as the rule doth require. In some cases and in som sins were the word of God doth require it, and when the rule requires it. Our confession of sin to God is not right without it. That it is necessary appears from the Example of such as have confesed their sins to man as well (19 Acts 18) as to God. (5 James) It is comanded. 16 Confess your faults one to another and pray one for another that your sins may be forgiven. Paule [offerd] [ ] confess that he was a great siner, a pursecutor. This confession that is a duty is not that the papist require [a regular] confession of every secret sin that a man commits. A man is not bound[13] to confess or evill workes that are secret and hidden, but it is in case of known sin and of publique scandall or private wrong and Injury that we are bound to confess our sin to man. This confession of sin to man is Either publique or private: There is publique confession and that is in case of publique scandall and wrong where there is a disorderly walking whereby the name of God is dishonored for the honor of God and [row lings] away the reproach [pr b]: confession is to be made. 2 There ought to be a confession of sin in private to man and that is either for our own help or for the sattisfaction of others or to promote the repentance of others.[14] 1 For our own help that we may hence council and Assistance from them and that especially in 3 cases. 1 In case of trouble of conscience

[13] This passage is underlined in the notebook.

[14] The reference to papist confession is made because Foster was defining and comparing the nature and superiority of Puritan confession over that practiced by the Church of Rome. This passage directly reflects the religious sentiments that underscored the original Puritan desire to be free from the bonds of Roman / Anglican practices.

fear and doubt upon our spirits. In such case it is necessary to make confession to some minister or able friend that may counsell and pray for us. Again 2 In case of strong Temptation when a Temptation doth follow us and is to hard for us we may and ought to make confession and desire help from others. 3 In case of some Extraordinary afflicition that doth follow when we think there is some speciall sin is the cause of it we ought to confess it and to seeke help and assistance agaynst it. It ought to be a secret sin confessed to a faythfull friend <u>that is faythfull</u> to keep secret when the conscience is [unboosomed]. 2 There is for private sin confession to be made to give sattisfaction for private Injurys don according to that rule. (5 Matthew 23.24) If you remember your brother hath ought against you goe first and be reconciled to him. If the injury be private and secret there may be restitution and reparation without confession, but where the Injury is known there ought to be confession. 3 There ought to be confession to bring to repentance those that have been companions and partners with us in sin to manifest our repentance to them. There are extraordinary cases when men are bound to confess to men their sin as in Abram's case and Jonah's, but those named are ordinary cases. Now the Reason why we are to confess sin to man is because sin is the breach of that law that is for the good of man, 2 is for the Honor of God. 3 It is for the credit of the [ch] of God. 4 It is a meanes to prevent sin in others. 4 It is an evidence of the truth of confession of sin to God. 5 It gives [more] ground of charity to us and to pray to God for us.

Use: it reproves those that are guilty of publique scandal and yet doe not make confession of sin to God. That are guilty of privat wrong and make no confession of sin. 2 Be Exorted to make confession of sin to God and to man when God requires it. Doctrine: Els your confession to God is not reale. 2 Without this you canot have mercy and you canot Expect forgivenes of God. Without you doe this make your confession of sin.[15]

<u>(Sunday) January 23, [1680][16] Mr. Foster.</u> (28 Proverbs 13) He that covereth his sin shall not prosper, but who so confesseth and forsaketh

[15] In other words, in the eyes of God, not confessing sins to man prior to confessing them to God, makes the confession less valid. There could be no secrets regarding sin.

[16] The notebook's author records the year as 168, but based on the continuation of the Proverbs sermon series the year was meant to be written 1680. The zero was accidentally omitted.

shall have mercy. As ever we would prosper and have mercy we must not cover our sin, but confess and forsake them that so we may find mercy. 2 There must be not only a confession of sin but a forsakeing of it. To hide and cover sin will bring judgment, but confession alone will not procure mercy without we forsake it. We must not have Jacob's voyce and Esau's hands. Speake against sin and yet keep it that will not doe. Forsakeing of sin is an evidence of true confession of it. (1 John 1:9) There fore confession is some times spoken of alone. If we confess our sins he is just and righteous to forgive, in forsakeing of sin we doe practically speake agaynst sin. A true penitent doth not only confess but forsakes it, but an hipocrit he doth confess but not forsake. This forsakeing of sin is one part of conversion. In conversion there is the confession of the mouth the contrition of the heart and the amendment of the life.[17] The acknowledgment of it, mourning for it, and departing from it. There must be a ceasing to doe Evill and a learning to doe well. (1 Isaiah 13.14.15) There must be a laying aside all filthyness and superfluity of Naughtiness. (4 Ephesians 22) There must be a departing from sin and a new life and conversation. This is that as God calls to in the law and commands in the gospell. The lord Jesus Christ begins his ministry with this. (Matthew 4) Jesus Christ calls men to repentance and this is a principle part to forsake sin. (26 Acts 18) It was the end of the ministry to turn men from darkness to light and the great promise that are made to the siner is upon this Tearm. ([ ] Isaiah 7) God promiseth mercy and that he will abundandtly pardon, but the Tearmes are he forsake his Evill way and forsake his unrighteousness. (34 Psalm 14) Would you have many dayes and [ ] good dayes depart from Evill and doe good. (4 Daniel 20) Brake of your sins by righteousness and thy iniquitys by showing mercy. If it may be a lengthening out of that Tranquility. Every true penitent is like Ephraime. What have I to do with idolls? A true penitent sayth I have kept my selfe from my iniquity. (1 John 2:1) Those things I wright to you that you sin not. You must forsake sin in affection and conversation in heart and life he must loath it and leave it. You must forsake it in heart and affections. If I regard iniquity in my heart God will not hear my prayer. (97 Psalm) You that love the lord hate Evill. You must not delight in it. (119 Psalm

[17] This is similar to the process known as the morphology of conversion, and is discussed at length by Edmund Morgan in *Visible Saints*.

163) I hate Every false way, but thy law I love. 1 The Law binds and requires it that we forsake it in our heart, and without we forsake it in our hearts we shall never forsake it in our lives. 2

There must be a forsakeing of sin in conversation,[18] there must be a ceasing of doeing Evill, (1 John 6) a chang in the heart and in the life. Allso, there must be a walking in the law of God. There must be a full [bent] and purpose of will against sin. 2 It requires our labouring against the strength of sin to mortify and subdue it. 3 It doth allso imply a hearty greife and sorrow for sin when we doe fall into it. It implyes a cessation from the act of sin that we doe cease to doe Evill and learn to doe well. It implys an Earnest desire and [t] must endeavor to be subject to the law and will of God. This forsakeing hath these properties: 1 it must be universall where one sin is spared there is no forsaking of sin. (141 Psalm 4) Inclin not my heart to any Evill thing. Let me not eat of the daintys of the wicked. There is non so holy as to be freed from the being of sin in his heart or practice of it in his life. Yet we must be pressing forward to the marke of our high caling in God thro Jesus Christ. It is the marke of an hipocrit he spares sin and alowes himself in it. (20 Job 12.13) A godly man doth not alowe himself or spare any one sin. 2 This must be constant we must forsake sin at all times and in all [companys] what ever we doe, and with whom ever we doe convers we should for sake our sin. (39 Psalm 4) When the wicked is before us we should forsake sin. (2 Philippians 12) 3 This forsaking of sin must be with an principle of love to God to his ways and a spirit of hatred to sin and Enmity against it.

The reason we are to forsake sin, because our not forsaking of sin will be a forsaking of God. Sin and God are contrarys. We canot follow sin and serve God. They are contrarys. It is our great duty and our happynes to se God, se and injoy him. If we do not forsake sin we canot Love God. Sin is contrary to God. 2 We shall forsake God as to communion with him. We shall Forsake God as to obedience. We shall forsake God as to his Gory.

2 Reason is taken From the unprofitablnes of sin. There is no good in sin [that] we should love it. [They] are unfruitfull workes of darknes. (23 Job [26])

---

[18] Conversation is meant as one's outward behavior or appearance.

3 Reason is because sin is so contrary to our good: it is the greatest enemie to man's happynes and the only cause of our misery. It makes us fall short of God and of his glory. It hinders our communion with God. It destroys the purety and peace of the soule. It is contrary to all good.

4 Reason is from the sinfullnes of sin. The Evill that is in it. It is the greatest Evill and therefore to be forsaken. Sin is a great Evill therefore not to be committed but forsaken. There is nothing of good in it for which it should be delighted in. It is wholly and absolutey Evill. See the Evill of sin in that it is contrary to the cheifest good. It is the cause of all the Evills and worss than all other evils what so Ever. It is contrary to God man's walkeing in sin. It is called a walkeing contrary to God. It is a resisting of God, a [contempt] and despiseing of God. It is contrary to the nature of God. It doth strike at the being and Essence of God. God would not be if the siner had his will. The siner is a hater of God. He would have no God. 2 Sin is contrary to each person in the divine nature, contrary to the Father as a law giver for it is a Transgression of his law. It is contrary to Christ as a redeemer it Tramples his blood. Contrary to the spirit that is a sanctifier, contrary to all the glorious attributs of God, to his soveranty. It is rebellious so to his holynes, wisdom and goodness. 4 It is allso contrary to the workes of God. God made all things good. Sin makes them Evill. It brings a deformity to the workes of God. It is contrary to his [pr c prion] will, which is a rocke to guide the creatures to their end and happynes. 6 It is contrary to the Image and Likeness of God. (4 Ephesians 22) (3 Colossians 10) Sin doth deface and blott out this image. 7 It is contrary to God's glory. It is a despiseing of God. 2 It is the cause of all other evils. There are but 2 Evills: morall Evill and [penall] Evill. Sin is the cause of it, by all man sin cam in to the world and death by sin hath passed over all. Sin brought the flood on the old world, all Evill upon the body and soule. Temporall and Eternall Evill all is the Effect of sin. Sin is the procureing cause of all. 3 It is worss than all Evills. Sin is worth their sorrow sickness and death. 1 The Evill of affliction doth not separate from God, but sin doth. Your iniquity cause [ae] seprat between you and God. An afflicted state may [consist] with Love to God but sin canot. Afflictions quicken [ ] [ate] not affliction worke for [a r] of [ ] glory afflictions make happy [ ] sin make miserable. We may be afflicted and get not under the wrath of God, but a man canot be in sin but he must be under the

wrath of God. Afflictions are contrary to man, but sin is contray to God. God is the author of affliction but not of sin. Affliction may make us sorowfull for the [present], but it brings joy with it.[19]

Use 1: It doth teach us that it is the greatest misery to be left in sin, for God to give us over and leave us to the hardness of our hearts. (1 Romans 24) God gave them over to a reprobate [i d] to things that were not right. This is the soorest Judgment to be left to sin. Such shall not find mercy. 2 It is the greatest blessing to be delivered from sin and it is the way to all other mercys.

2 Use: It doth Exort us to this forsakeing of sin. You have been Exorted to confess it to God to men. Be Exorted to forsake it. It argues greatest obstinancy to confess sin. It is all [ ] to say I will have my sin tho I doe confess it, but let us forsake sin. 1 Get under the pride and reigne of sin and forsake it. Labor to get it mortified in you heart or you will not forsake it in your life. But how shall I know when sin doth reign in me or no? Answer: they that doe yield to Every Temptation of sin are under the power of it. 2 If there by delight and pleasure in it. If you be under a bent of will to follow after it. 3 If there be a maintaining, defending, Excuseing, and hideing of it. 4 If there be a persevering in sin. (104 Psalm 23) If we doe make [provission] for the flesh it argues our being under the power of it: 2 Let us forsake sin in our actions. Let us cease from doeing Evill and doe good. And for direction and help as every one would forsake sin be sencible of your own inability to doe it and go to God for to help you. Your sufficiency is in him, you need his grace to help you. 2 Improve the word of God hide it in your heart as ever you would have mercy of God. 3 Resist and apose the first beginning and notion of Lust in your heart and shun all occasions of sin. Walke not in the way of wicked, pass by it, have a care or your own sins that you are most adicted too and shun Temptations to that sin. Shun all appearance of Evill. He that would shun it in realty will shun the appearance of it. 4 Be exceeding watchfull and walk circumspectly. 1 The Evill of our own hearts should quicken us to watchfulness. There is a lov of sin drawing aside. 2 There is a Tempting world and Saytn that is Exciting and stiring up to sin.

---

[19] More on the "joys" of affliction. This concept in the *Hartford Sermon Notebook* could be examined in more detail. Briefly, affliction was viewed as a sign from God, and how one dealt with affliction was a measure of that person's godliness.

5 Let us Ever set the fear of God before us that we doe sin agaynst. Thinke of the majesty of God agaynst whom you sin. 2 You sin against a God whose ey is upon you and sees you. 3 Ey God's holynes. He is a God that is angry with the wicked every day. 4 He is a just God and will give to Every one according to his [deserts]. 5 He is a God of power able to punish you for sin. Non can deliver you out of his hand. 6 Looke to the Lord Jesus for strength and grace to mortify sin in you. 7 Doe you maintain in your heart the thoughts and meditations as will make you afrayed of sin and thinke of the day of Judgment when Every secret sin shall be brought to light? 2 Thinke of the vileness of sin. It deprives you of that honor God put on you, and thinke of grace and holynes that make you like God and fit for communion with Him. Thinke of Christ's sufferings and of the happynes of the saints but, 3 if we thus confess and forsake sin we shall have mercy. 1 From man and then from God.

The fifth installment from Proverbs does not depart from the theme of sin and confession, but it does present the saints counter-weight to sin, which was the mercy of God. This final installment from Proverbs is also interesting because it was preached on the same day that Foster began his short sermon series from Ephesians. It seems he completed the Proverbs series in the morning service then later that day began the series from Ephesians.

(Sunday) January 30: 1680 Mr. Foster:[20] If we confess and forsak sin we shall have mercy. Before you heard the siner's duty you doe now see his priviledg. Sin lays open to judgment but mercy will pardon the penitent siner. (18 Jeremiah 17) The judgments of God are conditionall upon our impenitency. If we repent of the evill of sin God will repent of the evill of punishment. (55 Isaiah [ ])[21] God will have mercy and abundantly pardon the penitent. God's threatenings are to provocke men to turn to God, that is God's voyce to siners. All the Temporall judgments of God upon his people are upon those Tearmes, to bring them to confess and forsake sin that they may have mercy. From whom is it that they that confess and forsake shall find

[20] Even though the notebook's author does not indicate the opening text, this is clearly #5 in Foster's Proverbs series. The notebook's final sermon from Wednesday, February 8, 1680 is the only other sermon where the notebook's author failed to write down the scriptural reference for the sermon's opening verse.

[21] Probably (55 Isaiah 7) King James, p. 816.

mercy? He shall have mercy from those whom he hath offended by sin and to whom he hath confessed sin and that is God and man. 1 He shall have mercy of man. We always need mercy of God and need mercy and forgiveness one of another. It is man's duty to show mercy to his neighbour. If he confess his sin forgive him. It is pity compassion love favour pitty charity and forgivenesse as to the wrong, Injury, and offence. There should be mercy, and the sword of justice is not so sharp against the penitent as against the obstinate. 2 Such shall have mercy allso from God. We need mercy of God allways. Every penitent shall have mercy of God. God will be just in showing of mercy. God's mercy is greatest and we stand in most [need] of it and we shall be happy if we have it. It is as delightfull and more delightfull to God to pardon a penitent than to punish an impenitent siner. What is implied in this phrase of having mercy of God? Answer: The word doth noat pitty and compassion and Tender affection, that of a mother to a child, and intends all the good and the deliverance from all Evill. God will have mercy, that is, God will not punish, he will not cut off for sin, but deliver from that punishment that sin hath deferred. God delivers from Temporall judgments and from hell allso: as you may see. (2 Chronicles 7:14) I will heal your land and deliver from locusts and famine. 2 It implys pardon of sin. God will not Impute sin to them. They shall be pronounced righteous, they shall be Justifyed accepted as if they had never sined. Pardoning mercy is Especially here Intended. God will have mercy and abundantly pardon. 3 It doth imply allso the communication of all good, Temporall spiritual and Eternall. All good is called mercy and it is an Effect of this Favour love pitty and compassion of God. The Reason why such and only such as confess and forsake sin shall have mercy it is from the mercifull nature of God. God is a mercifull a gracious God and therefore we have mercy from God. 2 This is for the honor of God to show mercy to penitent siners. He that confesseth gives glory to God. It is God's glory to pardon such siners.

3 Reason is from the gracious promise of God. God hath given his word and promise he will pardon such and therefor he is just to doe it.

4 Reason is from the [mediation] and intercession of the Lord Jesus Christ. He hath made a way to mercy without wrong to justice.

5 Reason is that the people of God may be Encouraged for to trust and hope in God. It is for the Incouragement of saints and siners to confess to God with the there is forgiveness that thou mayst be feared.

6 Reason it is that the Justice of God may be more conspicuous to Impenitent siners and that they may be in Excuseable.

Use: this teacheth us that there is great incouragement for every siner to confess and forsake sin. He shall be sure of mercy. 2 Hence learn where we have obtayned mercy of God, the Tryall is have we confest [ ] and forsake. 3 It showes the misery of impenitent siners. They shall have no mercy. 4 We se the reason why there are so many without mercy they do not confess sin. 5 Sin is the cause of misery.

Use: Exortation to those that have made confession of sin and obtained mercy of God unto you. 1 Be Exceeding thankefull to God For this mercy. It is mercy you have confest sin. It is mercy your sins are forgiven you. Admire at God's wonderfull mercy your sins are forgiven you. Admire at God's wonderfull mercy to you. 1 God that shows you mercy did not show mercy to angells. 2 You hav had mercy when the greatest part of mankind have not had. 3 You have mercy tho: your sins have been Exceeding great.

(1 Corinthians 6:1) 4 After you have despised mercy God hath showed you mercy. 2 Doe not return to those sins you have confessed and forsaken. 3 Be exorted to continue in confessing and forsakeing it. [It is] a worke you are still to doe as long as you live. This will be an evidence of your sincerity if you persevere in it. 4 Be Exorted to walke as those that hav (2 Peter 2:1) been pardond and received mercy of God. 5 Be Exorted to show mercy to others. Be kind and Tender hearted, forgiving one another as God for Christ's sake hath forgiven you. (109 Psalm 15.16) It lays you open to cursing not to show mercy. 2 You that yet live in sin and never hav confest and forsaked sin be convinced of your sin and misery. You are Lyable to the curss. 2 There is no other way but this to find mercy but by confession and forsaking. 3 Be Exorted to take this cours to confess and forsake sin. Se God is ready to show mercy to Every penitent. 2 Consider God's mercy is free, Everlasting, and with him there is plenty of mercy. 3 Without mercy you are Exposed to Eternall misery. 4 The offers of mercy will not last allwayes.[22]

[22] Many sermons in the Hartford Sermon Notebook are built around the concept that time is running out for the unconverted, that they must waste no time in converting before it is too late.

CHAPTER TWELVE

CIRCUMSPECTION

Chapter 12 consists of two Isaac Foster sermons taken from Paul's letter to the Ephesians. The New Geneva Study Bible suggests that Ephesians is about the mystery of the church. "The church is an outpost in a dark world (5:3–17), looking for the day of final redemption. Above all, the church is the bride preparing for the approach of her lover and husband."[1] *Foster's January 30 sermon explores the concept of redemption.*

Mr. Foster. (Sunday) [30] January 30. (5 Ephesians 15.16 verse) *"Take hede therefore that ye walke circumspectly, not as fooles, but as wise," "Redeming the time: for the days are evil."*[2] Se then that you walke circumspectly not as fooles but as wise redeeming the time because the days of that Evill. This [cap] containes several dutys of holiness. The [2d] dutys of husbands & wives there are several precepts layd down. 1 To follow God as dear children. They should imitate God, follow God in that holynes. Goodnes appears in his workes. 2 He Exorts us to love and therein to imitate Jesus Christ (Verse 2). 3 To shun an avoyd severall sins here named from verse 3 to 6. We should shun fornication, uncleanes, covetosnes, because it doth not become saints. Verse 3. Because there is other matter that doth becom saints to be speakeing of giving thanks to God for his benefists. Because such sins doe exclude men from inheriting the kingdom of God and Christ, no unclean thing shall enter into Jerusalem. 4 Because of the special Evill that is in this sin it is Idolatry. He makes a God of the creature. 5 Because these things do provoke God and bring his wrath upon you Verse the 7th 4 precept layd down is to teach us to avoid the company of those that live in such sins, be not you partakers with them in their sin. And there ar 7 reasons of it:

1 Because of the chang wrought in them you were sometimes darknes but now you are light in the lord. Walke as the children of the light.

---

[1] *New Geneva Study Bible*, 1860.

[2] *The Geneva Bible, 1560 Edition*. 91.

2 Because the fruit of the Holy ghost is better than all those fruights. It is rightness, goodness, Truth, these are the fruits of the spirit.

3 Reason is taken from the unfruitfulness of those workes of darkness. There is no fruit, profit, peace to be had in these.

4 Because our contrary walking will reprove their workes of darknesse.

5 Because of that horrible vileness of such siners who sin in secrett it is a shame to tell of what they doe in secret.

6 Because all that they doe in secret shall be made known at the day of judgment.

7 Because of the call of the gospel and of the Holy ghost which is to rise men out of this work of darkness and to goe to Christ that they may have life. 5 Precept is in the words of the text se that you walk circumspectly not as Fooles, but as wise, the dayes are evill. In the text 1 there is a solem charg given 2 a description of those that doe attend the charge 3 here is the principle part of this wisdom redeeming of time. 4 The reason we should thus walke, because the days are Evill. Here is a solemn charg, see you walke watchfully, [ch rily], warily. The dangers we are exposed too, the dificultys we meet with calls for it. 2 The description of the persons that thus walke not as fooles but as wise men. The wise man's eys are in his head, but fooles walke in darkness. (23 Exodus 8) A wise man is stated as one that hath the eyes open. 3 Here is the principle part where in wisdom manifested in redeeming of his time. We [then] walk in wisdom when we doe redeem our time. Eternity doth depend upon it. [There] is the principle thing where in wisdom doth appeare. Now redeeming of the time. 1 It is taken from merchants that doe make the best of the market for their goods, make the best of their time. Make as much of it as you can, doe as much good [with] it and receive as much good as you can in it. 2 Others look at the words as a metaphor as one that hath mortgaged his estate and doth recover and redeem it again. We then redeem time where by the doubling of our dilligence we recover what we have lost by former negligence. 3 Som thinke the apostle doth alude unto that Expression of the king to the [caledens] I know you would protract and delay the time as men doe in danger to gaine time: we should make time as much as we can by doeing as much as we can in a Little time. 4 Others there are that thinke the words are a metaphor of men that goe to market. They will improve the market to buy and sell in. Soloman tells us that there are times when there are seasons of partake or fitt times to get gain and advantage by it. 4 The reason that

is given to press us to it, and that is because the dayes are Evill. In evill times then we should more Especially redeem time. Time is not evill in it selfe but in respect of man, the coruption of those that do dwell in those dayes that doth make them evill. It is the sin or suffering of man that dwell in those dayes. The last dayes shall be evill dayes because sin shall abound and love wax cold. The days shall be perilous. Men are lovers of pleasures more than of God. So the Evill of affliction is that as cause the daye to be Evill. (47 Genesis 9) Jacob [few and][3] Evill have the dayes of my pilgrimage 10 days of old age wherein infirmitys cam upon men. It is cald evill day and the day of affliction is called an evill time. Times of sin and corruption are Evill times. (11 Ecclesiastes 2) (9 John 4) (12 John 35)

Doctrine: that it is the duty of every [person][4] to walke circumspectly. 2 That it is a pricipall part of wisdom to redeem time Especially in Evill dayes. It is our great duty to walke circumspectly. The many dangers that we are exposed to, the shortnes of our time, the suddainness of death, should make us to redeem our time.

<u>(Sunday) February 6, 1680: Mr. Foster.</u> (5 Ephesians 15:16 verse) Doctrine: it is the great duty of every man to walke circumspectly not as fools but as wise. There ought to be a great deale of circumspection in the life of every [man]. Herby we shall Evidence ourselves to be wise and not fooles. A wise man's eys are in his head to see his wayes and to fore see danger, but the foole walkes in darkness. He hath no light to guide and direct him in his way. (12 John 35) He that walkes in darkness knowes not whither he goes, but the wise walkes in the way. We canot walke as [Christians] without we walke circumspectly. Example: What is implied in walking circumspectly? Answer: 1 It Implys wisdome and knowledge and understanding [through out] to be this in our lives and conversation. (4 Colossians 5) Walke in wisdom redeeming the time. The wisdom hath respect to the rule by which and the end to which we walke. We must know our duty befor we can doe it. We want wisdom to guid us in our way. (119 Psalm 33) Teacheth me oh lord the way of they statutes and I shall keep it to the end. (1 Colossians 9) The apostle prays for this that they may be filled with

---

[3] King James, p. 60.

[4] This symbol appears many times in the notebook and may translate as creature, Christian, or man. It resembles a slanted, headless stick figure with an extra set of limbs.

the knowledge of God, that thy may walke [worth] [ ][5] the lord to all pleasing. 2 It implys that watchfulness that ought to be in the life of a [Christian]. Circumspection is a looking about us. We should be watchfull in all our wayes. We stand in slipery places, are ready to fall, and therefore had need be watchfull. Be watchfull, be vigilant, for your adversary goes about like a roaring lyon. Every [Christian] in every action ought to be watchfull. (40 Psalm 12) Inumerable Evills compass me about. Have a care of negligence and securety. Watch over your hearts least you be insnared. 3 This noates allso that study and diligence that ought to be in all our actions not idles and sloathfullnes, but diligently a [Christian] must work out his salvation with all diligence. 4 Hereby is meant that exactness that ought to be in our conversation. Exactly, precisely, and accurately coming up to the rule of what the law requires, coming as neer to it as possibly may be. The same word that is used here of circumspection is allso used for perfect. (1 Luke 3) Having perfect knowledge. We walke circumspectly when we doe keep and obey Every command and 2 when our obedience doth reach the extent of the command. As [teaching] the law, we are blameless when we keep the law in our hearts as well as the mind. We must not walke loosely but com up to the command. It noates watchfulness and care. 2 Without a [Christian] to walke thus exactly.

There are many reasons: 1 because of the many Eyes that are upon us. To observe our wayes. Therefore we ought to be circumspect. There is the eye of God upon the way of a [Christian]. God's eys behold and his [eylid] consider the children of men. (139 Psalm 2.3.4) His eys doe behold the Evill and the good. He ponders all our goings, that is God doth examine and way them. This reason David gives to Soloman. (1 Chronicles 28:9) Know the God of your fathers with a perfect heart and a willing mind, for God searcheth all hearts. (12 Ecclesiastes [ ]) God's ey is upon you. He is alwayes before us. An idle servant will be diligent when his master's ey is upon us. 2 There is the ey of angels upon us both of good and evill. The good angells they watch over you keep you from evill. The divills ey is on you to get advantage of you. The Divill is a watchfull bishop in his [diocess]. 3 There is the ey of man upon us, the ey of good men. Therefore walke exactly, that you doe not greive, offend, and provoke them. Evill men's eys are upon you. Se therefor that you doe not give bad examples.

[5] "worthy of" King James, p. 249.

2 Reason: is from the many dutys a [Christian] is cald too and the great difficulties he meets with. Every day is full of duty to fill up our time and it is difficult to doe it. It is true Christ's yoake is easy. It is so to the regenerate man, but such are the remaynders of sin that it is diffcult to doe it.

3 Reason is from the great danger a [man] is exposed too. Innumerable evills doe compass them about. There is danger from our own hearts. Walke circumspectly because we have such desperate deceitfull hearts, such a sinfull heart, such a Law of sin that bring us to subjection, a flesh that doth lust against the spirit. 2 From Saytn there is danger. He is continually presenting object to draw from duty to sin, therefore ought to walke circumspectly. 3 The world is in danger to draw our hearts from God. Walke exactly.

4 Reason: the shortnes of our life and the uncertainty of the time when it will com this should move us to walke circumspectly. Watch, you know not at what hour the lord will com. It is but a little while.

5 Reason: is because God requires utmost perfection of us that we should be perfect as our heavenly Father is perfect. Be holy in all maner of holy conversation.

Use 1: Hence learn that it is no Easy matter for to live the life of a [Christian]. It is a hard and a difficult worke to be continually watchfull in all our wayes. It is no Easy matter. 2 It doth teach us how to Judg of men or fooles. We may doe it by their conversation he that walkes circumspectly, but there are but few that are wise. 3 We have need of continuall grace from God to enable us thus to walke.

2 Use: is of reproofe to those that doe not observe this precept of walkeing circumspectly who not withstanding that profession that they make. Yet their conversation being compared with the [rule] they are not exact walker, not only those that are openly profane and [true] [morall] men, but those that are true [Christians] fall short of what they are here called to. They doe not walke sircumspectly with the open profane that doe not profess holynes but professedly walk on in sin as they (3 Isaiah 9) they doe not hide their sin, but doe declare their sin as Sodom and hide it not. Woe to such, they doe not walke circumspectly, they are not ashamed of sin but doe glory and boast of their sin. Such are to be reproved and condemned. They are farthest off this exact walking. Those doe walke as fooles they doe make a mock of sin. It is a sport to such fooles to doe evill. They that thus goe in sin they are [posting] to hell, except the lord in mercy do stop their course. 2 Such are to be reproved as doe not com up to this rule, that

are meer civill honest men, not because they have this, but because they have not more. Such as these tho they are not notorious siners, yet they have no truce grace. (18 Luke 11) (19 Matthew 21) The young man did [this], but yet at last he forsooke Christ. (3 Philippians 6) As concerning the law, blameless Paule cam up to this before his conversion. God requires habitual soule conformity to his will. A meer civill honest man comes short of what is required of every [Christian] in these 5 things: 1 In respect of that righteousness that is by faith, that righteousness which he [hath] is his own. It is not the righteousness of Christ Imparted to us and [read] by us by fayth. Such they doe goe about to stablish their own righteousness. 2 The civill man coms short of what should be in the [Christian] in regard of that heart holiness that should be in him. All his attaynments doe not attayn to the new heart and to the right spirit. There is no heart holiness in Him. 3 He comes short in regard to the principle and the end of his obedience. It doth not com from true Fayth in God and love to God. The [Christian] doth Exceed him in that: the [Christian] doth all for the glory of God. 4 The meer morall man for the most part doth only minde 2 [table] dutys. He is a righteous but not a pious man. He gives to man his due, but he doth not give God his due. 5 Such as are meer civill men, tho they doe make conscience of greater sines yett they doe not of lesser. They com short of what is here required of them, they doe not walke exactly.[6] God requires more of you. 3 It reproves formall professors. Secret hypocrites have a form of godlynes, but deny the power of it. They doe not com up to that Exactnes that God requires. How many such ar there that are Externally precise? Their hearts are not precise. They doe not walke Exactly. They com short of what God requires. 4 It reproves true [Christians] that doe not walk exactly. They are farr short of Exact walking. They are not exact and precise to attend the rule: [ob] but is there any that can walk so? Is there nay that doth

[6] To the Puritan, the civil man was always less than the saint, as Edmund Morgan shows in *The Puritan Family*: "There was a type of man whom the Puritans never tired of denouncing. He was a good citizen, a man who obeyed the laws, carried out his social obligations, never injured others. The Puritans called him a 'civil man,' and admitted that he was 'outwardly just, temperate, chaste, carefull to follow his wordly businesse, will not hurt so much as his neughbours dog, payes every man his owne, and lives of his owne; no drunkard, adulterer, or quareller; loves to live peaceably and quietly among his neighbors.' This man, this paragon of virtue, the Puritans said, was on his way to Hell, and their preachers continually reminded him of it." Edmund Morgan. *The Puritan Family: Religion and Domestic relations in Seventeenth-Century New England* (New York: Harper and Row, 1966), 1.

good and sineth not [that] should [we] be so pressed: for Answer: 1 consider the faylings of the best of men is no excuse for us, but they should make us more carefull. 2 Tho we canot walke so exactly yet we ought to doe it. It is not our ability but duty so to doe. 3 A true [Christian] is not resting in any perfection but is pressing Forward. A true [Christian] presseth forward. 4 Though no [Christian] attayned to the hieght degree, yet Every [Christian] hath attayned to some degree of perfection. (1 Luke 6) They were both righteous before God walking in all the commands of God blameless and sincerity in gospell perfection and that every true [Christian] in some measure attained. 5 Every [Christian] doth repent of that where in he doth com short of the rule and he lookes to the righteousnes of Christ that he may be exact in Christ. We are compleat in him.

3 Use: let us all be exorted to walke circumspectly and to walke exactly. We must doe more than others doe to move to this. 1 Consider the honor of God is concerned there in. 2 The credit of religion is allso concerned here in. (4 Ephesians 1) Walke worthy of the lord to all well pleasing. 3 The conversion of others is allso concerned there in.

4 Consider their own salvation is concerned here in. As to the certaynty of it, you must walke as [Christians] if you will be saved. [1] You canot have the assurance of it without walking Exactly. To help here [would] you walke exactly study the law of God. 2 Often examine your selves. The neglect of this is cause of great [remisness]. 3 Rest not in any thing what you have atayned. 4 Goe to Christ for grace that you may walke Exactly in your life and conversation.

CHAPTER THIRTEEN

THE GOD OF THE WORLD

In this first sermon of chapter 13, Isaac Foster refers directly to Satan 49 times. By the end of this sermon, there would have been very little doubt in the minds of the congregation about Foster's theme for that day. Did any of them know that this sermon was merely an introduction to a series that would last through November? In this series, Foster addresses virtually every topic explored in this book. The themes of conversion, justification, redemption, sanctification, predestination, the Devil, and the natural man among others. In this series, these themes are subjected to the scrutiny of a maturing preacher, who by this time has clearly found his voice.

As with chapter 6, the problems within the church are the subject of the text, and Foster's overt references to the Devil were very likely intended to arouse Hartford's awareness of its own moral laxity. Foster's opening sermon of September 12 is an exhortation to be wary of the power of Satan and his temptations, but it is also about humankind's weapon against Satan, which of course is Jesus Christ. The Devil was clearly a pervasive presence in the lives of Foster's congregation.[1]

<u>(Sunday) September 12, 1680: Mr. Foster.</u> (1 Corinthians 10:13) *"There hathe no tentation taken you, but suche as apperteineth to man: and God is faithful, which wil not suffer you to be tempted above that you be able, but wil even give the yssue with the tentation, that ye may be able to beare it."*[2] Doctrine: that temptations are comon to man it is the portion [com] [ ] man in this life to be tempted.

[1] In his book *Power and the Pulpit in Puritan New England*, Emory Elliott discusses the figure of Satan in the lives of New England's Puritans, and based on Isaac Foster's sermon series from Corinthians, Elliot's assessment seems quite accurate. "During the 1660's and 1670's, when ministers had placed the blame for all of New England's troubles upon the people themselves, the figure of Satan had occupied a secondary position to the rising generation as the cause of evils in the colony. With the shift in the message of the sermon toward assurance of the young in the 1680's, Satan reemerged as the principal foe." Emory Elliott. *Power and the Pulpit in Puritan New England* (Princeton, Princeton University Press, 1975), 198.

[2] *The Geneva Bible, 1560 Edition*. 80.

Use 1. Inform: see hence the happyness of the saints in heaven. They are out of Saytn's reach. 2 Thinke not strang to meat with temptations. They are comon to men. No Temptation hath taken you but what is common to man. 3 Hence learn that the best of men have continuall need of grace in that they must be Tempted. They must withstand Saytn and therefor they stand in need of speciall grace and strength from here to withstand the powers of hell. (6 Ephesians 13) Wherefore take unto you the whole armor of God the whole stock of graces, that the spirit of God is the armor by which we stand against Sayten. We stand in need of grace and Especially of fayth by which we must withstand the fyry darts of the Devill. We need grace to strengthen agaynst temptation more than [to] [be] freed from it. We need grace 1 to watch agaynst the temptations of Saytn. (25 Matthew 25)[3] They all slumbered and [slept]. It is our duty to be vigilant and watchfull and great is our anger if it be not so and we want grace for this. 2 We do need grace to discover Saytn's Temptations that we be [not] ignorant of his devices. We need grace to find [o] [ ] the turnings and windings of this cuning serpant. We need special grace to resist and overcome Saytn so that we be not overcome by him, that we be not taken by his wiles and devices.[4] God hath promised if we doe resist [ ] Tempter and he shall flee from us. [ ] Saytn is not invincible he hath been and [n] be overcome. Saytn was conquered by the blood of Jesus. (12 Revelations 10.11 verse) The [lambe]: This great Goliah may be conquered by them that doe [oe] out against them in the name of God. It is true Saytn did [ ] never shall totally overcome any one saint. He that is be [ ] of God God keepeth him that Saytn doth not touch them [s] to have them. No they are gainers by his Temptations. He doth not suffer them to be drawn into sin. That unpardonable sin. It is [ ] true they canot apose him. (1 Samuel 28:15) 4 They need grace [so] for to get the [good] of Temptation. God hath promised all shall [worke] for [good] for those that feare him if all their afflictions Temptations and then surely we want grace to help that it may be soe. Those Temptations they sift the godly. They are [fined] and made more pure and holy, thereby God suffers his people to be afflicted for this very end that grace may be more conspicuous [ ] them. 5 We need grace that we may Honor God under Temptation.

[3] (25 Matthew 5) King James, p. 36.

[4] In other words, we need to be regenerated, and godly, a visible saint.

4 Use: Hence learn the guilt of Sayten and the great [ ] that lyeth upon Saytn. He is guilty of his own apostacy and of the sin of man because he is a Tempter of man to sin. ([1] John 3:8) He that commits sins is of the Divill:

5 Use: See the great sin of man in that man is so ready to comply with the Temptations of Saytn. Saytn's temptations may be our afflictions but not our sins against our wills. 6: Hence learn the great judgment of God on man for his hearkening to the voyce of Saytn in his first Temptation. Man did not resist sin in the First Temptation it [just] with God to let Saytn be a snare to men. 2 It learnt us not to be too secure nor selfe confident in our strength.[L]:[5] This Doctrine doth [ ] us the wonderful grace of God to man: In Saytn's Temptations [ ] that God doth restrain him. Saytn hath rage eno:[ ] power eno if God should permit him to destroy all [of] mankind. 2 Admire the grace of God that God should send [his] son to conquer Saytn for us. The lord Jesus Christ by death he destroyed him that hath the power of death the Divill. We have cause to admire that weake and frayle man is able to overcome this enemie by the strength of God. [ ] in that God hath found out wayes to bring us out of Tempatation. This is wonderfull. 5 That God should [ord] [tation] so as to bring about our [ ] 6. In that Saytn who doth Tempt us hence in this world shall be judged by us in the other world: Know (1 Corinthians 6. 3) you [not][6] that you shall judge angells. 2 It is of comfort to the godly [ ] this set against you. He sets upon you Especially. (7 Revelations 17) Saytn his designe is Especialy against the saint because they are of the image of God. 2 Because God loves them. 3 The saints are ther enemies and therefor is [wroth] against them. 4 Because they shall judg him another day. Yet there is ground of comfort for you. 1 In that Saytn can doe nothing without the heavenly father's permission. (1 Job 6) (2 Job 4) 5 Saytn can doe no more than God gives him leave. God hath him in his chain he is so far from being able to [ll] with man that he can deale with no creature without God's leave. Saytn canot touch you. He is under God's government. (10 Matthew 28.29.30) 2 It is ground of comfort that this enemie of yours is a conquered enemie by Christ Jesus the captain of your salvation. He hath bound

[5] This shorthand character appears to be an upper case L. It appears throughout the notebook, but I was not able to decode the symbol.

[6] "not" King James, p. 210.

the strong man [armed] by death he hath (2 Hebrews 14) overcom him that hath the power of death which is the Divill. 3 It is ground of comfort for you may be assured of a glorious conquest and victory at last. He that is born of God the wicked one touches him not. You may be sure by the conquest of Christ to overcome him. You shall have him under your feet shortly. God will bring Sathen under your feet shortly. Saytn may wound and hurt you, but you shall be sure to overcome at the last. 4 It is of comfort that in the midst of all temptations your grace is increased and you are the more fitted for glory. The Divills rath God doth cause it to prayse him. 5 Ground of comfort is that Christ hath been Tempted. The servant is not above his lord. The consideration that Christ hath been Tempted may comfort us in that we see we may be Tempted and not sin. Saytn's Tempting is not our sin but our complying with the Temptation is sin. We may be Tempted and not sin. It is ground of comfort allso in that Christ because he was tempted is able to save and succour those that are Tempted. He is the more inclinable to have compassion upon us and is the more readily inclined to succour us. 6 The many promises we have of releife is ground of comfort to us. God hath promised we shall not be tempted above what we are able. Another ground of comfort is whatever wound we doe receive from Saytn we may be healed of it by looking unto Jesus Christ. 8 Another comfort is the good angells are as ready to help us as the Devill is to devoure us. (1 Hebrews 14) They are all ministering spirits sent forth for the good of the heirs of salvation. (2 Kings 6:16.17) 9 Those temptations of Saytn are but for a short while, but for a season. Be Exorted that you have a care that you be not overcome by Saytn's temptations. (26 Matthew 4) Watch and pray that you Enter not in to temptation. Keep you hearts above all keeping. Watch your hearts especially when you are alone. Watch your hearts, thoughts, and meditations. 2 Watch the motions of Saytn that you be not surprized or taken unawares. His Temptations are often very suddain and very violent: 2 Let us be sober. (1 Peter 5:8) Be sober be vigilant. Watchfulness and sobriety they doe goe together. (21 Luke 34.35) And take heed that your hearts be overtaken with surfeiting and drunckenness and that day come upon you unaware as a snare. (1 Corinthians 9:25) 3 Let us be much and frequent in prayer to God. Hereby we fly from our selves and fly to God. Watch and pray that you may not Enter into Temptation. (2 Corinthians 12:8) 4 Let us resist Saytn in the beginning of his Temptation. (4 James 7)

(1 Peter 5:9) Whom resist stedfast in the faith they are fyry darts soone quenched at the first but no aposeing afterwards. We should stop our eares at the voice of this deafe addar. 5 Let us be diligent in our particular calling if Saytn find us [s] he will set us worke. They that will not be God's servants to doe God's will they shall be the Divills slaves. 6 Let us have a care of all occasions unto sin. (119 Psalm 37) Turn away mine eys from beholding vanitie. (5 Proverbs 8) Reprove of the way of sin. 7 Labor to be acquainted with Saytn's devices and with his wiles. It is a great part of heavenly wisdom to know and be acquainted with the devices of Saytn. (1 Job 8) Saytn considers man. 8 Let us labor to know and rightly Improve and make use of the word of God. The word is the sword of the spirit, that sword by which you must manage the war against Saytn. 9 Let us put on the whole armor of God. (6 Ephesians 12.13) It is the apostle's councill. Let those that want this armor labor to get it. Let those that have it improve and make use of it. Consider what an enemie he is, the only deadly enemie. 2 The End of his Temptations is to ruin and destroy you: 3 He sets you about the worst worke. 4 and the reward:[7]

Mr. Foster. (Sunday) September 26, 1680. (1 Corinthians 10:13) Doctrine 1: That temptations are common to man in this life, we must looke to be tempted in this world.

Use: to exort all to looke to Saytn to watch against his Temptations. For motive consider Saytn is your greatest enemie therefor resist him and flee him. He is the first enemie. 2 He is the worst enemie. Most powerfull enemie. A politick enemy that makes God our enemie 2. Consider Saytn never Tempted any man but that he deceived him. 3 Saytn's Temptations are directly contrary to your end. You canot glorify God as you should, neither you cannot enjoy God. 4 Consider the great Encouragement that God gives to Every one. Tho: the Enemie be great yet you may goe forth against him in the name of the Lord and you shall not miscarry: 1 The Divill he is a creature, he is a cursed creature, a conquered creature, and 1 he is a creature an enemie to your soules. (4 James 7) Resist the Divill and he will flee from you. 2 Consider he is a cursed creature. God is an enemie to the Divill as well as you. 3 He is a chained creature. He is a captive to God, an enemie that is not at liberty that is held in chaines by God. 4 The

[7] The sermon's ending is incomplete.

Divill is a [conquer] enemie Christ hath overcome. He has overcome the Divill for you. Be of good cheare. I have overcome this world. (2 Hebrews 14) Every saint that is in heaven hath fought his way thither and overcome this potent Enemie. 5 Though the Divill be your Enemie yet God is your friende and he that is for you is greater than he that is agaynst you. The Divill canot make God to be your Enemie though he moved God against you. ([J] 2): Principalities and powers canot seperat you from the love of God in Jesus Christ: When Saytn is casting you to prison God will give a [breathe] of life. 6 The Divill shall fly from you if you doe but resist him. (4 James 7) Be you stand fast in the fayth and resist the Divill and he shall fly from you. (4 Matthew 11) 7 God hath promised grace to resist the Divill. 5 Consider the sad fruits of your [yeilding] [to] Saytn. (2 [Ten] 2.26) Liberty [ ] but [ ] [loos] it [f] temptation all the misery and all the sin that is in the world is an effect of man's yielding to Saytn. How happy had man been if he had not bin led away by Saytn. 6 Consider the more you yield to Saytn the stronger Saytn will be and have greater strength against you. Therefor at first resist him now. 7 Consider the great priviledg and happyness of all those that are [creatures] in this conflict. The happyness of such is great. You saw their soules saved from the 2 death and ordained to life. Man had never been miserable had not Saytn overcome the first Adam. Made had never been happy had not the second Adam overcome the Evill one.[8] 8 Consider how great a comfort it will be to you in life and death to overcome the Quick one: 1 You will be [like] to Christ and that is a comfort. Your conformity to Christ it will be an evidence to you that you are born of God. He that is begotten of God keepeth himselfe and the evill one doth not touch him. (8 John 44) 2 If Saytn doe not overcom you while you live he shall have no power over you when you dye. 3 If you are a conquerer you shall be sure of a crown. We then fight the good fight when we conquer in our fight. 2 Man is Tempted from his own lust: It is the portion of man in this life to be Tempted from his sinfull lusts. The Divill is not only Enemie but our own lusts are. (1 James 13) Every man is Tempted with his own lusts when he is inticed and drawn away to sin. We have in our own hearts a wors Enemie than Saytn. Many doe [bely] the Father of lyes. (2 Peter 3.4.verse) Having Escaped the corruption of the word thru: lusts the whole word hence then is

[8] Second Adam is Jesus Christ.

corruption in judgment and corruption in maners. (15 Matthew 19) Out of the heart proceeds Evill thoughts, murders, fornications, and uncleanesses. (7 Romans 5.8) Example: What is meant by the lust that Tempts man to sin? Answer: it is that naturall inbred pravity and corruption of man's nature whereby he is Inclined to all Evill and averss to whatever is good.[9] This is that which the apostle calls in dwelling sin and the law of that [members]. In the fall of man there was 1 the act of sin in eating the forbidden fruit. 2 The [gift] of sin whereby man was liable to punishment and was a fruit and effect of sin. (1 James 14) [Christ's] want of righteousness. This pravity of nature doth show itself in corrupt Lusts. (6 Romans 12) The Effects of these sins are called the Lusts of the Flesh. (2 Ephesians 3) 2 How doth this Tempt man to sin? How is man tempted by his own lusts? 1 Man is Tempted hereby as he is strongly seduced and drawn to sin allured and perswaded to sin. (5 Galatians 17) The lusts of men's hearts are Impetuous and caryd on to sin. 2 It Tempts man as it doth hinder and apose and keep man from doeing what God commands. Are we called to hear [pras] here is an Evill heart that doth appose as in all that is good. (5 Galatians 17) The flesh lyeth angst the spirit so that we canot doe the good we should. Let me show you the power and effecasy this lust hath to Tempt man to sin. And this appears by the Titles of it. It is called the law of sin. It is an inward law of sin that is the power and effecasy of sin. 2 The subject of it this lust is in the whole man in the whole soule. It is in the understanding will and affection and whole man. The mind and conscience is defiled. Their understandings are (1 Titus 15) darkened and their affections bent to sin. 3 It doth appeare from the Effects of this lust in the lives and conversations of men. 1 In wicked there lives show it. The wickedness of man is great (6 Genesis 5) and every imaganation of his heart is onely Evill and that continually. (4 Proverbs 16) (1 Kings 21.5) (2 Samuel 2.13) 2 The Effects of lusts in the Lives of the godly show the power of Lusts. They canot doe the good they would, they doe the Evill they would not. 3 The power of it appears by the maner of its walkeing. It wars agaynst the spirit. This noates the greatest force and violence of it. It is deceiptful and allways Evill and that continually. 3 Where in doth appeare the evill and danger of Temptation from our own lusts? 1 It appears in that they are internall. They are in our own hearts. (31 Jeremiah 33)

[9] Natural inbred pravity is the state of man prior to regeneration.

Our Enemie is not only upon us but in us. 2 Lusts is a more constant enemie than Saytn. We allways carry it about with us. Sathen tho: he be a constant enemie yet he flys away from us for the present. 3 It is more powerfull. Saytn may persuade but he canot overcome, but this lust doth[ ] the will [ ] of Saytn are not sin, but the Temptations of Lusts they are sin. Though men doe not alow of it. The law of God requires conformity in our hearts as well as our lives. This lust in our hearts though we doe not comply with it yet it is our sin.

Use 1: hence learn what little cause men have to be proud and lifted up and what cause to be humbled that we are so full of sin. How should it take us off from all sin and humble and abase us? 2 Hence learn the sad Effect of man's first sin and Fall. Hence it is that his whole nature is corupted, that he hath this lust that dwells in him. Before his fall man had no lusts in him. 3 Hence learn man's destruction is of himselfe. So it was in his first sin. Man doth tempt himself to sin. 4 Hence learn the desperate wickedness of our own hearts in that we are by it tempted to sin. It is not enough to repent for actuall sin, but we should repent and be humbled for the sin of the heart as well as of the life. That we should be humbled for and repent of 5 it shows us where to begin the work of reformation. It must be in the heart. It is not Enough to lop the branches but to lay the ax at the root of the tree. Hence David prays Lord create in me a clean heart. 6 Hence Learn what need we have of restraining grace and what cause we have to bless God for it. By restraining grace I mean that God doth by his grace restraine and bound that coruption that is in the heart that it doth not overflow in your life.[10] (20 Genesis 5 verse) I withheld the from sining agaynst me sayth God to Abimileck. (76 Psalm 10) God doth restraine men. Admire at restraining grace: [L] See the need we have of renewing grace. To have the power and principle of it [I may] be renewed.

Foster's series from First Corinthians is still very much concerned with the temptations of the Devil, but there is also a shift toward defining the natural man and his sad, miserable condition. Foster believes the natural man is a slave to his lusts, and that while God may keep the Devil in chains, the Devil keeps non-believers in chains. Essentially, God allows

---

[10] Another instance where Foster addresses the congregation in the first person.

the Devil to exist so that man will be tested by the temptations of the God of the world.

(Sunday) October 3, 1680. Mr. Foster (1 Corinthians 10:13) There is no temptation taken you but what is comon to man.

Doctrine: that temptation is common to man in this life. Man is tempted by God to prove, try him, and doe him good, and is tempted unto sin by Saytn and by his own Lusts. Man is tempted of his own Lusts he hath an Enemie with in him. The Lust is that inbred pravity that is in the nature of man. Man's whole nature is depraved with sin. This pravity is the Lust that carys men to sin. This Lust tempts to sin as it doth Iritate provoake and stir up to sin. This Lust is that as doth move and stir up to sin. Sin wrought in me that [concupiscence]. 2 It tempts to sin as it doth hinder and apose in doing good. These are more powerfull, more takeing and sinfull then the Temptations of Saytn. 6 Hence learn man's need of renewing as well as restraining grace. Our natures must be renewed, our hearts satisfied, or we can never be saved. (3 John 6.7) That which is born of the flesh is Flesh that that is born of this spirit is spirit and therefore marveld not, that I say you must be born again, for except you be born again you canot enter in to the kingdom of heaven. This is necessary by the command of God. God comands us to be holy as he is, to be perfect as he is perfect. 2 It is necessary as a means to an end, for without holynes no man can see God. It is a means to hapynes and life. This Teacheth man the need of renewing grace.

[Use] Instruction: it teacheth us the sad and miserable condition of man by nature, and or Every naturall man. He is under the power and dominion of Lusts. He is held in Bonds and is under captivity to his Lusts. Hence the apostle of Simon says I perceive thou art in the Bond of iniquity. Consider man in a 3 Fold state in this, and a state of Nature is the worst. 1 There is man's created state. In that state man was [up]. He had the greatest liberty and freedom of will and non could take away this liberty without his consent. He had nothing in him for the Tempter to worke upon. [made had a] power to overcome Saytn. 2 Consider man in his Estate of renovation. There is spirit as well as grace. (6 Romans 14) Man is not free from sin, but from the power and dominion of it. Sin in this state dwells in man as an enemie that fights with them, but not as a lord that [u s]. Sin is like to those kings in Daniel that had their lives prolonged, but their dominion and power was taken away. Sin to the godly is as the Caninits were to Iserell. They wer as thornes in their sides. 3 Consider man in a state of nature and this is most wretched and miserable, he is a servant and slave to sin, held in bondage and slavery to Lust. 1 This bondage to sin is ever acompanyed with Bondage to Satyn. The reign of Sathen doth depend upon the reign of sin. He that is a slave to his Lusts he is a slave to Saytn allsoe. The Divill holds men fast to him by his Lusts. He doth the worke of the Divill. The God of the world Blinds the eys of those that doe not believe. He keeps them in chains [they] plow iniquity. 2 It is the worst because it is soule Bondage, soule slavery. It is worss because that is sin. Outward Bondage may be consistant with man's happynes, but this is not. To be in soule Bondage is worss Because that men are not sensible of it, they doe not feele it.[11] (2 Exodus 23) They make choyse of it. They are [Bowred] servants. They doe chose to be slaves. (49 Genesis 14) They are like Isachar: they bowe their shoulders to beare and become servants. 4 He that is a servant to his Lusts he serves many masters, Serving divers Lusts. 5 He that is under the dominion of Lusts he serves a master that is worss than himself. He is a servant unto servants: 6 This is the worst of bondage because the siners worke is never don. There is no End of it, as he serves his Lusts while he lives so he serves them when he dyes, and shall serve them Eternally. Except God [ ] mercy free from sin here it will rule over you forever. 7 It is the most miserable service because of the reward and the wages the siner shall have of his Lusts. His servants you are whom you obey, whither it be sin unto deth or of righteousness unto life.

8 Use: see where the guilt and the blame of man's sins and ought to ly. Is man drawn to sin it is of his own Lusts. Man must blame himself. A lewd life comes from a lewd heart. The guilt of man's sin it must not ly upon God. (1 James 13) God canot be Tempted with evill neither doth he tempt any man. (3 Genesis 11.12) Adam taxeth God with his sin the woman thou gavest [man]. God doth in his will permit it and in his decree determine it. God also concurs with man in all his action but not with the sin of those actions. 1 God wills it with the will of purposes, yet man commits sin contrary to God's will of command. God canot be the author of sin because God hates it as contrary to His nature. 2 God forbids it, it is contrary to his will. 3 God punisheth it in the principle offender and in the surety. When Christ stood in the roome of siners God did not spare him. He was holy seperat and

[11] Isaac Foster had a servant, as did many Puritans.

undefiled. He knew no sin. Sathen is not onely to blame. He is guilty, he is not onely guilty. Hence the serpent shared in the curss and in the punishment and therefore in the sin. 3 Therefore it must ly upon itselfe. Man was not forced but acted freely in his sin. It is from his own heart and from his own Lust.

2 Use: of confutation. It confutes that eror of the Paladians[12] that did deny the being of sin or any coruption of nature that might Incline him to sin. They hold man was born an Inocent not inclined to vice or virtue farther than by example, but this Doctrine confutes thereby there are Lusts in our hearts that doe lead us into sin. 2 It doth confute the Eror of those that have asserted perfection in this life. If there be this Lust in man in the best of men then there is no such perfection in us. If we say we have not (1 John 1:8.10) sined we are lyers and the truth is not in us. We are said to be perfect, but it is in regard of our desires and endeavours and parts and in respect of justification. But not in respect of [sanctification]. There is sin where is most grace.

3 Use: of conselation and comfort unto all those that are satisfied, to every true saint. Here is comfort not with standing you have suche an enemie Lust that dwells in you. You shall have this body of death this Lust about as long as you live. It will Easily beset you. Yet ther is ground of comfort that you have another principle. A principle of grace that dwells in you that is of Eternall duration that shall never be destroyed by you. It is ground of comfort that not withstanding the being of Lust in you yet the power of it is subdued. You have cause to rejoice that you are redeemed from such an Enemie. Out of such bondage you [ ] a captive but you are freed. 3 Here is comfort [to] a little time you shall be delivered from the being of Lusts. God delivers you now from the yoake of sin. You [ ] shortly be delivered from the being of sin in [glorifi]. (2 Corinthians 12:5) Of such a one will I glory. You may rejoyce in the hope of glory.

4 Use of Examination: Try whither you are under the power of these Lusts or now [whether] sin doth reigne in you or no, [whether] you

---

12 According to the *Encarta Dictionary*, Paladians is a classical Greek reference related to Athena. The *Oxford Classical Dictionary* refers to Pallas, which was a giant killed by Athena. *Oxford Classical Dictionary* (Oxford: Oxford University Press, 1970), 772. I was unable to locate a biblical reference for Paladian, but this is likely referring to the Pelagian heresy, and the notetaker simply misunderstood the preacher. The Pelagian heresy was a British heresy and well known in theory. It may reveal something about the note taker, that he or she listened carefully but without always comprehending.

are under the Bond of iniquity or whether the son hath made you free in deed. This a [L] of greatest Importance whether Lust raignes in you or not. Examine yourselves and prove your selves whether it be so or no. 1 Consider it is possible to know this: there are certaine rules whereby you may try your state. Possibility is the ground of endeavoure: 2 Consider as there is a possibility so it is our great duty to examine ourselves and try ourselves. 3 Consider many have been mistaken in this inquiry and passed a fals judgment upon themselves. 4 Consider it is Exceeding dangerous to be mistaken in this matter for this is a soule concern and an Eternall concern if we mistake in this matter. We may be Eternally ruined if we be mistaken. We shall miss of the use of means of deliverance. He that is not sencible of Bondage will not seeke for freedome. 5 Consider if we do not examine ourselves in this matter we shall loose the comfort of freedom from Lust without it. 6 It is hard and difficult for a man to know whether he be under the power of Lusts. 1 It is difficult because you may have convictions of sin and yet live under the power of sin. All convictions are not saving, neither doe they all end in conversion. 2 There may [be] repentance of sin and yet under the power of it. All repentance is not repentance to life. All sorrow is not godly sorrow. (27 Matthew 3) 3 There may be fayth and yet sin reign in you. All faith is not unfeigned nor the fayth of God's elect there is added fayth. The Divill hath faith. 4 You may resist the Temptation of Lust and yet be under the power of it. 5 The power of Lust may be restrained for a time and yet be under the power of it. 6 Consider you may reform many things in your life and yet Lust reign in your heart. John he reformed much and yet lust remained in his heart. 7 A man may doe that which is materially good and yet be under the power of Lusts. Thus the Pharasie I am noe [ext timer] I taste twice a week. So Paule [t ching] the law Blameless. So the young man I have kept all those commands from my youth. For tryall [that] which we may know our state. 1 Doe you resist and apose this Lust when it doth tempt you, are you not willingly subject but doe you appose it? Doth the spirit Lust angst the flesh? Consider it is not every resistance of every opposition that will doe, but this resistance and opposition it must be strong and vigorous. The whole heart and minde and strength must be engaged in this resistance. We must rather dye than yield to sin. 3 It must be constant, a constant opposition. Do you try this bent of spirit, is it continually resisting of sin in you? (6 Romans 23) (8 Romans 2) 3 It must be universall. Do you resist and appose all sin all kinds of sin, all degress and all appearances of sin? 4 Is this resistance of sin aganst sin as sin because contrary to God and his lawe? 2 Are you willing and desireous to com under the government of Christ that he should rule and reigne over you?

(Sunday) October 10, 1680. Mr. Foster.[13] (1 Corinthians 10:13) There is no Temptation taken you but that which is common to man.

Doctrine: Temptations are common to man in this life. 5 This resistance must be from a right principle. There may be much don to apose sin 1 from a principle of nature. The dictates of a naturall consciens may resist the inclinations of corupt will. (2 [om] 14.15) Those having not the law are a law to themselves. If lusts inclin to [mur] then the law of nature doth teach to resist this and it is because the law of God is [rivited] in nature. 2 A man my resist sin from acquired light, by the light of common grace bestowed upon men and by religious [Education]. They that know much of sin see much of the danger of it. They that have been inlightened may fall away in to sin. It is impossible for those that are truly in lightened to fall away, but a man may be in Lightened and fall away. 3 A man may resist this and that Lust from his [Temp] and yet be under the power of lusts. There be severall lusts that do attend the eyes rashness and Intemperance, youth and covetosnes old [eye]. (5 Job 2) Rath killeth the foolish one, envy slayeth the silly one. 4: A man may resist Lust from the contrarity of one Lust to another as the covetous man resists prodigality. 5 It is from a principall of selfe love that men doe resist sin. When the flames of hell are about them they resist their lusts because they make them miserable and not because it is sinfull. 6 This resistance of sin must be for a right end. See that you have a sinceer end at the glory of God not [then] profit honor, but because it hinders comunion with God. (6 Matthew 22.23) If [yi][14] ey be single then the body is full of light. (8 Acts 23) He desired the gift of the holy ghost. A good gift but his end was bad to make his gaine. 2 Tryall when we be under the power of lust is [ ] doe you feele sin in dwelling sin of your burthen and doe you groan under it. Others they play with their bondage and are not sencible of it. But Paule cryeth out oh wretched man that I am, who shall deliver me from this body of death? Every one that is burthend

[13] This sermon is in form a kind of catechism, with questions left for each congregant to answer on their own. There are other sermons in the notebook that employ the catechism . It appears to have been a form favored by Isaac Foster.

[14] "thine" King James, p. 9.

with sin cannot make use of this evidence for under conviction of sin sin may be a burthen, and a man may be willing to part with it. But have you felt sin as a heavy burthen to heavy for you? Have you flyed to Christ to be eased of it? 2 Is Every sin a burthen? Actuall sin, the sin of your nature and the wickedness of your hearts, is this a burthen to you? 3 Is it a dayly burthen to you every day as long as you live? 4 Try yourselves by this. 3 Do you heartily and do you Earnestly desire to come under the rule and government of Jesus Christ? Are you willing to part with the old master and have Christ to rule you? Other lords have ruled over us, but now we will make mention of thy name only. (60 Isaiah 1) Are you willing to be taken out of captivity to sin and to be put in to the service of Christ? Is your service of sin the greatest bondage to you and your service of Christ the greatest freedom? Have you seen the greatest excelency in Christ? Is it better for you to serve Christ than another? Is he better to you than others? 2 Do you see an excelency in the government of Christ? The law of Christ is better than the law of sin. The septer of Christ is a scepter of righteousness. 3 Have you seen an excelency in the subjects of Christ, that they are better than those that are the subject of sin? They are the fayrest among woman. 4 Have you seen an excelency in your sufferings for Christ? (11 Hebrews) Is the reproach of Christ esteemed and prized by you? Can you glory in the cross that you suffer for him? To you it is given to suffer for Christ. 5 Do you see an Excellency in the gifts of Christ, that grace is better than gold? 4 Tryall: what fruit do you bring forth? You may know your hearts by your lives. (7 Matthew 16) [Ye] shall know them by their fruits. A good tree brings forth good fruit and a corupt tree corupt fruit. If the fruit be good the Tree is. If the fruit be corupt so is the Tree:[15] (6 Romans 22.16) (8 John 34) He that is the comitter of sin is the servant of sin. (2 Ephesians 3) 5 Tryall: by Lookeing into your affections you may know your state. Affections are the powers of the soule whereby it doth act and move the soule. They are the goeings out of the soule. (5 Ecclesiastes) Keep thy foot when thou goest to the house of God. They are the affections. What is your love and hatred set

[15] Bonnie Strother points to images of fruit and flora in the sermons of Thomas Shepard. As with celestial bodies and images of the sea, these were generally quite popular devices in Puritan sermons. Isaac Foster seems to have had a particular fondness for honey, which he mentions several times in the *Hartford Sermon Notebook*. See: Bonnie Lew Strother. *The Imagery in the Sermons of Thomas Shepard*. PhD Dissertation, University of Tennessee, 1968.

upon? Doe you love the law of God? Doe you delight in communion with God? Is your Love first set on God and on other things for the sake of God? Is your hatred set upon sin that it be with a perfect and irreconcilable Hatred? If your affections be so then sin hath not power and dominion over you. As to your joy and sorrow doe you delight in sin? Is your Joy in the pleasure of sin? Are stolen waters sweet to you? Doe you delight to sin, is it a sport to you to doe evill, or is their delight in the law of God in comunion with God? He that is under the power of sin delights in the pleasures of sin, but he that is under the power of grace doth delight to doe the will of God. Is your sorow for sin as to desire? What doe you desire, long for? Is the same desire in you as was with David, that you may dwell in the house of God always? Doth your heart pant after God? Are the tabernackells of God amiable to you? Doe your hearts long for the word of God? 4 As to hope what is the object of sin? Is it the wayes of sin or is it fixed upon God alone? 5 As to your feare are you most afrayed of God, of sining against [ ]? 6 Do you [I y] your self for all known sin and live in the practice of all duty? Is there no sin that you doe wittingly alowe of? 7 Doe you goe unto Christ by fayth for strength aganst sin and lust, that you may overcome them and be more than a conquerer over them? (2 Galatians 19.20 verse) (1 John 5) 4 This is the victory that over cometh the world our faith, Faythe whereby we apprehend Christ whoe as our head hath overcom the world.[16]

5 Use: of Exortation. 1 They that through grace are deliverd from the power and reigne of Lusts and those that are under power of sin. [ ] to such as are made free from the law of sin by the law of the spirit. 1 Doe you own and acknowledge the free grace of God there in? The only Reason that you were freed from sin is the grace of God.

(3 Titus 4.5) According to his mercy and of his own free grace hath he saved us. 2 Be exceeding thankefull to God for this grace that you should be made free and not another is there any deliverance like to this. Be Exceeding thankful to God for this his grace to you. (15 Exodus 1) They sang prays to God for deliverance from the Egiptian bondage by an ordinance forever, and yet that was but a shadow of this deliverance. God be thanked for this. You wer the servants of sin but now you obey the word. And Simion prayseth God that hath raysed up a

[16] Overcoming the world is the same as overcoming sin, and overcoming the Devil, the god of the world.

horn of salvation to save you from all your Enemies. To quicken to this duty consider [now] but God could deliver you. Lust is to strong to be subdued by any created power. God alone can only subdue iniquity. Consider how sad and miserable your state was before you were made free. God delivered you when you were an enemi to God, you resisted God in the worke. Consider how great a person God imployed in this worke. God sent his son, his own son not an angell. He cam to proclaim Liberty to the captives. 4 Consider the price that was paid for your redemption. It was the blood of Christ not coruptible things. (2 Hebrews 4) By his own death he [rescued] us from death tho: he was Equall with the Father yet he became a servant to redeem us from being servants to sin. 5 The great priviledg we have by this freedom from sin should make (8 John 36)[17] us prayse God. If the son make you free you shall be free indeed, Free from sin the Greatest evill, and Free from death the greatest punishment. 3 Be exorted to remember what you were to keep you humble and to make you thankfull. The apostle minds the Ephesians of this, such were som of you. (5 Deuteronomy 15) Remember that you were a servant to sin and to Saytn, but God hath brought you out. 4 Be Exorted to humiliation. Be Exceeding humble. Tho your state be higher, your heart should be lower. 3 Things should humble you. 1: that you were so long a servant to sin before you wer a servant to Christ. That you spent so much of your time in the service of sin to which God allowed no time. That you were so longe before you engaged in the service of Christ. 2 It is matter of humiliation that there are remaynders of those lusts yet in you, that your sin is not destroyed, but ther are some remayns of it in your heart. Sin will dwell in this house till the Earthly house be dissolved. This is matter of humiliation. 3 It is matter of humiliation that after you are delivered from sin that yet it should so prevayle as to [harry] you captive agn. This is matter of humiliation. We have not kept our liberty after the [S][18] hath made us free. (5 Galatians 1) Stand fast in that liberty with which the son hath made you free. 5 Be Exorted to labour to get more power angst this lust: subdue it more and more. Let sin dye dayly in you and let no day pass but give him some blow whereby you may hasten his death. Do not thinke that satisfaction is

[17] Throughout the notebook, scriptural references do not always follow a clear pattern. They can be found at the beginning, middle, and end of sentences.

[18] Possibly shorthand for son or spirit.

perfect, but we should labour to be more and more satisfyed. 6 Let such as are freed from sin be Exceeding watchfull. Tho the dominion of sin be taken away yet his life is prolonged for a season, therefore be watchfull. Watch agnst it that sin may not get his power againe. Watch angst your sin, the sin of your nature, that you may be able to say as David I have kept my selfe from my own iniquity. If we over com this, other lusts will never overcom us, but fly Goliah is [slough] and all the Philistines freed. 7 Be exorted to be the servants of God. Hath God freed you from sin? Devote your selfe to his service that hath freed you from slavery to [ ] obey God's will. This is a great argument. I am the [ ] God that hath brought them out of their house of bondage, therefore keep those commands. God hath freed you from Saytn, sin. Be the servants of God. Your service is due to God. It is the end of your redemption, it is the only way to show your gratitude.

Mr. Foster. (Tuesday) October 12, 1680. (1 Corinthians 10:13) There is no Temptation taken you but that which is common to man.

Doctrine: 1 That temptations are common to man in this life. Be exorted to yield obedience to the law of God. (1 Luke 74) He hath freed us from all our Enemies that we may serve him in holiness all our dayes. Are you freed by God then serve God. Lay out your self and strength for God and for his service to quicken to obedience to God and to service of God: your service is due to God, but you ow noe obedience to sin. We are debtors to God and it is his due that we should serve him. You are the creatures of God, and you should serve him. All your strength is to little to serve God. We are debters but not to the Flesh to serve that, but obedience it is only due to God. 2 It is the end of your redemption from sin that you might serve God (2 Titus 14) who gave himself for us, that he might redeem to himself a peculyer people [zealous] of good workes. God is to be served without feare. (1 Peter 4:1.2) Christ hath suffered for us to this end that we might not suffer agn nor be the servants of sin. 3 This is our cheif way of expressing of our gratitude to God in freeing us from sin, it is by serving of God. (116 Psalm 89: 12.16 verse) Hath God loosed our Bonds we should say as David surely I am thy servant: What doth the lord thy God require that we should walke humbly with God? 6 It is Exceedingly dangerous for you to return to sin agn. God will certainly bring a yoake upon you. (28 Deuteronomy 47) 7 If you will not serve the Lord your God the Lord will put a yoake about your necks: 5 Consider you ought to obey the law of God that you might be like

Christ and conformable to him. In dyeing to sin so in newness of life we might allso serve God in holiness. (1 Peter 4:12) 8 Be you Exorted to pray to and depend upon God for grace and strength to preserve and keep you, that sin doth not get dominion againe over you. Depend upon God for grace that you be not overcom agn. (19 Psalm 1) (119 Psalm 133) Let no iniquity have dominion over you. If God doe desert and leave you it is certainly sin would get strength and overcome you, to quicken you to depend upon God. 1 Consider the best of the saints have been captivated with sin after the power of sin hath been subdued. ([ ] Rom 11) He was carryd captive sould under sin. Iniquity doe prevayle and innumerable Evils doe compass them about. 2 Consider that Sathen is yet striving to set sin upon the throne agayne: 3 To quicken consider you can doe nothing of yourself. You have no justification in your self. You can doe nothing without God. Therefore goe to God. If God withdraw from you sin will overcome you. 3 God hath promised his grace to us and presence with us if we doe seeke unto him for it: (2 Corinthians 12:7.8) 4 Be Exorted to labour to help others out of this Bondage and slavery. How many are there that thinke they are free and are servants to sin, slaves and in Bondage. (2 Peter 2.19) While they promise themselves liberty they are in bondage to sin. Remember those in bonds as bound with [them] those that are under spirituall bonds. 1 Consider hereby you destroy the kingdom of Sathen. It is ruined hereby. 2 Hereby you [can] worke with Christ whoe cam to preach deliverance to captives. 3 Hereby you honor God. You will bring a great deall of Honor to God and Jesus Christ in bringing many to him in the multitudes of subject is the king's honor. 4 Hereby you will procure a blessing to yourself. (29 Job 12.13) The blessing of them that are ready to perish com upon them. [L] Be Exorted to persever to the end in aposing of sin and yelling obedience to God. Stand fast in your liberty and yield not your [member] to be weapons of unrighteousness. Resist unto blood rather than yield to sin that so you may be kept from Bondage and slavery to it. It is hard 1 because it is a dayly conflick. Everyday [ma nt] there is no truce to be made with sin. There is no peace to be made. 2 It is such an Enemie as you canot fly from it. You are [habit s] for sin. You canot fly from it. 3 Lusts [hath] [eyd] from the Devill and from the world yet persevere to the end. Christ hath prepared a powerfull weapon for this warfare, they are mighty to God to caste down the strong loves of sin and Saytn. Be not discouraged but mayntaine this war and be strong as [t e i ous] in aposeing. Christ hath provided strong armor that

Jesus Christ hath provided to contend with this Enemie. The word of God the sword of the spirit is the weapon we are to weild in this conflict. Our weapons are not carnall. 2 That when you are most week in this conflict in yourself then you shall finde Jesus Christ to strengthen you. The power of Christ shall be with you whose strength shall be made powerfull in weakness. 3 Consider your continuall conflict with your lusts will be an Evidence of your grace. Your maintaining of this conflict doth Evidence that you have grace that doth mayntaine the conflict. If there were no grace in you there would be no opposition of sin. Where sin and Saytn rule all in the heart there is no enemie to appose: 4 Consider this lust in an Enemie that hath been often conquered. Lust hath Tempted and made war with the soule, but hath been overcome. Be therefore Encouraged to persevere. 5 Consider this lust the Enemie that doth assurest you it hath [received] his deaths wound and shall assuredly dye at last if dominion is taken away. 6 You are sure of victory over sin and that you shall at last posess a crowne. You shall have this day and sin shall not have dominion over you. Jesus Christ by his death hath [ited] the [d] death of sin. Sin must not reigne now, and after a litle while it shall dye. That is a good fight that ends in victory and that obteines a crowne. 2 Exortation is to those that are yet under the reigne and power of lust. Be Exorted to awake out of that secure Estate and condition. You are the worst of servants be awakened and be not secure. Your enemi is not only upon you but in you. He that serves one lust serves many lusts. Be not secure in your bondage, but be awakened and labour after the glorious liberty of the [s s] of God. (8 Romans 21) This is a great part of the miserie of those that are under sin. They see it not, but be you awakened to labour after an interest in that liberty that Christ came to give to you: You are born a slave and you are not free unless the son make you free. Let not your bondage to sin hinder you from the herkening to this Exortation. (25 [t] 10) (61 Isaiah) (1 Corinthians 6:2) Compare these two together and the year of jubille was a signe of your deliverance from sin, of gospell Liberty, that liberty Christ proclaimes, and yet how few are there that doe rejoice in it: but to quicken you to move after and to seeke liberty: As long as you are under the dominion of sin you are under the curse of the law. Under the condemning power of it. (6 Romans 14) Sin shall not have dominion over you. You are not under the law but under grace. (7 Romans 8) 2 Consider so long as you serve sin you are a servant to an enemie and that makes your bondage farr worss. You are servants to that which is an enemie to

God. The blessed glorious God, the carnall minde is emnitie against God. And how dreadfull a thing is that you serve an enemie to yourselves, an enemie to your soules. (1 Peter 2:11) Abstaine from [fleshly][19] lusts which war against the soule. It takes away the happyness of the soule. You serve a potent Enemy, a falls and deciptfull Enemie. 3 So long as you are a servant to sin and under the dominion of sin all your services canot please God. (8 Romans 8) They that are in the flesh they canot please God. Your prayers are sin and all that you doe are evill and unpleasing to God. You can doe nothing to serve God in an acceptable maner, and what a dreadfull thing is this to have all you doe unacceptable to God. 4 Consider to quicken to seek after this freedom. How much hath been done by God to redeem siners from the power of lusts? God the Father sent his son in to the world for this end to redeem captives. (8 Romans 3) What the law could not doe in that it was weake through the flesh, God sent his one son for this and to condemn sin in the flesh. 2 Consider that God the son hath given his life to be a ransom to free poore captives, redeemed not with silver or gold but with the precious blood of Christ. (2 Hebrews 14.15) (1 Peter 1:4) 1 The life of the son of God was layd down to take away the life of sin. 3 The gracious offer that is mad to the siner by God all that Christ hath [made] by his death, is offerd to the siner in the gospel. (1 Peter 3:19) 4 Consider both the father and the son, they send the spirit to worke this freedom from the bondage to this sin. 5 Consider the time past of your life is enough: that you have served sin it is too [tooe] much, but all our time is too little for God and the [last] of our time too much for sin.

<u>Mr. Foster: (Sunday) October 24, 1680.</u> There hath no (1 Corinthians 10:13) Temptation taken but such as is comon.

Doctrine: Temptation is common to all men in this world. Man is Tempted by his own lusts. 2 Exortation: to those that are under the power of lust to Labour for freedome for it. 1 For so long as you are under sin you are under the power and dominion of it. 2 As long as you serve your lust you serve an enemie, an enemie to God and you. 3 As long as you are under the power of your lust you canot please God. 4. What hath been don in order to your liberty? God hath sent his son. 2 Jesus Christ hath shed his blood for you. 3 There is the call

[19] "fleshly" King James Bible, 286.

of the gospell. 4 The spirit of God is promised. 5 To persuade you doe you consider how long you have been a slave to sin? Ever since you were born. You were not born free neither you have purchased this freedom. (16 Ezekiel [ ]) (1 Peter 4:2) The time past of our lives should suffice us. Will you both live and dy to all Eternity a slave to sin? 6 Consider what will be your end of continuing a slave to sin. (32 Deuteronomy 29) That is your wisdom, to consider the end of things. (5 Romans 20.21) What fruit had you in the things whereof you are now ashamed and death is the end thereof. 1 The longer sin raignes in you the stronger it will be. The power of sin is increased (13 Jeremiah 23) and strengthend by your long continuance in it. The older he growes the stronger he growes and it will have more power over you. 4 (for) The longer you sin the more bitter will your repentance be. The greater sorow and greater Teror. Peter went forth and wept bitterly. 3 You are by continuing under the power of sin and not seeking for freedom from it you are in danger to be left of God. To be given over to great ([Rom] 24.26.28) sin. They did not delight to retain God in their knowledge. God gave them up to all maner of wickedness. (69 Psalm 27) Ad iniquity to your iniquity 4(for) by your continuing under the power of sin you increase your punishment and miserie. If God deny repentance you make your torments the biger. You lay up treasures of wrath in hell. 7 Consider that happy condition of all those that are made free from the Treasures of sin. As there is no bondage like the bondage of sin, so there is no happyness like that to be freed from sin. (126 Psalm) You may say God hath don great things For you. Who of you shall be glad? 1 They are happy in their [ ] in their service in their fellow servant in their reward. 1 They are happy in their [ ] (144 Psalm). Happy is the people that is in such a case. God is the best master and hath the best servants. 2 They have the best service they doe the best worke. 3 They are happy in their fellow servants. Their company is delightful. A holy people a peculyer nation.[20] 4 They are happy in their reward. The end of those things is Ever lasting life: no master can give such ([ ] 22) a reward as God doth. 8 Consider how sad it will be for to remember when it is to late that you might have been freed from the slavery of sin and would not

[20] Peculiar nation is similar to peculiar people. In this case, the meaning is God's chosen nation or, Israel of the Old Testament, and New England in the seventeenth century.

be for to help you. Here labour to be sencible of your bondage, the worth of this liberty and of the want of it, know you are a slave to sin and Saytn. (2 Peter 2:19) You are a servant to lust and corruption. Labour to see the want of it. 2 Begin bee times, do not defer, doe not delay, but set about this worke be times. The children of Iserell they were glad of the 1st news of redemption. 3 Resist the first motions of lust. Parte not with your enemie, there is no peace to be made, but as soon as lust conceives doe you appose it? Yeild to the beginnings of it. Lust is as a sparke of fire that if not quenched will set all afire. Withstand the beginnings of sin. Imediately resist. 4 Labour to watch angst and keep yourself from your own sin. There is som sin that is the chief of sin in you and that may be called your own iniquity. Strive against this and watch against this. Know what is your master sin search after it. It is no great matter to know your master sin. It may be known. 1 That sin where conscience is awakened doth most Terify. 2 That sin that doth distract most in dutys. 3[21] 4 That sin you canot endure should be [touched]. 5 That sin you most seeke to hide. 6 That sin you have most in your mindes. Lust at night and [lust] in morning. 5 Shun all occasions of sin and all appearances of evill. They that can alow themselves in any appearances of evill will fall into evill itself. Avoyd all occasions of evill. Turn from the way of those that run to Evill. (23 Proverbs 2) Doe not enter in to [Joel] tent, sit not in Dalilahs lap. 6 Watch and be sober, all sins of intemperance put us under the power of lust. Be watchfull aganst your Enemie if you will not be overcome by it. Be sober. 7 Improve the word of God and attend the ordinance of God, that is a means whereby you may be turned From darknes to light. 8 Beg of God for his spirit and grace to be bestowed upon you, whereby you may be freed from the dominion and power of sin. It must be by the mighty power of God. (15 Deuteronomy 26) Beg of God to give you his spirit and bestow his grace upon you. (110 Psalm 3) 3 Man is Tempted to sin by the world. Man hath not only his enemies in the world but the world is his Enemie. Tho sin be not a creature of God, yet they are become Tempters of man to sin. The creatures God hath given man to enjoy while he lives are means of his death. Those things that were given to man as food for his body are Fuell for his lusts. Man is a slave to sin and allso to the world. The world is a temptation and

[21] In the notebook, there is no entry after point 3.

snare to man to draw his heart from God. (1 Timothy 6.9) They that will be rich fall into many foolish lusts and snares. (69 Psalm 22) Let your table be your snare and that which should be for your welfare becomes a Trap to them. They are Temptations to draw your hearts from God. (32 Deuteronomy 15) The children of Iserell they waxed fatt and kicked them. He forgot God that made them and did Lightly Esteem of the rock of their salvation. Ye (1 John 2:16) the Injoyments of this world are a Temptation. As first fruits and relations are a considerable part of man's Injoyments they are Temptations and snares. ([12] Proverbs) A friend Love [the] at all times and a brother is born for adversity. Man by [ ] is Tempted to sin. 1 By their Evill counsels they give they are Tempters. Jobe's wife tempted him to curse God and dye. When they doe it out of love they tempt us. Thus Peter (16 Matthew 22) master save they selfe. When they hinder from duty. 2 When they draw our hearts from God and draw Inordinate affections to them. 3 As they draw us to take of our trust and confidence from God. 4 As they hinder us from coming to and trusting [in] Jesus Christ. When they were bidden to the Feast they would not com. (8 Matthew 21) 2 A man's wealth and Estate, riches, plenty and abundance of the things of this life, They doe Tempt man and cause him to forsake God. (19 Matthew 29) How hard for a rich man to Enter the kingdom of heaven, because their riches be a Temptation to them to draw their hearts from God. God gave them their desires (106 Psalm 15) and sent [leaness] in to their soules. Riches and welth they do Tempt man to put confidence in the creature. The rich man's wealth is a city of refuge and a high [w e] to him. (31 Job 24) (1 Timothy 6:17) Charg them that be rich that they be not high minded and that they trust not in uncertain riches. 2 Welth doth Tempt men to pride and high mindedness. They were filled and their hearts were lifted up. 3 Welth doth tempt men to carnality and voluptuousnes. Soule take thine [ease][22] (12 Luke 19.20) at [rest] Eat drinke and be marry thou hast goods for many dayes. 4 Covetousnes riches Tempt to this. The more they have of the world the more they desire of it. Man's desire is unsatiable. He inlarges his desires as hell and it canot be sattisfyed. 6 It tempts to atheism, to a denyall of God and forsakeing of him. (30 Proverbs 8.9) Give me not richess least I befall and deny the.

[22] "ease" King James Bible, 93.

(13 Hosea 6) It tempts to a forgetfullnes of God: 7 It Tempt to unbeleife, they doe hinder our closeing with and Imbraceing of Christ by faith. (14 Luke 18) It is a temptation to man to neglect Christ. Treasure on Earth hinders from having Treasure in heaven. It Tempts to Idolitry and to a neglect of the word and ordinances of God. 3 The Honor and power and dignity man is advanced to in this life is a Temptation to man. All men are not Equall. Honor is a Temptation to ambition, to ostentation and [ca te ning] of others, and pride and lifting up of themselves above others. 4 The pleasures of this life they doe Tempt man to sin. Those lawfull pleasures and delights God alloweth to man in this life (3 Ecclesiastes) are Temptations to man. 1 They cause vanity in the heart. They fill us with vayne thoughts 2 and hinder our love to spirituall things and take off our hearts from the joys above. They Tempt man to fake happyness in the creature, they hinder us from goeing to the fountayne of all good: and draw our heart off from God. The implyments allso of this life is a Temptation to man. Reason why it is so it is because of the lust of men's heart after them. (1 Timothy 6:10) The love of money is the root of all evill, the inordinate love of it. They that will be rich fall in to temptations.

2 Reason is from the curss of God upon the creature.

3 Reason is from Saytn's working.

4 From man's ignorance of spirituall things and our not seeing the glory of spirituall things.

Use: this Doctrine should teach us to be contented with our portion. Envy not others that have abundance of this world. The greater is their Temptation.

Mr. Foster: (Sunday) October 31: 1680 (1 Corinthians 10:13) There is no temptation taken you but what is common to man.

Doctrine: that Temptations are common to man in this life. The world is a Temptation to man by Saytn's working in and with the world. Saytn is cald the God of the world because he doth dwell here. It is the place of his [t], and he improves those things that they be temptations to man. (3 Genesis 6) The serpent beguiled the woman. The Divill doth present those things to man as those things that are to be desired and are pleasant and lovely to the ey of man, and thus it was in the temptation of the 1st Adam and so in the temptation of the 2d Adam. He presented to him the glory of the world and said all those things I will give the fall down and worship.

4 Reason:[23] it is from man's Ignorance of spirituall things. The naturall man doth not re (1 Corinthians 2:14) ceiv[24] spirituall things, they are foolishness to him and they are spiritually to be discerned. (19 Psalm10) Man doth not discern the things of God. (11 Ecclesiastes 7) He takes no pleasure in them. He tasts no sweetness in them.

5 Reason: is from man's seekeing happynes in this world. (4 Psalm 6) Many say who will show us good? Men seeke good in the creature and so find no good from them because they place their chief good in them. Happy is the people that is in such a case, but happy is that people whose God is the lord.

6 Reason: from the judgment of God upon man in departing from God his cheife good to the world. 1 God leaves him to the creature and makes them as the waters of Marah[25] bitter to man.

Use: Learn we to be contented with our portion though we have not so much of the world. 2 Learn not to envy those that have much of the world. Envy them not. The prosperity of Fooles destroys them. They that have the world they have their Temptation with them. 3 This may teach us to moderate our affections too, and our desires and Endeavoures after the things of the world. Pray as Augur. (30 Proverbs 8) Give me not poverty nor riches. If men have been destroyed by prosperity doe not desire it, but be put upon it to [seek] after a better portion than any thing in this world. Mind those things that doe accompany salvation, mind and choose the better part.

2 Use: of Exortation: 1 let us be Exorted to be moderat in our use of the world if it be such a Temptation. (1 Corinthians 7) Let those that use the world as though they abused not. (2 Ecclesiastes 24) (3 [Cap.]

[23] The previous sermon ended with 3 Reason. This indicates that it is not only a sermon series, but the continuation of a longer sermon.

[24] The word "receive" is divided by the scripture reference. This is an example in the notebook where a word is separated by a reference, compared to the more common examples of phrases and sentences being separated by a reference. This must be a function of the minister's oral delivery and the notebook writer's ability to copy what is being said. I do not believe this notebook is a re-write. Instead, I believe the note taker is writing in-step with the sermon's delivery, or is "writing after the preacher" as suggested by Edmund Morgan in *Light on the Puritans from John Hull's Notebooks*. This does not explain why the word is split in half, but it points to what must have been the very challenging task of accurately recording every word that was being said.

[25] Marah is a place-name meaning "bitter." It was a "place in the wilderness of Shur, so named because of the bitter water found there by wandering Israelites." *Holman Bible Dictionary*, 1075.

12.22) (5 [Cap.] 18) 2 Be Exorted for to have a care of being Tempted by the things of this life. Let us watch, least our hearts be overcom by the world that is a Temptation to draw our hearts from God. (17 John 6) I pray that we may be kept from the evill of the world that we may not be tempted and drawn by it unto sin. It is a temptation to all men in all places. It will tempt a Judg to pervert Judgement. (16 Deuteronomy 19) Thou shall not rest judgment. It is a temptation to ministers to preach falls Doctrin. (1 Titus 11) (2 Peter 2:3) Through covetousness they shall [sin]. A Temptation to merchants to oppress and get (12 Hosea 7) gain:[26] It is a temptation to Every man (5 James 4) in his calling to oppress. It is a temptation to us in our generall calling in workes of charity and piety. Forget not to entertain stranger Laying aside covetousnes. Let us labor to over com the temptations of the world so as it may not be a temptation to us. For direction be sure you gaine not the world in any indirect way. Get it in a right way if you would get good by it. 2 Ever seeke after and use the creatures for a right End, and Labour not to seeke the creatures for themselves, but that you may serve God with them. God made all things for himself. Every creature is made for God's glory. Seeke them, use them for this end, and they will be no temptation to you. 3 Doe not place your happynes in those things, doe not use them for that end. You may be happy with out them and miserable with it, for you may gaine the whole world and yet be lost. 4 Seeke and use the things of this life with prayer and thankesgiving. [Let] God sanctify them they will not hurt us, but this is the means where by God doth sanctify them. All things are sanctifyed by the word and prayer. 6 Let not the cares of this world hinder you from better things. (10 Luke 41.42 verse) Our saviour commands Mary that had chosen the better [part]. (1 Timothy 6:19) Lay up for yourself a good foundation angst the time to com that you may Lay hold of Eternal life. Provide for thy soule for Eternity. Lay up Treasure in heaven. 6 Trust God's providence in the use of means, doe not distrust the providence of God. (6 Matthew 20) He provides for the [foules]. 7 Live above the world while you are in it. Our conversation is in heaven sayeth the apostle. Let the world be a crucifyed thing to you. Live by faith in Christ, and Esteem all things in the world nothing to Christ, and in comparason of him: 8 Labor to be convinced of the vanity of all the things in the world that you doe not

[26] Isaac Foster's father William was a merchant.

goe a whoring after them. All things in the world are vaine in order to make the soule happy. There is no good in them to satisfy the soule. (49 Psalm 11) Their inward thought is that their houses shall endure forever. 9 Be willing to part with that world at God's call. If you canot part with it it will be a snare to you. Be willing God should take from you as well as give it to you. 1 When we are called to workes of charity doe not keep it back. (1 Timothy 6:17.18) Be rich in good workes. God loves a chearfull giver. (11 Proverbs 24) 2 Be willing to part with the things of the world when God calls for it. It is a way of suffering for Christ. (10 Hebrews 34) They tooke Joyfully the spoyleing of their goods. 3 When God takes them away in [the way] of his providence.

4 When God is takeing us away from death be then willing to part with it and take nothing away with you. Bring your hearts and spirit to this to desire no more of the world than God gives, and to be willing to part with it when God calls for it. 4[27] Be Exorted to have a care of all inordinate love and affection to the things of the world. Love not the world and the things of the world, for because of our love to the world the world is a Tempatation to it: to stir you up to this duty consider the danger of those whose love is set upon the world, whose end is destruction, who minde Earthly things. They that will be rich fall into many Temptations and Foolish Lusts and fall into perdition. It causeth apostacy. The love of the world caused [Demos][28] to forsake us. 2 If your love be so set on the world you have no love for God, and God will have no love for you. If you love the world the love of the Father is not in you. 3 This doth hinder your service of God. As there is no love of God in the heart, so there is no service of God in the life. [L] Consider there is infinitly more to be injoyed in God and God is more worthy to be loved than all the creatures. God deserves our love. When is our love inordinately set on the world? 1 If the world be the object of your love, joy, sorrow, and feare and hope, if you be more afrayed of loosing the world than God [n] is a signe your heart your love is heare. If your cheife care and study and paynes be to get and keep the things of the world it is a signe you are Inordinate in your affections to them. 3 If you prefer seasons to gayne the world above

---

[27] Throughout the notebook the numbering of sermon sub-points is often incorrect, as in this case where 4 follows 4. I have not attempted to correct this, but have transcribed the numbers exactly as they appear in the original.

[28] Demos refers to the ordinary people of a community or nation, the populace of a Greek city-state. *Webster's Unabridged Dictionary*, s.v. > demos.

the means of grace, if you prefer the field before the house of God and the weekeday before the sabboth, it is a signe of inordinate love to the world. (1 Malachi 13) 4 If the cares (8 Amos 5) of this world doe distract us in the service of God that we canot serve God, but when we com to the house of God to serve him the cares of the world disturb us. When we canot part with the world when God calls for it in charity. When we doe Improve the world for a wrong end when we improve it in our lusts not for God's glory. To help aganst this inordinate love to the things of this life: often meditate and thinke upon the shortnes of this life. Set not your heart upon this world. You must shortly leave it. You are but a sojourner and stranger here. Your aboad is but for a short time. You are passing away from hence and must leave all those injoyments. (49 Psalm 7) He shall carry nothing away with him and his glory shall not defend after him. (49 Psalm 2 and 20) Man in honor abideth not, but is as the beasts that perish. 2 Often meditate on the things of this world. We doe not consider what they are. They are unprofitable, uncertain, mortall, and dangerous. They are unprofitable. We should take our hearts from them. They are unprofitable in life, there is not that profit in them in this life as we Expect. They are as the wind. Happy is that people whoe is in such case 2 They are unprofitable in death. No man can deliver himselfe from death with [those]. They are unprofitable in the day of judgment. God will not be bribed by them. 2 They are uncertain as well as unprofitable. Trust not in uncertain riches. 3 They are mortall. Wilt you set thy heart upon that [there] is not? They are dangerous they are Temptation and snares and their prosperity have slayn them. 3 Consider the Excelency of spirituall and heavenly things. God hath given us better things to set our hearts upon. 4 Labor to be sensible of your spirituall wants and your absolute need of spirituall things, and this will be a means to take off your affections off of those things. [L] Consider of eternall life. Your time is short but you are to live to all eternity in another world: 4 Man is Tempted by the instruments of Saytn to sin. Ev was Tempted by the serpent and Adam by Eve. Ahab by the falls prophets, Job by his wif and Christ by Peter. All evill companions may com under this head, instruments of Saytn. Reason why Saytn make use of instruments that he may hide himself. 2 Because of the influence that men have on upon another. By reason of relation and Imployment.

3 Reason is from the enmity that is in Saytn angst man and his earnest desire to destroy man.

4 Reason is from the readiness that is in wicked men to promoate the worke of the Divill and to carry on his designes. You are [o f] the Divill and his lusts you will doe. (4 Proverbs 6)

Use 1: let us walke sircumspectly if there be such tempters about us as Saytn. Our lusts the world the instruments of Saytn. 2 Have a care of Evill companion. He that is a companion of fooles shall be destroyed. 3 Be watchfull over one another. 4 Let us pray as Christ, Lead us not into Temptation.

Mr. Foster. (Sunday) November 7, 1680. (1 Corinthians 10:13) There is no Temptation taken you but that which is coman to man, but God is faythfull. Temptation is comon to man, that is their affliction. 2 There is the comfort that God lays down, but God is faythfull, you shall not be Tempted above what you are able to beare. The faythfullness of God is that which respects the promis. 2 God will make way for your escape that you may be able to bear it.

Doctrine: it is a unspeakeable ground of comfort to the people of God under Temptation to consider is faythfull, that will not suffer them to be tempted above what they are able to beare, and that they shall find a way to escape out of them. Or you may take it [thus] the faythfulnes of God unto his word wherein he hath engaged to his people. They shall not be overcome in Temptation is an unspeakable ground of comfort to them under temptation. God doth promise to keep his people in Temptation. God hath Engaged his grace shall be sufficient, and that the houre of Temptation shall be shortend for the elect. God hath promised that his people shall be Established and kept from Evill, and that he will confirm them to the End. Faythfull is he that [c l t]. (1 Thessalonians 5:23) You he will doe it you shall be Established. (6 Hebrews 18.19) Man under Temptation hath greater grownd of comfort than Adam in paradise. He had no promise that he should not be overcome, but God hath promised the believer he shall not be over com in this.

Doctrine: There are 3 [Propositions]: 1 God is faythful. 2 God hath promised we shall not be Tempted above what we are able, but [ ] the temptation he will find a way of Escape. 3 This is ground of strong consolation. [ ] God is faythfull. Ther is no deceipt with God. He is faythfull in dealing with the children of men. Let God be true and Every man a lyer. God is faythfull. This is an attribute of God. It is a virtue of God and one of the perfections of his divine nature. He is called a God of truth. (19 Revelations 1) He is called the faythfull one and (7 Deuteronomy 9) the lord thy God. He is thy God the True and faythfull one. (9 Isaiah 7) (1 Corinthians 1:9) God is faythfull, by whom you are called to the fellowship of his son this is attributed to God negatively. God is not a man (23 Numbers 19) that he should ly, nor the son of man that he should repent. (1 Samuel 15:29) The strength of Isrell will not ly. (6 Hebrews 18) It is imposible God should Lye. The word of God doth make known God to us to be such a God. The light of [nature] proves it to us. From the perfection of the 1st being and cheife good He hath no imperfection in His nature and good [but] be true. How or in what respect is God sayd to be faythfull? 1 In respect of his essence and being in opposition to all falls Gods. He is the only true and living God and is set so in opposition to all falls Gods. His being is not imaginary [duty] [but] God is the true and faythfull God as opposed to them. 2 God is true and faythfull in respect of his decree and purpose. It is imutable an unchangeable and shall have his accomplishment.[29] There be many Devices in the hearts of man, but the counsell of the Lord shall stand. He is of one mind and [who] can turn 2 [Betray] him. (14 Hosea 24) The Lord hath surely sayd: as I have thought so I will accomplish. God's counsell shall stand and he will doe all his pleasure. The purpose of God concerning the good he will bestow upon the Elect. They shall have their accomplishment. Whom he predestemant he calls, whom he calls he Justifys, and whom he Justifyes he glorifys.[30] 3 God is faythfull in all his workes in his workes of creation. The workes of God are great and wonderfull. Just and true are thy wayes Oh king of saints. They are don in deed and in truth. (7 Exodus 11) 2 God is true and faythfull in his works of providence. God is holy in all his workes and righteous in all his wayes, in the administration and government of the whole world. (19 Revelations 11) He is the true and faythfull one. (119 Psalm 175) In faythfullnes though hast afflicted me. (89 Psalm 35) If they breake my statuts I will visit them with the rods of men, but my faythfullness I will not take from them. 3 God is faythfull in the worke of his redemption. (1 Timothy 1:15) This is a faythfull saying Christ is cald a faythfull high preist in that he doth for siners. 4 God is faythfull in his

---

[29] This passage is very similar to Caleb Watson's sermons from Malachi on the immutable and unchangable nature of God.

[30] The Puritans may not have been strictly Calvinist, but Calvin's influence on Puritanism is evident.

word. Hath he said it and will he not doe it? (23 Numbers 19.20) God is true and faythfull in his word and commands. Thy judgments are the truth and the Law of God is the way of Truth. 2 God is faythfull in his word of prophesy. Every word of God shall be accomplished. All things must com to pass according to the prophesy. (2 Hebrews 3) The vision is for an appoynted time, at the end it shall speake and not ly, hence those prophesies that were future are written in the presen tence: as that in Revelations: Babilon is fallen. 3 God is faythfull in the accomplishment of his word and Threatening. The Fathers where are they and their prophets. Do they live forever, but my words tooke hold of you. (14 Numbers 13) (26 Numbers 24.25) (2 Genesis [17]) In the day thou eatest thereof thou shalt dy which is dayly fulfilled. 4 God is true and faythfull in his word and promise, Every word and promise is fulfilled. The promises are great and precious. They are precious because they shall be fulfilled. [ ] 6 Doe we not in the 11 of Zachariah 10 read of God's breaking of his covenant? And, (14 Numbers 34) you shall not com in to the land of which I promised. Answer 1: this is spoken according to the maner of men. They breake the covenant of their part and 2 this word hath in respect of what they had done to God as you have spoken to God so (14 Numbers 27.28) will I doe unto you. They charged God with breach of his promis. God sayeth as you have sayd so will do: 3 The promise was conditionall if they kept God's Testimonies. God is faythfull (7 Deuteronomy 9) to them that love him and keep his comandements. 4 The promise of God was not to the rebelious but to the faythfull Caleb and Joshua. 5 It was fullifiled. It was mad to Abram and his seed and to them it was fulfilled.

Use: is God a true and faythfull God? Then believe the threatenings of God. The soule that sins shall dy. 2 Let Every believer believe the promise of God. Let that strengthen your fayth in God. (77 Psalm 8) Doth his promise [fail][31] for Ever more: 3 Be all Exorted to Imitate God and labour to be like God in true and faythfull [ ] in our words when we speake according to our heart, in our workes when we doe according to our words that we speak. 2 God will not suffer the faithfull to be Tempted abov what they are able to bear, but will find a way of Escape all. God will find a way to deliver them out of their Temptation. God is faythfull to his word. (2 Thessalonians 3:2) The lord is faythfull that will stablish and keep you From Evill. (12 Revelations 14.16) The Divill

[31] "fail" King James Bible, 681.

persecutes the woman, the woman flys into the wilderness, and the Earth helps the woman.[32] (2 Timothy 4:17) The Lord stands by and helps the faythfull in the houre of temptation. Example: What is this ability spoken of here, you shall not be tempted above what you are able. It is not to be understood of the naturall power and ability [is in] man that is nothing. We have no sufficiency of our selves. If left to our selves Saytn would carry us captive at his will. 2 It is then meant of that ability that is given us of God that Temptation shall not exceed your grace. You shall have as much power as Temptation. I can doe all things through Christ. Strengthen me. It is that might that is in the inward man with might wrought by the (3 Ephesians 16) spirit of God. We can neither will nor doe of our selves. This ability is given to us by infuseing a principle of grace in to our hearts when we have new desires and new affections in our hearts. 2 By that supply of grace of assisting and strengthening Grace we receive of God. We are Enabled, for without this supply of grace we should com to nothing. 2 How doth God make way for our escape that we may be able to beare Temptations? God doth it by limiting and restraining of Saytn in his Temptations. The Divill if he were left to himself he would follow us everywhere, there were no escaping, but Saytn is by God restrained and Bound, Els Job had not Escaped for all his patience God would have Els kild him as he did his children. 2 God makes way for our Escapeing Temptation by strengthening our patience in Temptation and our fayth in God to beare and bring out of it. (12 Revelations 14) The [ch] Escaped how she had wings given her to fly from him. The wings were the graces of Fayth and hope. 3 God doth find a way of Escape all by giving [ ] the good of Temptations. (1 Peter 1:6.7) God makes Temptations a means of good. We are not led into temptation when it doth not hurt [ ]. 4 God delivers out of Temptation by takeing us to himself, out of the reach of the Divill and all his instruments.

[32] In his Ph.D. dissertation, Avihu Zakai argues against the notion that Perry Miller's Puritans sought to reform all of Europe using the model of New England's "City on a Hill." Zakai believes the Puritans "viewed the mother country as a Babylon…Their real aim was, instead, to fulfill the role of the 'woman in the wilderness' (Revelation 12:6) and seek an asylum in which to the fight against the Antichrist could be carried on." Theodore Dwight Bozeman. "The Puritans' 'Errand into the Wilderness' Reconsidered." *The New England Quarterly* 59, no.2 (June 1986), 237. It is difficult to know with certainty what the intention of Foster's use of the wilderness woman reference is here.

Reason [why or that][33] :it is so is from that promise of God. God hath promised and engaged this in the covenant of his grace. God will never leave and forsake those that do trust in him. (3 Genesis 15) He hath promised the seed of the woman shall bruise the serpents head.

2 Reason: is taken from the decree and purpose of God in election. The Elect shall not be Tempted above what they are able. (24 Matthew 22) Except those dayes should be shortened the elect should scarsly be saved.

3 Reason: from the Tenderness, love, pity, and compassion of God to his people. (104 Psalm 5) The Lord pitys his people considers there frome that they are but dust. (57 Isaiah 16) God will not contend forever.

4 Reason: is from the victory and [conquest] of Christ over all his and our Enemies, and there fore we shall not be Tempted above what we are able to beare. We overcome Temptations because Christ overcomes them.

5 Reason: is from the intersession of the Lord Jesus Christ. He doth Intercede for us, we overcome by the death of Christ and the blood of the Lambe. I pray that they may be kept from the Evill of the world and from the Evill one.

6 Reason: is from the great honor is brought to God thereby, and the great dishonor would com to God if he should not keep them. It would argue want of love in God or power in God that he is not able to [free].

3 Proposition: This is ground of great comfort to the people of God that they shall not be Tempted above what they are able to, that in the End they shall Escape. We are assured of escape [all]. God is faythfull that hath promised this. This the apostle mentions to the Corinthians as their comfort in the text, that they shall at last Escape. It is an adition to our sorows that there is no way of Escape. (14 Exodus 3) It is ground of comfort because of the miserable condition of those that are Tempted above what they are able.

2 Reason: from the unspeakeable mercy God bestows on us and that is our comfort.

Use: 1 the Doctrine doth teach us not to be discouraged and doe not faint under Temptation. 2 It should teach us patience in bearing of Temptation and trust in God under it. 3 It should quicken our courage

[33] This shorthand symbol translates as "why" or "that."

in resisting Temptation. You are sure to comfort. 4 It shows the happynes of those that have an interest in the promises.

Use: it doth exort us not to yield to temptation. 2 Doe not seek deliverance out of God's way he hath promised a way of [escaapeall]. Seeke deliverance in God's way and [wayts] God's time. [L] Seek to God for strength angst Temptation and that he would make a way for your [escapeall].

CHAPTER FOURTEEN

SACRAMENT DAY

Isaac Foster's vivid description of the torture and crucifixion of Christ is stirring. It is interesting that he chose the Old Testament rather than the New Testament as his opening text for this sermon, and the New Geneva Study Bible offers some possible explanations. "Isaiah predicted the coming of a Servant and Savior much greater than Cyrus. This anonymous Servant would bring justice to the nations, establish Israel in a new covenant with the Lord, become a light to the Gentiles, and take away the sins of His people. The Servant would suffer willingly to achieve these victories, and God would reward and vindicate him. The new Testament identifies the Servant as Jesus Christ, the incarnate Lord."[1] *The significance of typological themes was clearly an important aspect of Puritan theology. It is a methodology of connecting the Old and New Testaments that appears often in the* Hartford Sermon Notebook.

Of course, the covenant aspect of Isaiah spoke to the Puritans, but the New Geneva Study Bible lists many other elements of Isaiah that clearly fueled the themes of the Hartford Sermon Notebook. *"Isaiah's vision of God's kingdom is great, because it includes the history of redemption from his day until the fullness of redemption. It embraces the exile, the return of the Jews from exile, the mission, ministry, and kingdom of Jesus Christ, the mission and hope of the church, Jesus' present rule over this world, and the restoration of all things in holiness and righteousness."*[2]

As the end of New England's seventeenth century drew near, the need to restore holiness and righteousness was keenly felt, especially among the ministers. Increase Mather's Reforming Synod of 1679–80 is a clear indication of this general feeling, that God's chosen people in New England had begun a moral declension. Additionally, the lack of sermons from May 1680 might suggest that Hartford's ministers were attending that year's Synod in Boston.

<u>Mr. Foster. Sacrament Day (Sunday) November 14, 1680:</u> (53 Isaiah 10) *"Yet the Lord wolde breake him, & make him subject to infirmities:*

---

1 *New Geneva Study Bible*, 1020.
2 Ibid., 1021.

whe he shal make his soule an offring for sinne, he shal se his sede & shall prolong his daies, and the wil of the Lord shal prosper in his hand."[3] Yet it pleased the Lord to greive him, thou hast put him to greife, and in the booke are many prophesies of our Lord Jesus in gospell times, but non doth more set out the sufferings of Christ than this prophesie. He ushers in the sufferings of Christ without complaynt of unbeleife: who hath beleieved our report. It hath respect to the prophet's time. Few did then believe Christ should suffer so. Or 2 in Christ's time in gospell times few doe believe this [cap] [containes] a discourse of Christ's sufferings. 1 The sufferings of Christ he was bruised. 2 The blessed Effects, he shall see the [tra i ll] of his soule. 1 God bruised him. It pleased the lord to bruise him. Tho: he was not an actor of sin, it pleased the Lord to bruise him, to batter or to break him. (12 Exodus 46) The pascall lambe, a bone of it was not to be broken. That was a figure of Christ and of Christ it was said a bone of him was not broken. 1 It noats any greife, payn, whereby a man is broken. 2 He was put to greife. Sickness or payn puts to greife: (8 Matthew 17) He tooke our infirmities and beare our sickness. Those deseases Christ beare were the sickness of our soules. God put him to greife made him sorowfull. 2 We have the blessed fruit of his sufferings. 1 He shall see his seed, this is a greivious reward for his sufferings. He should see a number of the Elect believe in him. Hence this was the fruit of his death. (12 John 24.32) [ ] I am lifted up, shall draw men to me. 2 It is sayd he shall prolong his day. (9 Hebrews 28) (7 Hebrews 25) He should dye no more. He lives Ever [other] understand it of the seed of Christ and then Christ shall have a seed upon earth that shall abide successively to the end of the world. 3 It is sayd the pleasure of the Lord shall prosper in his hand. Jesus Christ shall atayn his end.

Doctrine: that it was the will and pleasure of God for to bruise the lord Jesus Christ and put him to greife tho: he was the well beloved son of God. The Lord Jesus Christ in the days of his flesh he under went all the sorowes the sins of the elect deserved, hence he is sayd to be a man of sorows made up with sorowes and acquainted with greifs, accustomed to it. He bore our greifs. Example: when was Christ thus bruised or put to greife? It was in his state of humiliation. It is not in his state of exaltation. He is not then bruised or put to greife. (116 Psalm 10.11) At thy right hand are pleasures for Evermore. Christ was

[3] *The Geneva Bible, 1560 Edition*. 302.

put to greife in his birth, in his life and death. When Christ put his foot upon the stage of the world he was bruised.[4] He was born of a man and Low virgin in the stable of an inn, Layd in a manger. 2 In his life he was put to greife all the days of his life in his private life (3 Luke 23) which was till he was 30 years of age. It is probable that in that part of his life he followed his Father's trade. He was hungry. (4 Matthew 2) (4 John 6) He was wearyd with his Journey. (8 Matthew 20) All these common miseries of man Jesus Christ underwent. 2 Allso in his publique life he was put to more greif. He appeared the son of man and had many Enemies to put him to grief. 1 Saytn Tempts him. (4 Matthew 4) 2 He was put to greife by the men of the world. He was rejected not entertayned by his own. He was despised and we Esteemed him not. There was the contradiction that he mett with all from siners. They despised him and entertained him not. 3 The Lord Jesus Christ was put to grief chiefly in his death. 1 In the Antecedents of his death, that which went before it, one of his disciples, a falls one, betrayed him. A True disciple denyd him and all forsake him. The Jews denyd him, the gentiles they despised him. There was the fear and [Teror] that was in Christ at the foresight of death. He was sorowfull to the very death. 2 At his death it [S] [then] Christ was cheifly put to greife: 1 Consider the kind of his deth and then you shall see how he was bruised. It was not a comon nor naturall death but a vyolent death. The death of the cross. The worst of death, it was a death that man's cruell nature had devised to punish the worst of malefactors. This death was the most shamefull deth. Christ endured the cross and despised the shame. It was the death of a slave. No free man was ordinarily put to that death, and it was inflicted on the worst of malefactors. He was to be carryd without the gates. He was not worthy to live with nor dy among the people. 4 There was his accusation set over his head. [S] This is the king of the Jews in dirision [ ] was the dirision and scoffing of all sorts of people. He died amongst theives, set betwein to as the worst of the three. 2 The death of the cross was painfull more than ordinary, and that appears in that they peirced his hands and feet. 2 There was the Extending or stretching of his body upon the cross. (22 Psalm 17) 3 It was a graduall and lingering death that held them in great paine six houers. 3 It was a cursd death. Cursed is he that hangs upon a tree. (3 Galatians 3) Christ hath redeemed us from the curss of the

[4] Shakespearian Puritans? Perhaps not, but they certainly knew his work.

law being made a curse for us. 2 Consider the weight of the wrath of God that Jesus Christ bore upon him when he was on the cross. All the sufferings of Christ on his body were nothing compared with what he did suffer in his soule. He suffered the Imediat stroke of God upon his soule and that made him cry, (26 Matthew 37) my God my God why hast thou forsaken me. God hid his face withdrew his favour, and Christ bore more upon the cross from God, then from the cross.

Reason why the Lord Jesus Christ was thus bruised of God. 1 Because he was made sin for us. He was made sin For us who knew no sin. He bore our iniquites upon the cross. (53 Isaiah 6) The Lord hath layd upon him the iniquities of us all. Jesus Christ was a siner imputatively.

2 Reason: he was put to greife that we might be delivered from greife, made a curss that we might be delivered from the curss.

3 Reason: it was that the prophesies might be accomplished.

4 Reason: that he might simpathize with his members, that he might be a mercifull high preist.

5 Reason: that he might overcom the Divill and have the victory of sin and Saytn.

6 Reason: that he might take away the cause of sin.

Use 1: The sufferings of Christ teach us the great Evill of sin. 2 Learn the wonderfull love of Christ to man that he should be willing to be thus bruised for man.

2 Use: of comfort to all that have an interest in Christ's death and sufferings, your comfort is your sufferings for Christ is not soe great as his. 2 What Ever sufferings you suffer the sting of all sin is taken away. 3 All your sufferings they are the fatherly strookes of a Father. 4 The Lord Jesus Christ doth and can simpathiz with us in all our sufferings. His greife is our joy.

Use: Exortation: Let us be exorted to love Jesus Christ that soe hath loved us. How should we love Christ? By mourning for all that heart enmity in us agnst Jesus Christ. 2 By your hatred of sin that brought Christ to the cross. 3 Show your love to Christ by your obedience to him. 4 By your studying to advance his glory. 5 By being willing to suffer for Christ. 6 By earnest desire of communion with Christ. 2 Be exorted not to put Christ to more greiefe by your unworthy carriage towards Christ. Doe not crucify him agn. 3 By an ey of Fayth, looke to Jesus Christ for an interest in his death and sufferings. Behold Christ in his word and ordinances, by an ey of fayth, fetch new supplyes of grace from God.

Foster's November 5, 1679 Thanksgiving Day sermon also chose a Psalm as its opening text, Psalm 103 verse 2. The Geneva Study Bible provides an insightful explanation of the character of the Psalms, which points to their prominent use as opening texts on days of Thanksgiving: "A psalm of thanksgiving is appropriate when the Lord answers a prayer of lament. The first three psalm types form a kind of triad. The psalmist sings hymns when he is right with the Lord, laments when he is out of harmony with Him, and gives thanks when the relationship is reestablished."[5]

Mr. Foster. Thanksgiveing Day (Wednesday) November 17, 1680. (68 Psalm 20) "*This is our God, even the God that saveth us: and to the Lord God belong the issues of death.*"[6] He that is our God is the God of salvation and to our God belongs the [issues][7] from death. This psalm is a psalm of David and pened upon som great deliverance God wrought for his ch. Som thinke it was pened upon the deliverance out of Egipt, others upon a deliverance from the Phillistins, and when the ark was removed from the house of Obidedom.[8] David doth bless God and gives him the Title of that God of salvation. We hav a description of God, our God, the God of his people. 2 Described by what he doth for his people, he is a God of salvation to them. 3 The psalmist describes God by his title. God the lord. Jehovah adoni. A God that gives [a being] 4. He is discribed from his sovraign power over the Lives of all his creatures. To him belongs the [issues] from death.

Doctrine: that it is matter of rejoyceing and that then the people of God shared glory in that he is their God is the God of salvation. He that is our God is a God of salvation. The psalmists boast of this. This is our God. We have wayted for (25 Isaiah 9) him and he is our salvation. The God's of the heathen, they that pray to them pray to a God that canot save.[9] Example: 1 God is a God of salvations. He is so to his people. He is cald the hope of his people and their salvation. He is cald

---

[5] *New Geneva Study Bible*, 754.

[6] *The Geneva Bible, 1560 Edition*. 249.

[7] The word is "issues" in the King James Bible.

[8] Obidedom is a personal name that refers to several different Old Testament figures. In this case, Foster is using the name to refer to Obed-edom the Philistine, who was loyal to David. Following the death of Uzzah, David entrusted Obed-edom with the Ark of the Covenant, which he kept at his house for three months.

[9] If the God's of the heathen was a reference to the spiritual beliefs of Connecticut's Indian population, Foster may be referring to the pantheon of Gods worshipped by New England's Algonkian tribes. See Steven F. Johnson. *Ninnuock (The People): The Algonkian People of New England* (Marlborough, Massachusetts: Bliss Publishing Company, 1995), 37.

a rock of salvation the tower of salvation. Salvation belongs to him it is his salvation. 1 Why is God cald a God of salvation? Answer: 1 because God is the 1st [contrive] and Inventor of that way of salvation. It is that contrivance of infinit wisdom. God is the author and finder of that way of salvation by Jesus Christ or it had been never found out, and had not that been found out there had been no Temporall salvation when man destroyed himself. God was his help when man had destroyd himself. God found a ransom. 2 Because God hath revealed this way of salvation to man in his word, and by his spirit and power effectually [convays] it unto man and confers it upon Man.3. God is called a God of salvation because of his providence whereby he doth [pe r t] and uphold all his creatures. The goodnes and mercy, power and goodnes of God is manifest in providence. All is upheld (1 Hebrews 3) by the word of his power. Oh Lord thou preservest man and beast in him. We live, move, and [have] our being. 4 God is cald a God of salvation because God doth delight and take pleasure in salvation. God's nature doth incline him to show mercy to his people in misery. (3 Lamentations 3) God doth not afflict willingly nor greive the children of men. Hence when God punisheth a people it is cald his strang worke. God doth not delight in the death of siners. (11 Hosea 8) How shall I give the up and marke the as [Admah][10] and 2 lov him. 5 It is from the soveraigne power of God. Dissposeing of salvations he can save whome he will and how he pleaseth. 1 No other God can save and so God is cald the God of salvation in way of distinction from other Gods. They canot save. (3 Daniel 29) There is no God can deliver after this sorte. 2 No meanes can save without God. Those that are most likely are most ineffectuall if God deny his blessing. (33 Psalm 16.17) A [horse] is a vayn thing to save and [no][11] the [king] canot save by his multitude of strength. (144 Psalm) It is God that gives salvation to [kings]. They canot be saved without God. 3 God can save with out meanes. (59 Isaiah 16) When there was no man [then] [his] right had wrought salvation. We have a strong [ity] he will [appoyn] salvation for walls and Bulwarke. 4 God can save by small means [ca] [ ] meanes thou canst saved by many as (2 Chronicles 14:11) well as fue. God can save by contrary means therefor cald a God of salvations. 2 Why is God cald a God of salvations? 1 Because of the kinds of

[10] "Admah" King James Bible, 994.
[11] King James Bible, 656.

salvation God gives his people, of Temporall, spirituall, and eternall. Saves from sin from death and from Saytn. 2 God is so cald because of the multitude of salvation that God workes for his people Every day from man's Evills. (40 Psalm 12) Enumerable Evills compass me about, no time, place of our abode but we need God's salvation. 3 That object of salvation. God is a saviour to all men and so a God of salvation. 4 From the many ways God useth to save [buta] by [a]. Christ loved [he] is the hope of all the ends of the Earth and the confidence of thos afar of on the sea:

Reason why it so. 1 From the love of God to his people in his Eternall [r] God will save them because they are chosen of God unto salvation and they are appoynted to salvation. It is not because they are better than others, but it is from the good will of God to them.

2 Reason: is from the merit and purchass of Christ. He hath merited it for them. He is the meritorious cause of all our salvations. (68 Psalm 18) (8 Romans 32 verse)

3 Reason: is from God's covenant with his people. God is engaged to them to be a God of salvation to them. (7 Deuteronomy 8) Because of the oath of God he will bring them out of Egipt. So David God made a covenant with him, and this is all [my] salvation.

4 Reason: it is taken from the great glory that comes to God by this salvation God gives his people. (63 Isaiah 12) (83 Psalm 18) That men may know the whose name is Jehovah: Help us for the glory of they name. Hereby God makes himself known in the Earth. 2 Here by fals Gods are put to shame, it quicken the people of God to fayth and obediens. It [puts] the people of God to rejoyce and glory in God. This fills the mouths of God's people with songs of thanksgiving. He that offers prays, glorifys God.

5 Reason: God is a God of salvation to his people and they seak to him and trust in him for salvation. 2 God's being a God of salvation is matter of rejoyceing and that the people of God should rejoyce in that there God is a God of salvation. (3 Hebrews 17) (41 Isaiah 16) Thou shalt glory in the holy one of Isrell. (64 Psalm 9.10) The Reason why it is so because we here by express our thankfullnes to God and give God the glory of our salvation. (1 Chronicles 16:8.10) Rejoyce in God. 2 Because this is the happynes of the people of God above those that have fals Gods. Their rock is not as our rock. 3 Because they are assurd they shall never want salvation for he that is our God is a God of it:

Use 1: Hence learn the misery and sad condition of all those that have no interest in God that canot say this God is their God. The reason of their misery is because God is a God of salvation. Their misery appears because they need salvation as well as others. 2 No other God can give them salvation. 3 He that is a God of salvation to his people will destroy the wicked. (78 Psalm 50) 2 It shows us the happynes of the people of God that have an interest in God. You serve a God that is able to help and save you. Ye, (144 Psalm 23) happy is the people that is in such a case. Happy art thou there is non like that people that is in such a case. Happy art thou, there is non like the a people to [s d] saved by the lord. 3 God is a fit object to be [h s d] [on] and prayd two because he is God of salvation. 4 It shows whoe we are to prays and give the glory of all our salvations to the God of salvations. 5 The people of God have no reason to be cast down in afflictions. Your God is a God of salvation. (1 Samuel 30:6) 6 It doth teach us that the enemies of the people of God have no reason to rejoyce or insult over the people of God when afflicted because their God is a God of salvation. Hence learn what engagements ly upon the people of God to love serve and prays God, the God of salvation. 2 Be Exorted every one to labour after an interest in God that we may say as the psalmist, our God is a God of salvation. 2 Be Exorted to acknowledg God as the author of our salvation. 3 Looke to God for salvation when we need it. 4 Be Exorted to rejoyce and glory in this that our God is of salvation, let us rejoyce in his salvation. God hath been a God of salvation to us. Consider the publique salvation God hath granted in our civill state [ch] state. Peace and plenty to our nation, to our Neighbours, and to our selves. God hath been a God of salvation to our persons famalys, let us rejoyce and glory in this. 1 God is worthy to be rejoyced in. 2 Consider God's salvations to us have been many, saved every day many ways. God hath saved us when he hath not (3 Deuteronomy 29) saved others. 4 If we doe not rejoyce in God's salvation it will provoke God to destroy us. God hath saved us not withstanding many sins that may have provoked God to destroy.

Foster's sermon series on (1 Luke 79) is about the saving quality and light of Christ, and an interesting question arises: how many of the people who were listening had seen the light? Estimates for the number of actual church members have already been discussed, but in view of the prominence of the notebook's exhortations for initial conversion and conversion renewal, the dynamics of regeneration in Hartford's First Church really begin to take shape. The message for Hartford's residents was two-fold: convert if you are unregenerate, then, once the skin of the natural man has been shed, practice continual conversion in a morphological progression like that described by Edmund Morgan in Visible Saints.

(Sunday) November 21, 1678. Mr. Foster: (1 Luke 79) *"To give light to them that sit in darknes, and in the shadowe of death, & to guide our fete into the way of peace."*[12] To give light to them that sit in darkness and the shadow of death we have the prophet blessing God for Christ. He gives a character of Christ. He blesses God for salvation by Christ. (Verse 69) Mor particularly we have the desent of Christ from David. 2 The accomplishment and fullfilling of the prophesie. (Verse 70 to 73 verse) 3 It is sent forth from the end, deliverance from our enemies, sin, Saytn and world, and that we might serve God in holyness and persever there in all our dayes. 2 In the prophesy we have the caracter of John Baptist described from his [office], he should be a prophet. 2 He tells us what maner of prophet he should be to prepare men to receive Christ and to give knowledge of salvation to the people by Christ and the remission of their sins 1 which is amplyfyed by the [e fiedant] cause the mercy of God. 2 The meritorious cause Jesus Christ in the words, observe the misery of man set forth by darknes. 2 The mercy conveyed to man by Christ is set forth by light. Man's misery is he is in darkness. In a proper sense darknes is nothing but the privation of light, but the darkness here is not meant of privation of Naturall sence, but it is taken in a figurative sence and so it sets forth man's sin and misery. Sin is intended here, man's abideing in sin is his abideing in darknes. If we say (1 John 1:6) we have Felowship with him and walke in darknes we ly. Hence the works of sin is Termed the workes of darknes. 2 Darkness noats all the Effects of sin, all that evill and punishment that comes upon man by sin. Externall sorow, misery that comes upon any man's body or state, that is called darknes. When I looked (30 Job 26) for good then cam darkness. Hence (8 Isaiah 22) they shall look into the Earth and behold trouble and darknes. Sickness and bodily affliction is called darknes and the grave is cald the house of darknes. 2 It is put for that misery which is internall on the soule, hence [Ex] and ignorance is called darkness. (12 John 35) Spirituall desertion is called darkness, God's leaving the soule. (50 Isaiah 10) If any man walke in darkness and see no light let him [stay] upon his God. 3 Eternall misery is hereby set forth. Hell is called the place of utter darknes. 2 Man's misery is set forth by the shadow of death. It is

---

[12] *The Geneva Bible, 1560 Edition*, 28.

such darknes as is like deth itselfe. 2 It is such darknes as brings under the power of death. The shadow of death is no other than a deadly shadow that doth bring death. 3 Man's misery is set forth by setting in darknes. There is the place of his abode and residence. He abides in darknes. 2 Here is the work of Christ. The Lord Jesus doth com to give Life to man and Light in this darkness. All joy comfort and happyness is expressed in light. God himself is called in him is Light and no darkness. Jesus Christ is cald Light, Joy, and comfort. The word of God called light glory is allso cald light.

Doctrine: that Jesus Christ it was the worke of him in coming into the world to give light to man that sat in darkness and the shadow man's misery without Christ sits in darkness. The mercy Christ gives he gives light. (2 Corinthians 4:6.7) God that hath commanded light to shine out of darkness hath shined in our heart. He is cald the son of righteousnes and the day spring from on high. He cam to Enlighten a darke world and to Enlighten dark hearts. The condition of man before he believes is darknes. They that doe believe (1 Thessalonians 5:5) they are called children of the day. 1 The state of nature is a state of darkness. He sits in darknes and the shadow of death. (82 Psalm 5) They walke on in darknes abide in darkness. (26 Acts 18) I was sent to preach Christ and to bring them from darkness to light. In what respect man is sayd to sit in darknes? Naturaly in regard of ignorance. The ignorance and blindness of men is called darkness. (15 John 9) (4 Ephesians 18) Every man is naturally blind and may be sayd to be in darkness. (1 John 5:9) He is the light that enlighteneth every man that comes in to the world. There is ignorance of God. A man naturally sits in darkness. He hath no light discovers God to him the world by wisdom knowes not God. There is the knowledge that there is a God and that he is to be worshiped, but as to any saving knowledg of God man is thorowly ignorant. There is no knowledg of God so as to enjoy Him. 2 There is ignorance of the will and wayes of God and of the way of worshiping God and the way to enjoy God. 3 We are ignorant of ourselves and know not what we are, in what Estate we are fallen. 4 There is ignorance of the way and means of salvation. 5 Ignorance of spirituall things, ignorant of grace and glory. (1 Corinthians 2:14) 2 A man naturally sits in darkness in regard of sin he walks in it: (1 John 1) 6 All sin is cald in darkness. Have no Fellowship with the unfruitfull works of darknes. The who were darkness are now light. All the ways and workes of sin are called the workes of darkness from the time and season men make choys of those workes of darkness. (24 Job 15) The ey of the adulterer wayts for the Twilight. 2 They are called so from their contrarity to the Law and word of God which is called Light. (6 Proverbs 23) (1 Peter) The word of God is that light that shines in a darke place. 3 Works of sin are cald workes of darknes from the cause of them. They proceed from that darkness in the heart and blindness in the understanding. 4 They are called workes of darknes from the author of them and that's the Divill, which is the tempter to them. (6 Ephesians 12) (1 John 6) 5 They are soe called from the End of them and that's utter darkness. Sin leads to it, to the blackness of darkness. There is nothing of the light of grace to be seen in their conversation. They doe abide in sin, sit in it. 3 Man is sayd to sit in darkness in regard of the misery, affliction, trouble and sorow that abides on men in this world. The darke places of the Earth they are full of the habitations of cruelty. 4 Man is in darknes and abides in it by reason of the horor and great feare that men are subject too. (2 Hebrews 15) Thro fear of death all their life time they are subject to bondage. 5 Man naturally sits in darknes in regard of death and Hell. Death is cald the place of darkness the land of darkness. Man is an heire of Hell and deserves to be cast in to that place of darkness. This is the misery man is in without Christ: when is it and what is the ground of this darknes? 1 Man's apostacy from God. Man departed from God or he had never fallen into this state of darkness.

2 Reason: is taken from the justice of God. Sin is the procureing cause, Justice is the inflicting cause.

3 Reason: is taken from Saytn's working. The first darkness man was brought into was by Saytn's Temptation. The God of the world doth blind the minds of those that believe not. He is the instrumentall cause that doth hold men in darknes. He hinders their coming to Christ, Endeavours to hold them in chaines of darkness.

4 Reason: is from man's abuse of that naturall Light that God gives. Light shineth in darkness and the Light comprehendeth it not. Men abuse their naturall light, hence God gives them over to blindness.

5 Reason: is taken from man's neglect of that means of light. (6 Proverbs 23) The law is a lamp and the comandement is a light, but men doe not give heed to it, are not inlightened by it, hence they abide in darknes. They love darkness and not the light.

Use 1: learn we hence to se and be deeply affected with man's misery by nature. Not to behold the sun is a great misery, but much more to se the son of righteousness. Light is sweet much more spirituall light. Man by nature hath no sight of God and grace and glory, is in misery, sits in darkness, danger, of sin hell and misery. Man's misery appears in regard of the kind of darkness man sits under, spirituall darknes of sin and want of the light of God's love and favour. 2 Consider the degree of this darknes, darknes in the shadow of death in darkness wherein is no light. 3 The misery of man appears in the subject of this darknes. The soule the best part of [ ]. Consider the danger man is in by this darknes, redy to fall in to the pit of destruction. [L] It is abideing darknes. (15 Job 30) He shall not depart out of it. Agn it is such darknes as the naturall man loves. He calls this darknes light, Loves it, delights in it. It is dedly darkness, it is condemining darknes, such darknes as is joyned to the shadow of death. It is like to death. 2 Learn the happynes of man in a state of grace. He is freed from darknes. The who wer darknes are now light in the Lord, turned from darknes to light.

2 Use: of examination. Try where you are in a state of darknes where you be of the number of those that sit in darknes. 1 Do you see any Excelency in spirituall things? He that sits in darkness he sees no Excelency in God Christ. 2 Do we love the bretheren, those that are godly for the sake of godlynes? (1 John 2 verse 11) He that hates his bretheren is in darknes and hath no light. 3 Try your states by your conversation. Do you walk as children of the light, doe you shine as lights in the world? Doe you set a good light to others? 4 Try yourself by this. Hav we no fellowhsip with the workes of darknes? As long as you doe the workes of darkness you have no communion with God.

3 Use: is of conselation to the godly that are brought out of this state of darknes. You are brought (1 Colossians 12) to light. 1 Your comfort is then darknes shall not return again unto you. 2 All though you are not totally freed from darkness, yet God will be a light to you in darkness. 3 You shall certainly be brought to that light wherein is no mixture of darkness at all:

4 Use: of exortation. You that are freed from this darkness be Exceeding thankefull to God for this and show forth the prays of him that hath called you from darkness to light. 2 Be exorted to walke as the children of the light. (2 Philipians 15) 3 Endeavoure to bring others out of darkness. 3 It exorts those that are in darknes be sencible of your condition. Se your misery. 2 Looke to Christ for light to bring you out of this darknes and to bring you to light, and consider there is light to be had. Jesus Christ is the light of the world and he cam to give light to those that sit in darknes. 2 It will be an aggravation to your sin that you abide in darkness when light is com into the world.

3 If you live and dye in a state of darknes you will go to the place of darkness.

Mr. Foster. (Sunday) November 28, 1680: (1 Luke 79) To giv light to them that sit in darknes and the shadow of death.

Doctrine: That is the worke of Christ for to give light to those that sitt in darkness. He is the fountayn of all spiritual light, the sun of righteousness that visits us from on high. 1 Man naturally sits in darkness. You have heard what the darknes is, ignorance of God, Christ, of heaven and glory. 2 Darknes of sin man lives in and abides in. 3 Darkness of sorow, afflicition. 4 Darknes of feare and horor that doth rise by sin. 5 There is darkness of death: 6 The darknes of hell that is called a place of darknes.

The Reason is from man's apostacy from God the Father of lights. 2 From the justice of God. 3 By means of Saytn by neglecting the means of light, God gives darkness. 2 It is the [ ] of Christ to Enlighten a darke world. All spirituall light comes from Christ. (8 John 12) Hence Christ is called the light of the world. (9 John 5) As long as I am in the world I am the light of the world. He is the true light that gives light to the world. [In] his [ ] to give light to the gentiles. (49 Isaiah 5) I will [give][13] the for alight to the gentiles. It is his work to give and [con y] light when there this light that Jesus Christ gives to those that sit in darkness it is all good. The whole of man's happyness that is confered to man in and by Jesus Christ's light is either in created or created in. Created light is God himself all goodness. (1 John 1:5) God is light and in him is no darkness. He is the father of lights. Created light proceeds from God and is begotten of Him. Created light is properly [to] be that which is so called by a figure. (1 Genesis 3) The 1st is in the sun by figurative light, and that is Temporall prosperity and Joy. (29 Job 3) Job sets forth his outward prosperity by light [ ] [h ter] 6. They had light and gladnes, joy and honor, a feast and a good day. (112 Psalm 4) Unto the upright there ariseth Light[14] darkness. 3 There is spirituall Light, Intellectuall in knowledg, or the light of holyness and grace. 4 And there is Eternall light, the light of heaven and glory which is called the Inheritance of light. Jesus Christ now is the author

[13] "give" King James Bible, 811.

[14] In the King James Bible, the words "in the" appear between light and darkness, but they do not appear in the notebook.

of all light, but the light in the text is the light that is given to man by the worke of redemption. 1 The Light of wisdom, Reason and understanding Jesus Christ doth give to man. Jesus Christ was given to open the Eyes of the blind, those that were spiritually blind. (1 John 5) In him was Light and the Light was the Light of man. There is the Light of spirituall wisdom. Jesus Christ inlightens our understandings with the knowledge of God in Jesus Christ. God that comands (2 Corinthians 4:6) the light to shine out of darkness hath commanded the light of the knowledge of Jesus Christ to shine in our hearts. The naturall man doth not discern the things of God.[15] 2 The light of joy and comfort is given by Christ. 1 Externall Joy and comfort is given to us by Christ. He is the saviour of all men, especially of those that believe.[16] 2 The light that doth shine from the favour of God, he gives it. It is called the light of lights. 3 The light of holynes and good workes cam from Christ. (2 Philipians 16) (5 Matthew 16) Let their light soe shine before men that they may see their good workes and glorify their Father in heaven. 4 The light of councill and direction is from God. (12 John 35) He that walkes in darknes he knowes not where he goes, to giud and light us in the way of salvation. 5 The Light of truth grace and truth com by Jesus Christ. 6 The Life of glory, heaven, and happyness, it all comes by Jesus Christ. He gives it to us this light, externally by his word, and internally by his spirit. (2 Peter 1:19) You have [c] [vr] word[17] to which you do well to take heed which shines as a light in a darke place. (4 Luke 18) How doth Christ give light to the gentiles by preaching the gospell to the poore? The law of God is a [clamp]. 2 Christ gives light to those that sit in darkens by his spirit internally. He inlightens the understanding that it may behold that externall light that is the word.

Reason 1: [when] is it Jesus Christ came to give light?

1 Reason is from the tenderness of God, his love pitty and compassion to poor man. God was full of pitty and compassion to man.

2 Reason from the great honor that is brought to God hereby as the wisdom, power of God appeared in the creation of the first light, so they doe most clearly shine out in the creation of this Light in the world.

---

15 Clearly, the natural man was seated among Hartford's congregation, and must have understood him or herself to be the object of Foster's sermon.

16 The Elect.

17 In the King James Bible, the phrase is: "We have a more sure word of prophecy."

3 Reason it was that Christ might destroy the workes of the Divill. (1 John 3:5) For this cause was the son of God manifested to destroy the workes of the Divill which are workes of darkness.

Use: did Jesus Christ come to give light to those that sit in darkens? Wonder and admire at the riches of the grace of God [in] Christ that he should give us light that sit in darknes. God might hav held us in darknes. 2 Hence learn the misery of those that are without the gospel, where ther is no knowledge of Christ. Their misery is they are without light they sit in darkness. Their darknes is spirituall. 3 It showes us the misery of all those that are without Christ that doe sit in darkness. They abide in darknes though they doe dwell in Goshen[18] and the light is round about them, yet they have no light in them. (5 Job 13) They meet with darkness in day time and group at noone day, as in the night. 4 This Doctrine teacheth us where to goe for Light if we want it, let it be of what kind so ever. Goe to Jesus Christ who is a fountayn of light and gives light, the light of knowledg of joy and comfort, the light of the favoure and good will of God. Christ is that fountayn of all light. 5 We se the Reason why there are so many abide in darkness and why so much darknes is in those that are in Christ. It is because they Improve Jesus Christ no more: 6 That shows the happynes of all those that have closed with Christ. They shall not walke in darkness but have the light of life:

2 Use: exortation to those that have received Jesus Christ and this light. Walke as the children of the light. That's our great worke and duty and do this. 1 By having no fellowhip with the workes of darkness (1 Thessalonians 5:5) but by reproving of them. 2 We walke as children of light when we Live in the exercise of grace. (1 Thessalonians 5:8) Put on the brest plate of fayth and love. 3 We walke as children of light when we walke according to the word of God, holding for the word (2 Philippians 5:6) of life by walkeing according to it. 2 Be exorted to believe in the light believe in Christ who is the light of the world. 3 Be Exceding thankfull to God for this light that he hath given us in this worke of redemption. This light that Christ gives unto us it is a marvelous light and therefore we (1 Peter 2:9) should be thankfull. It is marvalous compard with Natural light, compard with that light they

[18] Goshen has several applications in the Bible. Primarily, it was a territory or hill country between Hebron and Negev. It may have been of specific significance to Isaac Foster as the place of the "Hebrew Sojourn" in Genesis.

had in old Testament times.[19] It is marvelous in that it shines upon som and not others.[20] It is the light of life it is Eternall life:

Mr. Foster. (Friday) November 12, 1680: (9 Matthew 12 verse) *"Now when Jesus heard it, he said unto them, The whole need not a physicion, but thei that are sick."*[21] They that be whole need not the phisician, but those that are sicke we have a relation of Christ's healing the sick of the palcy. The place where he did this care his own city, the place where Christ aboad and lived. 2 The miracle it selfe the words Christ spoke to him, be of good chear thy sins are forgiven. He cam for healing of the body and he healed his soule. The Effect of his words. The [seribus] [cocl d] he blasphemed and Christ's Answer. (verse 5) (6 verse) 2 The effect is wrought on the multitude, they gave glory to God that had given such power to men. They did not se that Christ was God. 2 The other remarkable worke was the calling of Mathew. That is his name. 2 His office he was a publican. He sat at the receipt of custome. 2 His readyness to embrace Christ's call he rose and followed Christ. 2 By the Enterteinment he gave to Christ he Feasted Christ. (5 Luke 29 verse) The guests that accompanyd Christ at this feast were publicans and siners. 2 The offence of the Pharises seing and sitting with such guests, they are offended at Christ for eating with publicans and siners. 3 We have the Answer of Christ. They that be whole need not a Phisician, but they that be sick in the Answer of Christ is Implyed 3 things: 1 that siners are spiritually sick and sin is the sickness and deseass of the soule. 2 Jesus Christ is only the phissician of those that are spiritually sick: 3 This Implys the desperate prid the Pharases had in the opinion of themselves and their own righteousness and their disisteem of those that goe to Christ the great phisescian.

Doctrine: that there are many that are spiritually sick that thinke themselves to be whole and see no need of Christ to be their phisiscian, and doe neglect to seeke for healing from Christ. (3 Revelations 17) It is the great misery of many they do thinke themselves whole without Christ. In the Doctrine there are three propositions: 1 sin is the desease and sicknes of the soule the soule by sin is made sick.

[19] Natural light refers to Old Testament times. Those in the Old Testament were natural men because Christ had not yet come, and they were therefore unregenerate.

[20] The finale of this sermon illustrates perfectly the exclusivity of the church of the "visible saint."

[21] *The Geneva Bible, 1560 Edition*. 6.

2 Jesus Christ is the only phisissan for sick soules. 3 There are many that though they are sick yet think themselves whole and see no need of and never looke after the phisisian of the 1st sin is the cause of bodily sicknes. For this cause many are sick. Sin is often called a dis-sease. Bles the Lord oh my soule. (103 Psalm 3) Who pardons thy sin and heals all thy deseass? These are spirituall deseases. (1 Isaiah 5:6) A sinfull people is set forth by a sick people. They are full of wounds and putrifyed soares. Hence pardon of sin is set forth by healing. Healeth your deseases. Example 1: Why is sin cald a deseas and sicknesse of the soule? Answer: it is because of the likeness that is between sicknes upon the body and sin on the soule. They are like in their nature and like in their effects. Sicknes doth destroy the bewty of the body. (39 Psalm 11) When God by rebukes rebukes men, their bewty consumes as a moth. Sin takes away the lovelyness of the soule, the glory of it. Grace is an ornament that adorns the soule. The king shall greatly delight in her bewty. Sin is a spot and blemish to the soule. When sin is taken away the soule is without spot or wrinckell: 2 Sickness doth destroy the strength of the body. Sin takes away the strength of the soule. It makes the soule to be week. It takes away all the powers and faculties of the soule. (2 Corinthians 3:5) Hence we have no sufficiency of our own to thinke a good thought. 3 Sickness doth bring paine and misery upon the body and much sorow. So doth sin, it brings horor misery and torment unto the soule. It wounds the soule. 4 Sicknes if not cured doth bring death to the body. 5 Sin if not pardond it brings Eternall death upon the soule. 2 Example: wherein appears the danger of this sickness and spirituall desease? It is the worst sickness because sin is a mortall desease. All sin every sin is so in its own nature. It strikes at the life of the soule and brings death. No man nor means can cure this desease and sickness of the soule. It is mortall and that whereof many dye. 2 As it is mortall so it is universall. It is that plague that over spreads all. There is none clear of it. It is all men and in every part the head and heart is sick. 3 It is a desease that containes many in it. Every particular sin is a desease. 4 It is such a deseas as inflicts the body and brings bodily desease upon them. 5 It is such a desease as men are unsencible of: they see it not, they are not affected by it. They are stupifyed by it. 6 It is a deseas that hinders Indisposeth to seek after any help and cure: 7 It is a deseas that needs the most costly cure. There is no other way but the blood of Christ. It is a deseas if not healed that brings Eternall death. 3 Example: how coms it to pass, [wherein] is it that men are so sick? They were not made so:

What is the Reason 1: it is from their apostacy from God. Man by fall fell from that healthy state and it is hereditary. It comes to us by the fall of Adam. We are corupt in him.

2 It is our neglect of the Phisiscian, our not seekeing after a cure, and so we are sicke.

Use 1: Exortation: let us be exorted to labour after a sight of our spirituall deseases, and let us be affected with them and groan under them. We can doe [so] [when] we want bodily health, but let us be affected with our soule sicknes. 2 Be Exorted to looke to Jesus Christ this soule phisission for a cure and for healing. Let us not ly and languase in our deseases, but consider there is healing to be had. There is balm in Gilead[22] there is a phisissian there. 2 Consider the danger of these deseases that are mortall. 3 Consider that it is, but that some times that there is healing to be had. The day of grace is limited for direction and help. Labour to be sensible of our sickness and deseases.

2 Have a care of going to [r] phesitian. 3 Be found wayting for healing in the use of the means. Go [ ] appoynted wayt on the word of God as they at the poole of Bethesdah.[23]

Sermon number two from the Matthew series is another exhortation for the soul healing power of Christ. Like the previous sermon, it also carries the metaphor of a physical physician throughout, as Foster compares the physical and spiritual depravity of humankind. It is also a Jeremiad for the repentance of the backsliding generation of Hartford.

Mr. Foster. (Sunday) December 5, 1680: (9 Matthew 12) They that be whole need not the phissisian, but they that are sick.

Doctrine: there are many that are spiritually sick that yet they see themselves whole and no need that they stand of phissisian. 1 Sin is a desease and sicknes of the soule. 2 That Christ onely is the phisission of the soule that can heale us of those spirituall deseases. There is no balm in Gilead nor no phisission, but Christ he is the son of righteousness with healing under his wings. All receipts of healing are given to us by Christ. He is the author of them. It is implyed in healing our soules with Justification. [He] pardons all our sins and heales

---

[22] Gilead means "raw" or "rugged" and can be a personal or a place name. As a place, it was an agriculturally significant region famous for its flocks and herds. *Holman Bible Dictionary*, 651.

[23] The Pool of Bethesda was the name of the pool in Jerusalem where Jesus healed the man who had been sick for 38 years. *Holman Bible Dictionary*, 192.

our deseases. (33 Isaiah 24) 2 It allso implys [sanctification]. Christ cures by takeing away the giult of it. 1 In the understandings of men he heales the blindnes of their eyes ignorance and 2 Christ heales the will of hardnes impenitants and unbelief. He heals their memory, the conscience and the affections, by takeing them off of Evill objects sets them on good, and by moderating and composing of them. 3 How Christ heals us meritoriously by his blood the efficient [s] by his word and Efficaciously by his spirit.

Use: see what a suteable saviour Christ is where we should goe for healing, where we should ascribe the glory to Christ. It shows why many are not healed, they goe not Christ. Be not discouraged. You know where to go for healing.

2 Use: this is of comfort to saints that have an interest in Christ. They have an interest in him that is able to heale them. You shall not perish under any desease you have [on] to cure you. 2 It is of comfort to sick siners that are all over sick, full of wounds and bruises all over. Is their desease beyond the cure of man? Yet that is ground of comfort. He is able to save. (4 Matthew [verse] 25) Here is a phisissian is able to cure you and help you.

3 Use: of Exortation: to those that have Christ for their phisissian and have been healed by them. Hath Christ healed all [these] deseases can you say you are not sick? Your iniquities are pardond. Be exorted to love and honor and Esteem the lord Jesus Christ that hath healed your soules. You should Exalt Christ while you live that hath healed these diseases that would have brought your soules from the grave? 3 We should sing prayse and lift up the Name of God to provoake to thankfulness. The lord Jesus Christ was your phisisian alone when none els could heale you. 2 Jesus Christ by healing your deseases you are freed from eternall death, therefor be thankfull. 3 You have nothing to requit Jesus Christ for this cure. Christ hath wrought for you and Christ hath healed you by being wounded himself. Love this phisisian and be thankfull to him all your dayes. He hath born our sickness. Christ hath allso wrought an Eternall cure For you. You shall not fall into such a sin any more: 2 Be exorted to bring others unto this phisissian that he that hath healed you may allso heale them. Lead them to Christ and tell them what Christ hath don for you. 3 Be exorted to be carefull of your health if Christ hath cured you. Let your soules be nourished with the food of the word and not poysend by any sinfull lusts. 4 Hath Christ healed you, take heed of falling into relapses. They are dangerous. 2 Those that are yet under all their deseases and to

whom Christ hath been no phisisission be Exorted to looke unto this phisissian who goeth about cureing all maner of deseases of the soule. Is the Fame of Christ com among you? Flock to Christ that you may have healing for your soule. 2 See how dangerous it is to defer looking to Christ for healing. 1 Because there is no other means of a cure you shall never be healed until you doe goe to Christ. 2 Your desease that is upon you it is a mortall desease, and that which brings eternall death. 3 You are not sure of an houer more to looke after this phisissian. 4 The longer you defere and neglect your desease doth the more increase upon you. 5 The longer you defer to looke the harder the cure will be and the more painfull to. Your repentance will be more bitter the more sins you have to repent of: 6 It is but at sometimes that you may be healed not always. The spirit will ceas [tri n I]. It is but at sometimes the angells stir the watters. 2 Consider then never any that did seeke to this phisissian but they were healed. 3 There never any that have sought to other phisissians and not to Christ that have been healed. 4 Consider how excelent a phisisian Christ is, there is none like him to be compared with him. Be exorted to goe to him. His excellency appears in that he doth heale all deseases, all maner of deseases. Be they what they will he heales them. (17 Matthew 6) I brought my son to the disciples and they did [not] cure him. 2 Jesus Christ as he cures all disseases so he can preserv and keep you from all deseases that they may not com upon you. 3 He is such a healer as doth it freely, the cure shall cost you nothing tho it cost him dear. He takes no money, you may com and be healed without mony. (14 Hosea 1) 4 Never did any miscarry under this phisissian. (17 John 12) Of all that then hast given I have lost non. He is such a phisissian as cures all. 5 He is a mercifull compassionate and tender phissisian. (4 Hebrews) He is a mercifull and compassionate high preist touched with the feeling of the infirmities of his people. 5 He is such a phisissian as doth invite all sick to com to him. He calles us and doth not wayte to be cald by us. (3 Jeremiah 22) Return ye backsliding children and I will heale you. 6 He is such a phisissian as is all wayes present near to you. 7 He is omniciant he knows all.[24] No part of your deseass can be hid from him. 8 You are sure to be wellcom to this phisissian when you com to him. They are all wellcom that doe come to Christ for direction to goe to this phisissian to be healed of all our deseases. 1 Be sencible

[24] The omniscience of God is a popular theme in the sermons of Caleb Watson.

of them of your own sickness and deseases. 2 By prayer make your applycation to Christ. (30 Psalm 2) Oh lord I cryed unto the and thou healest me. 3 You must believe if you will have him cure you. Christ cures non but those that doe beleive in him. 4 Goe to goe no other if you would have Christ be your phisissian. 5 Improve and make use of those remedys prescribed unto you for healing: Attend upon the word and ordinances for this. 3 There are many that are spiritually sick and see themselves whole and see not the need they stand of the phisissian, and the Reason is from the blindnes of their mindes. There is a desease in that faculty that should judg of the desease. 2 It is from the judgment of God upon siners for neglect of the means. 3 From those fales cures that are wrought by our selves or others.

Use: [n ist] not in our own judgment, but try ourselves by the word of God. 3 Hav a care of having the conceipt of ourselves that we are whole when we are sick. This hinders lookeing after Christ, and Christ will not cure us if we doe not see ourselves sick. See all your deseases and goe to Christ cure and heale us of them.

In the sermon that follows, Foster thoroughly defines the saint and the glory that awaits God's chosen people. This sermon also contains some interesting references to the genealogy of the chosen generation.

<u>(Sunday) December 12, 1680. Mr. Foster.</u> (16 Psalm 2.3) "*O my soule, thou hast said unto the Lord, Thou art my Lord: my weldoing extendeth not to thee,*" "*But to the Saints that are in the earth, and to the excellent: all my delite is in them.*"[25] Oh my soule thou hast sayd to the Lord you art my Lord. My goodnes Extends not to the, but to the saints, the Excelent ones. This is one of David's Psalm's. It is called a [mictum][26] of David. It is a golden Psalm. The Psalm being most sublim entreaty of Jesus Christ and his Exaltation. In the beginning of the Psalm we have David's prayer and petition: save me oh God. 2 The grownd and reason of his petition five fold. 1 His trust was in God. (Verse 1) 2 His interest in God. (Verse 2) Oh my soule thou hast sayd to the lord thou art my Lord. As if he should say I hath no God but the. 3 His disclaiming any trust in his own goodness. My goodness doth not extend to the. 4 His charity to and delight in the saints of

---

[25] *The Geneva Bible, 1560 Edition*. 237.

[26] Michtam is the title for a psalm associated with the expiation of sin. *Holman Bible Dictionary*, 1120.

God. Lord be mercifull to me. I am mercifull to thy people, I doe good to them. 5 His hatred of Iodlatry. He would not sacrafice to other Gods nor worship them. In these 2 verse: 4

Doctrine: 1 They that have an interest in God and trust in him are in expectation of salvation from God. 2 Your goodnes of best of [non] Extends not to God. 3 It should Extend to the saints. 4 The saints are the only Excelent ones upon the Earth. 1 of the 1: Oh Lord I am thine. I have mad choyse of the to be my God. Preserve me therefor oh God. The Reason is from the promise and covenant of God, with such God, [when] such God is in covenant Engaged to them. All the good God bestows on man is in the covenant. The covenant is to them. 2 The goodnes of the best of men it doth not Extend to God. The goodness of the creature doth not extend to the creator. God's goodnes doth reach all his creatures. It reacheth us in creation. It was from the goodness of God that we were so made. 2 God's goodness Extends to man in providence and to all creatures. Oh Lord the Earth is full of they goodnes. 3 In the work of redemption the speciall goodnes of God extends to men. Oh lord how great is the goodnes that thou hast layd up for them that feare the, but man's goodnes doth not extend to God in these 4 respects. 1 It extends not to God to compare with or equall him in goodnes. My goodnes is not like thine. (1 Samuel 2:2) There is none holy as our God nor no rock like our God, who is a God like to the glorious in holynes. God's goodnes is infinit and essentiall. 2 The goodnes of men extends not to God to ad to his goodness. God is not made better by our goodness. God can receive nothing from our hands. Can a man be profitable to God as a man is to his neighbor? 3 Our goodnes canot Extend to God so as to merit any thing from God, so as to oblige God to doe this or that for us upon the merit of our goodnes. 4 Our goodnes doth not extend to God so as to requit or recompell God for any thing God doth bestow upon us, so as to make sattisfaction to God or pay God for any thing we have.

The Reason is from the perfection of God. God is so infinityly good that he canot be made better: and so can receive no good of us.

2 Reason is from the imperfection of man. As God is perfect so man is imperfect. A siner a vile sinfull creature.

3 Is from man's absolut dependance upon God. Man depends upon God for his goodness holy and absolutely, and therefor his goodness canot extend to God.

3 Doctrine: our goodness ought to Extend to and our delight should be in the saints that are in the Earth. Acts of Bounty and charity should Extend to the saints. 1 Our goodnes should extend to the saints. We should be kind bountifully and doe good to them Especially. Let us doe good to all, but Especially to the saints (5 Matthew 44) for these reasons: 1 Because they are more worthy than others, they deserve more from us. 2 The reward will be greater for the good we do them than we doe others. 3 Because God doth good Especialy to them, we should be like to God and bestow his speciall goodnes upon them. 2 Our delight should be in the saints and excelent ones. He hateth all the workers of iniquitie. Our delight should be in the saints because they are like to God and their conformity to God. 2 From the great good we shall gaine by such. He that walketh with the wise shall be wise. They are means of doeing of us good 3 from the Evill and danger of conversing with and accompaning wicked men. A companion of fooles shall be destroyed.

4 Doctrine: the saints ar the only excelent ones in the Earth. There is a beauty a glory and excelency in them. Not only saints in heaven who have no spots, but the saints on Earth they are excelent. All in the world have no excelency in them. The righteous is more excelent than his neighbour. [Samuel] to Saule God hath taken the kingdom from the and given it to one that is better than the. (62 Psalm 9) Men of high degre are a ly men of low degre are vanity. Though our gifts and accomplishments are never soe great yet without grace there is no Excelency in them. Grace and holynes puts an excelency upon man. Holynes is the excelency of man and of angells. Take away holyness from an angell and he is a Divill. Grace adornes a soule and makes it Excelent. Thou hast crownd him with glory and honor. It is not the things of this life make man excellent in the sight of God, but it is grace and holynes. (1 Job 8) God commands Job not for his riches but his uprightnes. Example: how doth it appear that the saints are so excelent how may it be proved they are so excellent? Answer: from the names and titles that given unto to them. They have most Excelent names and Titles given to them better than to others. They are called the sons of God. (1 John 12) To as many as received him to them he gave privilidg and honor to be cald the sons of God. (1 Peter 2:9) A chosen generation, a Royall [preisthood] , a holy nation. Kings and preists to God. Compare these with those titles given to the wicked children of

the Divill, a generation of vipers, dogs, sons of [Beliall].[27] 2 This may be proved from the things they are compared too. Hence they are cald or compared to Jewels, to a treasure. (19 Exodus 5) (135 Psalm 4) The Lord hath chosen Jacob for his peculyer Treasure. They are compared to choys silver. The [Tong] of the righteous is as choys silver, but the heart of the wicked is good for nought. They are compared to a crown of glory ([62] Isaiah 3)[28] and a Royall dyadem. The wicked are compared to dross, to reprobate silver, and to things that are vile and lowe. (22 Ezekiel 18 and 6 [ ]) 3 It may be proved from the love of God to them and price he set upon them. 1 How doth it appear you have heard in Two things. The love of God to them and the price he sets upon them shows that they are the most excelent. They only are prized and honoured by God. Precious is the death of the saints in (43 Isaiah 4) God's sight, So precious that God doth cutt off the wicked for the preser (21 Proverbs 18) vation of the righteous. The Lord doth destroy the wicked in your [roome] and for your sake. I will give men for the and people for thy life. God gave Egipt for the sake of Israell. God is very Tender and carefull of them, they are the aple of his ey most dear near and Tender to him, gives his angells charg over them to keep them in all their wayes. (105 Psalm 14) God is more tender of them than a mother of her child. God will be comanded and in treated to worke for his people in their behalfe. 4 The saints are so excelent appears from their likeness to God. He is most Excelent and the rule and measure of all Excelency in the creature. The saints are most like God, have that image of God, are partakers of the divine nature. 2 Wherein doth consist their excelency above others? 1 Negatively it is not in any thing that is in their natures above others. We are by nature children of wrath as well as others. Both are made of the same lump. In regard of their degree and purpose of God there is a difference. 2 This excelency of the saints above others is that in any thing that is Externall, or in their comon gifts and graces of the spirit of God, or in respect of the gifts of the comon bounty of God and his goodnes . It is not in wealth or Estate or in riches. God hath chosen the poor of this world. The wicked it is sayd God filleth their bellys with his [hid] Treasures. 2 It is not in honor of power or worldly grandeure that they Excell. They are

[27] Beliall means "useless" or "worthless" and may indicate the name of some specific malevolent power. *Holman Bible Dictionary*, 184.

[28] (62 Isaiah 3) in King James Bible, 822.

usually as Lowe in Esteem as in Estate. They are called kings but there kingdom is not of this world. 3 It is not in naturall guifts and endowments they Excell. (11 Matthew 25.26) I thanke the oh Father that thou hast hid those from the wise and prudent and revealed them to babes. 2 The saints Excell and are more Excelent in their birth and parentage. They are born of God and the [saints] of the most high. They are born not of Flesh but of the will of God. (1 John 11:12) Jesus Christ [thy] saints and angells are all the sons of God, Christ by generation, the angells by creation, and the saints by adoption. 2 They are Excelent in regard of their spirituall and supernaturall gifts and indowments. (45 Psalm 9) The [kings] daughter's glorious within. Their beauty is in the hidden manah[29] of the heart. It is not coruptable. The ornament of a meeke and quiet spirit then is of great price with God. All the excelent things of the spirit are compared to the. (16 Ezekiel 9 to 12) Most excelent things. 3 They are excelent in regard of their life and actions. They excell all others upon the earth. There life is [hide] with Christ in God. (2 Galatians 20). They live and act from a better principle and to a better End. They act from fayth and love to God and to the glory of God. (11 Hebrews) Their prayers, dutys, are more excellent than others. 4 They are Excelent in their death. (37 Psalm 37) Marke the perfect, behold the upright, the end of that man is peace: to them to dye is gain. They are excelent in death appears by the wicked themselves who wish they may dy the death of the righteous. [L] The righteous are Excelent in their reward, Inheritance, and portion. The saints are heires to a crown. (16 Jeremiah 19) (8 Proverbs 12) and kingdome. The inheritance of the saints is incoruptible and undefiled that fadeth not away. The inheritants of the saints is in heaven [when] it shal appeare. The saints are excelent in this lif. God esteems them so. And at the last day when they com to glory, the saints shall shine as the stars in heaven for ever.

Use 1: It should teach us how to judg and esteem of men for their holyness and righteousnes. We should love honor and Esteem them for such. They that fear God are the persons to be honored and Esteemed by us. 2 This may serve to humble the wicked though never so high and great, yet a [more] godly person is in God's eys prizd above them. (49 Genesis 3.4)

[29] Manna is a grain like substance and is considered a food from heaven. It sustained the Israelites when they were in the wilderness.

2 Use: of Exortation: be exorted to carry it to the righteous and holy as the Excelent doe not despise offend and greive them. (18 Matthew 6) Have thou nothing to doe with that [just] man. 2 Love priz honor and esteem them. 3 Let our goodnes our bounty benificen Extend to them. 4 Let us delight in them. 2 Let the saints that are holy and righteous [so] Excelent be persuaded to carry it as such as are excellent. Live and walke as those that are excelent, do not envy the prosperity of the wicked, be contended with and thankefull for your portion. 3 Let not your affection run out upon man low things. 4 Doe not [mare] your Excelency, be not as the low that wallos in the mire. 5 Live a more Excelent life than all others. 3 Be exorted all to labour after grace and holynes. Nothing els makes you amiable in the sight of God. Be purged from sin if you will be a vessell of honor. (4 Proverbs 7.8.9)

CHAPTER FIFTEEN

THE ROD

The New Geneva Study Bible describes Micah as "A book of judgment proclaimed. The prophet declares that the holy and righteous God will no longer tolerate the persistent evil of His people (1:3). Many of Israel's sins are mentioned, ranging from idolatry and sorcery (5:12–14) to deceit and fraudulent dealings (6:10, 11)."[1] Additionally, and perhaps more importantly to New England's ministers in 1680, was the covenant aspect of Micah. "Fundamental to Micah's proclamation of both judgment and restoration are the terms of the covenant relationship between God and His people. While God faithfully fulfilled His responsibilities under the covenant (6:1–5), the people wallowed in disobedience, and now the covenant curses were to be applied (6:13–16)."[2]

Foster's December 15 sermon is another Jeremiad, an exhortation to the people of Hartford that the rod of God awaits a backsliding people.

(Wednesday) December 15, 1680. Mr. Foster: (6 Micah 9) *"The Lords voyce cryeth unto the citie, and the wisdome shal se thy name: Heare the rod, and who hathe appointed it."*[3] The Lord's voyce cryeth to the city and the man of wisdom shall fear they name. Hear the rod and who hath appoynted it. This [cap] is the begining of the prophets 2nd sermon. In the beginning of the [cap] there is the preface of the sermon in the 1 and 2. 2 God's Expostulation in 3, an account of God's benefit verse 5, then hipocracy verse 6. Y our duty to return to God verse 8, and the way of it the text. The preface in the verse 1.2 it is not frequently used but in extraordinary occasion to set forth the stupidity of the people. They will not hear God's voyce. Speake to the mountaines. The like preface in (32 Deuteronomy 1) and (1 Isaiah [2])[4] Hear oh heavens and give ear oh Earth. 2 The Expostulation of God with his people. (verse 3) Wherein have I wearyd you what have I don to you. Have I Layd any burthen upon you? Testify against me.

---

1 The *New Geneva Study Bible*, 1422.
2 Ibid.
3 *The Geneva Bible, 1560 Edition*. 376.
4 (1 Isaiah 2) King James Bible, 765.

3 Here is the enumeration of the benefits God had don for them. (Verse 4.5) I brought you out of Egipt and redeemed you out of the house of Bondage. This is often spoken of as being a fruit of the promise of God made to Abram and it was a shadow of spirituall deliverance and God did lead them by the hand of Moses, Aron, and Miriam. 2 God delivered them from the plots of their enemies. Remember what Balak [ ] he would have Balam[5] curss Iserell, but what did he Answer he did bless you (Numbers 6:22) or els the counsell he gave to Balack to Intice them to idolatry and fornication: he puts a stumbling block before Iserell, and that from Shittim[6] to [Ballpeor]: This was the place where they began to fall to Idoalatry to [Gih gah]. (5 Joshua 2) That is the place where they entered into covenant with God. That you may know the righteousnes of the Lord, how faythfull he is to keep covenent with his people. 4 Here is the hipocrasy of that people in a fained show of returning to God. Wherewith shall I com before the Lord, with burnt offerings or calves of a year old. By these they would make a show of a desire to com before God. 5 The duty God requires of his people set forth negatively in the (8 verse), will God be satisfyed with sacrifices with Thousands of bullocks or with his first born? Ahaz[7] made his son to pass through the fire (106 Psalm 37.38), but will the Lord be pleased with this? No this will not doe, but this is 2 set down affirmatively. Now this thy God doth require the, that thou doe justly show mercy and walke honorbly with God. 6 In this chapter here is the voyce of God to press them to this duty. In the text, the voyce of God cryes to them to put them upon the performance of the duty. The text is the means that God useth with a sinful and backsliding people to bring them to repentance and that is his word. They that have wisdom they will heare the word, but if that do not doe then hear the rod. 1 There is the warning God gives. 2 The description of [those] that take the warning they are men of wisdom. God by his word cryes to the city, to the head city, to Jerusalem. It cryes it is loved and lifted up. Those that take this warning, [their] property, priviledg, the men of wisdom shall see they name. God will reveale himself to them. 3 Here

[5] Balak is a reference to the king of Moab "who sent for Balam the prophet to pronounce a curse on the Israelites". Balaam, however, spoke no curse; and Balak was denied a victory over Israel. *Holman Bible Dictionary*, 163.

[6] Shittim is a large area in Moab, directly across the Jordan from Jericho. It is where Israel camped before crossing into the Promised Land. *Holman Bible Dictionary*, 1495.

[7] Ahaz was an evil king of Judah (735–715) who participated in "monstrous of idolatrous practices". *Holman Bible Dictionary*, 37.

is the means that God useth with those that are not warned, and that is his Rod. 4 The great duty of those that neglect the word and are under the rod. They are to hear the rod. The rod is not dumb, it hath a voyce with it who hath appoynted it. It is in God's hand. He orders, apoynts it. Look to God that orders, apoynts it there.

1 Doctrine: that the message of God sent to a sinfull people by his word and servants is the Lord's voice. That message Micah brought to his people it is cald the Lord's voyce in the text. We are not to looke at men but at God in it. He is the author. It comes from God. They are his promises and his threatenings, and if we looked upon it as so, the word of God would be more Effectuall to us, if we received it as the word of God. The Reason is because they are sent by God. They have their commission from God and they have their instructions from God. Either immediately by his spirit or immediately by his word. 3 It is from God's speciall presence and assistance with them to the end of the world. 4 Because it is God's ordinance and appointment.

Use: of exortation. Let us hear the word of God spoken by his ministers as if God himself did speake to us.[8] Let us hear it with reverence and 2 with fayth. Let us believe it. 3 Hear it atentively. Take heed what you heare. (1 James 19) Hear it obedientially. So hear the word so as to give God the glory of it. Acknowledg God in it.

2 Doctrine: that God is wont for to give warning by his word before he corrects with his rod. God doth not send enemies to destroy a people before he sends his messengers to warn them. (3 Amos 7) Surely the lord will doe nothing but he reveals his secrets to his servants the prophets. To the old world before the flood there was Noah's preaching, and Jonah before Ninevah was destroyed, and John's warning to the 7 churches of Asia: the Reason of this is from God's love, pity, and compassion to his people. (2 Chronicles 37:15) (11 Hosea 8) God is backward and willing to spare his people. 2 God sends his word and gives warning that they may be prepared (4 Amos 12) to beare the rod and to meet God. 2 God doth it by the honour that is done to the name of God when his people take warning and are brought to repentance by his word. 4 That the Justice of God might be more conspicuous, and men may be excusable when God afflicts with the rod.

[8] God did speak through his ministers, at least many Puritans believed that he did, which clearly gave the ministers a special kind of power.

Use: be thankfull to God for his word. 2 Admire the patience of God in giving warning to a sinfull provoking people. 3 Have a care of despiseing of God's warning by his word. That is the great exortation. Take warning by the word of God. He that is often reproved hardens his heart, shall be destroyd sudenly. If you hate reproves you shall dy. (1 Samuel 2:24.25) If you do not attend to the voyce of God it is because he will slay you. (2[Chronicles] 25:26) I know God hath a purposs to destroy the because thou has not hearkend to my word. 2 Have a care doe not neglect the warning given us by his workes. Speciall and extraordinary workes of God and signes and wonders in the heavens are signes of (2 [J ch] 13) great callamity in the world. (2 Acts 19) These prophesy of signes and wonders are spoken of in gospell times and these signes are forerunners of calamity in the world. Christ speakes of such signes. (21 Luke 9.11) We have great reason to looke upon the present signe in the heavens to be a fore runner of some calamaty coming upon the world, and therefore it is not to be despised by us.[9]

3 Doctrine: that it is the wisdom of man to take warning from the word and workes of God.

Reason 1: from the great advantage and priviledg we have by soe doeing, because we escape a great deale of evill thereby.

2 Because of the danger of not doeing.

3 The word of God will most certainly be accomplished except we prevent by repentance. (1 Zachariah 5:6)

4 Doctrine: It greatly concerns a sinfull people [ ] the rod that have despised the threatenings of your word [ ] greatly conserning to see that rod and whoe hath appoynted it. They that have been deaf unto the word had need be carefull to hear the rod. But what is meant by the rod? Answer: any affliction whatsoever whereby God doth afflict his people for their sin. (89 Psalm 37) I will visit your transgression with a rod. If the stroke be imediately from God it is his rod, or if it be immediately from men.

[9] There are two interesting points that can be raised here. First, in the Fall of 1680, a great comet appeared in the New England sky, which was of great portents to the Puritans, and its appearance was well documented. See: Samuel Eliot Morison's "The Harvard School of Astronomy in the Seventeenth Century." Second, the fascinating implications of this passage are very similar to much of David Hall's work in his book Worlds of Wonder, Days of Judgment, where the interplay of magic, superstition, and Puritan Orthodoxy come together.

The [esirian] is the rod of God's anger. This affliction God lays on his people, for sin is called a rod. 1 Because of the smart and payn that is in those afflictions. No afflicition for the present is joyous, but greveious. 2 Because the author of those afflicitions it is a rod in the hand of your Father. 3 They are called a rod in regard of the end, which is corection not destruction. 2 What is it to heare the Rod? It implys our attention and obedience to the voyce of the rod. The rod speakes to us. 1 The voyce of the rod to the people of God is that they are siners against God. (89 Psalm 31) It tells us we have Transgressed agnst God. 2 It tells us that God is displeased with us. God is offended with us. The things that David did displeased God. 3 It tells us that we have despised the word of God, that we have not been humbled. 4 It tells us that God yet hath love for us, he doth love us as a Father. God corects us, then God loves us. We ar not bastards but sons. It tells us God is a Father to us in this respect: the rod of God speakes this comfort to us, that God hath love for us and hath not yet cast us off, els he would consume and not correct us. 5 The rod tells us that it is our duty to return to him that smites us. It hath the sam voyce with the word of God. Turn to God. The rod calls upon us to Examin our hearts and wayes to see [what] God contends with us. (8 Jeremiah 6) That is the first step in order to turning to God the prodigall considers before he returns. 2 The rod calls to confess our sins to God that doth correct. 3 It calls for selfe judging and condemning our selfes. 4 The rod calls for godly sorow. It tells we should mourn when we are chastised of God. 5 The rod calls us unto supplication. We must pray for forgivenes. Lift up our hearts with our hands to God in heaven. [ ] rod calls for reformation that we should be amended. (2 Chronicles 29:10) It calls us to make a covenant with God to walke more humbly and better before Him. 2 To hear the rod is to attend to and obey its voyce. Attend, mind it, and act according to it. Doe what the rod bids us doe. 3 Why doth it greatly concern us thus to hear God's rod when it folows the word? 1 Because of the author, Because of him that doth appoynt it. It is God appoynts whoever be the Instrument 1 as to the matter of the affliction, the Instrument, the season, the measure of it. Hear it is God's love and it is the last means God useth with a sinful people.

Use: Let us examin our selves what we have learned, the rod of God and voyce of God whither we have not been unteachable or incoragable. Have we not stoped our eares to the voyce of God? Have (2 Chronicles 36) we not mocked the messengers of God, despised the word of threatening and reproofe and command. Let us Examine where we have not been incoragable under the rod. Have we turned to him that smit us? Have we been convinced, judged ourselves, have we reformed, have we returned unto God? May it not be sayed of us he hath smitten us and yet we have not returned to God. Let it Exort us to heare the voyce of God that cryes to us. 1 Consider if we doe not hear the rod, the longer we neglect it the heavier it will be. 2 Our sin is greater under the rod. 3 If we hear the rod, God will remove the rod.

Mr. Foster. (Sunday) December 19, 1680. (5 Micah 9) We now com to the Reason why we should hear the rod. 1 Because of him that doth apoynt it. God is the author. Whatever be the instrument, God is the cause of it. There is no rod coms upon a people at anytime but God doth it. The Evill of sin man is the cause of it, but the Evill of punishment God is the author of it. I wound and I heal, I kill and I make alive. (3 Lamentations 38) Out of the mouth of the most high good and evill proceedeth. There is good and Evill com from the hand of God. They com not meerly from 2nd causes, but God is the author and appoyonter of it, therefore we should heare the rod. God's appoynting of the rod implys 1 the decree and purposs of God. It is the determinate councell of God that comes in Every rod. It is God that hath appoynted the rod and his people to be punished therewith. 2 It implyes the covenant and promise of God that it is that God is bound too in his covenant and that he will [performe] if they sin agnst them.

He is Bound by covenant to punish his people if they sin agnst God.[10] 3 It implyes God's provdentiall disspose of the rod as to the wayes, maner, and circumstances. God doth appynt the rod. As to the matter of it, what kind or sort of affliction shall be brought upon a people? Whither it be upon the soule Imediately and then it be the Temptation of Saytn. Paul was buffeted by Saytn. 2 The rod upon the soule is spirituall desertion [h] felt this. 3 By giving up to [penall] blindness and hardness of heart to a reprobate winde, thus God doth punish those he gives up. 2 Or if the rod of God be upon the body, som bodily weaknes, God doth appoynt it. 3 Or if it be upon our nam, reproach, shame and disgrace, this God orders. 4 If it be upon the Estat when

[10] The covenant of grace gave its people protection through salvation, but it was also God's standard for judging his people. The covenant was a contract, and when the contract was not honored, the result was punishment. Puritans used this theology to explain and accept the difficulties and tribulations of their physical world.

God sends [losses] croses, or if it be upon [relations] it is God appoynts it. 2 God doth appoynt the rod. As to the instrument that corrects his people, it is not in men or Divills to afflict God's people without God give leave, Saytn canot nor the wicked. The Asirian is the rod of God's anger and the staff of God's wrath. The instruments can do nothing without God. (17 Psalm 13) The wicked is God's scourge because God improves them to correct his people. 3 God appoynts the rod as to the measure and degree of it. Let it be greater or lesser that is from God. That it is heavyer or lighter it is all of God. (27 Isaiah 7.8) In measure he corrects them, and in the day of the east wind he stays his rough wind.[11] 4 As to the season and as to the time of it, it is of God. As to the beginning of the rod, when it shall com and end, it is of God and God appoynts how long it shall abide upon his people. (88 Psalm) Some are afflicted all their dayes as [his men].

2 Reason we should heare the rod of God from the relation that we stand in to God, and that when he doth correct. God is a Father and we are children, we should heare the rod. When God doth afflict it is Because we are as children. The rod speakes God our Father, and as children the rod speakes our adoption. In that respect therefor we should heare the voyce of the Rod.

3 Reason is taken from the speciall love and great condesentian of God to his children when he doth afflict. That he doth not consume us but afflict us, that he doth not suffer to go on in sin, but doth afflict and correct poore man. (7 Job 18) What is man that thou should visit him and try him every moment? (3 Proverbs 11) Despise not the chastisement of the Lord, for every son he loves he corrects.

4 Reason may be taken from the great priviledg and advantage we have by the rod of God. We are a happy people if we be corrected by God. Happy is the man whom God corecteth and teacheth out of his Law. (12 Hebrews 11) We have proffit and advantage by God's rod and therefore hear it. It makes us see the Evill of sin and convinceth of it and others that it makes us mourn for sin. (15 Ezekiel 15) The people of God had never seen sin to be evill as it is nor mourned for it, but yet the rod show it them. 2 The rod is a meanes to turn to God. It is a means to convert the soule. It is good for me that I (119 Psalm 71.[67]) have been afflicted. I have learned thy statuts. It brings to repentance.

[11] East Winds came from the desert and would often sear the land and dry up vegetation. *Holman Bible Dictionary*, 1673.

(22 Proverbs 15) Foolishnes is in the heart of a child, but the rod drives it away. 3 The rod doth make us scircumspect in our wayes and makes them afrayed of sin, and carefull to keep in the wayes of God. 4 The rod is a means to subdue the power of sin in us, to encrease the grace of God in us. Tribulation increaseth patience and hope and c (42 Job 12) the graces have been doubled by the rod in degre tho not in number. 5 The rod preserves from penall and eternall judgments, from wrath and death and the curs and damnation. We are christened of the lord that we may (1 Corinthians 11:32) not be condemned with the wicked world. 6 The rod prepares for and makes an adition to our state of glory, for our light affliction that are but for a moment worke for us a farr more exceeding and etenall waight of glory. That is your glory shall be increased according to your afflicitons.

5 Reason we should hear the rod and the voyce of it Because we have deserved it. Should God correct without a cause or did correct more than sin deserved we might murmur, but God doth not. So he doth correct us less than our sins deserves.

6 Reason hear the rod Because it is the last means God makes use of to warne and amend us. If this doth not do God rejects and casts them off with [ ] should I smite them anymore. (24 Ezekiel 13)

Use 1: Examination. Try ourselves when we have heard the rod of God and the word of God.

2 Use: Instruction. It may teach us what we may expect of God if we are not bettered and reformed by the word. God hath his rod as well as his word. If his word doe not warne and reforme then God will visit with his rod. The voyce of wisdom is turn at my reproofe, but if not God will mock when your destruction cometh upon you and desolation as a whirle winde. 2 Hence see the great and sin and foly of those that despise the rod. This we are in great danger of we are warned in the (12 Hebrews 5), my son despise not the chatisement of the Lord neither faint under it. (3 Proverbs 11) It is exceding dangerous to doe so. Behold you despisers, wander and perish. 4 Sorts of person guilty of this. 1 Those that do not regard or take notice of the rod of God upon them are guilty of despiseing God. They regard not the worke of God nor the operation of his hand: (5 Isaiah 12) Those that looke upon all afflictions as coming by chance as if afflictions cam out of the ground and sprang out of the dust, (2 Kings 6:33) they are worss than that prophane king, this Evill is of the Lord why should I wayte any Longer. 2 Those that are not affected by the rod of God, that doe not

feele the smart of it, that do not mourne for it. (7 Hosea 9 verse) Strangers hath devoured his strength, gray haires are upon him and yet he knoweth it not. God had corrected him till he was weak and yet they take noe notice of it. It becomes a child to mourn and be ashamed of the least stroke of the Father. So when our heavenly father's rod is upon our hearts, 3 those that doe not inquire into the cause why God doth correct with the rod, they are to blame and doe despise the rod when God is correcting of us. God is searching of us and therefore it is our duty to search ourselves. 4 When we doe not minde the end God aimes at in the rod 1 then we doe condemn the rod. One of the end of the rod is to convince and humble us for sin, 2 to judg ourselves, to convert us from sin and to turn to God. When this is not done by us we doe not minde God's end in correcting with the rod. 3 It doth teach us the great priviledg of the people of God and that is in this, that God doth not only give his word to correct and amend but gives his rod as well as his word. (15 Genesis 15) It is a great priviledg to be visited with the rod because it is not a cruell Instrument. It is not an Instrument of deth. It is to reform and amend, an instrumentall of discipline. 4 It should teach us not to censure not to condemn those that are chastened with the rod of God. It is no Evidence of a bad Estate but of a good Estate. Let us not censur them for it, but let us looke upon them as children. (4 Job 7) (5 Job 2.3) (73 Psalm 14.15) 5 It should teach us to stand in aw and not to sin. Offer to God the sacrifices of righteousness.

3 Use: of Exortation. 1 Let not those that are under the rod of God be discouraged and cast down. Despise not the chastening of the Lord nor faint under it, and for your Encouragement. 1 Doth God correct you with his rod when he deals with you as his children? (12 Hebrews 6.7) Home the lord loveth he chastens and what [ ] is there but the Father chastens. 2 Consider there is a great deale of love in the rod of God. It hath hony upon the end of it. 3. God is very mercifull, Tender, and full of compassion when he corrects. God doth not stir up all his rath. (103 Psalm 13) (1 Corinthians 11:13) 4 God will not correct you without there be need of it. (1 Peter 1:6) If need be you are in [heavines], but God will hear you if you cry unto him under the rod. (32 [Za] 6) Consider the rod is to make you better, it is to refine and consume your dross and Increas your grace, and the rod is but for a time. (1 Peter 5:6) It is but for a season. (103 Psalm 9) God will not always chid nor will not allways contend. 8 God corrects less than our

iniquities have deserved. 9 If we hear the rod humble ourselves and turn to God, God will turn to us and rejoyce over us more than ever. It should allso [for] to Exort us to prepare for the rod.

Mr. Foster. (Tuesday) December 28, 1680.[12] (6 Micah 9 verse) Doctrine: that it greatly concerns a sinfull people under the rod to heare the rod and who hath appoynted it: To Exort to hear the voyce of the rod of God. We should Labour so to live and walke as not to deserve the rod. If God should marke what is a [ise] we could not live so as to deserve the rod. God comes to corect not for comon faults but for great sin:

4 Use: of Exortation as not to be secure but to prepare for a rod. Be not secure but be prepared for a rod. 5 Let it Exort all to hear the rod and who hath appoynted so heares to be brought to repentance by it. Heare the rod of God so as to obey it. Do not ad sin to sin but be awakened and humbled under the rod. (2 Timothy 3:13) Evill men and seducers wax worss and worss. It is a sign of a wicked man not to be better by the rod. Let us not be like those that blaspheem God because of their [plauys]. Attend the voyce of the rod, and 1 Consider that the voice of the rod is the voice of God. God speake by it, hence it is sayd hear the rod by him that hath appoynted. If you will not be disobedient to the voyce of God then heare the rod. 2 Consider our hearkening to the voyce of the rod of God in time will be a means to prevent a heavyer Rod. When God begins to correct a people it is not useall that he lets them alone till he reforms or destroyes them. He doth punish them 7 times more if they doe not hearken to the voyce of the rod. 3 Consider it is a great agravation to sin not to hearken the voyce of God's rod. Your sin is greater since the rod came than it was before. It is a sin against a second meanes, against the word and rod. (4 Amos 6) I have given you [cleanness][13] of teeth and yet you have not returned to me. Sin is agravated under the rod Because you sin against conviction. The rod convinceth of sin. God by rebukes doth convince man of sin. 2 It is to sin angst the means of reformation and the means of takeing away sin, and that greatly doth aggravate sin. 3 It is sin agnst speciall lov. There is a great deal of speciall love in the rod that God doth not [leav] them to fill up the [casure] of their iniquities. It is to sin against love

[12] This sermon is a continuation of the previous sermon based upon the sequence of Uses. This and the fact that it is part of the sermon series confirm that the year is 1680.

[13] King James Bible, 1002.

and grace and mercy. 4 Sin under the rod hath in it desperat contempt of God, and it proceeds from desperet emity against God. 4 Motiv: consider to press you to hearken it would be a sore judgment to us for God to remove his rod before we do hear It: Why should you be smiten any more you will yet revoult more and more? 5 Consider if we doe heare the voyce of the rod God will delight in us. This is well pleasing to God. (31 Jeremiah 18) I have heard Ephraim bemoaning of himself saying I was chastised. Ephraim is a dear child. My bowels are moved.[14] Surely I will have mercy on him. There is no escaping the rod nor can we Expect to have it removed unles we be brought to hear it. 7 Be sure the rod doth not com in vayn, nor before we have need of it. Therefor heare it for a season if need be you are in heaviness. There is need of it in respect of the covenant. Their condition doth require the rod before it comes. There is need of the rod upon severall accounts. 1 To wean us from the world. They are apt to be weded to the world and need the rod to make them looke at the things which are not soon, that are Eternall. 2 It is needfull to Imbitter sin to them to make them loath. (22 Jeremiah 21) 2 There is need of the rod to purg away sin and to clens them from it. By this shall the iniquity of Jacob be purged and all the fruit shall be the takeing away sin. The rod is needfull to Exercise their graces and to quicken to obedience and holynes. God teacheth them obedience by the things they suffer. It is allso to fit them for speciall service in their places and generations. 6 Hereby they are prepared for glory, for heaven and happynes. (1 James 9) The captain of our salvation was made perfect by sufferings. 7 They are needfull to make us simpathiz with others of the people God in affliction. 8 Consider there is a great deal more than God doth show to his people in and by the rod. There is mercy in sparing of his people in that God doth not use the rod as oft as he may. 2 In moderating the rod he doth not stir up all his rath. 3 There is mercy in God's sanctifiing the rod, 4 in God's repenting and removeing the rod. 9 Consider how happy it will be for us if we heare the chastening of the Lord. Happy is the man whom thou chasteneth and teacheth out of they law. (119 Psalm 67) Consider we must Expect utter destruction unles we doe hearken to correction. If we be not purged by the rod the fury of God shall rest on us for direction.

[14] Bowels in modern terms refers to the intestines and the stomach. In the KJV, "bowels" refers to the human reproductive system, and figuratively, to strong emotions and excitement. *Holman Bible Dictionary*, 233.

1 Labour to see and feele the smarte of the rod. Be sencible of the strooke of God. 2 Inquire in to the cause of it. 3 Labour to be humbled under it and be reformed by it. Return to God, and beg of God to sanctify the rod to you. He only can doe it to us.

(Wednesday) December 29, 1680. Mr. Foster. (12 Hebrews 5) "And ye have forgotten the consolation, which speaketh unto you as unto childre, My sonne, despise not the chastening of the Lord, nether faint when thou art rebuked of him."[15] And ye hav forgotten the Exortation that speaketh to you as children, and [ ] in the text the apostle helps their patience by their memory helping that it is a seasoable truth. In the text we have the maner of the apostacy putting them in mind of it. 2 The loving appellation. 3 The Exortation it selfe, the maner. Have you forgot or do you forget. Hereby he reproves their forgetfullness. 2 Hereby he doth commend it to their memory the Exortation. There is no condition we can be brought unto, but there is something suitable in the word of God for us. 2 The loving appelation given in the Exortation: to the affliced it speake to you as children for to enforc the exortation that they may be more affected by it and take the more heed to it, and to encourage you under affliction. God is their father. Thy children their affliction is an evidence of their children. Here is the title God gives to his afflicted. They are children, God speakes to them as such. The branches of the exortation: teacheth us to avoyd those vicious extreames we are apt to run into. 1 Despiseing the chastisment of the Lord or, 2 to faint under it. We are apt to make litle of it, to take care no about it. Chastening is 1 the corection of a Father. Judgment is upon God's enemies, but chastisement is for God's own children. Chastisement belongs to God's children and the word chastisement denotes the relation between a Father and a child. 2 Chastening is that which God lays upon his people for their sin and thus they are distinguished from such things as are for tryall of a person or people, and these are upon the most eminent saints. The chastisement are upon all God's people when they sin. 3 It is the affliction which is for instruction. God's rod is to drive out folly out of the heart of a child. It is not to destroy, but to instruct a people and reform them. 2 Faint not when you art rebuked. This is the 2 branch of the Exortation: be not weary of correction: this is a higher decre of weariness.

[15] *The Geneva Bible, 1560 Edition*. 106.

Doctrine: that God is a Father to his people when he doth afflict. It ought to be a great care of the people of God not to faint when they are aflicted: 1 The afflictions of the people of God they com to them from a Father. (12 Hebrews 6.7) He scourgeth every sin whom he corrects. 1 God is not an enemie. He doth not afflict a people as an enemie, for God doth not delight in the afflictions of his people. He calls it his strong act. How shall I doe it? God is afflicted in their afflictions. God doth not seek their destruction. 3 God doth not afflict them to take vengeens of them, nor properly to satisfy God's justice. God is not implackeable in the afflictions he brings on his people. God doth correct a people as a Father. If you consider 1 his love in the affliction, 2 his fatherly anger to them: God doth not hate them, but as a Father doth pity and hath compassion on them. There is moderation in their affliction. 4 The Lord doth afflict. He aymes at their good: and for that [cofit] God as a Father is ready to forgive when they aske forgivenes: When his people repent God will repent of the Evill.

Use: it should teach us not to censure those that are afflicted. A man may be a dear child of God not withstanding. 2 It should teach us not to be discouraged. 3 It should teach us to revernce the hand of God when he is correcting of us.

2 Doctrine: that it is the great duty of the people of God unafflicted to have a care of despiseing the chastening of God or fainting under his rebukes. We are ready either to make to litle or too much of God's chastisement. We are ready to [cary] as if we had no sence to feel or strength to bare afflictions. It is hard and dificult to carry aright under the providentiall will of God. (5 Jeremiah 3) Thou hast smitten them but they greived not. Thou hast broken them but they were not moved. The afflicted they must have a care of despiseing the afflictions or chastments of the Lord. We should not thinke them small nore despise them. It is the counsell of [Eliphaz] to Jobe in the (5 Job 17) Despise thou not the chastisement of the Lord. Who are they that despise the chastisment of the Lord?

(Wednesday) February 9, 1680.[16] When doe they despise the chastisment of the Lord? When we are not affected by, nor warned and awakened by God's chastisement. When the signs of God's rod doe not

[16] Based on the theme of this sermon and the language of the minister, I believe that it is the work of Isaac Foster.

put us upon doeing that as may prevent the rod. (27 Deuteronomy 19) [Con] men bless themselves under the threatenings of the curss and yet bless themselves and say we shall have peace where [y] [they] despise the rod at a distance when we are not awakened to prevent it. This is a despiseing of the chastment. God is want to give warning before he strikes. There is a Lightening before the Thunder of his judgments. God doth not useuly take his people at unawares, but God comes gradualy and visibly upon a people. These warnings God gives his people are by his word. God speakes before he smites. At what time I speake (18 Jeremiah 7.8) concerning a nation to pluck up (2 Chronicles 36:16) God warns his people not only by his prophets Exterordinarly Inspired by his word, but by (3 Micah 7) his ordinary ministers. 2 God warnes a people by his workes, by his Judgments upon his people in Former times. They are warning to us go to Shiloh,[17] se what God did there. 2 In part God warnes by spirituall Judgments when God [leaves] them to obstinancy in sin and Impenetenly in sin they warne of judgments. 3 In the speciall actings and workings of divine providence we may see it in the efflicitng and instrumentall causes of judgments. There (36 Job 37) 4 sometimes by extraordinary signes and wonders that God workes in the heavens or in the Earth these have been want to be accounted signes of judgments. [ ] that they have been so by experience. (21 Luke 12) There shall be famin and fearfull signes and wonders of aproaching iminent danger and Evill approaching.[18] (2 Joel 30) (2 Acts 19) The end of those warnings is that God's people may prepare to [meet] God in the way of his judgments that we may meet with him in a way of repentance and reformation. When we are not affected with this, when God's hand is lifted up we will not see. This is a despiseing of God's chastisment. 2 The chastening of God is despised when we doe make light of it and are not affected with it, when it is upon us when we looke upon it as a small light matter not to be minded by us. Lord thou has smitten them, but they have not greived when we carry it as if we were not chastized or we doe not feale the rod of God when it is upon us, when we doe not mourn or bewayle it. (12 Numbers 4) When we carry it as if we had no sence to feele the chastisement of God nor no sin to procure it. Our owne pain and misery, the sence of

---

[17] Shiloh is a city 30 miles north of Jerusalem that for over a century was the location of Israel's religious center.

[18] See: David Hall's *Worlds of Wonder, Days of Judgment.*

the wrath of God, sin procureing it, all these should afflict us. 3 The chastening of God is despised when we doe not consider and take notice of the hand of God in it. When we do not look upon it as coming from God. When we doe not consider the operation of God's hand in it. When we looke upon our afflictions as coming to us by chance. (3 Lamentations 38) Good and Evill com out of God's mouth. (10 Matthew 29) He orders all things and is the principle efficient, but when this is not considered. (1 Job 21) (5 Job 8) We despise the worke of God when we doe not own it to be his. (3 Amos 5) (6 Micah 9) It is he that doth appoynt the rod, as to that matter the end and the measure when we doe not consider that this comes from God. 4 The chastening of God is despised when we doe not inquire in to the cause why God contends with us. What is the cause, what is the controversy, why doth God contend with us? When this is done we make to light of it, we doe not atend our duty. Such is the mercy of God that he doth not allways afflict when there is a cause, yet such is his justice that he doth never afflict without a cause. 5 The chastening of God is despised when we doe not minde the end of the chastisment of the Lord. It is for the good of the people that God afflicts. (12 Hebrews 10) He doth chastiz for our proffit to make us a holy people.

(27 Isaiah 9) God afflicts to take away sin, to convinc and Turn from sin. (36 Job 8.9.10) God brings His people into affliction to humble and to [prove], (11 Daniel 35) to sanctify, purge, and make them white, to ween us from the world and bring near to themselves. He sends a Flood that they may return to him more fear and reverence God, to make them more zealous and watchfull, when this end is neglected. We despise the rod when we do not turn from sin for which we are smitten, nor to God that smites for sin. This is a despiseing the chastizment of the Lord. 6 When we do not put a due valuation and Esteem upon the chastisement of the Lord, the contrary duty is not atended by us. When we doe not price and esteem and reverence the hand of God. When is it that men despise the chastisement of God?

Use: it calls upon every one to consider whither the chastening of God hath not been despised by in. Have we not despised it in the threatening and in the Execution? Have we inquired to the cause, have we been humbled as we ought? This is mater of consideration and if it hath not been [it] matter of humilation.

CONCLUSIONS

Deciding which elements to discuss in the conclusion of this book began with a question. What did the book accomplish? A thorough transcription has been completed. Sixty-two formerly unknown sermons from seventeenth-century Hartford no longer hold their secrets, at least in a written sense. Unpacking their meaning may take some time, and I hope will involve the close attention of other scholars.

Transcribing the *Hartford Sermon Notebook* has been both a personal and an intellectual odyssey. From the beginning, the scope of the project seemed to grow increasingly more daunting. Throughout the life of this project, I have frequently stated that the most important purpose of this book would be the transcription itself. I believe this transcription of the *Hartford Sermon Notebook* is very accurate. Every sermon was examined at least four times, and several received even more attention, due mainly to challenges with the paleography. Ultimately, I believe this transcription can be taken as a true reproduction of the notebook's sermons, as they were "heard" over three centuries ago.

Having said that, what does the analysis show? Specifically, what does the transcription tell us about Hartford's Puritans in the late seventeenth century? Primarily, the *Hartford Sermon Notebook* confirms that the style and content of the Puritan sermons of Hartford, circa 1679–80, are in fact a part of the wider movement of New England Puritanism. I did not imagine that Hartford's sermons would be radically different in style or tone from the rest of New England, and in fact, they are not. David Hall's assertion is correct, the ministers "all thought alike," at least in terms of their preaching. In addition, what about the specific messages of the notebook's "occasional" sermons as opposed to the more frequent "regular" sermons? The sermons preached in Hartford were diverse, including several Day of Thanksgiving sermons, ordination sermons, and sacrament day sermons. These sermons adhere very closely to Harry Stout's classifications in *The New England Soul*, and the "regular" sermons in the notebook should contribute to Stout's plea for a scrutiny of regular preaching in colonial New England.

The theology contained in the sermon notebook covers a wide range of Puritan and reformed concepts. The terms I chose to explore included conversion, regeneration, justification, redemption, and the Elect. More broadly, I wanted to explore the importance and appearance of the covenant in the *Hartford Sermon Notebook*, since the covenant was one of the most important elements of Puritan theology.[1] I refer to the statistics that follow in terms of relative importance. In other words, if the word "conversion" is used in every sermon, and in this case, it is nearly the literal truth, then that concept was an important one to the minister, relative to the other terms used in the sermons.

The processes of conversion and regeneration are closely related. Conversion is the initial process of realizing a work of grace within oneself, which if properly conveyed to the congregation will lead to acceptance as a visible saint. Regeneration is nearly the same idea, in which the "natural" or unregenerate man comes to accept Christ as his savior, in what is more commonly referred to as "born again." Of course, to the Puritans these were not one-time events, but rather were part of a continuous process whose ultimate goal was redemption. The principle source for a detailed explanation of this process of "conversion morphology" is Edmund Morgan's *Visible Saints*. "Conversion" appears in 18 of the sermons, or approximately 30%, while regeneration appears in only 3 of the sermons, or 5%.

Justification, what Perry Miller calls "the first act of regeneration" is a stage in which God is fully satisfied that the criteria of his justice and law have been met; hence, the individual is absolved of their sins. Justification appears in 12 of the sermons, or 20%.[2] Redemption or "salvation," the final and eternal union with Christ, and the ultimate goal of the Puritan, was at least as important to the ministers of Hartford as conversion. Redemption also appears in 18 of the sermons, or 30%.

My findings for the term "covenant" are interesting. Relative to the other terms explored, covenant appears somewhat less often. Only 11 of the sermons refer to the covenant, or 18%. Assuming the accepted importance of the covenant in Puritan theology, the relative scarcity of the term is interesting. I acknowledge that the notebook does not contain every sermon preached in Hartford during the years 1679 and 1680, but if the average number of "regular" sermons preached was

---

[1] See David A. Weir's, Early New England: A Covenanted Society, for an in depth history of both civil and ecclesiastical covenants.

[2] Perry Miller. *The Puritan Mind, the Seventeenth Century*, 27.

2 per week, or around 100 per year, the *Hartford Sermon Notebook* contains nearly 1/4 of all the regular sermons preached during that two-year period. While the figures above do not necessarily offer conclusions, they do fuel questions, which usually lead to some kind of understanding. For example, was covenant theology less important to the second generation than it had been to the first? Declension studies suggest that it was, and so may the *Hartford Sermon Notebook*.

The numbers associated with the Elect are relatively small. Only six of the sermons refer to the Elect, but this term can be combined with "saint," a term I stopped exploring when I discovered its appearance in nearly every sermon. This suggests that in terms of relative importance, the "Elect" or "saint" is one of the most prominent of the notebook's theological concepts. Ironically, the Devil maintains a close second to the saint, and appears in 24 of the sermons, or 40%. The God of the World was very much on the minds of Hartford's ministers and their congregations. I admit that these figures are unscientific snapshots at best, so I do not intend to make hard scientific claims based on them. Instead, the stated goal was to look at the occurrence of these important terms relative to each other, simply to explore and compare the kinds of verbal expressions that mattered to Hartford's ministers.

The most important result of the transcription of the *Hartford Sermon Notebook* may be its awakening of the knowledge that Connecticut's preachers were at least as adept as any from "The Bay" at delivering the word of God. The ministers of the *Hartford Sermon Notebook* were Puritans. Clearly they battled over a number of issues, and their Presbyterian/Congregational differences generated sacramental anxieties that would last for many years, but otherwise they were Puritans. They were an interesting people, who pose something of a paradox relative to the secular character of our modern television/internet society, whose science and technology have replaced "the word" of the sermon as the central feature in the lives of people.

It is with both relief and regret that this project is ended. Relief because it is finally completed, regret because it is time to say goodbye, especially to Isaac Foster. Your life was cut short by a deadly disease, but your sermons are regenerated, reaching across three centuries of history, and teaching us still.

BIBLIOGRAPHY

Allin, James. "Serious Advice." Boston, 1679. Early American Imprints, Series 1: Evans. Central Connecticut State University, New Britain, CT. 14 Aug. 2008 <http://infoweb.newsbank.com/.>

Benham, J. H. *Contributions to the Ecclesiastical History of Connecticut; Prepared Under the Direction of the General Association*. New Haven: Published by William L. Kingsley, 1861.

Benton, Robert M. "An Annotated Check List of Puritan Sermons Published in America Before 1700." *Bulletin of the New York Public Library*. (New York: Peter Smith, 1941).

Bercovitch, Sacvan. *The Puritan Origins of the American Self*. New Haven: Yale University Press, 1975.

——. The American Jeremiad. Madison: University of Wisconsin Press, 1978.

Bernier Paul. *Ministry in the Church: A Pastoral Approach*. Mystic, Conn.: Twenty-Third Publications, 1992.

Bozeman, Theodore Dwight. "The Puritans 'Errand into the Wilderness' econsidered." *The New England Quarterly* 59, no. 2 (June 1986): 231–251.

Breen, T.H. *Puritans and Adventurers: Change and Persistence in Early America*. New York: Oxford University Press, 1980.

Bremer, Francis, J. *Puritan Crisis: New England and the English Civil Wars, 1630–1670*. New York: Garland Publishing, Inc., 1989.

——. *The Puritan Experiment: New England Society from Bradford to Edwards*. Revised Edition, Hanover, NH: University Press of New England, 1995.

Bush, Sargent, Jr. *The Correspondence of John Cotton*. The University of North Carolina Press, 2001.

——. The *Writings of Thomas Hooker: Spiritual Adventure in Two Worlds*. Madison: The University of Wisconsin Press, 1980.

Butler, Trent C. *The Holman Bible Dictionary*. B & H Publishing Group, 2003.

Cohen, Daniel A. "In Defense of the Gallows: Justifications of Capital Punishment in New England Execution Sermons, 1674–1825." *American Quarterly* 40, no. 2 (June 1988): 147–164.

Cohen, Charles L. "The Post Puritan Paradigm of Early American religious History." *The William and Mary Quarterly* 54, no. 4 (October 1997), 695–722.

Collections of the Massachusetts Historical Society. Vol. VIII.—Fourth Series. *Letters of Increase Mather*. Boston: Wiggin and Lunt, 1868.

Connecticut Church Records, Reel #500, LDS #1009610, Hartford First Church of Christ, V1-1684-1910.

Danforth, John. *An Almanack*. Cambridge, 1679.

Danforth, Samuel. "A Brief Recognition of New Englands Errand into the Wilderness." Cambridge, 1671. Early American Imprints, Series 1: Evans. Central Connecticut State University, New Britain, CT. 11 June 2008 <http://infoweb.newsbank.com/.>

Ditmore, Michael G. "Preparation and Confession: Reconsidering Edmund S. Morgan's Visible Saints." *The New England Quarterly* 67, no. 2 (June 1994): 298–319.

Earle, Alice Morse. *Home Life in Colonial Days*. Stockbridge Massachusetts: Berkshire House Publishers, American Classics Edition, 1993.

——. *The Sabbath in Puritan New England*. New York: Charles Scribner's Sons, 1891.

Elliott, Emory. *Power and the Pulpit in Puritan New England*. Princeton: Princeton University Press, 1975.

——. “The Development of the Puritan Funeral Sermon and Elegy: 1660–1750.” *Early American Literature* 15, (1980): 151–164.
Foster, John. *An Almanack*. Boston: Henry Phillips, 1680.
Foster, Stephen. *The Long Argument: English Puritanism and the Shaping of New England Culture, 1570–1700*. Chapel Hill: The University of North Carolina Press, 1991.
Gardner, E. Clinton. “Justice in the Puritan Covenantal Tradition.” *Journal of Law and Religion*, 6 no. 1 (1988): 39–60.
Gordis, Lisa M. *Opening Scripture: Bible Reading and Interpretive Authority in Puritan New England*. The University of Chicago Press, 2003.
Graham, Judith S. *Puritan Family Life: The Diary of Samuel Sewall*. Boston: Northeastern University Press, 2000.
Habegger, Alfred. “Preparing the Soul for Christ: The Contrasting Sermon Forms of John Cotton and Thomas Hooker.” *American Literature* 41 no. 3 (November 1969): 342–354.
Hall, David D. “A Reader’s Guide to The New England Mind: The Seventeenth Century.” *American Quarterly* 34, no. 1 (Spring 1982): 31–36.
——. Ed. *Puritans in the New World: A Critical Anthology*. Princeton: Princeton University Press, 2004.
——. *The Faithful Shepherd: A History of the New England Ministry in the Seventeenth Century*. Cambridge, Massachusetts: Harvard University Press, 2006.
——. *World’s of Wonder Days of Judgment: Popular Religious Belief in Early New England*. Cambridge, Massachusetts: Harvard University Press, 1990.
Hambrick-Stowe, Charles. *The Practice of Piety: Puritan devotional Disciplines in Seventeenth-Century New England*. Chapel Hill, University of North Carolina Press, 1982.
Hartford, Connecticut: Records of the Second Church of Christ, 1669–1731. Hartford: Connecticut State Library, 1914.
Hiner, N. Ray. “The Cry of Sodom Enquired into: Educational Analysis in Seventeenth-Century New England.” *History of Education Quarterly* 13 no. 1 (Spring 1973): 3–22.
Historical Catalogue of the First Church in Hartford, 1633–1885. Published by the Church, 1885.
Holifield, E. Brooks. “Peace, Conflict, and Ritual in Puritan Congregations.” *Journal of Interdisciplinary History, XXIII:3 (Winter 1993)*, 551–570.
——. *Theology in America: Christian Thought from the Age of the Puritans to the Civil War*. New Haven: Yale University Press, 2003.
Hooker, Samuel. “Righteousness Rained from Heaven.” Cambridge, 1677. Early American Imprints, Series 1: Evans. Central Connecticut State University, New Britain, CT. 14 Aug. 2008 <http://infoweb.newsbank.com/.>
Hoyt, Albert Harrison, Ed. *The New England Historical and Genealogical Register and Antiquarian Journal 49*. Boston: Published by the Society, 1869.
Hubbard, William. “The Happiness of a People.” Boston, 1676. Early American Imprints, Series 1: Evans. Central Connecticut State University, New Britain, CT. 14 Aug. 2008 <http://infoweb.newsbank.com/.>
Indian & Colonial Research Center. Foster, [Isaac?]. MsBd F811. Abstracts of sermons, mostly those of Mr. Foster, 1679–1680.
Johnson, William Stacy, and John H. Leith Eds. *Reformed Reader: a Sourcebook in Christian Theology, Volume 1, Classical Beginnings, 1519–1799*. Louisville, Kentucky: Westminster/John Knox Press, 1993.
Johnson, Steven F. *Ninnuock (The People): The Algonkian People of New England*. Marlborough, Mass.: Bliss Publishing Company, 1995.
Kempis, Thomas A., translated by Rev. William Benham. *The Immitation of Christ, Harvard Classics* vol. 7. New York: P.F. Collier, 1937.

Kraus, Joe W. "The Development of a Curriculum in the Early American Colleges." *History of Education Quarterly* 1 no. 2 (June 1961): 64–76.
Lepore, Jill. *The Name of War: King Phillip's War and the Origins of American Identity.* New York: Vintage Books, 1999.
Lesser, Marvin Xavier. *"All for Profit": The Plain Style and the Massachusetts Election Sermons in the Seventeenth Century.* PhD Dissertation, Columbia University, 1967.
Lossing, Benson J. ed., *The American Historical Record and Repertory of Notes and Queries.* Philadelphia: Chase and Town Publishers, 1872.
Lovin, Robin W. "Equality and Covenant Theology." *Journal of Law and Religion* 2 no. 2 (1984): 241–262.
Lucas, Paul R. *Valley of Discord: Church and Society along the Connecticut River, 1636–1725.* Hanover, New Hampshire: The University Press of New England, 1976.
Madden, Etta. "Resurrecting Life Through Rhetorical Ritual: A Buried Value of the Puritan Funeral Sermon." *Early American Literature* 26, (1991): 232–250.
Main, Gloria L, and Jackson T. Main. "Economic Growth and the Standard of Living in Southern New England, 1640–1774." *The Journal of Economic History* 48, no. 1 (March 1988): 27–46.
Mather, Increase. "A Call From Heaven." Boston, 1679. Early American Imprints, Series 1: Evans. Central Connecticut State University, New Britain, CT. 14 Aug. 2008 <http://infoweb.newsbank.com/.>
——. "Pray for the Rising Generation." Boston, 1679. Early American Imprints, Series 1: Evans. Central Connecticut State University, New Britain, CT. 14 Aug. 2008 <http://infoweb.newsbank.com/.>
——. "Renewal of Covenant." Boston, 1677. Early American Imprints, Series 1: Evans. Central Connecticut State University, New Britain, CT. 14 Aug. 2008 <http://infoweb.newsbank.com/.>
——. "The Times of Men." Boston, 1675. Early American Imprints, Series 1: Evans. Central Connecticut State University, New Britain, CT. 14 Aug. 2008 <http://infoweb.newsbank.com/.>
——. "The Wicked Man's Portion." Boston, 1675. Early American Imprints, Series 1: Evans. Central Connecticut State University, New Britain, CT. 14 Aug. 2008 <http://infoweb.newsbank.com/.>
Mignon, Charles W. "Christ the Glory of All Types: The Initial Sermon from Edward Taylor's 'Upon the Types of the Old Testament.'" *The William and Mary Quarterly* 37, no. 2 (April 1980): 286–301.
Miller, Perry. *Errand into the Wilderness.* Cambridge, Mass.: The Belknap Press of Harvard University Press, 1956.
——. "Errand Into The Wilderness." *The William and Mary Quarterly* 10 no. 1 (January 1953): 3–32.
——. "Preparation for Salvation in Seventeenth-Century New England." *Journal of the History of Ideas* 4, no. 3 (June 1943): 253–286.
——. "The Half-Way Covenant." *The New England Quarterly* 6, no. 4 (December 1933): 676–715.
——. *The New England Mind: The Seventeenth Century.* Cambridge Massachusetts: The Belknap Press, 1982.
Miller, Perry and Thomas H. Johnson, Eds. *The Puritans: A Sourcebook of Their Writings.* Mineola, New York: Dover Publications, 2001.
Mitchel, Jonathan. "Nehemiah on the Wall." Cambridge, 1671. Early American Imprints, Series 1: Evans. Central Connecticut State University, New Britain, CT. 10 June 2008 <http://infoweb.newsbank.com/.>
Moran, Gerald F. "Religious Renewal, Puritan Tribalism, and the Family in Seventeenth-Century Milford, Connecticut." *The William and Mary Quarterly* 36, no. 2 (April 1979): 236–254.

——. *The Puritan Saint: Religious Experience, Church Membership, and Piety in Connecticut, 1636–1776.* Ph.D. Dissertation, Rutgers University, 1974.
Morgan, Edmund S. "Light on the Puritans from John Hull's Notebooks." *The New England Quarterly* 15, no. 1 (March 1942): 95–101.
——. *The Puritan Family: Religion and Domestic Relations in Seventeenth-Century New England.* New York: Harper and Row, 1966.
——. *Visible Saints: The History of a Puritan Idea.* Ithaca: Cornell University Press, 1963.
Morison, Samuel Eliot. "The Harvard School of Astronomy in the 17th Century." *The New England Quarterly* 7, no. 1 (March 1934), 3–24.
——. *The Founding of Harvard College.* (Cambridge: Harvard University Press, 1935.
Morrissey, Mary. "Interdisciplinarity and the Study of Early Modern Sermons." *The Historical Journal* 42, no. 4 (December 1999): 1111–1123.
——. "Scripture, Style and Persuasion in Seventeenth-Century English Theories of Preaching. *The Journal of Ecclesiastical History* 53, no. 4 (Oct 2002): 686–706.
Murphey, Murray G. "The Psychodynamics of Puritan Conversion." *American Quarterly* 31, no. 2 (Summer 1979): 135–147.
Nowell, Samuel. "Abraham in Arms." Boston, 1678. Early American Imprints, Series 1: Evans. Central Connecticut State University, New Britain, CT. 14 Aug. 2008 <http://infoweb.newsbank.com/.>
Oakes, Urian. "New England Pleaded With." Cambridge, 1673. Early American Imprints, Series 1: Evans. Central Connecticut State University, New Britain, CT. 4 Aug. 2008 <http://infoweb.newsbank.com/.>
Oxford Classical Dictionary. Oxford: Oxford University Press, 1970.
Oxford World's Classics. *The Bible: Authorized King James Version With Apocrypha.* New York: Oxford University Press, 1997.
Pettit, Norman. The *Heart Prepared: Grace and Conversion in Puritan Spiritual Life.* Middletown, CT: Wesleyan University Press, 1989.
——. The *Heart Renewed: Assurance of Salvation in New England Spiritual Life.* Lewiston, NY: The Edwin Mellon Press, 2004.
Phelps, Virgil V. "The Pastor and the Teacher in New England." *Harvard Theological Review* 4, (July 1911): 388–89.
Pope, Robert G. *The Half-Way Covenant: Church Membership in Puritan New England.* Princeton: Princeton University Press, 1969.
Public Records of the Colony of Connecticut, Volume III, October 1679.
Robinson, David M. "The Cultural Dynamics of American Puritanism." *American Literary History* 6, no. 4 (Winter 1994), 738–755.
Ryken, Leland. *Wordly Saints: The Puritans as They Really Were.* Grand Rapids, MI: Zondervan Publishing House, 1986.
Scobey, David M. "Revising the Errand: New England's Ways and the Puritan Sense of the Past." *The William and Mary Quarterly* 41, no. 1 (January 1984): 3–31.
Schultz, Eric and Michael Tougias. *King Phillip's War: The History and Legacy of America's Forgotten Conflict.* Woodstock Vermont: The Countryman Press, 2000.
Selement, George. "Perry Miller: A Note on His Sources in The New England Mind: The Seventeenth Century." *The William and Mary Quarterly* 31, no. 3 (July 1974): 453–464.
——. "Publication and the Puritan Minister." *The William and Mary Quarterly* 37, no. 2 (April 1980): 219–241.
Shepard, Thomas."A Short Catechism." Cambridge, 1654. Early American Imprints, Series 1: Evans. Central Connecticut State University, New Britain, CT. 14 Aug. 2008 <http://infoweb.newsbank.com/.>
Shipton, Clifford K. "A Plea for Puritanism." *The American Historical Review* 40, no. 3 (April 1935): 460–467.

Sibley, John Langdon. *Biographical Sketches of the Graduates of Harvard University, Vols. I,II and III.* Cambridge Massachusetts: Charles Williams, 1873.

Simpson, Alan. *Puritanism in Old and New England.* The University of Chicago Press, 1955.

Sproul, R.C. General Editor. *New Geneva Study Bible: Bringing the Light of the Reformation to Scripture.* Nashville: Thomas Nelson Publishers, 1995.

Stannard, David E. "Death and Dying in Puritan New England." *The American Historical Review* 78, no. 5 (December 1973): 1305–1330.

——. *The Puritan Way of Death: A Study in Religion, Culture, and Social Change.* New York: Oxford University Press, 1977.

Stiles, Henry R. *The History and Genealogies of Ancient Windsor, Connecticut.* Hartford: Case, Lockwood & Brainard Co., 1854–1879.

Stout, Harry S. *The New England Soul: Preaching and Religious Culture in Colonial New England.* New York: Oxford University Press, 1986.

Strong, James. *The New Strong's Compact Bible Concordance.* Nashville: Thomas Nelson Publishers, 2004.

Strother, Bonnie, Lew. *The Imagery in the Sermons of Thomas Shepard.* PhD Dissertation, University of Tennessee, 1968.

Thacher, Thomas. "A Fast of God's Chusing." Boston, 1678. Early American Imprints, Series 1: Evans. Central Connecticut State University, New Britain, CT. 14 Aug. 2008 <http://infoweb.newsbank.com/.>

The Geneva Bible: A Facsimile of the 1560 Edition. Peabody Massachusetts: Hendrickson Publishers, 2007.

Ulrich, Laurel Thatcher. "Good Wives: Image and Reality in the Lives of Women in Northern New England, 1650–1750." New York: Vintage Books, 1991.

Webster's Unabridged Dictionary. New York: Simon and Schuster, 1979.

Weir, David A. *Early New England: A Covenanted Society.* Grand Rapids, MI: William B. Eerdmans Publishing Company, 2005.

Weis, Frederick Lewis. *The Colonial Clergy and the Colonial Churches of New England.* Baltimore: Genealogical Publishing Co., inc., 1977.

Wertenbaker, Thomas Jefferson. *The Puritan Oligarchy: The Founding of American Civilization.* New York: Grosset & Dunlap, 1947.

Whiting, John. "The Way of Israel's Welfare: Or an Exhortation to be With God, that He May be With us." Boston, 1686. Early American Imprints, Series 1: Evans. Central Connecticut State University, New Britain, CT. 14 Aug. 2008 <http://infoweb.newsbank.com/.>

Willard, Samuel. "The Duty of a People." Boston, 1680. Early American Imprints, Series 1: Evans. Central Connecticut State University, New Britain, CT. 14 Aug. 2008 <http://infoweb.newsbank.com/.>

——. "The Heart Garrisoned." Cambridge, 1676. Early American Imprints, Series 1: Evans. Central Connecticut State University, New Britain, CT. 14 Aug. 2008 <http://infoweb.newsbank.com/.>

Wilson, Lisa. "Ye Heart of a Man: The Domestic Life of Men in Colonial New England." New Haven: Yale University Press, 2000.

Winship, Michael. "Contesting Control of Orthodoxy Among the Godly: William Pynchon Reexamined." *The William and Mary Quarterly* 54, no. 4 (October 1997), 795–822.

——. "Were There Any Puritans in New England?" *The New England Quarterly* 74 no. 1 (March 2001): 118–138.

The Wyllys Papers: Correspondence and Documents Chiefly of Descendents of Gov. George Wyllys of Connecticut, 1590–1796. Hartford: Collections of the Connecticut Historical Society. 1924.

INDEX

INDEX OF BIBLICAL REFERENCES